SUNSHINE BEAM PUBLISHING

Sunshine Beam Books is published by Sunshine Beam Publishing, Inc.,
Box 786, Hollywood, CA 90072

Design by Anna Huff

Photographs by Lisa Whiteman, lyrics by S.G. Wilson

A hearty thank you to the wonderful Kurt Braunohler

First Printing, January 2022

This book is a work of satiric fiction. Nothing in it happened.
Or so say the libs.

PRINTED PROUDLY IN THE U.S.A.
(that's why it's more expensive)

ISBN PAPERBACK 978-0-578-32949-9

ISBN E-BOOK 978-0-578-32950-5

A Memoir from the Award-Winning Host and Creator
of Satellite Radio's *Passing on the Right*

PASSING ON THE RIGHT

My Ups, My Downs, My Lefts, My Rights, My "Wrongs"...
and My Career (So Far) in This Bizarro World of Comedy

★ By Skippy "Batty" Battison ★

About Skippy Battison

After a decades-long, award-winning career as a stand-up comedian and extremely successful writer for hit television comedies, Skippy eventually turned his attention full-time to the world of conservative values, creating and hosting his own popular satellite radio show and weekly podcast, thereby making millions laugh while, also, *learning*.

Battison now comes clean for the *first time* in this astonishing memoir too *hot* for traditional mainstream publishers, touching on his beginnings on the streets of Bethesda, Maryland; his wild experiences as a stand-up in Ocean City, Maryland; his life in the topsy-turvy world of sitcoms and late-night television, including a very successful stint on *The Simpsons*; and befriending and working with such conservative powerhouses as Donald Trump, Supreme Court Justice Brett Kavanaugh and Rudy Giuliani, among many, many others!

Skippy lives in Great Falls, Virginia with his parakeet Andrew Jackson and his pit bull mix, John Galt.

Warning:

This book isn't for the faint of liberal heart. Seriously. If you're easily offended by "words" and "thoughts" and "convictions" and "honesty", then go read something else, maybe a book by Rachel Maddow. There has been no "sensitivity reader" to protect you. Warning you now ...

Okay. You've been warned.

Table of Contents

The Story Behind This Book

Before we get into the meat and gristle of the story (and apologies to all you vegetarians out there ... but this book is comprised mostly of *meaty* stories), I would like to give you a little background on the history of this tome that you're either reading or listening to me read to you on the exquisite audio version available everywhere.

It's been a long journey.

You might have already heard most of it.

But for those who haven't, here it is:

In August 2018, my former literary agent sold a pitch to Viking (owned by Random House) for a memoir of my very successful career as a popular stand-up comedian, comedy writer, and eventual podcast and satellite conservative radio star.

(Please note that the word "conservative" is used throughout this book but it's just a different way of saying *sensible* and *intelligent*. Again, if you have a problem with this, go find another book.)

I wrote weekends and even holidays and managed to squeeze out a first draft by January 2020, which was sent to my editor at Viking for her edits.

I received the edits back April 2020 and I immediately went to work rewriting and making the editor happy with thousands of cuts and tweaks and all the rest of it, some of which I agreed with, most of which I did not. But a "clean" manuscript was submitted.

A second round of edits came back from the editor in July of 2020 and I then went to work on fixing what the editor *still* felt needed help, passages she thought needed some "boost."

A third round came back to me in August 2020 and by working all nighters and through a planned beach vacation, I had all these requested changes finished by September 2020.

This version was then sent to the editor and she signed off on it. *Hallelujah!*

Meanwhile, the book had been designed and the front and back covers created.

We were all set for a May 2022 publishing date!

Think about that, then: the first version of this book was finished in September 2020, two months *before* the Presidential election, which was just fine with me.

I wasn't the one running after all.

The book was going to be about *me*.

And *my* life.

But then came ... January 6, 2021, the "insurrection."

And then *everything* changed.

Social media went haywire, beserk, bananas, blaming me and like-minded conservatives for *everything* that happened that day.

(Blaming me for January 6th is like blaming the cigar for Bill Clinton's downfall.)

My book was officially cancelled on February 1, 2021.

Viking released a statement wishing me the best of luck with my book and hinting that perhaps I could return the advance I was paid.

Gee, thanks for fighting for me, assholes!

(I haven't seen fighting this lame since the French rolled over and exposed their tender, flaky tummies after the Nazi's invasion of their country, which *we* then had to clean up, per usual.)

And no. I did *not* fucking return the money.

So here we are.

And there I was with a finished book and without a publisher.

And also without an agent. She had quit, citing "differences in political and moral beliefs."

I sent out the manuscript *myself* to 25 publishers, all of which turned it down.

And then to 53 literary agents.

Every single one of *them* turned it down.

"Too hot."

"We love it! But we just can't take the chance. Sorry!"

"Times are too dangerous. Maybe in a few years?"

What a waste, I thought. All that time writing a book.

And for what?

I've talked about all this on my satellite radio show, *Passing on the Right*, and my podcast, *Podding on the Right*, endlessly.

And then, as you know if you're a listener, which I imagine you to be if you're reading this book, fortune smiled upon me: one of my fans, one of my *Passing on the Righters*, emailed me with an explanation of GoFundMe and Patreon and self-publishing and NFTs and all the rest of what I needed to learn in order to pilot my own success through space and beyond ...

Whammo! And that was it!

Fuck it!

What did I *need* traditional mainstream book publishers for anyway?

Could I not make *any* book a bestseller by just having some friends and colleagues buy thousands and thousands of copies for me as a favor? (Joking, joking!!)

What I'm saying is that all of the "offensive" words and phrases I had previously eliminated are now inserted *back* into this book. *This* is the unexpurgated version, meaning that everything I ever originally wanted in the book has *remained* in the book.

Better yet, this version includes what happened to me *during* and *after* January 6th.

How great is that?

This book will bring you up-to-date on what happened *after* I completed the *last* version: what happened *after* the election, *after* the "insurrection," *after* the accusations about my role in it, *after* the lies, *after* all the bullshit nonsense.

Why did I *ever* need "traditional" publishing?

Were they going to put this book in airport bookstores? Pay to send me around the country to promote it?

The people in the marketing department, at least the few I had talked with, didn't know *shit* from *shut*. They knew *nothing* about politics or comedy or anything worthwhile. They were useless. In a sense, I consider myself lucky.

And so should you.

Why?

I'll tell you:

Because you get to read the version I always *wanted* you to read. There are no rules about how long this memoir has to be. There are no rules about what I can say and what I can't say. There are no rules about *anything* … beyond me telling the truth as I only know how to say it.

There's no bullshit here, folks. Rare, ain't it?

I'm not a soothsayer but I can already predict the criticism I'll receive for this book:

Hey! Why didn't you hire a "real" editor or a "true" legal team? Are you sure that all you've written is true? You're not holding anything back? How can we confirm the veracity of all this?

I find that very funny. I can assure you that I'm quite capable of editing my own work—or not editing my own work, if the need arises—and as far as a legal vetting, my father's old D.C. pal, Harold Robinson, has graciously taken it upon himself to go over the entire book for possible legal issues. Harold is a partner at a huge D.C. law firm and is quite skilled at telling me what to avoid.

Yes, there were a few chapters and lines that bothered him, and I took those out. I'm not suicidal. If you want to know what they are, just email me. Or I can tell you in person, over some cool beers.

Like Kavanaugh, I enjoy some fresh, chilled suds. What can I say?

And also like Brett, I'm a friendly guy. Specially if you're a woman around twenty-two who's hot as shit. (And now I'm *not* joking.)

What I'm saying is that I made this book *exactly* how I wanted it to be.

If it doesn't sell, it's my fault.

If it *does* sell, it's also my fault.

I have no one else to blame.

Consider this book the "ultimate director's cut" version of my life.

This book is *my* version. No one else's. *This* book is the real me.

For better or worse. But I'd like to think for the better.

Thank you for purchasing it.

I'll see you soon enough ... after we pass all the other losers ... on the *right* ...

— Skippy Battison

Great Falls, Virginia, September 17, 2021

Foreword

It's October 2010.

The weather outside, as that horrid song doesn't go, is perfect. Just like it was yesterday. Just like it will be tomorrow. Perfect every day. Sunny. Mid seventies. Perfectly normal. So perfect you want to kill yourself. This is Los Angeles, the city of spray-tanned angels. It's been more than ten years since I moved from the East coast and I'm *still* not used to the sun.

It is strong.

It's *too* strong. It's *too* pure. It *zaps* your brain. I want it to be hidden. I want the swampy, milky-white sky to hide the sun like it did back when I was a kid in Maryland. Please. This is all I'm asking: Just *one* goddamn overcast day of some clouds to ease my aching conscious.

Is that too difficult?

It seems so.

Inside the writing room at *$h*! My Dad Says*, where I'm perched on an uncomfortable chair bought in bulk at Office Depot, in front of a huge, leaning tower of Styrofoam boxes (this back when we were still allowed to store hot food in a container that actually kept the food, you know, *hot*), things are only getting hotter.

It's already 2:00 P.M., five hours into the day, and we've been arguing since ten about the same joke in an episode we're writing.

You may even remember the particular episode.

The middle-aged character of Ed, played by the great (*ahem*) William Shatner, is mistakenly invited to an orgy and is asked by a young female attendee to get the party started. But there's a problem. *He can't*. He left his reading glasses back at home and is now unable to decipher the directions on the three-speed vibrator that he's clutching.

Do you have a magnifying glass? asks Ed.

Looking down at Ed's crotch, the woman replies, *That bad, eh?*

It's a *great* joke and it would have killed, but there's a reason you don't remember it. .

It was cut.

Why?

Because it failed to make the character of Ed more *likable*. In fact, my entire orgy plot was cut.

Have you heard about this word?

If you work outside Hollywood, probably not.

It's rarely, if ever, used in every day life.

But it's a word used *every single day* in the world of Hollywood. *Likable*.

Everything and every character has to be *likable*. You know, just like in real life, where everyone smiles at everyone else. All the time. Because everyone's so *likable*.

Or something like that. If you were this likable in real life, you'd be labeled *insane*.

But not here in the Hall(ywood) Land of Distorted Mirrors.

It's a word I quickly became used to.

Hundreds of my jokes—maybe even *thousands*—over the years have already been shot down like clay pigeons because they weren't deemed *likable*.

I tune out and stare out the window. This is my joke and I should be fighting to keep it in. There's no reason why we can't have a joke about a vibrator and a guy too old to figure out how to use it.

It'd be a huge hit. Jokes for actual adults, not children and too easily offended morons.

But the fight has left me.

I spent a lot of time that season, and others, staring out a window.

$h! My Dad Says* eventually went off the air.

No huge surprise.

But sometimes, especially when I'm stuck in traffic or just soaking in my above-ground jacuzzi overlooking the George Washington Parkway, I imagine an alternate reality, a Narnia-type world, in which my jokes somehow and mysteriously made it through all that likability haze of bullshit and actually made it onto the air.

Would *$h*! My Dad Says then* have been cancelled?

Would any of the other shows I wrote for over the years?

Who knows?

Probably not.

But I do know this: that show, and all the others, would have been a *hell of a lot funnier*.

A whole world always existed just beyond that claustrophobic writer's room, and within every other writer's room I've ever worked: a world that seemed infinitely more amusing than any joke being created within the virtual prison that always came with bad snacks and worse air circulation.

As I write this, I've left Hollywood more than seven years ago. But when I did work there, I wrote for twelve sitcoms. Five making it to air. The rest gathering dust in a storage unit somewhere in the San

Fernando Valley, next to that empty warehouse where they shoot all your favorite "amateur" porn.

"Too edgy."

"Too raw."

"To real."

I've heard it *all*.

You know what I never heard—or very *rarely* heard?

My jokes being told on the air.

So so *so* many hours spent in those writing rooms, staring out a window.

I'd gaze out the window, day after weatherless day, to a place far, far away, to a world so many more times beautiful than the one George Lucas had ever envisioned, to a different time when comedy meant something, when comedy was rock and roll, and when weenies weren't in charge of our laughter, when making someone laugh came without strings attached, when a joke wasn't analyzed to death, before the canned applause turned watching TV into the equivalent of the noise machine blasting outside any therapist's office.

It all started so far away, this dream of mine, to make a difference in comedy. To be respected.

To be loved. To be adored for something I was actually *good* at. To earn smiles. And joy for all.

A time when I actually had true aspirations, a time before I was forced to quit that life and molt into an entirely new version of myself.

And then re-emerge as my *real* self.

Which is why you hold this book in your hands.

The journey has been long and fascinating and filled with humor and sadness and every other cliché ... including, yes, *likability* ...

I'm sorry. I *had* to say it.

So let's get to it.

A long, long time ago, in a state far, far away ....

★ Chapter One ★
BEGINNINGS

I've *always* been able to make people laugh, whether they wanted to or not.

I can't help it. It's something I was born with. Like a vestigial tail.

I'd often wonder if the success that eventually arrived for me was due to one fact and one fact only: *that I kept at it while others quit.*

Maybe that had something to do with it. But I think, really, most of my success is due to a higher power bestowing upon me something quite special.

Does that sound egotistical?

I'm sorry if it does.

But that's how I feel.

I had friends who could kick a football a million yards. I had friends who knew advanced calculus at the age of ten. I had one friend who got drunk off stolen beer and lit ping-pong balls on fire and then escaped before his neighbor discovered what was happening on his front lawn. Wait. That was me.

The way I explain it to people is that there are those who have the Humor Gene and there are those who *don't* have the Humor Gene. That's it. It's not any more complicated than that.

If you don't have that gene, there's nothing that can be done. And you might never come to learn the Humor Tongue.

You can feed the Humor Gene and pamper it and improve on it ... but if you're not born with it, good luck making a career out of it.

You can look at it like DNA. I forget the number, but we each have a certain number of DNA or Chromosomes. Say, 23. But some might get more, which is great. And some less, which is *not* so great.

I had the extra Humor Chromosomes. You probably didn't. I'm not saying that I'm in any way better. It's just a fact.

Then again, *everyone* has something they can't help being great at, right?

My childhood friend Skinny in Maryland was a genius at flirting with girls. When we asked him how he managed to work beyond his pay grade, he'd just shrug. I mean, this guy was no looker. *He was born with it*. Simple. No other explanation necessary. An impish glance here, a batting of his eyelashes there, the girls would succumb. He couldn't help it. It was programmed right into his very being. Hardwired. He was also hung like a petting zoo donkey but whatever. That's who he was. Skinny, by the way, first got laid at fourteen. The girl? Twenty. Skinny now sells household siding in Rockville, Maryland. Hey, Skinny! You *still* owe me for the Rusted Root tix!

But anyway. Humor. It's always come naturally to me. The first joke I remember telling was when I was six, maybe seven. On the playground, at Seven Locks Elementary in Bethesda, Maryland.

I can see her now, Mary Chester-Clark, not bothering a soul, alone as usual, muttering to herself about Lord knows what. She's also six or seven. She's on that playground, as innocent as an angel's kiss. She's kneeling on the blacktop, tongue out in concentration, taking her time, with great care, to draw a human figure with a piece of colored chalk.

What are you drawing? I ask.

A clown! she answers proudly.

I look at the drawing closer.

And then, so quickly as to not be stopped, I step forward and, with the bottom of my Keds, rub out the smile on the clown's face. I grab a piece of chalk and hurriedly draw an upside smile.

That's one sad clown! I say.

Not the nicest move in the world but the joke works, right? And best of all, it received a huge laugh, at least from my moronic crew of dimwits.

Mary cried.

It's 1985.

Now I'd be jailed.

Then I was *lauded*.

Ain't that nice?

A reputation quickly and effortlessly began to form.

All eyes would be on me, and me alone, in *any* situation that needed a laugh.

The class gerbil escaped from its cage and was found dead in a corner?

Look to Skippy. He'll have a joke.

The teacher just accidentally farted?

Look over to Skippy. He'll have a joke!

The teacher just suffered a heart attack and died outside the cafeteria?

Look over to Skippy. He'll *definitely* have a joke.

It was all in good fun, even if it was often at another's expense.

Little Mary Chester-Clark, the chalk drawer, later became a doctor or something. Good on her. Wherever you are, Mary, I apologize, okay? But you just got yourself a free mention in a famous personality's book, right? You can't beat that! (You're welcome.)

Cut to junior high school, a few years later. We're in band class. Eighth grade. I'm in the back, slapping away on the drums, looking good. And that's all that matters at this age, right? We're each doing a solo. Mine kills. Five piece drum set, cymbals, the whole thing. It really looks like I know what I'm doing. In reality, I'm trying to copy my favorite drummers I see on MTV. My dad bought me the drumset.

I finish my solo. There's applause. Now it's the rest of the students' turns for *their* solos. I wait impatiently. *Flutes, clarinets, trumpets. Jesus. I hate classical music.* I only got into drumming to play like Neal Peart of Rush or the drummer from Van Halen. I hate this Kennedy Center shit.

But what's this? Jessica Styward is squeaking away on an oboe, the worst instrument known to mankind, not counting the knee cymbals. Or *any* cymbals that don't use a drumstick and that you have to hit *really* hard.

Ooooh, this is bad. Like *embarrassingly* bad.

Like, so bad I almost want to help her.

So I began to rap.

Rapping out a song about how bad Jessica is at the oboe.

While playing the drums at the same time.

All eyes turn away from poor Jessica. And back to me.

"Jess! What a mess (drum fill), can't help but guess (cymbal crash), she never practiced for this (bass drum kick), this definitely ain't bliss (tom-toms), what I wouldn't now give (cowbell), for a kiss!! (CRASH!)"

Everyone *loved* it. Even Jess—or so I heard. Everyone except for Mr. Jenkins, who later died in a car crash. Not a bad guy. Just not the biggest fan of humor. At least *authentic* humor; not the crap doled out by the bucketful from the same generic troughs everyone scoops out of with their daily government-approved allotments of comedy buckets.

That particular rap cost me a week of detention. But when I attended my 20th reunion, people were *still* talking about it.

So ... let's weigh if it was all worth it. Goddamn *priceless*.

One week detention.

A career in comedy.

Yeah.

Worth it.

I'm *lucky*.

Why could I always get away with the things that I did?

Simple:

Here's the thing: I'm a *nice* guy. Always have been. This may not always come through to others but I am here to tell you that I am definitely a *nice* fucking guy. Women have always told me as much — or they would have told me if I hadn't cut them off at the pass before they yibber-yabbered me into an irritating state of malaise.

Like most nice guys, I don't want to hear that I'm nice.

I just don't.

I'm far too nice for that.

So I'm a nice guy who doesn't want to hear it.

Real simple.

Ain't that nice?

As any listener to my satellite radio show *Passing on the Right* or my *Podding on the Right* podcast knows, if I ever did actually believe in God, I'd say I was blessed.

The humor that has worked so well for me throughout my life and career has been innate. Experience can be overrated. Trust me. Some of the worst comedy writers I know were born poor and struggled.

You know what's more important? *Having a naturally good ear.* And just being born a decent guy.

So.

High school.

Sadly, my parents felt the need to send me to a certain private school, otherwise known as the very same school that a particular very famous person earlier attended as a high school student.

On advice of my lawyers, I wasn't going to include his name or story in this book but I thought about it for a bit ... and you know what?

Fuck it. I will.

Life is short.

Back in high school, a friend of mine had an older brother (at least 15 years older) who worked at a bar in Georgetown that served "yards," or really long glasses of beer. They also served crab cakes and other bar food. This older guy would always let us into the bar on

Friday and Saturday nights without forcing us to produce a real driver's license and all that bullshit.

When he wasn't working, this older guy would hang out with us at a backyard pool in the Whitehall Manor area of Bethesda.

One of the dudes who'd always show up to these informal parties would be *another* older guy who knew the bartender back from high school. This particular dude now worked as a lawyer in D.C.

I would see this older guy around the pool and we would get to talking about life, baseball, pussy, whatever. I'd express my frustrations at not being old enough to "legally" drink and he'd always just smile and nod his head, as if to say, *I was there too, pal. Hang in there, gooch. It'll get better.*

He was a cool dude. I liked him a lot.

One day just before I graduated, this lawyer was at the pool, drinking a six pack of Natty Bohs.

Just chatting, making small talk, I told him my plans to perform comedy after I graduated. He said he was a big fan of comedy. He told me to tell him a few jokes. I did.

He laughed *very* hard. Like, *super* hard.

I appreciated his reaction and his support. I didn't always get that reaction back at home. And I was new to the humor game.

"I'll tell you what," I said, after he stopped laughing. "One day when you're on the Supreme Court, I'll write jokes that you can read from the bench."

He smiled and said, "That's a deal! And when I'm on the Supreme Court, if you ever need anything, just let me know."

We both laughed and shook on it.

And that was not the last I heard from future Supreme Court Justice Brett Kavanaugh ...

More to come on this later.

Back to me:

Every era has its peak. Rome had its downfall. America had 1776 and all that fun shit that had to do with that particular time.

For me, and my legend, my peak was high school.

You may not believe that with all I've achieved since school, but I'm telling you the god's honest truth.

High school was my high point.

This was when I reached cruising altitude.

Everything was clear sailing. The tracks were cleared for me to launch. And every other traveling cliché.

Years before Tom Green, and *way* before *Impractical Jokers*, and a decade before *Punk'd*, and years before *Nathan for You*, and years and years before *Jackass*, years before *anything* really, there was me, with a few of my friends, in Bethesda, Maryland, pulling pranks on unsuspecting victims.

I was the king of fucking Bethesda pranks.

I was a prank-slinger.

I was fearless. I guess I felt I had nothing to lose. And to be honest, I didn't.

I'd run nude into ice cream shops and ask for "human flavor."

I'd fart into grocery store microphones.

I'd show up at a barber shop and request that they shave a Batman logo into my pubes.

I'd toilet paper the house of a foreign exchange student.

I'd rent a horse under a fake name and leave it within a shopping center's parking lot, in the one handicapped spot.

I'd hang a sign over the Beltway that had my friend's phone number on it ... with "FREE BJs!" written next to it.

It was *glorious*.

Maybe I shouldn't be putting this down on paper.

I was never caught or got into any trouble for these pranks.

And I don't want to start now.

I wonder what the statute of limitations would be for pitching a huge dookie in front of one of your teacher's houses?

Can you imagine *that* on a court docket?

"Sir, we're sorry to tell you that the shit you took on the doorstep of your teacher's house in 12th grade could still put you away for life."

But even beyond the fun aspect, I became an expert at *phone* pranks, which was *way* ahead of its time.

I loved calling suicide hotlines and pretending I was going to kill myself. I loved ordering pizzas with "fromunda cheese." I'd play the cassettes in the car as my friends and I drove around the Pike, eating takeout from Bob's Big Boy and Roy Rogers. We use to laugh our asses off. There's one gag where I'd have a Chinese accent and I tried to order a dog from a shelter for "today's special." There's another prank in which I called a male teacher in a real femmy voice and pretended to be a former lover who wanted to blackmail him for "what happened back in college." Hours and hours of phone tomfoolery.

Remember *Crank Yankers*? Or the *Jerky Boys*?

I've played some audio from these pranks on my satellite radio show but I've never really done justice to what I accomplished back then. John Lennon always claimed that the best work the Beatles ever did wasn't on their albums but back in their early days, before they ever became famous, playing live for just a few fans. I'd say the same.

I was there *first* and have the evidence to prove it.

It's frustrating to think back on how much this type of humor influenced the prankers who came after me. Tom Green grew up in Canada and not in Maryland but I have no doubt that my tapes made their way up to him.

I do know that my style of comedy is evident in Spike Jonze's early skateboarding videos, and then later in his movies, like *Being John Malkovich* and *Where the Wild Things Are*. I know someone who knows the guy who represents Spike in Hollywood, and Spike denies it supposedly, but I can *still* see it.

Whatever.

Spike's a good guy and he definitely has some talent. But he's originally from Rockville, Maryland! How could he have *not* heard about these tapes?!

He *must* have!

But again, whatever.

All the best to him. Honestly.

(Now will you appear on my satellite radio show, Spike?! *Please*?!)

My high school days disappeared in a laugh-infused flash.

I'm seventeen and about to graduate in a few months. The last few years have been fun but not as fun as it would have been had I attended a public school where *anything* went.

I'm about to graduate 219 out of 347, with a solid C plus.

There was really nothing I could do about my inglorious academic career.

Seriously, mom and dad. You wanted me to get better grades?

Ha!

No thanks.

That left one thing:

Having more pranky fun.

I knew I had at least one more caper left in me before I graduated that June and I knew that it had to be a *big* one.

Something the school would be talking about for generations.

There were a lot of opportunities to choose from.

I was never at a loss for prank ideas.

In the end, I went with a *doozy*.

I had a writing teacher named Miss Bailey. I had her for two years and she kept giving me C's.

Fair enough. A lot of teachers I had for two years gave me C's.

A lot of the teachers I had for *one* year gave me C's.

But what bothered me most about Miss Bailey was that I was actually turning in *good* work and she was *still* giving me fucking C's.

I was terrible in a lot of subjects but I was always very good at writing. It just came naturally, especially when I was allowed to *really* let my funny out.

Like the essay I wrote that was called "Emily Dickenson is Great But I Wish She Was *Way* Hotter."

It was a joke. Obviously, Emily Dickensen is a genius, or so I've been told many times. I personally never understood her poetry. What I *do* know is that she was no looker. Maybe that's why she stayed home all day, every day, and never left her house, and wrote all that poetry that students would later lie about enjoying. But let's be honest here, and I'm all about honesty: she ain't someone you'd invite to your senior prom. Maybe *that's* why she was always so down and unhappy. I don't know. I'm no therapist.

I wrote a shit ton of funny stuff back then. I wrote an essay about how Shakespeare would have been a hell of a lot funnier if he had only performed pranks in the 17th century instead of writing boring plays.

Miss Bailey gave that one a D. As for the Dickensen essay, that one got a C minus.

Miss Bailey and I did not get along.

I think that's pretty obvious.

Miss Bailey had it coming. So, what to do?

Well, here's one thing:

I learned that Miss Bailey owned a backyard hot tub. I found out where she lived in Bethesda.

And I then took care of the situation in my own, very special way.

Picture Miss Bailey coming home from a long day of trying to teach morons like me how to write. She's exhausted and rightably so. Try to envision her slipping into a warm hot tub ... bubbling over with citrus-flavored Surge soda. Picture Miss Bailey screaming. Picture her jumping out and slipping and falling and crying.

Picture me videotaping the entire event on an early version of a digital recorder.

I should point out that my father worked for years as a lobbyist for the American Beverage Association.

I could get as much soda as I needed.

Which definitely didn't hurt when I threw parties around my pool when my parents were off traveling to St. Barts a few times a year.

Anyway, does this type of prank sound familiar?

If it does, there's a *damn good* reason for that: Tom Green later performed it. And millions saw "his" prank and loved it and thought that Tom was doing it for the first time.

He wasn't.

Hey, Tom, thanks for paying me for this prank idea!

Just kidding. I love your work even if it does seem … *familiar.*
Come on my podcast, now?! No reason to remain mad at me!
Specially when I'm telling the … truth.

Miss Bailey left that summer to work in an office as a secretary at a
medical office on Old Georgetown Road. She never did teach again.
She wasn't all bad. She just did not have the best sense of humor in the
world. What can I say? Another one bites the dust.

*Regardless, thanks for teaching me how to write. Wish you were
still alive to read this book.*

*I might have even given you a discount and a "thank you" at the
end. How cool would that have been?!*

Graduation came and went without a clear picture as to what
exactly I was going to do for the rest of my life. I hit Beach Week with
some pals in Ocean City, Maryland, and partied damn hard in a condo
my father owned on 96th Street.

My father would call and ask if I was ever coming back home.

I'd ignore these calls. I had better things to be doing. Beach Week
came and went and then merged into summer. And I made no effort to
head back to Bethesda. Why should I have? I was having a ball! I was
doing a ton of fun stuff!

Like watching hours and hours and hours of TV.

I could do that *real* well.

I *adore* television. If television were a woman, I'd make love to
her for fifteen hours a day, while sitting on the couch, eating snacks
and watching TV.

If television were a hot dog, I'd fuck it every which way but loose,
and then suck off that hot mustard before ever touching those warm
buns.

If television was a 64-ounce cup of soda, I'd drink the entire damn
thing and then burp out my love in various flavors and scents.

That's how much I love television.

When I wasn't hanging with friends on the boardwalk or on the
beach, I'd be inside watching TV, mostly sports. When it came to
comedy, I didn't care. As long as it wasn't too fancy.

I loved *Sister Sister, Mad About You,* and *Family Matters.* I liked
Friends a lot, of course. *The Simpsons* was okay. But what I really
loved was *Wings.*

I just wanted to laugh. End of story. It wasn't complicated. It never
has been.

I hate when comedy gets way too up its own patootle for its own
good.

And I especially hate it when TV gets way too up its own ass. It's almost as if the creators are trying to prove how smart they were, rather than just having fun.

It's all about fun, people!

I mean, comedy should be fun, right?

I hated *Seinfeld* and I still hate it. I hate the whininess. I hate the outfits Jerry wears. I hate that none of the men bang Elaine. I hate how the show had nothing to do with my own life in Maryland. I hated the phoniness of the laugh track. I hated the horrible bass-heavy interludes (it always sounded like shitty jazz). I hated comedy about *nothing*. I wanted it to be about *something*. Preferably something that *interested* me. And if not, just make me laugh, okay? This isn't physics. Why make it all about anxiety and being bored?

If the characters are that bored, let me tell you something: the viewers are definitely *also* going to be fucking bored.

There was one episode of *Seinfeld* that I semi-liked, and that was the one in which Jerry has a girlfriend who is either ugly or beautiful, depending on the way the light hits her at any specific moment. That one made me laugh. Otherwise ...

When I did eventually get into comedy, I wanted to shake things up. I wanted to bring to the stage, as well as to television, the excitement I had felt hanging out with friends and pulling pranks and busting each others' balls. I really wasn't seeing that at the time.

That, however, was down the line.

So I had a pretty good idea that I wanted to devote my life to comedy in some way. But I still wasn't completely sure that I *could* pull it off. So I figured I'd take a gap year and figure it all out.

After Beach Week ended and after my friends left, and after Beach Week turned into Beach Month, and then Beach Month *After* Month, I sort of fell into a comfortable, relaxed groove.

Every day at the beach, I'd hit the boardwalk and read *The Washington Post,* supposedly looking for job listings but mostly just trying to appear smart for the passing chicks. Typically I'd hold out the front section of the paper so passersby would think I was reading about the most important issues of the day. In reality, I was most likely checking out the comic strips in the *Style* section, which I've always loved. Comedy for the sake of comedy. Nothing too fancy. Hit the joke, then it's over. No dissertation, no classes, no big shot book author telling you why you should have laughed when you didn't.

Fuck that. I hate know-it-alls.

I've never understood why anyone would ever take a course in comedy. Isn't that *why* you get into comedy? So that you won't have to ever take another fucking course for the rest of your life? Who the hell wants to do homework about anything, let alone laughter? The people teaching these comedy classes typically can't even make a living at the skill they're teaching *others* to do!

Now *that's* funny.

My advice to a young comedy fan is to read books by those who have *made* it. Now *they* are the ones you should trust.

I'm not talking about books like *Poking a Dead Horse* or whatever, which is about as boring a book as you'd ever hope to *never* find.

No, I'm talking about real *books*, like this one. I've paid my dues and I'm now going to give it to you straight. No academic bullshit attached.

I stumbled into it. You will too.

Back to the newspaper comic-strips …

Momma always made me laugh like crazy. So did *Pluggers* and *Zitz*.

Least favorite: *Doonesbury*.

Insufferable!

Just a constant stream of illustrations of the fucking White House. Panel after panel, cartoon after cartoon. With dialogue that never ended. *Way* too much writing. And who gives a shit about politics when you're a kid, anyway?

One afternoon, most likely deep into October, with no jobs on the horizon, still staying at my father's condo, still hitting the boardwalk every day to "read" the paper, someone sat down next to me on the boardwalk bench. He had a book in his hand.

A real academic: *Needful Things* by Steven King.

One of my favorites.

My kind of dude.

This turned out to be Benedict Hutchinson III.

Does that sound like a British monarch?

It most definitely wasn't.

And yes, that was his *real* name.

Never heard of him?

Well, you might know him better as … Tim-Tam-Flimm-Flammery, my ever loyal sidekick on my podcast and satellite radio show.

You just read that correctly. Tim, believe it or not, started off life as "Benedict Hutchinson III"!

So that alone is worth the price of this book, right?

When Tim-Tam-Flimm-Flammery and I first met, he was working as a house painter and doing the occasional stand-up gig at both Dickens Bar on the bay side and the Sand Bar and Grille closer to the boardwalk.

He wasn't exactly leading a royal life, beyond his fancy name.

He'd spin records for "Bucket of Rocks Nights" at The Bearded Clam and at Big Pecker's Bar & Grille for some extra cash. (For those not from Maryland, "Bucket of Rocks" basically means you get a bucket of cheap-ass bottles of the worst beer known to man, Rolling Rock.)

Tim-Tam-Flimm-Flammery and I quickly became best pals. We shared *a lot* in common. Both the funniest in our high schools. Not the best when it came to school. Loved pranks. Loved women. Not exactly laser-focused at a young age on knowing what exactly we had to do to make a living. Not smart in the "traditional" sense.

But ...

Super smart in the *street* sense.

The comedy world has the Flammer to thank for turning me on to stand-up comedy, a world I never really cared much about. I mean, I knew about stand-up but I always thought I'd be a writer of comedy films and television. It seemed to be the easiest way, right? Sit on your ass and not travel and write jokes for a lot of money?

Or I'd just be a host of a funny TV show.

What could be better than that? Easy peasy!

Flammer also wanted to get into comedy and figured performing as a stand-up was the best way to break in.

Shit, what did he know?

What did *either* of us know?!

We were two dipshits from Maryland. It sounded good to me! What else was I doing? And if it took performing stand-up to make a lot of money in comedy, that was just fine!

When I was growing up, my father loved comedy but he wasn't exactly my "in" to this world. He made an okay living but, sadly, he knew no one in entertainment. He was a comedy fan, that was true, and he owned all the albums that were huge in the 1950s and '60s and '70s, such as Bob Newhart, Lenny Bruce, Richard Pryor, Bill Cosby, and all the rest of them.

Truth be told, I never loved that stuff. I found it too dated. Too slow. And the material had nothing to do with *my* life. I mean, I *liked* Richard Pryor. I thought he was smart and I could see that he could do funny characters. But growing up in a whorehouse in Ohio or wherever ... what did that have to do with *me*?

I grew up in a nice house in Bethesda, Maryland, in a cul-de-sac, surrounded by other suburban homes.

I'm just being honest.

I don't look down on Pryor's life for any particular reason. Or his comedy.

I just don't know it—*at all*.

That sort of life worked for *his* comedy. Not for mine. My comedy would never have been honest if I had copied his style.

And only when the comedy is the most *honest* can it then become the most *funny*.

That's hard-won advice, by the way. (Yet *another* reason that the cost of this book has *already* been worth it. By the time you finish, there will have been *many* good reasons to have purchased this book.)

As far as Pryor goes, I did love one of his movies called *The Toy*. If you haven't seen this movie, check it out. It's hilarious. I think it's his best role.

I guess the style of comedy that I loved the most when I was younger would be the glory years of *Saturday Night Live,* with David Spade, Chris Farley, Adam Sandler, Rob Schneider. Classic. This for me was the "golden time." Forget the early years of *SNL.* Forget anything on that show *since*. This specific period is when everything *clicked* for me. I've never laughed harder. And I bet *you* haven't either.

I *still* have all those seasons' episodes on VHS tapes.

I know, I know. I've heard from my "Staller Callers" who claim that these particular years at *SNL* were "offensive." That the characters were insulting to women. That there shouldn't have been men playing women characters.

But men have been doing this shit for literally decades, going back to Aristofones. And I'm sure even *before* the Romans!

Monty Python definitely did it, even though I hate them and everyone else who has a foreign accent who attempts comedy.

Here's a pop quiz:

Please name me one *SNL* character funnier than Chris Farley playing the fat Gap worker who's always "famished."

I'm waiting.

Right.

I still laugh the most when I watch reruns from those years. All of those characters, so brilliant:

The fat lunch lady.

The fat Gap girl.

The fat male strip dancer.

The fat *anyone*.

I know it's not the politically correct thing to say nowadays but that shit was *funny*.

Period.

End of story.

It's like the North Korean character in *Sixteen Candles*.

Funny.

Correct to say so?

Probably not, which is why I'll be hearing soon from my Staller Callers. That's fine. There's an air horn waiting to blast you away into infinity.

If I liked any stand-up comedy as a kid it was probably Dice, as in Andrew Dice Clay. He was raw and I suppose he was "offensive," but is that a bad thing? Anything wrong with rhyming dirty poems?

I'm not overly familiar with Emily Dickensen's work but I can only imagine she rubbed out a few dirty one-offs as well.

I do know that Walt Whitman was gay and penned a few odes to the male body. I have nothing against that. If it's funny and well-written, I'm fine with it. In fact, the dirtier the better. There was a high school close to where I grew up that was actually called Walt Whitman High School.

The mascot was a homosexual Civil War male nurse.

Joking.

So I guess you could say that comedy was my "thing."

I thought comedy, talked comedy, lived comedy. But to go from being a fan of the form to making a living at it, well, that was a bit of a mystery.

Again, it was my dream to write comedy professionally, either for TV or for movies.

But how to pull it off? I had no idea.

So when I first went to see the Flim-Flammer perform stand-up at the Sand Bar and Grille in Ocean City, just off the boardwalk, it was like entering an entirely new world. I was more used to TV and movies. As much as my father loved to listen to his lame comedy albums, he never took me to a comedy club. My dad didn't have the time. Or the interest. He was too busy protecting the soda industry.

But as soon as I walked into the Sand Bar—instantly, *bang*!, without a *moment* of a doubt—I *knew* this was the world for me. I loved the smoke-filled air (back then, in the 1990s, I was a smoker, and so was half of America). I loved the sounds, the smells, the cozy feeling that I was someplace *special*. It felt as if I was in a cave in which only laughs resounded and the happy chatter of people echoed and echoed repeatedly into and beyond the early dawn hours.

The waitresses didn't hurt either. Most were about my age, blonde and more than willing to try just about anything. These weren't wall flowers at Sara Laurence University. These were girls who were *living* life.

Like I was.

I liked that.

14

A lot!

I knew that this would be my office for the next few months. But first, I had to learn stand-up. Does a comic need an agent? Are promotional photos necessary? Black and white? Color? How does one hold the mic? How long does it take to go from performing stand-up to then writing for television or the movies out in California?

I just didn't know.

So I sent myself to school.

The first *real* school that ever meant anything to me.

The Flammer quickly moved into my father's condo as my roommate. He began to pay me for the privilege of sleeping on my father's couch in the living room. This gave me the opportunity to earn some real money and it also allowed me to watch, up close, what I very much wanted to do: write jokes and then perform them up on a stage. And then quickly move to New York or California to make a ton of fucking money.

Every stand-up has a character. I learned that pretty quickly.

The Flammer's on-stage persona was "horny virgin." I know that's a common stand-up character today. But trust me when I tell you that it was fresh in 1996. It was the opposite of what most stand-up acts were all about.

Every other comic wanted to be seen as "Joe Cool."

You know the type: *Hey, look at me! I'm funky in bed, I've got it all figured out, I might pretend that I don't, but I really do have it all figured out! Ain't I cool?*

In reality, *no one* did better with the clubs' waitresses than the Flammer but he could also play the comedic virgin role to perfection: never been laid, never had oral sex, never did a thing, except with himself. The audiences lapped it up. Here are some of the jokes he'd perform:

"I tried paying a prostitute last night but she didn't have change for a one."

"Anyone wanna see a photo of my girlfriend? (Holds up photo of a beautiful woman) Isn't she *gorgeous*? We haven't yet had the pleasure of meeting."

"I'm not a member of the mile-high club. But I am a member of the *half*-a-mile-high club." (Makes jerkoff motions.)

You get the picture. Stand-up is hard to describe on the written page. It's even harder to pull off, which is why I hope that everyone reading this book will also listen to the audio version that's read by yours truly.

That would be more of the *stereo* version, while this book might be more of the *mono* version ...

But you know what I'm talking about, right? Every hand movement, every facial tic, every single pause that takes place up on that stage is impossible to describe on the page. Flammer had it *all*. He was what the comedy lifers call a *keystone*, solid enough to be a terrific performer, but maybe not big enough yet to be a headliner.

He was *good*. Real good. And I learned a ton.

Meanwhile, my father finally reached me (on the land line) and he gave me six more months and then I had to vacate the apartment.

Ain't that nice?

The week before, I had told my pop about all of my plans to get into stand-up full time.

And, no surprise, he was a bit confused.

"Are you even funny?"

"Yeah, dad. I am. Maybe not according to your 1960s sense of humor, but yes."

"You can get into whatever association you want as a lobbyist," he replied. "American Petroleum is looking for someone, I do know that."

"Yeah, dad. That's not what I had envisioned for life, y'know," I replied.

"Your mom's upset," he exclaimed.

"Wow, I'm impressed. You somehow managed to reach her on the golf course?" I retorted. "Congrats!"

(My parents were members of the Chevy Chase Country Club. My mom never left the golf course. She also never shared my sense of humor. Maybe she felt it was too edgy, I don't know, I never asked.)

"I'll give you six months," he replied. "And then the money flow stops."

Looking back, I really can't blame the guy. My pops grew up in a working class family in Boston. His father shoveled coal. His mother worked nights at a sewing factory. His brother, my uncle, was in a wheelchair because of cerebral palsy and he died when my father was six, after being hit by a milk truck. Poor Uncle Benny. Not easy for anyone in that family. My grandfather, Charles, died when my father was eleven. My father's mother, Helen, died when my dad was eighteen. My father put himself through college at Boston University by working at a small grocery in the North end.

And the older I get, and the more years that have passed since my dad passed away, the more I've come to appreciate what he managed to succeed and the life he provided for me. I think about him all the time. My mom? Not so much. She's *still* out on the golf course. This time with a *new* husband.

Her third.

Back to me.

So I was an adult now, living at my father's condo, trying to learn all I could about stand-up comedy. And I had six months to succeed or I was out on my young ass.

There were a lot of comedians coming through Ocean City at that time.

Some of the headliners were lifers, meaning they never got into comedy for the direct purpose of making money. I kind of felt sorry for these idiots. There was an air of desperation about them. Middle-aged men, wearing cheap shoes, they'd travel from town to town telling jokes about all their ex-wives and the children they were not allowed to see anymore. They appeared about as bored as any government worker and appeared about as inspired.

"I don't talk to my divorced wife anymore. At least not within six feet."

You know the type.

There's a *sadness* to these jokes that I always hated.

Why not talk about the *fun* things in life that are *real*? Like that time you were partying and you threw up out of your nose and you were in a Kentucky Fried Chicken and the manager kicked you and all your friends out? (This happened. You've probably heard about it a million times on my show.)

Or that time you borrowed your father's Beemer but you somehow forgot to eject the cassette of *Dice Rules* and you also forgot to turn down the volume, which was blasting when your father turned on the car the next morning with a client in the car. (This happened.)

Or the time you showed up at a friend's lake house and ran through a plate glass window with a mask and holding a knife. (This *happened*. Have the scars to prove it. But that scream and then that *laugh* ...)

In other words, make it *fun*.

What was wrong with fun?

Apparently *everything*. Because one can't just be fun, I suppose. One has to be *likable*.

And that's the problem with comedy then. And today. But I'm getting ahead of myself.

The Flammer had introduced me to the owner of the club, Martin "Matty" Barth, and we seemed to get along well. The guy was in his thirties and he always wanted to own a comedy club. Not a bad guy–or so I thought. Just more business than funny, if you know what I mean.

After a few weeks, Matty was letting me enter the club for free, although I did still have to pay for drinks and food.

No problem. I would have paid *anything* to have had the honor to come in every night.

And to eventually get up on stage and strut my own stuff.

After about a month of watching comedians every night, soaking up all I could, trying to learn as much as possible, I approached Matty at the end of one evening behind the stage. The conversation went something like this:

"Hey, Matty."

"Hey, Skippy."

"Listen, I have a proposition."

"To sleep with my wife? She's all yours!"

"Ha, no thanks! A different proposition. How long does it typically take for a comedian to become an opener and to then eventually become the headliner? Like, the Flammer is the opener, the keystoner, the first one on stage."

"Gee, Skip, it takes years. I mean, if you're lucky. Most drop out long before then. Why do you ask?"

"Because I'd like to become a headliner."

"Are you serious? Sometimes even I can't tell when you're joking!"

"You're a comedy club owner. You'd think you would!"

"Maybe ... but I really can't tell right now. Have you ever actually *performed* stand-up comedy?"

"I haven't. But I'm as funny as it gets! And I've been living with the Flammer for the past few months."

"It takes more than that, Skip. It takes *devotion*. Like *any* profession. Maybe *more* than other occupations."

"I think I can handle it."

"Handle what?"

"Me headlining."

"That's impossible."

"*Nothing* is impossible."

"Well, *this* is."

"Why?"

"Because we have headliners booked through the end of the year."

"Cancel one."

"Doesn't work like that, pal."

"Name your price?"

"Excuse me?"

"Your. *Price*."

"For what?"

"For me to *headline*."

"Without ever having performed stand-up?"

"I've been performing since birth."

"Not in front of a paying crowd you haven't."

"Name your price."

If there's one thing I learned from my father, it's the following: There is *always* a price. Whether my father was talking with a politician or a Senator or just another lobbyist, there was *always* a price that could be made to make something *happen.*

Or not happen.

A child died in your home state because he drank too much Mountain Dew? That's a shame. How much would it take to set things right? Maybe a new community gym?

A woman drank so much Mr. Pibb that she had to have kidney surgery? Gee, that sucks. I'm so sorry. What might help with this situation? A college scholarship in Mr. Pibb's name?

Well, life is no different. And guess what? With Matty there was … a price. *Shocker!*

I've talked about this a lot on my show and podcast. I've always said—and if you don't believe me, go back and listen to the older shows because it's all there—I've always said that sometimes you …

Just have to do what you have to do.

It's as simple as that.

You gotta play the fucking game. You gotta take matters into your own hands.

You can't *wait* for success.

If you do wait, you'll still be waiting a hundred years from now. You just can't sit back and wait for others to help you.

I mean, you can … but you'll get nowhere in life.

Do *whatever* it takes to succeed. *Make it fucking happen!*

I've talked all about this on my show and podcast.

But I've never specifically told you how much I had to pay Matty to make my own dreams come true.

Well, for the first time ever, I'm *now* going to reveal that exact price:

Hang on. Not quite yet. You know why? Cause I'm in charge.

As my favorite author, Ayn Rand, once wrote, "The question isn't who's going to let me. The question is, who's going to *stop* me."

Love that quote!

Let me back up a bit and first tell you what my roommate Flammer's reaction was when I told him that I'd be headlining right off the bat without "paying my dues."

Now most comedians would have been, to say the very least, a tad *annoyed,* as they'd have every right to be. I skipped *over* the Flammer. If anyone was due to become a headliner, it would have been the Flammer, someone who put in countless hours up on that stage as a host and an opener.

I mean, I was not just skipping over him once … but *twice*: two positions up to headliner.

And, to be fair to Flammer, the poor guy *deserved* the shot. *More* than deserved it. He had every right to be furious!

Every right in the entire fucking world!

But when I told him, he took it like a man.

He could not have been more kind and gracious.

I mean, not at first.

But when I threw in the incentive for him to stay at my father's apartment free of rent, he came around. He really did. This is no shit.

He was *proud* of me. I'll *always* give him that.

For all the shit I've given him on the air (for not getting me lunch fast enough, for not being able to book a certain guest, for not handing me the correct cartridge, for fucking up left and right), I love the guy. He was there for me when it counted and I'll never forget it.

If he had been rude, I might have said, "Fuck you. Get out of my pop's apartment," and never thought of him again.

But he didn't. And that's why you know him as Tim-Tam-Flimm-Flammery, production assistant extraordinaire.

Now, to be honest, the first thing he said to me after "congratulations" was: "How much you paying Matty?"

I thought that a bit rude. It's like asking someone how much pussy they got the night before. I mean, you *could* tell, but it does a bit of a disservice to the woman who gave out that pussy, m'thinks. (Said with pinkie in air, all fancy like, and with my chin up real high, smelling of … pussy.)

So I didn't tell him then. I just thanked him for congratulating me and then got busy prepping for my first night as a headliner.

And I didn't tell him for *years*. Actually, I *never* told him.

So now, for the first time, right here in this book, even the Flammer will be learning the specific figure, just like you! (*For that alone, this is worth what I'm charging! I mean, c'mon! What a fucking bargain, right?! I'm telling you! This book is worth every goddamn penny!*)

So here's the price I paid …

Hold on.

Just kidding.

Here's the price:

$75,000.

That's a lot of money.

I'm not going to deny that $75,000 is a lot of money.

Especially when I was just starting out and I was pretty much flat-on-my-ass broke.

But look at it this way:

Some people go to college. Some people intern. Some people travel overseas for a year or so on their parents' dime.

I looked at this $75,000 as being an *investment*. An investment my father easily could have paid—and did, when I explained to him the situation.

In many ways, I *saved* my father money.

I know *so many* people who attended an expensive university, paid $70,000 a year, and then ended up working for peanuts.

Would *that* have been worth it?

Also, keep in mind, I insisted to Matty that I would headline *five* times. Not just once.

So the final tally came out to … what?

Only $15,000 per headline gig?

That's pretty good.

I know high school classmates who left for Yale and Harvard and wherever else they went and they were just fine with their parents spending a fortune on their educations.

Well, this was *my* education.

Some parents buy their kids an expensive first house. Some parents buy them an expensive first car. Others buy them both, as well as a first, a second and a third expensive business. I know a lot of people my age who got *everything*. I got none of that.

I was living in a shitty one-bedroom condo my father owned in Ocean City Maryland, and eating crab fries every night. I was doing my time. I was paying my dues.

And I even had to live in my *fucking car* for a few nights when the apartment was infested with bed bugs. Yes. I was once homeless.

All I ever wanted was … *a damned opportunity*. Just like everyone else. And that's all I've ever asked for. An opportunity to *succeed*.

To show that I *could* succeed. So I paid the club owner the money–after much negotiation. In fact, Matty Barth first asked for $100,000.

I talked him down. The deal we eventually worked out was for me to headline five times over a period of three months for $75,000.

Always on *off* nights, never on weekends.

Regardless, at least I was finally fucking *headlining*!

This was exciting. But now what?

If you want to succeed in comedy and make a lot of money out in Hollywood–or so I was being told by Flammer–you had to become a success as a stand-up comedian first.

Could I become one?

That, dear readers, very much remained to be seen ….

Chapter Two

KILLING IT

The mid to late 90s was a *super* exciting time to be in comedy. When I look back, it practically seems like a golden period, one that I could tell my children, or even grandchildren, all about, in wonderful and nuanced detail.

Since that's not the case, since I have neither children nor will I ever have grandchildren, let me tell you this:

I met *everyone*.

Some today are even considered "legends."

Not by me, necessarily, but by others.

When I tell random people outside of showbiz these stories, they look at me in wonder, almost as if I've come back from a magical land, such as Narnia or Oz.

But I just consider the guys I met along the way "fellow travelers" in this long and crazy road that's called Comedy.

For most people, this road is a dead end or cul-de-sac. Lucky for me it was more like a thoroughfare.

Granted, it took a bunch of time on numerous back roads to reach this thoroughfare, but reach it I did.

Let me give you some names of people I've come across on my travels.

All readers, including you, come to books for names:

Marc Maron. Joe Rogan. Bill Burr. Louis CK. Dave Chapelle. Kevin James. Chris Rock. Mitch Hedberg, Martin Lawrence, Jon Stewart, Dave Attell, Sinbad, David Cross, Andy Kindler, Jay Moor.

And yes, even Eddie Murphy.

I met them all. And I have the stories that go with it. More on that later.

For now, though, it was time for me to put my nose to the kidney stone and start working hard on my new stand-up act.

What character should I choose? Every comedian is basically a character even if that character is just an extension of their true selves. So what would mine be?

I went through a long list of possibilities: the stud, the loser, the cheapskate, the nerd, the jock, but I kept coming back to just being *honest*. Pryor was honest with his character. That's who *he* was, a sex-crazed black guy born in a whorehouse.

Carlin was honest with his comedy, too. That's just who he was: a sharp-tongued white guy from New York City with a ponytail.

There was really no choice for me. I had to become who I was but *more* so.

The Flammer was gracious enough to help me bring my semi-fictional character to life. And, again, I can only thank him for his generosity.

Both of us would retreat to my apartment after we were done hanging at the comedy club, get baked, and then start riffing, attempting to one-up each other. We'd go until five, six in the morning, sometimes even later.

I would just start talking and would literally not stop.

If the Flammer liked what he heard, he'd write it down in a notebook. We did this for about two weeks. Go to bed when the sun was rising, wake up around noon, hit the boardwalk for a quick fried lunch (either fried clams or crab cakes), and then retreat back into the apartment to create more material.

That was me, anyway.

The Flammer, after helping me all night, every night, usually had to get up at 7:00 A.M. to paint houses.

Poor bastard.

I've been told that it took Carlin about a year to come up with sixty minutes of material. It took Cosby less time and he could perform a fresh set only a few weeks after retiring his last set. He was a creative monster who never stopped. (By the way, say what you want about the Coz, but the guy could write a *ton* of material. I'm not saying he's innocent when it comes to dosing women with drugs and then raping them, but the guy could *write*, even if it's a little too vanilla for my taste.)

What soon became pretty clear was that it was going to take me a lot *less* time to come up with sixty minutes than the run-of-the-mill comedian. Maybe not as fast as Cosby but pretty damn fast.

Within days, I had *hours* of material. *Hours.*

The Flammer told me he'd never seen anything like it. Pages and pages of observations, jokes, thoughts on the world, thoughts about women, thoughts on the government, thoughts about old people, thoughts on blondes, brunettes and even the red haired, who sort of freak me out as they remind me of albino mice, which you obviously know, as you're no doubt a listener to my podcast, hopefully a longtime listener.

I can only assume that you know me *pretty damn well* by now.

You've been listening for years.

But here's the thing: Audiences back then, and this was in the mid 90s, did not know *squat* about me: beyond that I was a good-looking, young buck ready to take on the world of comedy.

Matty, the owner of the club, gave me a call one afternoon and asked how I was doing. *Was I ready?*

Yeah, I'm ready, idiot!

Matty then told me that they weren't typically open on Thanksgiving night but this year was going to be different. They were going to do an early show at 4:30 in the afternoon and then everyone could go back to their families to eat dinner. It'd be a good excuse for them to leave the house for a little while, to escape their nagging relatives.

Was I interested in headlining?

Did a grizzly bear just take a huge shit in the pope's mouth?

Why yes, one just did!

I *was* very much interested!

Besides, I had already paid Matty the damn $75,000 and the check had cleared.

It really wasn't so much a matter of *if* but *when.*

Now I knew: Thanksgiving.

Which was just fine with me. I wasn't headed back to Bethesda for a holiday dinner, my first away as an adult, as my parents were headed to their place in St. Barts and my older brother the doctor and his fancy wifey-poo (also a doctor) didn't invite me to *their* dinner.

I was free-floating on my own.

I was a man without a plan.

There are worse things to have to do, right?

Perform comedy in front of audience members escaping their family members for a few blissful hours?

Hello?

Thanksgiving afternoon it would be then.

November 28th, 1996.

My routine was pretty much entirely finished and I was only fine-tuning my delivery *technique*.

This was pretty damn exciting for an 18-year-old!

And please remember: this would be only the first *of* five headlining gigs to come! There was a *lot* more excitement down the road!

But first I needed an outfit. So much of the success of a stand-up has to do with what he *wears* onstage.

Even *I* was aware of that and I had never before been on stage!

I knew that I couldn't get too fancy or I'd end up looking like I was out of touch with the "common man" down in the audience. This would especially hold true on Thanksgiving. I didn't want to look like an unfunny uncle telling pussy jokes. I wanted to look like a well-dressed *nephew* telling pussy jokes.

So I hit the shops along the boardwalk to find just that *perfect* outfit. You remember what Eddie Murphy wore during his famous concert in the 1980s? The one that was taped for a film? It was a red leather getup that looked incredible. I wasn't looking for that. One key to comedy is to know what you can get away with and what you *can't*. I wanted to choose an outfit that said at least two things:

Take this guy seriously. But *don't* take this guy *too* seriously.

It wasn't easy to pull off, but, in the end, I chose a nice pair of work slacks (this *was* a new job, right?) and a fun T-shirt that read:

I WOULD
never use the word
FUCK
in front of
YOU

If you glanced at the shirt quickly, it read:

I WOULD FUCK YOU.

If you looked more closely, it did *not* say that.

It didn't say that *at all*.

It said just the *opposite*.

That's my favorite type of joke. You take a look, or a quick listen, and it reads or says one thing. But you take a longer, harder look, or a listen, and it says something *entirely* else.

That's good comedy.

That's comedy that *lasts*.

I arrived early to the club, around 3:00. Flammer joined me. The crowd was sparse, if non-existent. That was fine. I knew people would be arriving a little later than was typical as it was a Thanksgiving afternoon. Beyond that, I had already won. My name was on the marquee as the headliner. I took a million photos on a Walgreen's disposable camera as evidence to insert into my resume.

No matter what happened from now until I died, no one would ever be able to take this away from me.

This was *huge*.

I had *already* proven to the assholes back in high school who had doubted me that I wasn't a total and complete failure.

There was some talk later by comedians that I had Photoshopped the photos I took of the marquee.

But guess what?

Photoshop did not exist then.

And to this day I don't even fucking know *how to use* Photoshop.

So suck my nutz. My name was on the marquee and that's a fact.

Inside, I met the two openers, Jim Accord and Danny Fago, both super solid stand-ups who had been at the game for years, but who hadn't yet gained the name recognition to refuse a Thanksgiving afternoon gig at a comedy club in Ocean City, Maryland.

The cliché in the comedy world is that no stand-up remembers their "first time." Jay Leno once said that your first time on stage is similar to your first time with a girl: you're a bit clumsy, it's over all too quickly, and you can only look forward to your next time.

It wasn't like that for me.

I wasn't clumsy. I wasn't quick. In fact, just the opposite.

It was like I had been *born* to be up on that stage.

That's not to say, however, that the entire experience didn't feel similar to my first time making love to a girl.

The difference, though, was that *that* incident took place in the back of my father's '94 Audi Quattro Coupe, when I was sixteen, behind Wintergreen Mall, with Phil Collins blasting. The lucky lady's name was Marie and she later rated me to her friends as a "very quick study," which meant a lot. Also, she was a Holton-Arms girl, so I'm pretty sure the "control group" was large enough to make an *extremely* accurate efficacy rate.

Back to my first night as a headliner:

Jim Accord and Danny Fago were both extremely competent openers. The small crowd liked them—they were both very solid professionals. Jim's shtick was that he was a "blue-collar" type who liked to drink beer and fuck his way through life. The shtick wasn't far off from his real persona: Jim grew up in Philadelphia, on a bad side of town, and scratched his way to the middle. When he wasn't on stage, he was working as a mechanic for lawn-care vehicles. He's still out there, making a very decent living at corporate events. I remember a few of his jokes, which I'll paraphrase here:

"The only ribbon I've ever won was of the Pabst variety. But I traded it in for another six-pack."

"My father really paved the way for me in life. He drove his motorcycle off an unpaved road."

"Why do people always *think* they're going to be sick? Don't they *know* that they're about to be sick? Can't they at least give us the damn *benefit of the doubt?*"

"I come from a family where Thanksgiving was a frozen turkey, sucked *piping* hot."

The last joke did very well.

When he walked off the stage, I gave him a high-five in a show of solidarity, which he appreciated and later mentioned on a Joe Rogan podcast a few years ago, at least according to a few of my podcast's callers who told me as much. (Talkin' to you, *Bang Bangers*.)

Next up was Danny, a stand-up who's no longer on the comedy scene. He's now a spokesperson for a Seattle tech company and is supposedly content outside the "life." I say, good on him.

Danny's persona was … a little less polished than Jim's.

His comic character was that of a solid pal, someone you might know from the local bar. But Danny didn't work dirty. He worked clean, or not "blue," meaning no curse words or ribald tales. Looking back, it was the perfect crowd that afternoon for Danny's jokes, although at the time, and for many years after, I thought it was an opportunity missed, like a jogger with one foot tied behind his back.

Why not go full speed with what you have at your disposal rather than limit yourself?

I always thought it childish to not fight to the full extent of your capability.

Danny's jokes did well but they didn't kill. Here are a few that I remember, or close enough to which my memory holds true:

"I do a lot of flying between gigs. On my last flight, the pilot said something you never want to hear: 'We're now making our final approach and we should be on the ground in about twenty-five minutes. *God willing.*'"

"I was watching reruns of *Fantasy Island* the other day. That's it. I was watching reruns of *Fantasy Island* the other day."

The reception for Danny was good, polite clapping and scattered laughter throughout.

By the time the host (I forget her name) introduced me, it was nearing five and the waitresses were already busy handing out the Thanksgiving appetizers and the (third) round of drinks. The place had filled up some. This audience was ready to let loose. "Primed to go bananas," as Ricky Seizmer, owner of the Ban-Nan-Naz Comedy Club in Athens, Ohio, used to say, according to friends who performed there.

Ricky's since died from a terrible illness. I forget what.

The young female host for the evening (I'm still forgetting her name) made a few jokes and then she got the crowd pumped for the headliner's arrival—*me*.

Time slowed when my name was called.

It reminded me of that time I was in a car crash in Georgetown, when an asshole ran a stop sign and plowed directly into the side of my car, nearly killing me. He was drunk.

Sadly, so was I.

So we negated each other.

Ain't that nice?

Reality in both instances had become a slow-motion picture show, everything connected, but spread and expanded into infinity. It's hard to explain. I think Einstein talked about this. Time moves at different speeds depending on the situation. When I was up on stage, time was moving both quickly *and* dragging. I was like a spastic stuck in amber. It's hard to explain to a layperson, such as yourself. Unless you're up there, you can't really know—*truly* know—what it feels like.

I do remember the host's smile as she handed me the mic. I remember how she retreated back to the bar to watch me perform with the rest of the comics. I remember how *bright* the stage light was shining, and how much I liked that feeling.

It felt *right*.

There's been a lot of talk, both on my show and on others, about this first performance. I do know that Marc Maron has played the bootleg tape from it often and Joe Rogan has played it more than a few times. I know it's online and it's elsewhere, including on Youtube, but this is my book and I'm the one who gets to tell you the truth.

And here it is, something I've mentioned on my show so many times already:

If one records a bootleg recording and if that recording is plugged into the soundboard, then you are ...

NOT

GOING

TO

PROPERLY

HEAR

THE

CROWD'S

REACTION!

You're not going to hear the crowd's reaction.
Right?
Make sense?
It does to me.

Okay? You're not going to hear a reaction from the crowd. You know what you *are* going to hear? The person up on stage. And what he says into the mic. *That's it.*

That's why there's a soundboard and an engineer controlling it all. So the audience can *hear* what the performer is saying. That's the one purpose of a soundboard and its engineer.

The soundboard operator doesn't care about crowd noise.

The Rolling Stones can be playing in front of 200,000 people and the sound engineer's job is to record *them*.

Not the fucking crowd.

That's it.

I *killed* that night.

That's a fact.

That's what listeners to Mark's and Joe's podcasts need to know.

Not sure why one wouldn't be able to discern this difference between failure and major success by the confidence in my voice as my set went on and on. It was a thirty minute set and you can hear me only growing in confidence as it reached its conclusion. There was no panic. There was no desperation. Just a headliner who sounded for all the world like he, at last, and after a few months of floundering, finally found his life's purpose.

Also, please keep in mind, this was *years* before iPhones and other devices that could so easily record a comedy set. There was no one in the audience capable of catching the reaction to what they were witnessing up on the stage. No one. If the set had been performed today, I can guarantee you that it'd be *all over* the Web.

1996 was a different time entirely.

If you're listening to the audio version of this book, rather than actually reading it with your own eyes, you can now hear the entirety of that performance. Keep listening. If you're only reading the book, that's fine. I'm going to transcribe the performance, along with *accurate* audience reactions in brackets. And I *assure* you, nothing is being left out. *Nothing* is being inserted.

Everything you are about to read, or hear, really and *truly* happened.

I introduced myself, told them I was thankful for their presence, and then I launched into the routine itself.

I started off with joke-joke-joke.

There was no time for the audience to catch their collective breath. That's the way I wanted it. Just a joke. Then another joke. And then another. Unrelenting. A cascade of comedy. A rolling waterfall of hilarity.

My goal was to grab each of the eleven or so audience members by the balls and say, without even saying a word: *Look at me. I'm funny. I'm worth listening to goddamnit!*

Here's *exactly* the way it went down, no bullshit:

[Sound of me adjusting the mic but leaving it in the stand]

"Thank you, um, thank you—"

[Even then I didn't know the host's name]

"Just thank you, great. And thank *you* for coming out this afternoon. I know you had other things to be doing—like being miserable at your parents' houses. [HUGE LAUGH] I'd be looking miserable, too, but my parents are off in St. Barts. Knowing my parents they're making *somebody else* miserable. [BIG LAUGH] So my name is Skippy Battison and I'm the headliner tonight, as you might have seen on the marquee outside. Yeah, this is *exciting*. So let's see, what have I been up to? I will say this: I'm tired. Man, am I tired. Was up for most of last night. Word of advice: never get together with a whore named after a domestic car. [HUGE LAUGH] *Porsche* the whore is fine. [HUGE LAUGH] *Chevrolet* the whore? Not so much. [HUGE LAUGH] What other names work for whores? Junk food works well. [HUGE LAUGH] Candy. Sugar. Or pricey alcohol. *Brandy* works well. Fancy foods, not so much. [HUGE LAUGH] *Fois grois*. No. That doesn't work. [HUGE LAUGH] Cheap booze. That doesn't work either. [HUGE LAUGH] *Malt liquor. Strawberry wine,* no. [HUGE LAUGH] Expensive jewelry works great. *Diamond* is a good one. You know what *doesn't* work? *Cheap* jewelry. [IN VOICE OF A PIMP] '*Cubic Zirconia*, get yo fine, fake ass in this room!' [HUGE LAUGH] I have a long and complicated history with whores. Lost my virginity to a whore. Her name was Chastity, which I've always loved. *Chastity.* I love it when whores nickname themselves the complete *opposite* of who they are. [HUGE LAUGH] I *love* that. [IN VOICE OF A NURSE] 'Dr. All Thumbs is now ready to perform your brain surgery!' [TREMENDOUS LAUGH] So what I'm saying is that I did end up meeting a whore last night. But negotiations broke down when she didn't have change for a one. [HUGE LAUGH]"

I should probably now point out that I had paid the Flammer for the "Asking a prostitute if she had change for a one" joke.

Headliners will do this *often* with openers. In a sense, you're paying for the joke to become yours and for them to retire it. It's a well-known industry standard. For what it's worth, Flammer used to tell me that I made the joke even *better*. When I was up on that stage the first time, I couldn't see his reaction, but I could hear it: it was seismic. I don't remember how much I paid him. It might have just been for the opportunity for him to stay another month on a couch in my father's apartment for free but that's payment enough.

A damn good deal for the Flammer!

Okay, back to the set:

"So that didn't work out. But I do have a girlfriend. Anyone wanna see a picture of her? [HOLDING UP A PHOTO TAKEN OF A CROWD SHOT] Isn't she fucking beautiful? Yeah. We haven't yet had the pleasure of meeting. [HUGE LAUGH] So what do I look for in a girl? I can tell you what I *don't* look for: someone who can beat me in an arm-wrestling competition. [BIG LAUGH] Somebody who's ever called themselves President Clinton's intern. [BIG LAUGH] Someone featured in *Playboy* before I was conceived. [BIG LAUGH] Anyone who screams in bed 'Less *please*, less!' [TREMENDOUS LAUGH]"

Let me just break in here.

At this point in my set, I launched into Flammer's mile-high club joke, but I switched jerkoff motions to something more appropriate for an afternoon Thanksgiving crowd at a comedy club in Ocean City, Maryland. More restrained. Not as heavy on the *jerking* motions.

That went *amazing*. Tremendous laughter.

I then talked a bit about airplane travel versus bus travel. I did a few minutes about AOL versus the Pony Express and how settlers in the West were inundated with early versions of CD-Roms (they were made out of wood).

I did some crowd work, which is incredibly rare for a first time performer. But I was in the groove. I was in the fucking goddamn zone!

I was *killing* it.

I improvised a bit. And then it was time to show the world just exactly what I was bringing to my very own, freshly conceived comedic persona.

Richard Pryor had his whorehouse in Nebraska to talk about. And that's fine.

I had my *own* history. One that took place in Bethesda, Maryland.

And why wouldn't *that* childhood be just as worthwhile as one that took place anywhere else?

Because I grew up upper-middle class and white?

Whatever.

As if there's something I can *do* about that.

Actually, there *is* something I can do about it:

I can *talk* about it and I can *write* about it.

And I can make it all funny.

Back to the set:

[Sound of me aggressively grabbing the mic and pulling it from the stand.]

"So I'm from a place not far from here. You might have heard of it. Bethesda. Nice community, few miles west of D.C. Cherry blossoms in the spring. Hotter than a yeast infection in the summer. [LAUGH] Total chaos in the winter when it snows two inches. [HUGE LAUGH] You know what I'm talking about. [IN VOICE OF PANICKED WOMAN] 'Oh, honey, I'm stuck in a three-inch snowdrift at the Giant Grocery on the Pike. Can you *airlift* me home?' [INCREDIBLE LAUGH] But there's more to Bethesda than what you'd see in the movies or in all the books. It's what I grew up with. It's *my* story. And I'm here to tell you some stories. I hung with a crew. And we got into some *mischief*. [A SOUND OF INTEREST FROM THE CROWD]

"I had a friend named Jimmy—not smart. Bit of an idiot and proud of it. You know the type. [KNOWING LAUGHTER] The one person in your neighborhood, and there's always one, who rams their sled into a tree and is never quite right. That would be Jimmy ... but he used to do that *every* winter. [HUGE LAUGH] How do I explain this? Jimmy had a big scar across his forehead. Not really what you'd call handsome. But not *totally* brain dead. Smart enough to know how to act dumb and manage to get away with it. [BIG LAUGH] *Every* group of friends needs a guy like this. Almost like a mascot. God, you can get away with *so much* when you have a lovable idiot on your side. [BIG LAUGH] Like a big, moronic dog who can talk. [LAUGH] And it gets you *anywhere*. [LAUGH] I'm talking *anywhere*. There was a club in D.C., more like a bar, where there was some dancing. This was the big thing for a while. The club was called The Dome. We used to call it the *Do*-Me. [LAUGH] You get in, you get laid. But we weren't yet twenty-one. Fake ID? No worries! Just bring Jimmy! [IN FUNNY JIMMY VOICE] 'Oh please let us in. It is my birthday. And I can't drive because I have a brain injury!' [VOICE OF BAR BOUNCER] 'Jesus, okay, okay. Just stop spitting.' [HUGE LAUGH] We used to bring him everywhere. God, the things we got away with. No one's going to check a brain injured guy for his driver's license. Brain injured guys don't drive. I mean, they do, but not *well*. [LAUGH] Plus, he *already* looked fucked up. He *always* looked buzzed! [INCREDIBLY LONG LAUGH] Dude could buy as much booze as he wanted—and *then* some. [SUSTAINED LAUGH]

"Gonna tell you a story now. This is all completely true. *Maybe*. [HUGE LAUGH] Friend's older brother, he owned an ice cream truck. Used to ride through the neighborhood during the summer months. Used to play a harmless tune like 'Turkey in the Straw' or some such shit. [KNOWING LAUGH] Never understood that song myself. Turkey can go anywhere the fuck he wants. He's a *turkey*. So why hide in *straw*? [LAUGH] So our friend's older brother heads out of town for a few days. A funeral or something. All my friends and me, we look at each other. [COLLECTIVELY, AS FRIENDS] 'Ice cream truck! And we need *Jimmy*!' We head over to Jimmy's house. 'Is Jimmy busy?' [IN MOM VOICE] 'Um, no.' [IN MY REGULAR VOICE] Of course Jimmy isn't busy. He's *Jimmy*. [LAUGH] Jimmy comes out. 'You doin' anything, Jimmy?' [IN JIMMY VOICE] 'Nah.' [REGULAR VOICE] 'No shit. C'mon, we're going adventuring.' Jimmy's mother looks at us like, [FEMALE VOICE] 'Oh, *what* now?' [REGULAR VOICE] 'Relax, Mrs. Jones. We *got* this.' [HUGE LAUGH]"

[Someone in the audience yelling 'Get out!' although it did sound like 'Get off!']

"First thing we do is change 'Turkey in the Straw' to 'Highway to Hell' by AC/DC [HUGE LAUGH]. Next thing we do is we dress Jimmy in a 1950s type ice cream outfit, basically just all white: pants, shirt, hat, everything. [LAUGH] Next: blast the hell out of AC/DC and I take control of the truck. Jimmy is spastically waving out the little window. Kids are yelling at him to stop. [AS KIDS] 'Stop, mister! *Stop*! We *want* ice cream! We *have* money!' [AS JIMMY] 'Huh? Uh, okay. I guess...' [AS KIDS] 'We want chocolate! We want a milkshake! We want *strawberry*.' [AS JIMMY] 'We got shit.' [AS KIDS] 'Huh?' [JIMMY] 'Literally. We have shit-flavored ice cream. [BIG LAUGH] Or frozen yogurt, if you want *that*. Up to you. It's *healthier*.' [HUGE LAUGH]"

Now, let's just to stop here for a second for me to explain something: you might remember this particular bit being used years and years later on the television show *Nathan for You*, right?

It was stolen.

My thinking is that Nathan Fielder heard the bootleg version of my show, which had been going around in tape-form long before it ended up on the Web, and filed it away. I'm not saying he *stole* it. I'm just saying the *idea* was stolen. This, as you'll see, became a frequent happenstance throughout my career. We'll get to that later.

Okay, back to the bit:

"[IN SERIOUS VOICE] Here's the thing about telling people that they're about to eat shit, okay? The thing is ... they don't seem to really ... *mind*. [LAUGH] It's a strange thing. I mean, they're *curious*. They're intrigued. It can't *really* be shit, right? [LAUGH] And then they're worried about the size. And the price. 'How much for the small?' [BIG LAUGH] And then they want to know about the backstory. 'Is this a *new* option?' [LAUGH] And then when you do pull out a cone filled with frozen shit, there's a look in their eyes that's hard to explain—picture the wide-eyed innocence of a child about to receive a treat ... and the saucer-sized terror of a memory they're going to remember until the day they die in a hospital bed, shitting themselves— [INCREDIBLY HUGE LAUGH, PAINFULLY SO]"

And then the red light appeared and my mic went off.

This was the signal that my time was up.

Later, after I listened to this tape, I realized that I wasn't wrong when I felt time had gone by so quickly, almost too quickly: 30 minutes became about 22 minutes, more or less, owing to a "mistake" by the guy running the light. This could be true or could not be true.

Honestly, I think it had more to do with the club wanting me to get off stage so they could serve more expensive Thanksgiving turkey, but I could be paranoid. I wouldn't put it past them—or any comedy club owner. There was one club owner I later came to know in Tampa who'd cut every performer's time by five minutes. Over the course of a night, that's *twenty* extra minutes for the waitresses to serve drinks and food, and all that extra time for the incoming crowds to spend on food, when they, too, came in early. It's a scam but an acceptable one, as Lord knows that it's tough to run a comedy club, or so I've been told by plenty of penny-pinching owners.

When I got off the stage, I was really jazzed. It was like being high on coke. It was the best high I've ever experienced that didn't involve shooting something up my nose or asshole.

The money I had spent in order to get up on the stage to show off my stuff was looking to have been *more* than worth it!

When I listen to the show now, what strikes me as much as anything is just how *solid* the act was from so early.

What also strikes me is that I wasn't a *mope* up on stage.

I wasn't complaining about civil unrest.

I wasn't complaining about women not having enough "rights."

But I *was* talking the truth.

Realism plus *Enthusiasm* equals *Hilariousism.*

Realism is the *spice.*

Enthusiasm is the *filling.*

You mix these two together and you bake for years in the oven of your own mind, and well ... you have yourself a *tasty comedic offering.*

It would only be later that I would discover the missing *third* ingredient.

That's when I really learned to fly. *That's* when I really hit cruising altitude.

Or *attitude.*

But that was still years down the road.

When I climbed down from that stage for the first time, I immediately noticed that all the other comics were gone, including the Flammer, which was understandable, I suppose, as it was Thanksgiving afternoon.

Even a house painter in Ocean City has things to be doing on Thanksgiving afternoon. I talked with a few people who made up the crowd, shook hands, wished them well, and then went back to talk with Matty. He was in his upstairs office but he had listened to the entire set through a pair of speakers next to his desk.

"Solid set," he said. He, too, seemed as if he was in a rush to get out of there.

What is it with this crew?

I thought people loved hanging out in comedy clubs?

"I *told* you I could do it."

"You did."

"When do I headline next?"

"Tuesday at 2:30 P.M."

"2:30?"

"Yup."

"In the *afternoon*?"

"Yes."

"You have to be *shitting* me. Did you hear their reaction?"

"That's when you're headlining next. I never said you'd be a *night* headliner."

"That was the assumption," I declared, growing angry.

"On *your* part perhaps."

"On *anyone's* part. Why would I pay that much to have a mid-afternoon headlining? I can understand an early show during Thanksgiving but why after?"

"That's my decision."

"And you've cashed the check."

"I have."

"Do you know who my father is? And how many K Street lawyers he knows who can ruin you?" By now, I was *steaming*. All my good will to Matty had burned away.

"I don't."

"A lot."

"Scary."

"I'll take you to court."

"Take me."

"You're a bastard. I will fucking remember this."

"Remember away."

Where was the nice Matty from before? The one I'd kid around with?

"I *will* mention your name when I become famous. Maybe even in a book," I screamed.

"Spell my name right. In the meantime, you have four consecutive Tuesday afternoon headlining gigs open for yourself. They're yours if you want them. If you don't, that's your decision."

I gave Matty Barth the finger.

He was an asshole then.

He's an asshole *now*.

Fuck him and the rented pony he rode in on.

And I'm spelling his name right:

Martin "Matty" Barth.

Asshole.

Now and forever.

I told you, Matty, that one day I'd be writing about you. And here it is.

Ain't that nice?

You can also look forward to me talking more about you on my shows.

So I left Matty's office.

I never saw the shithead again.

Years later, after I had my own podcast and satellite radio show, I sicced the Batty Boys on Matty. You may have read about all of this on various websites, and that he wasn't exactly thrilled when my fans met him outside his club's door, holding huge signs that read MATTY IS A DOUCHE. Or that my *Fanatic Fans* wrote JUDAS across his car's windshield with spray-paint. Or that my fans screamed FUCK THIS PLACE! during live sets at the club, stopping the shows in their tracks.

Or that the IRS received reports of improprieties with tax deductions over a certain $75,000 cash payment.

I'm not a vindictive type of guy. *But fuck him and fuck his place.* And if you're reading this now, Martin Barth, as I'm sure you are, you still owe me *four* headlining spots.

And I'll *take* the evening gigs, this time.

And you'll be happy about it, you little fucking bitch.

One more thing: After I left your office that night, Martin Barth, I fucked the host who had introduced me on stage earlier.

I *still* forget her name.

But I *do* remember hiding the used condom beneath the ice maker after the act was consumed.

That visit by the Ocean City food inspector a week later to check out the unconfirmed report of hygiene issues at the club?

Did you ever wonder who called for that inspection?

I'm not saying.

You know why, Matty?

I tell it like it is. If you can't handle it, get out of my way. I'll be passing you ... on the fucking right ....

★ **Chapter Three** ★
AN EPIPHANY

The job of any stand-up comic is to hone his craft while up on the stage — and to think about it all the time *off* the stage.

Nothing else works. You can't perfect this very specific art form anywhere else. You can practice for years in front of a mirror, but unless you're in front of a crowd, you're not going to grow as an artist.

I was now in a bit of a pickle.

I was now banned from the only good comedy club in the Ocean City, Maryland area. And I *lived* in Ocean City, Maryland.

The decision wasn't a tough one: I had to move *away* from Ocean City, Maryland. There was really no other choice for me: as much as I loved the place, as much as I loved hanging at the beach and on the boardwalk, I had to head to where the comedic action was happening.

But I wasn't yet ready to move to New York or Los Angeles.

Or Chicago.

Or Toronto.

So I decided on Washington, D.C.

I gave the Flammer Jammer the keys to my condo and wished him the best of luck. For all he'd done for me, and all he'd do for me in the future, I felt it only fair to give him my father's apartment to stay in. He'd continue to paint his houses and perform his stand-up at the Sand Bar and Grille and he'd continue to stay for free at my father's apartment (unless I *really* needed some money, in which case I'd just ask for the rent). I wished him the best of luck and I meant it.

We'd meet again down the road.

My father also owned a condo in the Watergate building in downtown Washington that he would use whenever he was working too late to drive back home after a long day of lobbying in the city. It was a small apartment, four bedrooms, two baths, overlooking the Potomac River, with access to a 24-hour doorman, but it would suit my needs just fine. I was still way under the six month time-limit my father had arbitrarily placed on me, so I felt zero compunction to ask him if I could stay there full time. After some hemming and hawing, he said yes, as I knew he would, and I moved in just before Christmas 1996.

It was a heady time. I was young, I had an adequate-sized apartment in a thriving city, and the comedy scene—not just in Washington, but around the country—was booming. There was nothing standing in my way of achieving success—except for *me*.

And I didn't intend to stand in my *own* way.

It was a Thursday or a Friday when I stopped by the Improv on Connecticut Avenue and spoke with the manager, I'm forgetting her name. I asked what it took to become a performer at the club. Not necessarily a headliner, per se, just *anything*. There were a few other clubs in D.C. that specialized in comedy, but this one was clearly the best—or so I'd been told by friends.

The manager told me to talk with the *owner* of the club.

I asked what time was he coming in. She said it's a *her*. She told me her name. I'm now forgetting it. She said: "She's already here, in the back but she can't talk. Come back later." "What time?" I asked. "Try three o'clock. She's usually off of her calls by then." "Fine. I'll come back in a few hours."

So now I have some time to kill. Part of me wants to hit Georgetown University to see if I run into anyone I knew back in high school. Maybe visit the bar featured in *St. Elmo's Fire,* one of my all-time favorite movies–

Hey! *Wait a second.*

Movies ... now *there's* an idea!

I have nothing else going on, besides working on my stand-up comedy material (or "comedy stylings," as previous generations put it), so I decide to take a walk over to the Dupont Circle theaters and check out the listings.

There's a movie playing named *Phenomenon*. The poster features a retarded looking dork pointing his finger up to the sky. No thanks. There's also a movie called *Mr. Holland's Opus*. The poster features another dork holding a conductor's stick. He also looks a bit retarded.

Again, no thanks. But I'm still in the mood for a *good* movie.

Sadly, it looks like it'll have to be a rented video from Blockbuster. (Note to the kids reading this book: There used to be things called "video stores" in which a "person" could "rent" items called "videotapes" or "DVDs." Now, let's return to the "present" ...)

When I look back at certain moments of my life, I sometimes wonder if there was always a higher meaning. In other words, if certain moments or events were *meant* to happen. I don't believe in a higher power. As I once wrote in an episode of *The Simpsons,* but that was later cut, Homer (while standing on an office chair) screams: "I don't believe in any power higher than nuclear. And I don't understand that one either!!" But, like I said, this joke was cut. For various reasons, none having to do with the quality of the joke, which is very solid.

An hour or so later, I was back in my new apartment, eating a pizza from the great Italian takeout Vace in Cleveland Park, and watching a movie that I picked out at random from Blockbuster because I liked the cover.

I'll watch *any* movie that features an illustrated cover. To me, this is always a good sign that the filmmakers went out of their way to spend extra time and care on the product they're offering. It's not just a photo, or a still from the movie itself, which is lazy. For instance, the posters to *Rushmore* or *A Simple Plan*, two movies I really hate: could they have at least spent at least a *few* minutes drawing something creative and fun and maybe sexy? Nowadays, it's true, movies don't have to worry about VHS or DVD covers, only posters, which is fine, but I *still* prefer to see a cartoon or an illustration of the characters *somewhere*.

Why? Because it shows that the producers have actually put time and initiative into the project.

It's a sign of *respect*.

I should make this clear before I go on: I knew very little about Judd Apatow before renting this particular movie. I had heard his name but nothing really more than that. I wasn't familiar with his work as a stand-up and I had never seen his television shows. I came into this movie fresh, without any preconceived conceptions about the man. Today, it's easy to say, *Oh, sure. I knew Judd Apatow would become the king of comedy*. Back then, there was nothing so *sure* about it. If there had been, more people would have been kissing his ass, you can trust me on *that*.

There are certain movies that one can never forget watching. For a lot of people, it might be *One Flew Over the Cuckoo's Nest*. Or *Amadeus*. Or *Taxi Driver*. Or *Apocalypse Now*. Or *The Godfather*. *Whatever*.

For me, it was *Heavyweights*.

You might have seen this movie. You might not have seen this movie. But I'm here to tell you that it changed my life.

The premise is simple: a group of fatso kids take back their summer camp from a nut ball exercise obsessive played by Ben Stiller. (By the by, if you're still reading this and are okay with the words *retard* and *fatso*, then god bless. If you're not, stop now. Or just substitute "neuro atypical" or "thin atypical" in each and every case, thanks.)

Again, the movie has a simple premise. But like anything of worth, there's a *lot* going on beneath the surface.

I should backtrack. Most movies bore me, even the ones I'm *supposed* to like. *Especially* the ones I'm supposed to like. Admit it: every "classic" movie that the critics adore, especially the ones in black and white, are unwatchable. *Citizen Kane.* Can't watch it. Anything by Fellini. Unwatchable. *Casablanca.* Total shit. *Schindler's List.* Depressing as all get out. *It's a Wonderful Life.* Is it? Not for me, it ain't.

I ain't no small town loser.

No movie *really* ever spoke to me growing up. Sure, there were some I liked a lot, like *Encino Man* or *Bio-Dome* or *Blues Brothers 2000*, but there was never a movie that really *spoke* to me.

It's difficult to explain on the page but I'll try my best:

I don't like much.

I really don't.

Or, I should say, nothing much has a huge effect on me. It's there, it's fine, I listen to it or watch it or eat it and then I get on with my life. It's like the "Rainy Day" app I use on my IPhone whenever I want to fall asleep or experience an orgasm faster. The noise is just *there*. It's barely existing but I don't think much of it.

But every so often something comes out and it takes a really solid hold over me. The music of Lenny Kravitz would be one example. From the moment I heard *Are You Gonna Go My Way,* when I was a sophomore in high school, I just *knew* it would remain with me for the rest of my life.

(Side note: I once met Lenny at a roast for Eddie Murphy. I was a writer for the roast that was going to broadcast on Comedy Central. Before the show, I was backstage punching up jokes. I had one joke that went something like "There's just been a bomb threat and we have to empty this studio. Hold on a second—wait, no. The bomb was discovered to be *Pluto Nash*...." That joke didn't make it. Or any of the others. More on that later but let me just say that Lenny was *incredibly* nice and had some very sweet words to say about my date for the evening, an actress on the sitcom *Sister, Sister*. She was black. Incredibly, they later dated.)

So I sat down in my apartment to watch *Heavyweights*.

But there was no inkling—not in the least—that this movie that I had just rented from the Cleveland Park Blockbuster would change my life.

At first.

Quickly, however, I recognized that there was a *huge* difference with his very special film and all the other trash out there. There was a darkness just beneath the surface, which I had never seen in a comedy before. These kids were fatsos and they were being treated like shit. Granted, some of them were also assholes, but they didn't deserve to be treated like alley rats by the Ben Stiller character, who played the same version of the asshole that he always played.

I also grew to really *like* most of these fat kids! They were sweet and kind and, yes, fat ... but that didn't prevent them from wanting to be like everyone else who was normal at that age and had more friends. The jokes in the movie were fresh. They weren't of the stale variety that you would see in any other comedy from the era, such as *Fargo*. They were super sharp, while, at the same time, really down-to-earth. That's an amazing combination in comedy and I can't really think of another movie off hand in which this is so evident.

Beyond all that, these kids talked like *normal* kids. They talked exactly like the fatsos I knew when I was growing up. They were annoying but not unrealistic-to-life fatso annoying. I was enthralled.

I mean, just to have the balls to have *realistic* fat kids portrayed in a movie was pretty amazing! It was a risky idea. But they went for it. And that was a lesson I never forgot. Why *not* go for it?

When I finished *Heavyweights*, I rewound the tape and watched it again, but not before I checked the end credits to see who wrote it. It was a name I'd come to know so well farther down the road in my career. The name was *Judd Apatow*. And, even though we later had a falling out, I have to be honest here because I'm an honest guy: it was his work in particular that changed the course of my comedy career. His movies, for me, remain the high marks of this era in comedy filmmaking. *Celtic Pride. Drillbit Taylor. Year One.* All of them amazing, all of them classics.

But the reason why *Heavyweights* remains my absolute favorite is because it showed me what was possible as a writer of comedy. And the fact that I could be laughing at this movie *years* after it was made, showed me the *power* of writing. Making a room full of people in Ocean City, Maryland laugh was amazing. But to make the *world* laugh? Years later by way of VHS technology?! Now *that* was *real* power! *And more money!* It's all I ever wanted from the beginning!

Later that night, I made my way back to the Improv comedy club to speak to the woman owner.

She was a bit aloof when I suggested that I headline in the upcoming weeks. So I asked about being the "keystone" performer, meaning the comedian who's solid enough to be the opener but maybe not yet the headliner. Again, she was a bit aloof. To be fair, she wasn't mean or nasty. She just had better things to be doing. Or so she said. When my request to headline failed to gain any traction, I tucked my vestigial tail between my legs and asked for an opening shot. She suggested that I come to an open mic *before* anything definitively was set.

I asked when that would be.

11:00 P.M. on Monday and Tuesday nights.

Are you fucking kidding me? Who the hell is here at 11:00 on a weekend night?

If you want to begin, you have to start at an open mic.

D.C. fucking closes after eight! I'm from this town! I know that!

Plenty of people get started at open mics.

I just headlined up in Ocean City!

That means nothing to me.

I could only just stare at her. *Nothing? To me, it meant* everything.

So what could I do? I gave her my name and phone number and I told her that I'd be back the following Monday at 10:00 P.M. to audition for this open mic shit. Meanwhile, I returned to my apartment to rewatch *Heavyweights*. I was supposed to have the rental for three days. There was a *tremendous* amount to take in. And I intended to take in *everything*.

I ended up just keeping the damn thing. I *still* have it. Sue me. By the time Monday night came around, 10:00 P.M. sharp, I was still at home watching the movie. Fuck the open mic. And fuck the owner of the D.C. Improv. I had *better* things to be doing.

I had a new path.

But where would it lead?

God, to be able to write for the movies! How amazing would that have been!

I knew that the path would probably be long and windy.

I never did see the owner of the D.C. Improv again. Fuck her.

Years and years later, after I had already become a huge success, the *new* owner contacted me and asked if I could host a charitable event for a children's hospital in Maryland.

I declined.

Instead, I visited the hospital myself (yes, without permission) and handed out *Passing on the Right* swag, including hats (for the bald kids), bumper stickers (for the parents), and condoms with funny wrappers (for the nurses).

I no longer had any more time to waste on stand-up. Or that shit hole of a comedy club.

See, after seeing *Heavyweights*, I just *knew* that I wanted to devote myself *full time* to something so much *better* and *bigger*.

Screenwriting. That's it. Simple!

I had a new path, yes. But would this new path eventually lead to where I wanted to end up?

That remained to be seen … I had so much left to learn ….

★ Chapter Four ★
MY STUDY PERIOD

It was time to buckle the fuck *down*.

My free period was over.

It was fun, but there comes a time in any man's journey when you're no longer a child, and if you want to succeed—I mean, *really* and *truly* succeed—you have to get your ass through a Kung Fu phase in which you practically become a goddamn monk, studying all the time, keeping out any annoying distractions, in order to become ... *wiser*.

And then you come through the other side a better, more enlightened Asian person. (Joking, joking!)

So, if I was never exactly a wise student, I'd become a wise *teacher*—wiser than any I ever actually had in real life. And I'd start to teach *myself* comedy.

More specifically, how to write scripts for comedy films.

And there was only one way to go about that.

Watch *every* great comedy movie that had ever been made.

And not just watch.

But *study* these motherfucking movies.

What did they do right?

What did they do wrong?

How could I improve on a joke or a plot line?

I worked my way through the entire comedy aisle at Blockbuster's like a damn animal, starting with *Ace Ventura* and ending with *Zapped!*, a little known movie starring Scott Baio as a high school student who suddenly has telekinesis powers and can make shit happen with just his mind. I loved it. (Hi, Scott!)

Most movies I didn't love so much:

Being There
Network
Marx Brothers shit
Four Weddings and a Funeral
Magnolia
Man on the Moon
Modern Romance
Broadcast News
Anything by Woody Allen
Anything foreign or in black and white

These are just the movies that I remember not having liked. They were *plenty* of other stinkers, believe me.

Typically, the movies I didn't like were written by screenwriters *way* too pleased with themselves. *Look at me! I'm a dialogue writer! Oooh, I'm so fancy because I attended film school!*

Gives a flying shit?!

Certainly not me.

Show me a squirrel farting and I'm the happiest guy in the world. The squirrel doesn't even have to be animated.

I saw things I could improve upon with each movie that I didn't like.

For instance, in *Broadcast News*, I would have made the Holly Hunter character way hotter and without that annoying Southern accent. *Magnolia* was way too long and confusing. Again, I'd have gotten rid of the accents. The people in *Network* were too old, as were the Marx Brothers themselves. Maybe even too ethnic for my taste. I hate when old people try to act young by bouncing around and shit. And is Groucho's mustache real or a fucking facial deformity?

And with the movies that I *did* like, or even, dare I say, *loved*, movies such as *Zapped!* or *Nothing But Trouble* or *Hot Shots!* or *Problem Child 2* or *Mannequin 2: On the Move*, I took notes, sometimes lengthy ones, on exactly what worked and why, and how I could perhaps use these same techniques for my own scripts.

My brain was abuzz with amazing movie ideas!

So many ideas, truthfully, that I could *barely* sleep.

It seemed as if the moment I pulled that trigger to go *all-in* as a comedy scriptwriter, the gates were opened and the ideas just came *sluicing* through.

Here are a few "elevator pitches" for movie ideas that I came up with around that time:

An Amish family ends up going into space in a spoke-wheeled spaceship, hauled up by horses wearing wooden astronaut helmets.

A high school kid promises a girl that they'll meet on a certain date in front of the White House. He eventually shows up, twenty years later, but she doesn't, and he falls in love with some other girl who just happens to be there, someone way hotter anyway.

A dentist afraid of spit must get over his phobia by joining a sex club specializing in non-sanctioned "cuddle parties" where spit is used as a lubricant and as a "turn on" kink. The dentist's name is Dr. Sputum.

A talking donkey joins a baseball team and quickly becomes the star pitcher until he blows out one of his four elbows and gets hooked on cocaine that he sniffs through a huge donkey nostril.

A retarded guy becomes a genius but is still *ignored by his co-workers at the science lab where he now works until he meets a really nice girl willing to put up with all his stupid and annoying shit.*

A movie about crazy, rich dudes (Sound familiar? Yeah. *Crazy Rich Asians* would later steal this idea.)

Two adult cousins live with each other in a basement. (Sound familiar? *Step-Brothers* would later steal this idea.)

A film remake of Growing Pains.

I was vibrating with creative energy. Any one of these ideas would have been a winner, but I decided to go with an idea I had been thinking about for a long time.

The Holocaust has always fascinated me, as I'm sure it has with all of you.

Obviously, it was an ordeal for everyone involved. I'm not the first to say this nor the last. And I mean it when I say that there's nothing funny about the Holocaust.

But …

I've always wondered why there were never any *funny* movies about the Holocaust.

Turns out, I was once again ahead of my time.

Have you heard of the movie *Jo Jo Rabbit?*

Pretty good right?
Have you heard of *Life is Beautiful*?
Guess what?
I got there first.
I did. And I can *prove* it.
I should probably point out right here and now that I am *not* officially "Jewish." My mother's father's father was born a quarter-Jewish in Montreal. That's about it as far as Jewishness in my family. But I should also point out that I know a lot of Jewish comedians and comedy writers and, for the most part, I find them to be just acceptable enough to hang around with during working hours.
With that out of the way, I want to tell you about *Petey*.
Now there's been a lot of talk about *Petey* on various podcasts and on the Web and in books and on radio programs, and wherever one might get their fake news.
But I'm about to tell you the *real* story behind this film and everything that I'm about to tell you is 100% true.
Ready?
I'm serious here.
Are you fucking ready?!!
This is *definitive*.
Listen up:
I sat down before my 1996-era computer and I began to bang out a movie script.
My *first*.
And it turned into something ... even *beyond* what I could have ever imagined.
It was *amazing*.
I'm not going to lie.
It was everything I dreamed a comedy script *should* be.
It had laughs.
It had heartbreak.
It had realism.
And yes ... *likability*.
Damnit. I just *hate* using that dreaded word!
But it did!
It was perfection!
Think *Alf* in Auschwitz.
Picture an animated mouse, Petey, who lives inside a Jewish person's skullcap (the Jew, himself, isn't animated) during the Holocaust. Like Dick Van Dyke in *Mary Poppins* but with a fresher, more contemporary twist.
The mouse will say *anything*.

Think Mark Wahlberg in *Ted,* but living in, say, 1942 Poland.

The specific idea first came to me when I saw *Schindler's List* on a date. This wasn't in the theater, this was at home. In retrospect, there are *so* many better movies to watch when you want to get laid with a girl you've never met before, who had both sets of great-grandparents murdered in the Holocaust. 20/20 hindsight and all that.

But this was an artsy chick, and I thought it would work, as most of it was in black and white. It didn't. After she vomited, and after she left, I watched the movie by myself.

Not bad.

Sad in a lot of places, and, as I've said, I'm not the biggest fan when it comes to black and white and foreign movies, but this one held my attention. I hated that last scene when the old man was wearing a Members Only jacket and standing in front of some graves, holding a rock, and crying. But there *were* a few parts of the movie, especially in the death camps, that made me think that a lot could be done with such an idea in a comical way.

Let me explain my theory of comedy.

Comedy is like a trampoline.

The more rigid the trampoline, the *higher* you'll fly.

The less rigid the trampoline, the *lower* you'll fly.

I call it the "Comedic Trampoline Effect."

You can't get much more rigid than six million innocent people being murdered for no reason. That's about as rigid as it gets.

But you can *play off* of this rigidity.

And you can then jump as *high* as you want.

With this first script, I wanted to jump all the way to the fucking *moon*!

So the idea for *Petey* came to me after my date had left in a huff, with vomit on her bra, and I was getting stoned and watching *Schindler's List* by myself, eating from out of a box of Buffalo-chicken-flavored Bugles. And I thought: Everyone loves animated mouse characters but they're always so boring! Mickey Mouse has always put me to sleep, even as a five-year-old. There is no duller cartoon character.

Personally, I always thought he was a closeted homosexual, which is fine I guess.

But just fucking admit it, for crying out loud! I hate bullshit!

Even as a five-year-old I knew something was up with that asshole.

I much preferred the madness and the violence of the Warner Bros. cartoons. My favorite was always Foghorn Leghorn, who I found hilarious, although I suppose that's not something I should admit to as he's Southern and owns a bunch of chickens as slaves. I also thought

Minnie Mouse was totally fuckable, specially with that cute hair bow. I always pictured her with a big black bush.

So just the thought of a tiny mouse in Auschwitz with a big mouth who says nasty shit made me laugh like crazy. Combine that with putting this endearing and engaging mouse into a horrific environment that he's forced to deal with, well, you got yourself a comedy.

People ask me all the time if I'm upset that there exist "ironic" live readings of this script among celebrities like Jon Hamm and Busy Phillips and Paul F. Tompkins and Andy Richter and Janeane Garofalo, in which they act out the script for an audience to sit there and laugh. Can you guess my answer?

Not only do I not mind … *I fucking love it!*

Assholes, the script was *supposed* to be funny!

And the fact that it was never actually produced makes it all that much cooler that it's *constantly* performed live and that you can see hip teens performing it on Youtube and on TikTok and everywhere else!

I love it when young comedians and teenage fans of comedy act it out before a camera or even live! I love it even more when women play the role of Petey, even though it was specifically pointed out in the script that he was a man in his thirties, or he had the voice of one anyway. To me, the script has become like a Beatles song that's been reinterpreted by a *new* generation of musicians.

That's not to say that some of the criticisms haven't stung.

I should point out that this was my very *first* screenplay.

How was your first screenplay? Award winning? There are inevitably going to be a few glitches. Some of the jokes won't work. Some of the plot strands won't eventually pull together.

But I have to say that after re-reading *Petey* recently, the damn thing holds up *really* well and I *still* think that it would make for a great fucking movie!

So, yes. There are some things I would have changed in the script. If I were writing it today, I'd get rid of the scene in the crematorium.

This is the scene when Petey starts listing all the things that he hates about cheese and why all humans mistakenly feel that mice *love* cheese. The concept is still really funny but if I were to write it today, I would have the scene take place at a water park or something.

I'd also get rid of the scene in which Petey's owner, Herschel, annoys one of the head guards by having Petey mimic him from a distance. Audiences always seem to find it confusing as to whether Petey is siding with the guard or not. *He's not.* He's only *pretending* to be another Nazi guard.

I guess my dialogue is *too* convincing.

I'd also get rid of the food fight scene and the karaoke scene and the scene that takes place in a blow-up balloon kids' birthday castle that Pete mistakenly deflates with one of his sharp nails.

But there are still *so many* scenes and characters I just love!

I love the scene in which Petey and Josie (the female mouse) fall in love in front of a sunset but then immediately start fighting like humans. I love the scene when Petey starts conducting the camp's orchestra and he makes them play a Pearl Jam song. (And yes, obviously, I *am* aware that Pearl Jam did not exist during World War II, but I just thought it would be super funny that a Nazi-era orchestra would be playing "Jeremy," a song about having a crush.)

I love the picnic in the hot-air balloon gondola and the adventure that Petey gets himself into in the officer's quarters when he gets drunk off stolen wine and wakes up with a Hitler wine mustache.

I just like the damn movie, what can I say?

I'm not sure it was "*Heavyweights* good" but it was solid.

And, again, this was *years* before Mark Wahlberg (who I think is Jewish) came out with *Ted*.

The script was clearly ahead of its time. Even more important, it allowed me to improve my writing ability for my *next* comedic script, this one about a locked-in stroke victim who blinks out jokes.

The script was called *W-A-N-T T-O H-E-A-R S-O-M-E-T-H-I-N-G F-U-N-N-Y?*

This one was technically a very tough project to crank out, especially for a beginner like myself, and I kind of painted myself into a corner with this idea. In the end, though, I felt (and *still* do) that the premise was strong enough to work with.

There is a thing in Hollywood called the Black List which catalogs all the best unproduced screenplays in any given year. There's also a "Bad List" which records what are deemed the worst unproduced screenplays in any given year. I wrote *W-A-N-T T-O H-E-A-R S-O-M-E-T-H-I-N-G F-U-N-N-Y?* in 1997 but it *still* makes the Bad List to this day, which I think is unfair. The creators of this list honestly must feel that I didn't get the irony of a movie that would feature a main character who can only move his left eyelid. They must truly think that I wasn't aware that this would have make a great parody of all those shit "serious" movies that win Academy Awards. They must have honestly felt that I wasn't aware that the movie would run over six hours. And that it would feature a car chase, driven by this locked-in guy. How can the author of a script *not* have been aware of all this?

Of course I was fucking aware!

Whether people understand my particular brand of humor or not is not something I can ever control–trust me on that.

There's only so much a comedy writer can do to win over a reader, and if he or she doesn't get it, it's not my job to show up at their place and literally stretch back their mouths in order for them to smile.

I have enough on my plate without having to deal with *that*.

Here's the thing: If all you've ever grown up with is absolute garbage, that's all you're going to want to eat.

Sometimes when you're *too* new, too ahead of your time, you can upset people. This happened with Einstein, I'm pretty sure, and it happened with the Beatles and it happened with many other greats.

I wasn't the first person ahead of my time ... nor would I be the last. But that's okay. I can deal with jokers.

I was born out of due time and I've had to deal with the consequences.

I am more than okay with people mentioning the *Petey* script when they give their Academy Award speeches, in jest of course. I'm more than okay with bands such as the White Stripes and Radiohead writing songs based on the locked-in script. I know that both Harmony Korine and Vincent Gallo think of that script as having been *major* influences on their own amazing films.

I'm okay with the world's "sexiest man," Paul Rudd, appearing on talk shows and reciting a few lines from *Petey*. I really am!

There were also some solid, interesting reviews for both of my scripts in some of the trades and independent newspapers and magazines, especially later on, although I'm not really sure how the reviewers came across copies of them. Maybe eBay?

Marco Rollan of *The Los Angeles* called *Petey* "disturbing in a very unique way."

Kurt Ballard of *The LA Blade* wrote that the locked-in script was something you "will never forget. It is H-O-R-R-I-F-Y-I-N-G-L-Y singular."

I had so many ideas for scripts and I spent all my time working on them.

1997 is just basically a blur.

So many more scripts arrived in quick succession and I just sat there and wrote one after the other, no problem at all:

Run! (a slave comedy *years* before Tarantino's *Django Unchained*)

You Want Fries with That? (an abortion comedy years *before* *Obvious Child* and *Juno*)

Dumb-Ass Donny (years before the Simple Jack character in *Tropic Thunder*)

Poppin' That Wrinkled Cherry (at least a decade before *40 Year Old Virgin*. To be fair, *my* character was in his eighties. I hold no grudge against Judd Apatow, though. More on this later.)

I should point out that once I hit it big on satellite radio and in the podcast world there arose a renewed interest in these scripts, a few of which are now in development with non-traditional production companies, one having produced the Kirk Cameron *Left Behind* series about Christian rapture.

I'm not a religious person and I'm not personally a fan of those movies, but I respect the fact that scripts that wouldn't find a home otherwise tend to find a home with this company.

I think it's pretty cool and I'm grateful that they are showing *any* interest in my previous work. (My lawyer, Harold Robinson, told me not to mention this as I might jinx the opportunity, or it may not come to pass by the time this book reaches readers' hands, but Jack Black is now reading *Petey* and has expressed a strong interest to voice the main character, albeit with a few minor tweaks to the script, like the mouse is no longer in a concentration camp but in a circus and it's 1988. I can make that change! You know why? There are 500,000 reasons. Maybe *750,000* if I get lucky.)

Word started to build around the D.C. area, especially within the tiny film community, about my scripts. One day I was hard at work on another script (*Horny Hindu Harry* which was *years* before *The Love Guru*), when I received a call at my father's condo. How this person got my number I'll never be sure. But I knew right away that this guy wasn't messing around. He was a local filmmaker, had shot a few low-budget horror movies, and absolutely *loved* what he had read. I asked him how he happened to come across my work and he said that he had attended a comic-book and horror convention at the Aspen Hill Holiday Inn and he had bought bootleg Xeroxed versions of two of my scripts. Supposedly the owner of a local comic book store was selling them. If this happened today, I'd be furious. *Where's my cut, asshole?!*

Back then, I was *thrilled*.

Remember, this was just before the internet really exploded. To get word out about one's art then was never easy. Just the fact that someone (*anyone!*) was calling with nice words to say about something I had written meant a lot.

The phone conversation went something like this:

"Hey. I read your work. And I *loved* it. It's fantastic! So good! It reminds me of some of my favorite films. The scripts are just beautifully written and incredibly well put together. You have a really wicked sense of humor!"

"Thank you. I feel I should hire you as my publicity agent."

"Ha, that's very funny."

"But seriously, what did you like about my scripts?"

"Pretty much *everything*. All of these scripts work on *so* many different levels that it's kind of spooky. How long have you been writing scripts?"

"I just started."

"You have to be shitting me."

"No. I'm not kidding at all. It's 100% true."

"Holy crap. That's outrageous!"

"Yeah. I wouldn't ever lie to you."

"You just joked about me being your publicity agent. But in all seriousness, have you ever thought about finding a manager?"

"I thought about it. You must be kidding, right? Are you saying you'd be interested?"

"I'm definitely *not* kidding. I want to get into managing. So, yes."

"I would love that more than anything."

"Well, you've just found yourself a new manager!"

And that was that.

It really was as simple as that.

I had found my manager for my script-writing career!

Little did I know that this relationship would very soon come to change my life forever.

And not necessarily for the better ....

★ Chapter Five ★

DOUBLE-DIPPED AND COMICALLY FLIPPED

His name was Larry Van Wylde (yes, real name) and he didn't really need to work, as he was extremely rich. Or his dad was.

He was a huge fan of comedy and had befriended many comedians over the years as they came through town. He'd buy them drinks, dinners, the works.

He was very generous and the comedians loved that. And they genuinely *liked* him. He was a good guy.

But when he wasn't meeting up with comedians, Larry thought of himself as a showbiz type of guy. He desperately wanted to be funny but didn't have the chops. What he *did* have was balls. And an eagerness to become involved in show business. He felt the easiest "in" would be to become a talent manager for comedy screenwriters.

Not a bad idea. There are plenty of wannabe writers out there!

At first, Larry and I got along really well.

I'd visit him at his parent's home in Potomac and we'd lie by the pool and smoke weed and talk about our Hollywood aspirations. We seemed to share a similar sensibility when it came to humor and *Heavyweights* in particular. We'd go out drinking at the bars in Dupont Circle, just talking film and comedy and music and girls and all the rest of it, and what we'd ever do if we landed in L.A. Cool dude. Or so I thought.

The first of our problems kicked off when Larry told me I wasn't his only client. He had *five* other screenwriting clients. One used to work in Hollywood but moved back to D.C. to be with family. The others, also in the D.C. area, were young writers with a supposedly "amazing" future ahead of them.

I guess I couldn't blame the guy for taking on more than one client but I wasn't overly thrilled by the idea of *sharing* a manager.

It wasn't jealousy. It was more that I looked at myself as a powerful airplane engine that needed to be kept finely tuned or it would simply overheat and explode. I was a force of nature who needed my own guardian angel attached at all times. I needed a boutique handler, someone who could take the time and effort to polish a somewhat rough diamond into something worth more than any *other* diamond.

Jump on my engine and the sky's the limit! But if you're too busy with other engines, well, we both might just fall onto a house below …

When Larry refused to drop his other five clients, I made a stink but he held firm.

I should have just left him right then and found a new manager but I was too green in the industry, and I didn't yet have enough self-confidence to pursue what I needed to pursue.

But the truth of the matter—and I really can't deny it—is that I *needed* some help to propel myself to the next level. If I wanted to sell one of my scripts, and I *knew* that they were worth selling, I had to play the damn game.

For the time being, Larry Van Wylde was going to be as close to Hollywood as I was going to get.

So I had to deal with the fact that I wasn't Larry's only client.

The second problem arose when Larry had "notes" for all of my scripts.

Remember when I was telling you earlier how I hated the term "likability"?

Well, I also hate the term "notes."

The word "notes" for anyone outside showbiz basically means shitty suggestions from anyone not capable of writing scripts themselves.

It basically means your script is going to be *ruined* before it's even bought. But if you *do* want it bought, then you just have to be *okay* with it being ruined.

Smile and say, "Wow, these notes are *tremendous*!"

I can deal with suggestions, if they're helpful. I have no problem with *helpful* notes.

But if the notes I'm provided are *useless*, forget it.

I have no time for that.

Larry got in touch with me because he loved my scripts. And now he was telling me that they needed work?

C'mon, man. This was all a bridge too far.

After much thinking and contemplating, I told Larry to shove off.

Nicely, of course. But all the same.

It occurred to me that I was far too big for D.C.

Far too big.

Like an enormous, beautiful bobcat that had long outgrown its store-bought cage.

This bobcat needed a bigger pond to swim in.

Ain't that nice?

I'm just being honest here. That's what I do. I trade in honesty.

Yes, I needed help achieving success. But not from someone who had "notes" on how to improve my already hilarious scripts. Sometimes I look back and I wonder if my career would have been at all different if I had made those changes in my scripts that Larry had suggested.

I don't think it would have made *much* of a difference, truthfully. I look at where I am today, with my hundreds of thousands of listeners of my satellite show and my hundreds of thousands of listeners to my podcast, and with my one million users on Rumble and a stake in Truth Social, and I think, *Batty, you did okay.*

I did just fine.

Larry?

How did *he* end up doing?

Well, the fact that Larry later moved to L.A. and took his clients with him, two of whom went on to win Academy Awards for movies they wrote (it's easy to look up but I won't mention the movies here), doesn't bother me in the *least*.

Larry is no longer just a dreamer. He made his showbiz dream happen.

I say, *Bully for him!*

Honestly! I'm happy for him!

My voyage is *my* voyage and it's the only voyage I *know*.

And Larry's voyage is *his* voyage and I wish him the best of luck.

What *does* annoy me—and it annoys me quite a bit—is this:

Larry denies ever having represented me.

Larry denies ever loving my scripts.

Even more than that, what *particularly* galls me are the accusations that Larry has made against me over the years. I'm not exactly Mister Sensitive, but all of them are quite hurtful.

What accusations, you ask? I've never spoken about this before but I will now:

Larry has been telling the press over the years, and anyone else who'll listen, that I "stole" his business stationery in '97, with his name at the top, in order to "wheedle" my way to New York City and into the comedy scene up there.

Larry has also told anyone who'd listen that I "stole" $22,000 of his money by thinking of it more as a "gift" than a "loan."

Let me explain:

Larry had a lot of friends. He was a good guy. Some might even say that he was *likable*—AND THERE I GO USING THAT GODDAMN WORD AGAIN!

But, in truth, Larry really truly was *likable*. And the reason for this mostly had to do with him being very generous with his time and money. So when I reached my nineteenth birthday, Larry was nice enough to gift me $22,000. We both figured it was capital against future earnings.

I was a big talent. I needed some money in order to not have to work so I could devote myself full time to screenwriting. It just made *sense*. And I was *very appreciative* that Larry was giving me that much. It would surely tide me over for a few months or so.

Once I eventually hit big, Larry's 15% (yes, fifteen fucking percent) of all of my earnings would *more* than pay off the gift he was giving to me. I swear to you this was a birthday gift and not a "loan". Larry thinks of it differently and the case is still wending its way through the Rockville, Maryland court system.

As for the other hurtful accusation ...

As I previously mentioned, Larry had a lot of friends who were comedians. And some were from New York. I won't say who in particular. But I will say that if one of these comics just happened to receive a letter of recommendation written on Larry's stationery suggesting that they might want to take a certain "Skippy Battison" into their loving arms if I were to ever move to New York City, that this certain person might have listened.

I'm not saying I did this. I'm just saying that this *could* have happened. That the letter *could* have made it very clear that I was an up-and-coming comedy writer with a "terrific" mind and a "driving need" to become successful. That this letter *could* have gone on to say that I wanted desperately to hang with "like-minded comedic minds" and that, while I had much to learn, I also had much to *teach*.

One stand-up got back to me out of the fifteen or so I might have sent.

Again, I won't mention his name.

But ... I *will* say that this particular comedian was later accused of some sexual improprieties that he at first denied and then later came clean about.

I, for one, never saw anything wrong with what he had done. And it was only later, after I, too, was accused of sexual improprieties, that I saw how easily one could label others a "pervert."

But all that came later.

So a recommendation letter that Larry might or might not have written was sent out to fifteen comedians. And this one comedian friend of Larry's might *not* have checked with Larry before telling me to come up to New York, that he'd like to meet with me.

Wow! Nice! Looks like it was time for a cool change!

It was time to move out of D.C. and experience the vibrant energy of the exploding comedy scene in New York City! It was time to make it as a comedy writer in one of the biggest cities in the world!

The fact of the matter was that I was becoming a little bored of D.C. anyway.

It just all seemed so damn small!

And my talents were far *too large* to ever be contained within such a small city. This hit me one day when I was in a D.C. bar talking up a woman. She had no ideas or thoughts about comedy or showbiz or movies or television or anything else that was *fun* or *important*.

It was all about politics *this* and politics *that*.

I did end up fucking her. But after I left her bedroom at her parent's house where she still lived as a high school student, I got to thinking: *What am I doing here exactly? How am I going to ever make it big in a wonky city such as D.C.?*

Besides that, it was quickly coming up on the six month time limit that my father had given me to "make it."

He was now going to cut off funding.

Fine.

Whatever.

But things *were* starting to look up.

With some newly acquired funds (the $22,000 gift), and with a freshly written recommendation on Larry Van Wylde's stationery that was strangely very similar to my own voice, it seemed that I had a new lease on life.

Strange how little it takes to change one's lot in life.

In June of 1997, I finally pulled the ripcord by moving out of my father's Watergate apartment, leaving everything behind, save for my computer and my scripts, and I made my way up to New York City by way of Amtrak train, first class, thank you very much.

When I arrived, I took a cab over to this particular comedian's apartment and let myself in. The key was under the doormat, just as he had instructed. The apartment was small, nothing too fancy, but it was clean enough and there was some food in the fridge.

And his two dogs who greeted me were friendly and very eager for their afternoon walk.

Not only was it my job to soak up as much comedic knowledge as I could in New York City but for the next two months it would *also* be my job to take care of these two dogs, feed them, walk them, play with them, while this unnamed comedian went on tour across this great big ol' country.

For now, I was Mr. Dog Walker and I intended to perform this job to the best of my ability.

In the meantime–as I was now looking for a new manager–I started working on new film scripts, as well as television writing submissions.

I figured: *Why not, right?*

I was in New York City and comedy writing didn't only consist of writing for the *movies*. One could make a really amazing living writing for *television* as well. And while I was never particularly a huge fan of most late-night or sketch television shows, I figured I'd give it a damn shot.

Again, *why not?*

Now was as good a time as any: staying for free in the West Village with a gusty $22,000 wind behind my sails.

I mean, if not now ... when exactly?

When I wasn't cleaning up this comedian's two French bulldogs' shit—and it was *copious*—I was back in this stand-up's apartment, glancing through his ideas journals, which I had his permission to go through, and watching television—mostly comedy.

I wanted to live, breathe and, yes, even shit copious amounts of comedy.

I wanted comedy to come oozing out of every one of my goddamn motherfucking pores.

Helping matters was that comedians and comedy writers were *constantly* stopping by this apartment to see and talk with their friend, unaware that he was already out on tour. I got to meet David Cross this way. The conversation was brief but noteworthy for how much he taught me.

For instance, I learned from David—or *Dave*, as his friends call him—to never spend longer on a set-up to a joke than was absolutely necessary. Dave isn't the most patient of people. All he wanted, really, was to hear when exactly his friend was returning from the tour.

He then took off *before* hearing the gag line to my joke. But it was a good lesson. Always cut straight to the joke without making a big preamble out of everything. (Come on my show, Dave! Why *still* the cold shoulder?!)

Marc Maron stopped by.

So did Joe Rogan and Bill Burr and Dave Attell.

Jay Moor stopped by one afternoon and we spent a few minutes talking. He was a cool guy.

Most nights, I'd hit the Comedy Cellar and talk with the best of the best in comedy, whether they were stand-ups or just comedy writers. Once it became clear that I wasn't a "hanger on" or merely just a comedy "wannabe", but actually someone connected in a major way to their scene, they opened up very quickly.

I learned from the great Chris Rock that if you're in the field of comedy, then laughter can sometimes come in short supply. I suppose it's like gynecologists not wanting to talk about pussy once they're out of the office. I mean, it's fine to talk pussy, you're just not going to get very excited over any of it. Same with comedians. They're very stingy when it comes to laughter. Sometimes just a nod or a "that's good" will suffice. Sometimes even just a look. Sometimes nothing outward but a sense that inwardly they're *really* enjoying it.

Chris was a good man and always treated me right. I have no bad words to say against Chris. He's also a pretty good stand up comic. We really got to know each other well when I ended up watching Chris's dogs and fish while he was away on tour, and I have no complaints. But he was never the chattiest of dudes or one for small talk. He's also not great about returning my emails or phone calls but, c'mon, the fucker is busy!

(I once showed up at a performance by Chris at Comedy Cellar with a date, who later ended up sleeping with Chris. I laugh about it now. Whatever. And as he knows, he's always invited to come on my satellite radio show or podcast. Literally. Any. Time.)

It's funny. But a lot of people who know of my relationship with Chris have told me that they thought that I was the inspiration for his "Nigg*s vs Black People" bit. Maybe. I don't know. (Note the asterisk. I'm fearless but I ain't *dat* insane.)

Chris was workshopping this bit at the club one night. A few people were in the crowd. They were taken aback by the language he was using. I told Chris that perhaps he was better off using the term "Nigg*rs," rather than the more colloquial "Nigg*s." Chris shot me a glance but obviously kept the suggestion in mind.

I *do* know that I *was* an inspiration for a few of Chris's *other* bits, although he's never admitted as much.
How do I know?

Take a listen to "Crazy White Kids," his routine off his *Bigger & Blacker* CD. And then tell me that the "crazy" white kids don't remind you of some of the antics I, myself, pulled as a "crazy" white kid.

I used to sit with Chris after he'd perform his sets. He'd buy me a beer or two. Sometimes he'd even buy me dinner. He'd launch into me, similar to how he'd treat any heckler. To me, it was like playing against a professional basketball pro who'd basically beat you to a pulp on the court, dunking over you, whacking you to move away, just because he wanted to hone his chops. That's how I felt with Chris. I was his punching bag and he was a boxer. It was his *training*. Nothing more. Nothing less. I never took it personally.

But I *can* tell you that when I did speak about growing up in Bethesda, Maryland, Chris listened. Stories that I told you earlier in this book. And some stories that I *didn't* tell you earlier. Chris's fascination with my background only encouraged me to move deeper into the world of comedy. If Chris was this fascinated with my background, who *wouldn't* be?

Who else was around at this time? Let's see ... Patton Oswalt made a few appearances, and it was always fun to talk with him about the D.C. area. Patton was from Northern Virginia and we reminisced about record stores and restaurants and such. He had some good comedic ideas but I was never blown away by his material.

It didn't matter. I was living in *New York City*.

Marc Maron took me aside one night and gave me some fatherly advice about a packet I had insisted that he read just before he was about to hit the stand-up stage. This was for *SNL*, a show Marc had applied to recently himself.

In the back of the bar, Marc told me that he liked my *Jeopardy* sketch. But he felt that my premise that Alex Trebek had Tourette's Syndrome probably wouldn't have made it to air. He also really liked my sketch about Big Foot's bitch of a wife, but he suggested that I perhaps delete the part when Big Foot stomps on her neck. He loved my sketch about the White House temp agency that only sends out female interns willing to give blow jobs and take it up the ass.

Or maybe he didn't like that one. I can't remember.

Anyway, Marc *did* have one very interesting bit of advice for me and it's one that I took to heart.

Marc told me that he had just applied for *SNL*, for both writing and performing, and that he had met with Lorne Michaels in his office.

To get this far in the *SNL* hiring process is a *major* achievement!

Very few people who apply to the show will *ever* meet Lorne Michaels, and if you do, it typically means that you're *super close* to nailing the gig.

But Marc told me that he fucked up.

And fucked up *big time*.

And here's why:

Lorne is a popcorn fanatic.

You read right.

Lorne. *Loves*. Popcorn.

He eats popcorn all day, every day. He *lives* for it. We all have our addictions, and I suppose there are a lot worse vices than eating popcorn all day.

Everyone in the comedy world knows it.

So when Marc was meeting with Lorne and there was a lull in the conversation—as there often is with Lorne—Marc then did the wrong thing by ... reaching across the desk and grabbing some of Lorne's own popcorn to munch on.

Bad move.

To this day–and it's been, *what*, twenty years after the fact?—Marc is *still* convinced that this is why he wasn't hired on the show.

When Marc told me this I thought he was joking. He wasn't.

"So never, ever taken Lorne's popcorn," he said. "Never!"

To this day, I haven't. And if we ever meet, I don't plan on it either.

When I spoke to Marc again about this recently, after a Ricky Gervais roast that I wrote a joke for that was never used ("Ricky's a fun guy! This New Year's Eve, he plans to stay at home and watch his balls drop"), Mark claimed he *never* told me this story and that I only read it in his memoir.

That's bullshit. I find it difficult to believe that he can't remember me watching his pets for three weeks when he traveled around Europe on tour in March 1998. I even have photos of his apartment and pictures I took of his ideas journal, if any evidence is needed. But it's not. Because I'm telling the truth.

I *never* lie.

And you, as my faithful listeners, already know this.

Mark also denies that I ever told him to get into the interview business.

I thought he'd be absolutely *terrific* as a celebrity interviewer.

And please understand, this was *years* before the invention of the podcast. *Any* podcast, let alone Marc's very own podcast, *WTF with Marc Maron.*

I remember exactly where I was when I told him that he should get into interviewing celebrities and other comedians: we were at a deli, with him buying me lunch and telling me how to feed his aged cat.

He smiled. And obviously filed it away for another day.

Again, I'm not upset that Marc's never had me on his own podcast or given me the proper credit for success. Not complaining here. I'm just telling you what happened!

Regardless, and I say this sincerely, it was nice to run into Marc at the Montreal Comedy Fest in 2019. He looked fantastic for someone who spent most of his life drinking and smoking and eating like shit, and I have nothing but good memories about hanging with him back in the 1990s, and he waved and I waved and all is fine with the world. I guess you could say that we're competitors, as we're both big podcast and satellite radio stars. But I don't look at it like that.

What can I say?

I have a soft spot in my heart for the guy.

See? I'm not *all* bad.

Ain't that nice?

So ...

I sent off all the packets to the television shows that I was applying to—including *SNL*—and I sat back to await my fate.

In the meantime, and since I thought it'd be important to network with more comedy writers, I hung a few fliers around Rockefeller Center, as well as outside the Ed Sullivan Theater where David Letterman was then shooting his show. I made it clear that I was a new kid in town and that I had many comedic talents to offer and that I thought it'd be super cool to meet other like-minded comedy writers.

After hanging the fliers, I hit the apartment to wait for the calls I was certain would soon arrive.

You have to understand that email and internet were both somewhat new at this time. It's hard to look back and understand why I would do such a thing, but this was my world back then.

Yes, I'm *that* old.

So I reached out in the only way I knew how. By taping hand-made fliers around town on light poles and at construction sites.

Call me naïve, but I expected at least a *few* calls.

Perhaps in my naiveté I figured that New York wasn't as cold as I had always heard it was. And I'm not talking about the weather.

Perhaps in my gullibility, I also thought I could find some new friends and we could bond over our common love of comedy.

Call me whatever you want.

But I heard nothing.

Zero.

Zip.

Zippo.

A bit depressed, I placed a call to the Flammer back in Ocean City.

He worked early mornings and was in bed early, and I wrote at nights and I was never asleep until probably just as he was waking up. Poor schmuck was *still* working as a house painter and it took a few days to get through to him.

He was exhausted when we finally connected. He began to talk about himself and about the soreness he felt all throughout his back from being on his feet all day and up on that tall ladder in the freezing cold and how his father was terribly ill but I cut him off at the pass. I was more concerned, perhaps selfishly, about my situation in New

York. *Did he have any advice? Did he ever talk to New York City comedians coming through Ocean City? How does one actually meet people in the comedy scene here? How could I begin to make a name for myself?*

Improv, said the Flammer.

What's that? I asked.

It's when you get up on stage and improvise sketches and shit, said Flammer.

Just do whatever you want? I asked.

Yeah, said the Flammer. Play characters and shit. I mean, if you don't want to do stand-up anymore.

It's not that I don't want to perform stand-up, I said. It's just that I'm learning all I can from the big names. And it's a bitch to break into. It's all politics. And what I still want more than anything is to write comedy for TV or movies and make a ton of money.

Improv is *perfect* for TV writers, said the Flammer. A lot of successful comedy writers got their first start in improv. You should give it a shot. Couldn't hurt, right?

Huh, I said.

Yeah, he replied.

How's the apartment? I asked.

Fine, he said.

Thanks for the help, I said.

He started talking about his father having cancer and less than two weeks to live and all this other shit, but I cut him off and hung up.

So there it was.

Improv.

This was the first time that I had ever heard this particular word. *But I can assure you, dear reader, it would hardly be the last ....*

★ **Chapter Six** ★
THE UBC INCIDENT

I was still waiting to hear back from the television producers I had submitted packets to.

And I was *still* picking the brains of the best stand-ups in the business while watching their animals.

And I was still writing my comedic movie scripts.

But it was time to branch out. And the Flammer seemed to be correct: improv appeared to be a very nice way to achieve success in comedy, at least according to the people I asked. At the very least, no one seemed to *disagree*.

It seemed that everywhere I looked, there was another improv class to choose from! There were *so* many options! Literally, improv groups seemed to be on practically *every corner*!

I took a cab around the city and checked out a few spots.

They all seemed adequate, I guess. I didn't really know if one was any better than any other.

But I did know that I wanted to be taught by someone who *knew* what they were doing! Not some asshole who couldn't make a career at the very thing they were teaching!

Does that make sense? Do doctors study from professors who can't actually make a career in medicine? No. They study from real doctors who have been out in the real world making a fucking living.

I wanted the same with my improv teacher, preferably some big shot who had already been on *Saturday Night Live*. Some guy who could make shit *happen* for me.

After a few days of traveling around, checking out different improv spots, I finally settled on a group called The Upright Citizens Brigade.

If the name sounds familiar, this is where Amy Poehler and Tina Fey sharpened their razor-bladed sensibilities and later emerged as huge stars. Even later, Aubrey Plaza would come out of this same scene (*after* I was there), as well as performers such as the two broads from *Broad City*, I'm forgetting their names. It was also the epicenter for a ton of comedy writers who later went on to write for hit shows, such as *The Office, Bob's Burgers* and *30 Rock*.

The concept of improv was simple.

You pretended to enjoy improv for a while and then you got a nice-paying job through connections.

There were two options that I could have chosen from the start: one was to work there, as either an usher or a ticket-taker or as a bathroom cleaner. The other option was to pay for the "privilege" to learn from "the best."

Around this time, and this was in April of 1998, the tuition was about $250 for eight improv lessons.

One might think that comedy and improv are like masturbation. You don't really have to teach it and you certainly don't have to *pay* for it.

Wrong.

If it all sounds like a racket, it was.

A *huge* racket. But a *necessary* racket in order to network and to eventually "make it."

Or so I thought at the time.

I looked into the improv world even deeper. When you first join, you're at the bottom. You have to work your way up the ladder, higher and higher, by way of an improv method called The Harold, which is a long-form improv structure invented by a douche back in Chicago.

You keep moving up, through more and more classes, paying as you climb, until you at last reach the very top, by which point you can then perform for people willing to pay $10 a ticket so you can be "discovered" and get on a show like *SNL* or—and this seemed to be the most popular option—you can teach younger students the art form that you yourself can't make a living doing professionally.

The basic philosophy behind improv is a sense of "trust."

You must *trust* the others in your group. Others must *trust* you. We all should *trust* each other. Never in my life did I hear the word "trust" as much as I did when I joined UCB.

That was one philosophy that you had to abide by. *Another* was that while up on stage or in a class exercise, one always had to say "yes." One can never say "no." For instance, if a fellow idiot student wants to take an improv scene in a certain direction, you can't refuse.

You can't shake your head. You can't walk off the stage. You can't just tell them to fuck off.

No. Instead, you have to just stand there and go in the direction that this idiot sends you.

Is there any other occupation where one has to do this?

If you're a pilot of an airplane, and your co-pilot wants to go to Pittsburgh but you're supposed to go to Cleveland, do you just say "yes" and go to Pittsburgh?

If you're a surgeon and your fellow surgeon starts to operate on the left leg but it's the right leg that needs to be operated on, do you just smile and say "yes" and then operate on the left leg?

Saying "yes" to anything and everything is *not* my philosophy.

And I don't think it's the philosophy of many very successful people.

I'm not picturing Bill Gates saying "yes" a ton to shit he doesn't agree with.

Or anyone, really, except for simpletons and people who teach improv.

Yes is not my philosophy.

My philosophy is more street-based and perhaps more closely aligned to where I grew up.

One didn't say "yes" on the streets of Bethesda.

If you did, you could have easily wound up in the woods, nude, tied to a tree. By me.

But this was a different world I was entering. I was naïve. And I was young. And I was desperate to meet like-minded people in the comedy "scene."

We all have to start *somewhere*.

What can I say?

I joined a Beginning Improv class that was to begin in early May. It was held on a late afternoon, during the week. I imagine that a lot of the students were either waiters, bartenders or just plainly and simply unemployed. They seemed to have a lot of time on their hands.

I hated them instantly.

Most were older than I was and were looking to "break into" comedy long after it was perfectly clear that they had zero fucking talent.

One was a thirty-five-year-old who was doing it for "fun."

One was a twenty-something lesbian who wanted to free herself from the "binds" of society in order to "find" her sexuality in a "non-threatening atmosphere."

A few had always dreamed of being on *Saturday Night Live*.

None, as far as I ever found out, had ever lived, breathed and bled comedy since they were too young to remember.

And none was what one would call a "natural born talent."

One worked in an office as a paralegal. I'm forgetting her name. There was a guy named Chester who professed himself to be a "freak for comedy," but he was an accountant in Manhattan. A few others were around my age, and three or so wanted to pursue comedy full time. One was a nice woman whose name I'm forgetting. She had a handicap of some sort and couldn't really walk without a cane.

Truth be told, she really couldn't walk *with* a cane.

Another student was a dude named Stuart who was quite talented. I knew this immediately. I can just sniff it out. Like dogs sniffing another dog's asshole. How could I tell? When we first arrived, Stuart was walking from person to person on his knees, sniffing assholes.

My type of guy!

Seriously, no joke. What type of guy does it take to fucking perform a comedic move like *that* on the first day of an improv class?

Shit, even *I* wouldn't have had the balls for that one!

The teacher was about thirty, a strange dude named Robbie who used to work in retail but was now in the comedy scene full time. Or at least said he was. He had risen through the ranks of the improv world and, when not teaching improv, he would go out during the days on auditions for TV roles and commercials. Then, at night, he'd teach this beginning improv course to make some extra coin. He was a positive guy and, right away, this pissed me off.

One of my theories on comedy is this: one can't be *too* thrilled with life in order to be funny.

Another theory on comedy: This isn't a fucking team sport.

This is a *competition*.

Why should I be left behind if someone on my "team" isn't up to par?

Is that fair?

To me, it would be like being a part of a chain gang. One person trips and falls over a cliff. There's no other option but to have to go over the cliff with that first asshole.

Thanks, diiiiiiiiiiiiiiiiiiiick ....

If that wasn't annoying enough, I had just entered a "No Judgment Zone."

That was the sign hanging over the room where all the classes were taught. It looked like it was created by a ten-year-old at summer camp. I had no choice but to pass under it. But if I could have entered from the back door, I would have done that instead.

Here's the thing about me that you need to understand:

I *like* to judge.

That's where I find my best comedy.

That's the zone where I do my best work. If everyone loves everyone else, where are the fucking laughs? I doubt heaven is a very funny place. Hell is probably a hell of a lot funnier. It has to be, right? You'd be surrounded by total assholes doing funny things. I'm not saying I'm headed to hell for all the things that I've done over the years. I'm just saying that I'd probably enjoy it a fuck ton more than up in the clouds, kissing the huge ass of that one big guy in charge.

I always did have a problem with authority.

I'm going to get in trouble for saying this with some of my listeners, and with you, my readers, but I'm going to say it anyway:

Cute shit is for women.

Real comedy is for men.

There.

I said it.

And if that offends you, *buzz* off, pansy!

I'd like to digress a bit here and talk for a moment about Christopher Hitchens. If you're not familiar with the Hitch, he was a writer for *Esquire* magazine who said some things about women not being as funny as men. I think it was *Esquire*.

I never read the piece but I will tell you that I agree with him wholeheartedly.

Listen, I love women. I fucking *adore* them. I love talking with them. I even love cuddling with them (don't you dare tell *anyone* about this!). I just *fucking worship* them, okay?!

And that's not a lie. In some ways, they're smarter than men and "stronger," but obviously not in the physical sense. Or in the emotional sense. But they *are* willing to shop for hours on end for an item that you couldn't really give a shit about. I've had many women friends over the years and I intend to have many more. They're so much better than men in some ways.

But this is different.

I'm talking comedy here. And comedy—at least the *best* type of comedy—is down and *dirty*.

Nasty.

At times, even *vicious*.

It's war, man!

It's where anything can happen and you have to expect the worst at any moment.

I was once talking to Mitch Hedberg about this—not about this particular subject but about a lot of other things. Mitch and I weren't friends, per se, but there was a deep, mutual respect. Mitch was no dummy. He was a sweet man and a genius. I asked him what he thought about women in comedy. He was very diplomatic, as he probably *had* to be. His female handler was by his side. Or his wife. Whatever.

This is what I said:

If you're a woman, the best you can be is 15% less funny than a man.

Let me try to put this in Darwinistic terms. Men are awful, horrible, smelly creatures. I admit to that! I'm not denying it! We're horrible!

On the other hand, women tend not to be. Women don't club each other over their heads with mallets. Women tend not to get into bar fights or into stadium brawls or relish showing each other the size of their cocks.

I mean, *some* women do.

But the majority don't. Do we actually *want* women to do any of this shit? To wrestle in the mud like two primitive beasts, hurling shit at each other, making the dimwits on the sidelines laugh?

Not me.

I'm not saying women shouldn't get into comedy. They can get into it all they want! They can get into comedy just like they can get into the Olympics. But they're not going to beat the men's championship time. They're just not. They're not going to beat the men at Wimbledon. They're not going to quarterback for the Washington Redskins—whoops, I meant the Washington No Offensives.

They're just not. *And that's a fact.*

It just fucking is!

You can whine and complain and y'all are free to call my show and tell me off for saying as much ... but I don't care. I really don't.

I don't want women to be in the fucking mud.

Let *us* troglodytes wallow in the fucking shit and piss. We're beasts anyway.

Now, with that said, there *are* a few women I find funny. I won't name them in this book. Why? Because after I mentioned their names on my podcast and satellite radio show, I heard from a lot of them. And they weren't happy.

They said I shouldn't ever again claim that I find them funny. *Ain't that nice?*

Gee, thanks. And here I was thinking I was doing a *polite* thing ...

So I shall do them, and *all* women in comedy, a favor by not mentioning their names. But they make me laugh, what can I say?

I admit it! They act funny ... typically by acting like men, but they do have a humor bone or two in 'em!

(And if they play their cards *right*, they might just have *my* humor bone in 'em! *Joking, joking!*)

So I walked into this beginning improv class—beneath the obnoxious "No Judgment Zone" sign—and waited to see what all this shit was about exactly.

And at first, I had a *good* attitude.

I swear to it!

I was giving this garbage thing a fucking chance!

We all took seats in front of the stage and there were about eight or nine of us. We introduced ourselves, talked a bit about what we liked about comedy and what we'd like to accomplish not only with this class but down the road.

Stuart made a few wisecracks that I found very funny. We were obviously on the same comedic plane. The rest of the class went fine and we planned to get down to brass tacks the next time we met, a week from that day.

Fine. No problems.

By the second class, the problems began when our teacher, Rob, requested that I get up in front of the class and pretend to be a chicken hatching an egg.

Who am I, Farmer Fucking John?

Any reason why he picked *me* first?

I guess there has to be *someone* to do anything the first time but it just seemed so strange that out of all eight or nine people in the class, *I* was the one he chose to get up there first and make an ass of himself.

I should have known that there'd be a problem right then and there.

I grew up in Bethesda, Maryland. All I knew from chickens came from ordering them from the Hunan Delight in Cabin John Mall covered in soy sauce.

I did not get into comedy as a career to act like a fucking chicken. So I refused. I asked for another prompt. Rob told me about the "yes theory." No, I said. I'm paying for this shit, give me *another* prompt. We can only learn to escape what we think we're capable of achieving if we take a chance, said Rob. Suck my nuts, I replied. A few of the women gasped, which I took offense to.

How do you know I'm not improvising now? I asked.

What character would this be? asked Rob.

How about I show you this character? I announced. After this class ends? You'll like him.

The stage is *yours*, he replied. I am passing over to you the *improv baton*.

I'll give you a fucking improv baton, I thought. But said nothing.

I climbed up onto the small stage in front of my fellow classmates.

Without so much as even a second thought—or maybe even a *first* thought—I launched into a character that had just formed in my mind.

The character was *me*, pissed off that I had just wasted $250 on this shitty class for the "opportunity" to study with these unfunny morons, with the exception of Stuart.

I was shocked at how easily this character came to me. It was me plus 25% or so. It was me on steroids. Me on LSD. Me on the moon.

God, I *loved* being this character! For the first time in my life, I felt totally free, as if I was floating in space.

As great as my stand-up character had been, this character was even *better*. This was the *real* me. It felt like slipping into a warm bath. Any of the restraints that I had felt in the past were now diminished to zero.

The great George Carlin has talked about this.

That it's only when a comic or performer sheds their previous persona—your *fake* persona, the one that never quite *fit*—that it's only *then* that can you truly explode into an atmosphere of astonishing success.

I now knew what he was talking about. It felt like an orgasm.

But with *others*. Which I wasn't used to. (*Joking!*)

See, everything sort of just came together when I was up on that small stage. Like an out-of-focus camera shot that suddenly came into focus. I've never really experienced anything like it before or until I eventually hit a studio mic. And I *knew* that I had found the persona that I would come to use throughout the rest of my life—and that I would later achieve so much success with.

I could see it in my fellow classmates' eyes. It was almost as if they *knew* they were witnessing the start of something very magical and special.

There was almost a fear in their eyes, as if they were seeing something beyond anything they, themselves, were capable of producing: *Why even continue with this charade? Will I ever be as good as this guy?*

I also saw a look in the eyes of the idiot teacher. They were *blazing*. Out of jealousy.

Jealous because I had taken over the class and made him and his own complete lack of talent so clearly evident for *all* to see.

Jealous because I had mastered an art form that he had been attempting to master, clearly, for so many years, and probably never would.

I have very few regrets about my life. But if there *is* one regret that I will probably take to my grave, it would probably be that I never asked anyone to record my performance.

From what I remember—and it was all pretty much a spice dream—I went on for about thirty or so minutes, without a break, without so much as taking a breath, until the class ended and it was time for all of us to shuffle out, except for me, who was held back by Rob, the idiot teacher, who wanted to "talk."

He asked if we could speak outside of class. At first I thought he wanted to fight me. Then I thought he was coming on to me, which I would have been fine with in theory as I have no problem with the gays, but no, he really did just want to speak with me outside of the classroom. So we stepped outside of UCB and down the block a bit for privacy.

What was that? he asked.

Improv, I said.

Not the type of improv that I teach.

Maybe you *shouldn't* teach improv. Or maybe you should teach *that* version.

Improv isn't meant to be hurtful or mean-spirited.

And?

And that was both hurtful *and* mean-spirited.

How in the world was that both?

I asked you to come down from the stage many times. You ignored me.

I didn't hear you. I was in the zone. Clearly *you're* not in the No Judgment Zone!

Skippy, if you want to stay in this class there are things that I want you to do. And also *not* do.

Why can't I decide for myself?

I'm the teacher.

Are you, though?

What does that mean?

Because I'm well on my way to becoming the comedic persona I want to become. And I'm teaching *myself*.

And who would that be? This new persona?

Skippy plus 25%. Skippy *Extra*.

In spite of himself, Rob laughed very hard.

When he finally stopped, he said:

Listen, I like you, Skippy, okay? I like you a lot. I see a tremendous amount of potential. But I'm not sure that I can teach you anymore. You might have whatever you already need and I can't be of much help. I just don't know.

I replied: You're not a bad guy after all, Rob. Thank you. But I've already paid. Would you mind if I just came and maybe taught the students from my own standpoint?

I *would* mind.

You would?

Yes, I would. I'm afraid that you'll have to leave the class.

But it was improv, right? I mean, what I did *was* improv, right?

Not my kind of improv, no.

You asked me to portray a chicken laying an egg. I portrayed a man making fun of anyone who would ever ask me to portray a chicken laying an egg.

Skippy, you obviously have a tremendous amount of talent but I'm afraid that it's just not a good fit. There are other improv schools you can attend.

So that's it?

That's it.

We shook hands and we went our separate ways. He wasn't a bad guy, just a bit naïve. And not the most supportive of teachers.

Like a crotchless jockstrap. No *support*.

Okay then.

So that was it.

Game over.

The sound of the Final *Jeopardy* theme.

Kicked out of my first and only improv class I'd ever taken, or ever *would* take.

I strolled back to the apartment, just as calm as could be. I had to walk the dogs. Not mine. Joe Rogan's.

I then sat down to a dinner of takeout. *No problem here, folks! Nothing to see! Just move along please!*

I was surprisingly calm for a guy who had just been kicked out of an improv class he paid $250 to take.

I was real, real calm. Until I wasn't.

And then I lost my shit.

What happened next is sort of a blur.

I guess you could say that if I happened to be drunk at the time it would be deemed a "blackout." Actually, I was drunk, so I suppose that, in official terms, it really *was* a black out.

I phoned Joe Rogan, who was more than patient with my outburst. None of his dogs were harmed and neither was his collection of tapes from various shows and performances. There was quite a bit of damage to silverware and dishes, some of which had been in the family for generations. I felt terrible and when I calmed down, I actually called Joe just as he was about to go on stage. I told him about the improv class and my anger at how I was treated and about my talk with the teacher outside UCB and why I had just felt the sudden urge to break a lot of Joe's dishes and silverware.

I didn't leave anything out. He was patient enough, at least for the first ten or so minutes, but his performing nerves eventually shone through and a bit of his temper, truth be told. This scared me as he was a martial arts fanatic and could have easily put me in traction until the 22nd century. Luckily, he soon calmed down enough and told me not to worry about it, that we'd talk about it later. I'm still waiting for that call but I can't in any way blame Joe on this one. This entire episode is on me, no one else, and Joe's been nice to me over the years, not necessarily having me on his show, per se, or in accepting my invitation to appear on *my* show, but in not talking despairingly about me when others do so on his show.

So thank you, Joe. Sincerely. I appreciate it. You're a good guy.

Obviously I remember nothing of the call and was only told about it the next day by Joe's manager, Christopher something. He's no longer Joe's manager. It's pretty clear why. He was *not* a good dude. He told me to clear all of my stuff out of Joe's apartment and to never return.

How about the dogs? I asked. And the fish? I'll take care of all that, he replied.

Sure you will, I thought.

I still don't know if the animals ever lived. But it was no longer my problem. The next morning I called UCB and spoke to management. Rob, the teacher, had already talked to them and gave them *his* side of the story. We went back and forth a few days, culminating with my father's lawyer calling UCB to threaten that if they didn't allow me back into the class, he'd take them all to court.

It worked.

Like a goddamn charm.

Truth be told, I didn't even *want* to come back to the class. But what I *did* want was to force UCB to allow me to perform with my *own* improv group.

To *really* show them what improv was truly about.

One night only.

The performance would be free to watch. *Anyone* could come. I'd be in charge of *everything*. From the hiring of the improv actors to the subject matter.

I later learned that it was a big joke for all of the members of UCB, that my performance became "the thing" to attend. Irony and all that. That word had gotten out that this was going to be hilarious but for all the "wrong" reasons. And because they were scared of being sued.

That's fine. I *knew* that at the time. All I wanted was for people in my improv class, and all the other classes, to see just what I was capable of pulling off.

To show them that I wasn't a student and didn't need to be. That the teachers would now be the *students*. I wanted them to see what I could do when not tied down to stupid chicken-laying-eggs exercises.

The night of the show was to be a Tuesday at 8:00 P.M., just after the mid-level Harold group was to perform and just before the top-level group would cap off the evening. So it was a nice, tasty improv sandwich, and I was the filling, the meat, the protein, and maybe even the "man mustard."

The place was packed. All of my former improv class was there, as was my former improv teacher, Rob.

I had to hand it to the guy. Maybe he *was* capable of providing *some* support, after all. Maybe he was a jockstrap with actual crotch support.

A few movies have been written about this evening. Not huge blockbusters, but movies you can find on Youtube written and performed by the bozos who were there this night. I mean, real low-rent, real low-budget movies seen by nearly no one.

All of the movies—or most of them, anyway—seem to take the view that I was the butt of the joke, whereas it was just the *opposite*: the idiots in the audience were the butts. I knew exactly what I was doing, and I was in total control from the words "suck my asshole."

My goal was to show the rest of these neophytes what *real* comedy was all about. That the comedy world could contain a *lot* more than just goofy improv exercises taught by morons. That for *authentic* comedy, realism had to be striated throughout like fat within a marbled piece of meat.

I put together my own very special improv group. And I showed up to the theater about fifteen minutes before the start of the performance.

I didn't want to get there *too* early.

We entered through the alleyway. I wanted not only the audience—but also the other performers—to see us up on that stage as we emerged from backstage, fresh.

In the business, it's called a "hot take."

In other words, I wanted everyone in the audience to be as excited and as surprised by what they were seeing as possible. I didn't want any of the jokes to lose their power or to dissipate *before* we climbed up on that stage.

The improv group's name was The Found Items.

The ages of the performers ranged from nineteen to fifty-eight, both men and women, white and black.

Whoever fit the role best was included, a total of nine, including myself.

This was a truly talented bunch.

I'm not even sure that if I had been given one full year, I would have found a group more talented.

When it was our turn to perform, the lights dimmed, the introductory music stopped playing and the stage sat bare.

I wanted this to be the case. I wanted a sense of mystery as to what was about to happen.

The thing about comedy is that it's *all* based on *mystery* and *expectation*.

Let's analyze that a little deeper.

The worst type of comedy, in my opinion, is when you *know* something is going to happen. To me, that's humor for pre-schoolers.

Adult humor is *not* knowing what's going to happen next.

I mean, not even knowing who the fuck will be performing. Who they are. What their backstory is. Knowing *nothing*.

Who the hell were The Found Items?

That was the first surprise.

The second surprise was what The Found Items were about to do.

Now I *do* know that there are some bootleg recordings of this performance.

I do know that Les Claypool, the lead singer and bassist for the band Primus, used to play this performance before the band came out on stage. I know that Dave Cross has talked about this performance on a podcast or two. I know that Nathan Rabin for *The Onion AV Club* once wrote about it and that *Vulture* even played a portion of it on their website. There was a rumor going around that I sued *The Onion* and *Vulture*.

Not true.

I don't care.

Honestly.

I don't.

What I *would* like to point out is that this was a *visual* performance.

So when you listen, you're only experiencing *half* the magic.

Allow me tonight, or this morning, or this afternoon, or whenever you happen to be reading this book, or listening to this audiobook, to bring this story into the full and complete world of Technicolor.

Out onto the stage I bounded. I couldn't see into the audience but I knew it was packed. And I knew that most, if not all, of my own improv class were there, as well as my idiot former teacher Rob.

I could sense them.

Call it an itch in my dick.

A third *sense* in my *first* appendage.

"To begin," I announced on the stage, "I'd like for an audience member to yell out a year. It could be *any* year in history!"

An audience member shouted "1776." Someone else shouted "1976!" A few others screamed out random dates. One person shrieked "1921!"

"Great! 1921! And I'd like for someone to now suggest a city!"

"New York! Chicago! New Orleans! Paris! London!" I could hear.

"*Paris*! 1921. And now I'd like to have an occupation. It could be anything. Painter. Plumber. *Whatever*!"

"Doctor! Wet nurse! President! Lawyer!"

"Doctor!" I said. "Perfect. A doctor in 1921!"

The very excited crowd quieted down a bit. But you could still sense a *tremendous* buzz in the air.

"So we have Paris in 1921 and the profession of medicine!"

"YES!" someone screamed.

"HELL YES!" someone else screamed, or I imagined they screamed.

Whether they did or not doesn't matter. They very well *could have*.

"Lights please," I announced.

The lights went down.

Ten seconds later the lights went back up.

When they did, the stage was packed from left to right, front to back, with my improv team, The Found Items.

There was a collective gasp.

I think what the audience was reacting to at first was the smell.

It's hard to describe.

Earthy.

Alive.

Fecund.

A bucket of gravy that's sat out too long in the sun and that had long ago roped in the tremendous heat.

Ain't that nice?

Truthfully, it was a smell that I had grown accustomed to over the past few days, although it did take some time to get used to. The audience, however, was decidedly *not* used to this particular odor.

I heard a collective cry. The lights went back down, except for those lights aimed at the stage.

See, my improv group consisted of eight homeless people.

With me, the group made nine.

On the stage were those who clearly *relished* performing in front of a audience.

Do you know why?

I'll tell you:

In a sense, they'd *already* been *performing* for years!

It goes without saying that it's not easy earning nickels and dimes on the streets, especially the streets of New York City.

Each homeless person has to sort of adapt a "character" and then play this character to the hilt.

But the stakes are high. If these homeless on the streets don't amuse, or even interest, they don't earn.

And if they don't earn, they don't eat. And if they don't eat, they die. So *everything* came down to their ability to perform.

But this was an entirely new realm for them. Under the lights and up on an actual stage!

I look back at what I did for these guys, and two gals, and I imagine they *still* talk about it with their friends. Let's face it, the homeless don't have *too* many happy memories.

Usually it involves death or disease or being beaten.

This was something *novel*.

And the group *really* came through.

There was a woman named Mary Mother of the Sun. She was around thirty-five or so. Or maybe twenty-five. It was impossible to tell. Addicted to drugs since a young teen, she had traveled from Oregon to New York to make it in the world of fashion and make up. Obviously that didn't happen. But in a sense, she really did have a terrific eye. I had found her begging near Houston Street. She had an earth-toned towel wrapped snug around her head to keep away the "devil thoughts." It was definitely a *look*. I gave her six cardboard boxes out of ten, which is not a bad rating.

Rating the homeless was something I had been doing since arriving in New York City. I can't remember anyone who received anything close to a ten. But six was still a pretty good rating. I'd do this as I strolled around the city with the dogs I was walking. Just something to think about. I'm not sure what attracted me to all of those who were living on the streets. Maybe they were just fun to gawk at.

Mary was eager to be a part of the charade. If only for the $50 and a hot breakfast at McDonald's.

There were others.

There was a homeless man in his fifties who called himself Mr. Brandywine. The name was fitting as he was forever drunk off brandy and wine. I found him in the East Village, next to a movie theater. He was very eager for the money, as well as the companionship, I suppose. He had a lot of stories about once having been married but losing his apartment and wife and children to drink. I tuned out after the first few minutes. You could tell that he had some semblance of creativity, as he told me he used to work in advertising and he also claimed he was working on his written memoir. I don't know if either were true but he made me laugh. I gave him seven cardboard boxes.

So Mr. Brandywine came along for the ride.

I'm trying to remember who else was a part of the troupe. There was someone I named "Chatty Ratty," as her name was Ruth and she was chatty. She was also pregnant. She wasn't much for talking about her past but she did want to get into secretarial school, which I thought was a dream that sounded pretty reachable. She had a sparkle in her (lazy) eyes and I felt that she'd do just fine up on stage, which she did.

There were two guys in their twenties, one named Wake, the other Bake. They had come from Seattle. And then there were a few others whose name I'm now forgetting.

This was my troupe.

The script I had written and handed to them the day before was relatively simple.

I told them just to follow the audience prompts. Once they had something to work off of, they could then act it out the best they saw fit.

Be creative.

Have fun.

Be happy. This is a big opportunity for *anyone*, let alone you guys! "A doctor in Paris in 1921," I announced loudly, on the stage.

Ratty took the first line of dialogue and I thought she nailed it: "My pussy! It itches!"

There was laughter from the crowd, especially from my pal Stuart in the front row.

"Let me take a look at *that* pussy," announced Mr. Brandywine, in an "official" and "professorial" voice. He walked over to Chatty Ratty.

"Nice pussy, miss," he grandly announced, kneeling down and pretending to inspect it up close.

Big laugh from the crowd. They were *really* enjoying this.

I was genuinely curious to see where the gods of improv would take us.

Where could we possibly end up?

I mean, I knew where we'd end up but what adventures would we get to experience *along* the way?

I suppose, in retrospect, I can mostly blame Wake. Or Bake. I'm still not sure which one dropped his pants and took a huge shit up on stage.

Or which one slurred, "I'm a mayor doctor in town, 1981."

"*Paris, 1921*," I corrected, smiling.

The rest of the improv troupe then dropped their trousers and *they* started to take shits.

Or tried to anyway.

To be fair to them, they were only following my script. It just came a lot *sooner* than I had anticipated.

I figured them good for at least fifteen minutes of solid improv.

Ultimately, it was closer to one minute.

"So that's what a lawyer in 1971 in London looks like," Mr. Brandywine declared proudly.

"*Paris, 1921*," I corrected. "*Doctor!*"

The lights went on and the sound went off.

I could see the crowd fleeing.

Everyone except for my pal, Stuart, who remained seated, in hysterics.

That's a damn *loyal* buddy!

I searched for Rob, the teacher. He was sitting in the front row with a few of the other members of my former improv class.

Grabbing the microphone, I turned to Rob and declared: "*There's your egg, Rob. How you like them chickens?*"

He smiled.

I think he smiled.

It was hard to tell with all the commotion. (And all the homeless people behind me who were still taking shits.)

By this point, and even though I was used to it, the smell was even bothering *me*.

Time to end the show.

I figured it'd take a while to clean and prep for the next group of unlucky bastards to come on stage, not that I'd be helping in any way.

I've constantly been asked why I did what I did and why I found a group of homeless to act as my sketch team.

I'm not sure.

I think for a few reasons:

One, I wanted to show what *true* improv was really about. That comedy could be dangerous and funny and interesting and one didn't need *lessons* to perform it.

Two, I just felt like it.

Life is short.

Do what you feel like whenever you feel like doing it.

Especially if it feels *right*.

Right?

Right.

Fuck it.

Years later, I ran into the comedian Jason Mantzoukas at a comedy club in Los Angeles. He asked me if I was the guy behind that night. I said I was. He told me that he had been in the audience. That he was thinking about joining UCB and he was a fan of great comedy and that he, at first, thought it was all just an act. When he learned that it wasn't, he was even *more* impressed. And that's what made him want to join UCB and get into comedy full time.

I'm not sure if this is true but I have no reason to doubt it.

I *think* it was Jason Mantzoukas.

In certain areas of the entertainment world, this performance is viewed as being similar to the first show that the Sex Pistols ever conducted in Britain, where there were at most thirty people in the audience, I don't know. I hate that fucking band. But I've also heard that everyone in London around this time period—and since—has bragged that they were there at that first Sex Pistols show.

Or at least they want people to *think* they were there.

At the birth of punk.

At the start of a new revolution.

A schism between past and present.

The *before* and the *after*.

Which brings me back to my own situation.

I can't tell you how many fucking people now claim to have been at this *Found Items* show.

One hundred?

Two hundred?

One thousand?

It's impossible to tell.

I do know Tim and Eric have re-created this performance around Hollywood at parties and such (*without* the actual defecation and urination, I hope!).

Whether it influenced their specific brand of comedy, I don't know. I wouldn't be surprised if it did.

(Funny enough, I once attended a party in Los Angeles with a beautiful date. She wanted to become an actress and she was absolutely drop-dead *gorgeous*. Couldn't have been older than twenty-five. By the end of the night, she had left with Tim. I didn't mind. She was horrible, without a good sense of humor. I forget her name. Eric already had a date.)

For me, the "chicken hatches an egg" request was *always* demeaning. It was a waste of my time. And it was also a waste of my money, not that I ever actually paid.

I suppose I wanted to "get back" at Rob the teacher but, really, my main purpose was to show him, and everyone else at UCB, that I was miles ahead of everyone else.

That I had *nothing* to learn from them. That it was okay to keep traveling down my own comedic path without useless help from others. That my career was a *solo* outing, not a *team* outing, and that I did comedy like I did everything else: *alone*.

This was over twenty years ago as I write this. A long time. I still keep in touch with Stuart, who's out of the comedy game but doing well in Athens, Georgia as a mechanic for the town government. According to him, he'll *still* get down on the ground and pretend to sniff women's asses, which I find amazing.

I look back in fondness at this time in my life.

I miss those early, struggling years.

When anything could happen.

And often did.

Here's a postscript if you're interested: a number of years later I was walking down Broadway. I was in New York to write jokes for (or "punch up") a reality show called *The Apprentice*. None of my jokes eventually made it in and I never did get to meet a certain television character by the name of "Trump."

At least then.

Anyway, I was walking and thinking and not really following where I was going and I nearly tripped over an older man, holding out a paper cup from a diner.

It was Mr. Brandywine!

But it couldn't be, right?

I looked closer.

It was! *How could I forget that face?*

"A doctor from Paris, 1921!" I blurted out. "How are you doing, good sir?!"

At first, there was zero recognition from the old man. But I could sense in him a slow and painful attempt to recall through a booze-addled brain just *who* this successful looking guy was standing before him.

How did we know each other?

The wheels were turning, I could see that. Creaky as shit, but turning.

It didn't look at all easy for him to move but he went to stand. It was taking forever and I had an appointment to keep.

Where is he going with this? I thought.

God almighty, I hope he's not going to hug me! After all these years, he still stinks like holy hell!

Should I wait? Or take off?

A simple hello would have sufficed. Was he planning on something else? Maybe I shouldn't have said anything and just kept on walking?

He dropped his pants and dropped into a crouch. I hightailed it down the street and never looked back. *Once a performer, always a performer!* I'd now give the good man *eight* cardboard boxes.

Talk about *sticking* with a bit!

I wish him well wherever he now is. I imagine he's in the same exact spot or flat out dead.

But at the very least, he now has an awesome story to tell to his fellow homeless pals down here on earth or up there in heaven.

And that's at least worth *something*.

I don't know where any of the other members of my improv troupe ended up—I wish them *all* well. That's the way I am. All magnanimous and shit.

As for my story, well, my life would soon change *tremendously*. A new and different type of success turned out to be waiting for me just around the corner.

All I had to do was keep heading down that lonesome, dusty comedic path to a future I had always believed possible.

Little did I know, however, that the type of success I was about to experience (sooner rather than later) was *not* necessarily the type of success that would lead to happiness.

No.

But I'd find all that out soon enough.

Boy, would I ever ....

★ **Chapter Seven** ★
THE ACADEMY AWARDS INCIDENT

I have a few theories about comedy, all of them correct.

You've heard a few already. One that you *haven't* heard is this: You know what matters the most *when* it comes to a career in comedy?

Is it *quality*? Or *quantity*?

You're guessing quality, am I right?

Wrong.

It's *quantity*.

Most jokes suck. That's just a fact. The trick is to *keep* producing jokes and never, ever, *ever* stop.

Woody Allen said that showing up is 45% of success.

I'd agree with that.

Just fucking *show up*.

I mean, you don't *literally* have to show up.

But at least have your *work* show up.

After I left the world of improv, I doubled-down on packet submissions for TV shows, both for sitcoms and for late-night television shows.

I started submitting a packet *a week*. That's about twenty to thirty pages of *fresh* material each and every seven days. I also started to submit to shows out on the West coast. I was spending a ton of money at Kinko's faxing these submissions off to producers and executives, and if you don't remember what a fax machine is, you can *fux* off.

Yes, I was faxing in submissions.

I'd write up my pitch, print it out on whatever printer I happened to be using, and then walk it over to a Kinko's. This wasn't cheap. At that time, it cost about twenty-five cents a page. If each packet had about twenty pages, that would be what ... I'm not sure, but it added up.

So I started faxing from the library. That went well until I mistakenly left a packet behind and a kid ran over to his mother with a batch of penis jokes. My name was on the packet and I received a call from the head librarian telling me I was no longer welcome back at the library, which was a shame. I was also using the library's computers to jerk off with porn. But in the Quiet Room.

Anyway, my name was getting out there, as was my work. This was now summer of 1998 and I applied for a writing gig at Letterman, Bill Maher, Jay Leno, Conan O'Brian, and, my personal favorite, Craig Kilborn.

A sample of some of the jokes:

"The Mars Polar Lander was launched earlier today by NASA, with some help from Israeli engineers. They're biggest hope is to find signs of life, such as seltzer water."

"Bill Clinton was acquitted in his impeachment proceedings in the Senate. To celebrate, he's changing the image of a bald eagle on the $1 bill to a spread eagle."

"Anyone here seen The Sixth Sense? *I'm not going to give away the ending. Oh, the heck with it, I will: Bruce Willis's wig looks terrible."*

Not award-winning work, I suppose, but *extremely* solid. I received some very nice rejections, one that was even handwritten and encouraging: "Please keep sending more!"

It was written by an intern but that was fine. A handwritten rejection–encouraging you to keep on writing and never stop–is a *great* honor.

I could do that. I could keep submitting. I was nothing if not a hard worker when it came to writing jokes.

After a ton of calls home, I had convinced my father to extend my monetary "safety rope," as I called it, and I was thankful for that.

My former agent Larry was still trying to reach me so I could pay him back the $22,000 gift he had given me, still claiming it was a loan. Thankfully, I managed to evade his annoying calls and emails.

I hadn't seen my family in a good long while and I made sure to head on down to Maryland that year for Thanksgiving.

Looking back, I can see that this is precisely when my current political convictions started to form.

Notice I didn't say "fully formed."

"Started" to form.

It was a *gradual* process that took years.

Before this, you could say that I was an agnostic when it came to politics. I believed that politics existed but I didn't think we were capable of ever figuring it all out. I grew up in the D.C. area. I was surrounded by politics no differently than people who grow up in L.A. are surrounded by show business.

Politics bored me. My father worked in it. He'd try to talk to me about his day at work and I would never have the slightest interest in listening. As far as I was concerned, it was all bullshit. One person bullshitting another. And another bullshitting yet another. And so on down the line. Into infinity. What difference did it make if one person felt that the government should be more or less involved in our lives? What did this have to do with *my* life in comedy? Or my life as a kid? It didn't. It was all white noise to me and I barely listened.

But I must have been primed to change my tune. The stars were aligned in a certain way. I don't believe in astrology but I do believe that sometimes things happen at a certain time for a good reason.

For instance, I'm a Virgo.

And I've noticed over the years that the girls I've hooked up with the most are Scorpions.

I don't know what that means but there's a reason for it.

They also tend to have blond hair and are really young.

There's another reason for *that*.

As any long-time listener to my podcast and satellite radio show would know, you're aware that I have a brother whom I call "Da Dumb Doc." I've never mentioned his *real* name because he's a bit more reticent about the limelight than I am. One could say he's shy but I don't believe that that's the case. He just doesn't like the media attention, which might be a good thing, as he's not exactly an entertainer: he's a surgeon who operates on eyeballs.

Da Dumb Doc and I have never particularly got along. He's nearly six years older than I am. And he was always considered the "good one" to my "bad one."

The Yin to my Yang. The Chang to my Eng.

The Ring to my Ding-a-Ling-*Ling*.

Blessed with a high IQ from a young age, Da Dumb Doc never had any problems with the lame-ass subjects that bored the shit out of me, whether it was science or history or math or social studies.

That's not to say that I couldn't have done well if I had *tried*.

I was just too bored. It was later confirmed on one of my podcast episodes that I have an IQ in the "genius range."

But due to the stupidity of all of my teachers, no one ever bothered finding that out. The woman who finally tested me was later arrested (*long* after she was on my podcast) for making up some college credentials but she was *still* an IQ expert, or at least she proved as much on the *Dr. Oz* show. Regardless, the possibility for my being a genius is *very high*.

Da Dumb Doc could always play the game.

"Why yes, Miss Teacher! Anything you say, Mister Teacher!"

Yes, teacher.

No, teacher.

Sure, teacher!

Right away, teacher!

Never had a fight with the parents.

Never wrote a joke in his life.

He would laugh at certain jokes in movies or on TV but he was always trying to be analytical about "why" he liked those jokes. *Why am I laughing? Should I be laughing harder? Should I be laughing less?*

He was, truthfully, a bit of a bore to be around. And we fought. Constantly. To the point where my parents had to put us in separate wings of the house. We'd only run across each other in the kitchen or in the driveway, passing each other with our own cars, each with our own friends, each with our own dreams and aspirations.

Da Dumb Doc got into one of the best medical schools in the world, Johns Hopkins, after graduating near the top of his class at the University of Maryland. There he met a woman named Adrien and they married after both graduating with medical degrees, his in ophthalmology, hers in gynecology.

Two more boring people in this entire universe you'd never hope to ever meet.

Sadly, I did have to meet with both of them at family functions at least twice a year.

The first time I met Adrien, my sister-in-law, we got into an argument over whether or not Disney World was fun.

My vote was definitely in the "NO" category. She was a superfan of Mickey and voted yes.

Fine. We all have our Disney opinions. Mine just happens to be that Disney sucks. And that Minnie has a huge bush. And you can write that across your fat ass in large, loopy Disney font, for all I care. I think Disney is for children, and the mentally disabled, and for adult morons. That's my opinion — and, as always, it's the correct one.

(If I may digress, I love *any* tattoo written in silly font. For instance, I once saw a tattoo that spelled out "Winner" but in Dunkin' Donuts font. When I think of Dunkin' Donuts, I don't necessarily think of "winners." I've seen a few tattoos in "sperm font." One spelled out "YOLO," which stands for "you only live once." You'd think if you only lived once you could spend more money for a better tattoo font. And, one time, down in Florida, I saw a tattoo that read I LOVE MY WIFE but it was in balloon font. How all encompassing is your love if you're using a font children giggle to? Probably not *that* big a love.)

You may know my sister-in-law from a few phone pranks I've pulled over the years. I once called her in the midst of her bikini waxing and I told the receptionist that it was an "emergency." When she got to the phone, I told her that I loved her. "That was the emergency?!" she asked. "I just love you *so* much," I answered and hung up.

Success!

Another time I pretended that I was a DJ from a local morning zoo radio show and that she had won $500,000. All she had to do was a quick dumpster dive behind a Popeye's Fried Chicken in Cabin John Mall to find the money. She drove over there (as I was still talking with her), got out of her car, jumped into the dumpster ... and found nothing except for grease and chicken bones. She filed suit against me for that one, claiming that she had cancelled a few surgeries at her medical practice and that *she* had then been sued for neglect by her *own* patients. Turns out one of them nearly died. I mean, what can I say? Medicine is hard. Comedy is harder.

Another time I called and pretended I was Jon Hamm, her favorite actor. Jon's a *huge* fan of comedy. We've never met but I know he really digs my podcast, or so I've been told. I pretended I was Jon asking for medical advice for his girlfriend. She sued me for that one, too, claiming that I caused "irreparable harm to her reputation as a medical officer." She lost both times but not before I broadcast the court proceedings on my satellite radio show with canned laughter and other jazzy effects. She sued me for *that* and *also* lost.

It goes without saying that my relationship with my sister-in-law is not the strongest. The second time we met, we fought over whether men playing women in comedy sketches is acceptable. I think you know my opinion on this one. She chose the wrong subject to fight over. Or she chose the wrong subject to bring up and then for me to fight about. I happen to know a lot about comedy, whereas I wouldn't say that Adrien's Humor IQ is exactly up there in the "genius range."

We went back and forth for a few days, which stretched into a few weeks, which stretched into a few months, which continues to this day. I still hold to the fact that there's nothing wrong with a man playing a woman in a comedy sketch. I heard Shakespeare did this and if it's good enough for the Spear, it's good enough for me, although I have yet to find anything the dude wrote that I find in any way funny.

As far as I'm concerned, he sucks.

It hurts me to say that my relationship with my own brother is even less healthy. I suppose some of it has to do with his feelings about how our parents treated me (according to him, anyway) versus how *he* was evidently treated. It is true that my parents might have spoiled me a bit more than they did him. I was eager for attention and I needed extra help when it came to school and such.

But I can rightly assure you that this is not the *full* story. I think a lot of my older brother's jealousy is due to the fact that I would receive laughs at the dinner table.

I remember once imitating Dana Carvey's the Church Lady at a dinner and my parents crying with laughter. This was the same dinner in which my brother announced that he wanted to become a doctor. He had just told my parents that he had gotten straight As. But they had heard all that shit before. And they'd hear it again. They had *never* heard my Church Lady impersonation. What Da Dumb Doc didn't realize was that material has to be *fresh*. You can't keep repeating the same fucking stories. So you got straight A's. *Yawn.*

Who cares?!

I took a chance. I did not know how my parents would react when I launched into this impersonation. For all I know, they could have sent me to my room. My mother is very Catholic and takes jokes against religion seriously. So it was a risky move to launch into this character and I did so while doling out mashed potatoes. But it was a *huge* hit. I even reprimanded my mother for taking too large a serving of mashed potatoes in the Church Lady voice.

When I returned home for Thanksgiving in November 1998, my parents begged me to keep it "civil," which is like asking the Pope to attend an electronic rage concert with a pacifier up his ass. It's not going to happen. Well, it might, but it won't look good even if it *does* happen. I guess I'm one of those people who calls a spade a spade. If it's a four of spades, I'm not going to say that it's a "two of clubs."

I don't have much going for me in life, but I *do* have my honesty. And as I've often said on air, "When I lose my honesty, let me know, and I'll quit. *Honestly*."

I forget how this particular Thanksgiving argument started. It could have been about Bill Clinton or about taxes or abortion or government spending overseas or feminism, I honestly just don't remember. I *do* know that the turkey had just been served by Miss Benda, who's our long-time maid, although we like to think of her as more a family member.

In a sense, it was Miss Benda who raised me. Now retired, she'll regularly appear on my shows every now and again, and she loves it. To say that she's harbored a secret desire to act funny over the years might be an overestimation but she *is* funny in an inadvertent way and my listeners love to hear her mispronounce certain words in her strange, lilting Caribbean accent.

She's a big hit and I love her.

I *do* remember how the argument ended.

With food on the floor, with Doc Da Dumb and his wife leaving the table, with my poor mother crying, with my father screaming that we ruined yet another Thanksgiving and then retreating into his study to drink Diet Pepsi laced with rum and watch a college football game with plenty of advertisements for carbonated beverages.

After Miss Benda cleaned up, and after I made myself a turkey sandwich with all the forgotten trimmings, I made my way to my room. My mind traveled back to my killer Thanksgiving set at the Sand Bar Club now almost two years earlier. Time was flying!

Fuck did I have to be here for, suffering because family members were idiots?

I hate to use this term but I *was* a victim of my family's ignorance. (I'm not typically a victim, I *hate* victims, but in this case I was a *victim*.) And it felt terrible.

I had better places to be. Better things to be doing. And I had to deal with *this* shit?

But I wasn't going to retreat into the corner and just cry and moan all night.

That's not my style.

I got to thinking.

I *had* been right about the things I had said, right? I do vaguely remember they were about politics and how I was leaning more toward the Republican side of things.

If I was wrong, I could admit it.

But *was* I?

I *never* lie but I will sometimes get so caught up in the verbal action, all that back and forth, that I can lose track of what I'm fighting for.

Was this the case here?

I started investigating. And what I found changed my life.

I found that I wasn't alone. That a *lot* of the thoughts that I had about politics and current events and feminism weren't *only* held by me. I know this sounds strange when reading a book in the present day, but back in 1998, I was a bit of a newbie when it came to the online world. I only ever downloaded porn or looked up medication information concerning venereal diseases. I never ventured into more serious matters, such as politics or additional information on VD. Mind.

Blown.

Pah-Wow!

So there were *others* who felt that big government sucked?

There were *others* who didn't like being told what to do and what *not* to do by school marms?

There were *others* who felt free to say whatever they wanted about any race, religion, culture (including my own), as long as it was *funny*?

There were others who felt the same way about limited immigration?

I dug deeper and deeper, and before the night was over, and long after my turkey sandwich was finished, and just before Miss Benda made me a new one, I came to the conclusion that I had very much *not* been wrong about the things I had said at the dinner table.

In fact, I had very much been correct, even if I didn't always know why I preferred government "small" to "big."

This started my long journey to where I am now — enlightened, aware and *laid bare*.

Much more on this later.

When I returned to New York City, I doubled-down on my television writing submissions — and to my delight, I received my first joke acceptance. I'm known as being a somewhat pessimistic guy on my show, always a bit down in the dumps over the state of affairs, but I can tell you that when this joke was bought, I literally jumped for joy.

It was my first professional sale. To say that I was thrilled would be an understatement. That night, I took out a girl I knew from the comedy scene (she was a bartender at one of the clubs) and we went for a really nice dinner and then over to a bar where comedians and comedy writers hung.

She ended up leaving that night with Jon Stewart.

Whatever.

She had bad breath anyway. (As far as Jon is concerned, I never liked him and still don't, and not because he slept with my date. His politics I find childish. His comedy I find boring. His attitude I find insufferable. He's smarmy and I despise smarm.)

It didn't matter. I was high for a week. Literally. I was so happy that I went out bought and took drugs and then was high for a week. Here was the joke that was bought:

The Barbie doll, famous throughout the world, just celebrated her fortieth birthday. In other news, Ken is now dating an eighteen-year-old.

It's a fantastic joke. Better yet, the person who loved it was a known legend in the comedy world: Bruce Vilanch, the head writer for many of the Academy Awards that have taken place over the years, the *best* ones. Bruce has been around forever and is a real character, in the *oldest* sense of the word. He wears funny T-shirts and always has a smile. He's a great guy.

Now, it has been said that Bruce invented the funny T-shirt look.

I'd have to disagree with that.

I invented the funny T-shirt look for comedy writers!

Or at least I came up with the idea on my own and didn't need his help in that department.

I've always worn funny T-shirts and I always will. There's no better way to break the ice without saying a word than wearing a shirt that makes someone else laugh.

But there are limits.

I once went to the doctor and totally forgot I was wearing my *Suck It Fuck It Lick It Raw New Orleans* shirt.

Whoopsy!

Luckily, the doctor was a urologist and he was used to cock jokes.

So back to Bruce ...

He *loved* my joke.

He bought it for future use for a TV show or whatever, just to have in his back pocket, where he kept a lot of jokes. He worked on a ton of shows and would often outsource jokes and gags to other writers.

Now ... what happened next, I don't at all blame on Bruce.

The dude, without even knowing me, gave me my first shot, and I'm eternally grateful. We come from different backgrounds and sexual orientations and political views, but I love the guy.

He's a goddamn font of comedic knowledge.

So you understand that I don't hate him, right?
Okay then.

Bruce *loved* the jokes that I emailed him and he bought one.

He had his assistant call me with the number I provided in my email.

Although I forget the details, the call went something like this:

"Skippy? Hello! My name is [I'm forgetting her name] and I am the assistant to Bruce Vilanch, who is a humor writer for various shows out in Hollywood. We received your packet submission. First off, where did you get our fax number, can we ask? Because it's not public."

"I found it."

"Can you be more specific? The reason I ask is because we don't want this number necessarily available and out there. It's a private fax number."

"I can't say where I got it, no."

[In truth, I had found it on the desk of Jay Moor when I was walking his dogs.]

"We find that a little discomforting."

"Okay."

"So ..."

"So did you like what I sent or not?"

"Well, we did. It was very, very well written. The jokes were *great*."

"I can submit more?"

"We are looking for writers for the Academy Awards to be hosted by Billy [Crystal]. But you'd really need to be out here for that. You're located in New York? Your fax number had a 202 area code."

"Yeah, that's Jay's."

"Jay's?"

"Moor. We're good friends."

"Oh, okay."

"So I can come out to write for the Oscars?"

"Probably not, no. We just want to know where to send the $50."

"I'd love to come out. It would be a dream come true."

"Again, we're just looking for freelancers at this point."

"But ... it's a *possibility*?"

"I ... *guess* so," she said. "Anything's a possibility, right?"

I told her the best way to pay me would be to send the money to a Chinatown Western Union (remember, this *was* the 1990s) and I thanked her and hung up, a bit deflated.

Well, it was nice that they liked the joke.

But how much better would it have been to get hired to write for the goddamn Academy Awards?!

To write for a show watched by billions?!

But this was just a pipe dream for a young comedian and comedy writer with only an intense hunger to better himself and the world through laughs, right?

I went for a long walk that afternoon with Jay's mutt, Garanimal.

I had much to think about.

How did *most* people succeed in life?

By hanging back and letting others take control?

I knew so many of my father's friends (and my father himself) who only succeeded by showing extreme gumption and a willingness to put themselves out there.

Granted, they weren't in the comedy business, but still. These were successful fucking people I'm talking about!

And they didn't become that way by sitting around like assholes, just waiting for permission.

In order to fly, you have to take off.

It was time for me to *take off*.

I packed up what little I owned, wrote a quick note to Jay apologizing that his dogs would be alone for a week, and then rushed over to another apartment owned by a comedian whose cats I was supposed to be watching for the next few months.

I patiently explained why I had to take off so suddenly and why he might have to hire a temp agency to take over the visitation and the feeding of the cats and that I was sorry that it was going to be so expensive for him, but I really did *have* to leave, I hope he understood.

After all, it was for the benefit of his two cats.

I then did something I never did before or since: I just went straight to the airport and asked for the first first-class ticket to Los Angeles, California.

I took a chance that at least *one* airline would have *something* going out that night.

They did.

Ten hours later, my American Airlines flight landed in sunny, beautiful, perfectly normal Los Angeles.

Or it would have been if it had been daytime.

It was 11:00 at night.

But the next day, guess what? The sun came out and it was all perfection.

So perfect you wanted to kill yourself.

But I didn't!

I *loved* it.

At first, anyway.

Everything was clean. Everything was new. Everything was fresh!

I felt stupid for not having made the move sooner. New York, in the rearview, looked only gray and unfriendly. *What had I been thinking?*

I didn't want to write for a late-night show in New York anyway. Just the thought of cranking out jokes all day, every day didn't at all interest me.

I wanted each of my jokes (even though there would be a lot, as I am quite prolific) to be what *I* wanted to write, and not what *others* wanted me to write.

Just the thought of having to write for Letterman or Jon Stewart now gave me the sick chills. Fuck that nonsense.

I was an artist.

And an artist should only create what he wants.

I didn't get into comedy to have Letterman turn down 95% of my jokes. I *did* get into comedy to be my own boss. To be in charge of my own art.

I quickly found a nice house near Malibu, just off the beach with a little help from my father, and I got in touch with Bruce's assistant, I'm still forgetting her name. She had blonde hair. She expressed surprise that I had moved out just based on selling one joke.

But to give her some credit here, she *did* seem amenable for me to meet with Bruce to discuss the next steps. In the meantime, I was free to contribute as many jokes as I wanted by fax, and I got straight to work.

It's been said that over five billion people watch the Academy Awards—or did back in 1998—and I fully believe it.

Growing up, it was one of the few shows my family would gather around collectively to watch. I can remember watching it as a kid and rooting for certain movies that I loved, and my parents doing the same.

(For instance, one year they were rooting for *Goodfellas*, while I was rooting for *Harley Davidson and the Marlboro Man*, even though *Harley* hadn't been nominated for a single award. I *still* think it's a better movie.)

Within the first few days of arriving in L.A., I had faxed a few hundred jokes having to do with all of the movies that had been nominated that year in various categories. I had my own fax machine, so there were no visits to the library or to any Kinko's. I felt like I had a direct line with God. Just the image of five billion people laughing at one of my jokes was almost too much to even think about. I imagined all of my former teachers and asshole fellow students literally crying with laughter as they cackled at my jokes.

It was a feeling of *immense power*.

They had written me off, but *I* would be the one who would make the entire world laugh!

And I didn't even care if anyone knew that it was *me* who had written them!

It felt good just to think about.

It was beautiful and I was *relishing* it.

The main problem, though, was writing jokes about movies that I *hadn't* seen. I suppose it wasn't too late to watch the movies in the theaters but I was lazy back then (*still* am, I suppose) and I really had no interest in them anyway. Besides, my job was to *make fun* of them. Fuck did I need to watch them for? And if you ever caught me in a theater, alone, watching *Titanic* with a load of teenage girls and homosexuals, well, please drown me in the icy north-Atlantic sea.

No, it was pretty easy coming up with gags for these shit films without ever having seen them. On the list that year was *Good Will Hunting* (yawn), *As Good As It Gets* (double yawn), *The Full Monty* (please, bitch), *L.A. Confidential* (I fell asleep after reading only the title), and, as mentioned, *Titanic*.

I threw all my golden testicular eggs into the leaky *Titanic* basket.

I figured I knew enough about the Titanic story already to have enough working knowledge to write jokes about it.

The story of the Titanic (not the movie but the *real* version) has always bothered me for a few reasons.

I'll begin with the obvious reason:

It's up to the men to die first? I never understood this. Granted, one doesn't want children to die, but why should the women be saved before the men? From a logistical standpoint, what exactly is the point of having women on a tiny dinghy in the Atlantic Ocean, with only a thin layer of rubber between them and their demise (doesn't that sound like a condom joke)?

If anyone would be needed on a dinghy, it'd be a *man*. On top of that, who fucking paid for the opportunity to go on this journey to begin with?

Shouldn't the man have more of a say in how the journey ends, just as much as how the journey had begun (or even that it began at all)? I've gotten in some heat on my podcast and satellite radio show about this but it wasn't said in jest. I've also talked about my theory — the *true* theory — on why the Titanic went down. You've no doubt heard me talk about it already, but I'd like to explain it more at length in this book.

It's *my* book.

My rules.

The reason for the crash of the Titanic has long been proven to have been caused by a woman. This has been discussed elsewhere but I'll do my best to try to summarize the findings:

[By the way, everything I'm publishing about the Titanic comes directly from a website called TitanicNews. If it sounds like someone else wrote it, they did. Hopefully they don't sue … but whatever. I have a ton of listeners who are lawyers.]

On April 14, 1912, the seas were calm. This has been proven by meteorological reports, as well as diaries kept by sailors and fishermen in the Nova Scotia area just off Canada's eastern coast. Calm, smooth, no storms within hundreds of miles. The Captain of the Titanic, Edward Smith, was on deck, in charge. Smith was an expert in spotting, and avoiding, icebergs, having already logged countless miles and hours as captain of other passenger liners. This was not his virgin ride across the Atlantic, far from it.

At 11:40 P.M. EST, the Titanic hit the "iceberg." But according to numerous amateur radio operators in Canada and in the United States, there were at least fifteen transmissions sent out from the ship as early as 11:00 P.M. EST. Using digitized information management systems, antenna modeling software, and radio wave propagation analysis programs, researchers have determined that at last seven of these transmissions are "credible," meaning that they surely took place and weren't other transmissions sent out by fishermen or teenagers in the area. What these analyses determined was that Captain Edward Smith had smuggled a cheap little chippie (not his wife) on board by the name of Daphne Rynkins and was attempting to impress her by having her take over the controls of the ship. While he stood back and most likely ogled her from behind, she steered directly into not an iceberg but into what was later determined to be a dead whale. *How do we know it was a dead whale?* Days later, a large whale floated onto shore on Long Island. Inside it's stomach? The steering wheel of the Titanic.

One of these "credible" transmissions was recorded by a 42-year-old Maryland housewife named Mabel Dakelmeyer. She had stumbled on the message while scanning her home short-wave radio. The tape was later bought at a yard sale in Pennsylvania for $2 by an amateur Titanic historian, Nick Astasios. From there it was sent to the U.S. government, where it was pieced back together and analyzed. What they heard was astonishing. This is what she recorded:

Captain Edward Smith: What are you doing up here? You need to get below deck.

Daphne Rynkins: I love you so.

Smith: And I love *you* so. Do you wish to bring this beast into port?

Daphne: How I wish for you to become *my* beast.

Smith: For that, I would give *anything*. But first this ... grab the wheel like you mean to— [HUGE SOUND] What is that?! Can someone tell me what ... what might be that most frightening sound?

First Assistant: It sounds like we just hit an iceberg, sir.

Smith: Couldn't be! It sounded too soft. Almost as if what we hit was a large animal—O, GOOD CHRIST, YOU WHORE, WHAT HAVE YOU DONE TO US AND TO SOCIETY?!–

This is where the transmission cuts out.

So *that's* why the story of the Titanic always bothered me. The ship came down because it ran into a giant fish of some sort and because a cheap whore was distracting the captain with effeminate silliness.

And that's why I didn't want to see the bullshit movie version. Who the fuck *needed* to?

But I didn't let that hold me back from writing a ton of jokes about that godawful movie, none of which I can remember now. One joke had to do with Leonardo DiCaprio winning the gambling bet in order to get on the ship and what he would have received if he had *lost* the bet. Another joke had to do with the line "I'm on top of the world," or whatever the fuck Leonardo screams from the front of the ship. I think the punch line was something like: "Maybe ... but that feeling won't last for long." And there was another joke about the size of the jewel that Kate Winslet wore and if they bought it at a Zale's in the mall.

Actually, there *is* one joke that I do remember, and it's a good one:

"Where the hell was Gopher from *The Love Boat*? Probably handing out leis up on the Titanic's Lido Deck!"

That's a great fucking joke.

Bruce Vilanch *loved* all of the jokes I was faxing over, as did the producers for the Academy Awards.

That's what I assumed anyway.

Within a week or so I had sent in close to five hundred. I was relentless. Day after day, night after night, mostly at night, I can only imagine how busy their fax machine must have been as my jokes scrolled through endlessly, without stop.

"Can You Come IN?" read the fax that came across my machine one day.

"YES!" I wrote back.

Could I come in?!

To my first writing room?!

Yes, I could come in!

Does the Pope shit in *my* mouth?!

I still forget Bruce Vilanch's assistant's name but I told her I'd be in the next day, around 2:00 P.M.

I then made it my mission to go out and find a *very* funny T-shirt I could wear to meet Bruce.

As I mentioned previously, Bruce *adored* funny T-shirts. According to comedy lore, he'd wear a new one every day. It reminded me of searching for just that perfect outfit for my first night up on stage as a stand-up comic back in Ocean City.

In a sense, I looked at this meeting as the start of a new life and I didn't want to fuck it up. I definitely *did* not want to fuck this up.

I thought a good way to impress Vilanch would be to show that I respected his age and his experience in the comedy world.

His "humor wisdom," as it were.

I wanted to show that I wasn't at all bothered by the fact that he was fucking old. I wanted to show that I was "in" with the ancient tradition of showbiz and that I respected it, rather than feared it.

The T-shirt I eventually picked out read:

You Know You're
Getting Old When ...

everything that works hurts, and what doesn't hurt, doesn't work

I love this joke. It works on so many levels. It's one of those gags that I wish I had written. I know a joke is good when I'm jealous of it. Typically, I'm jealous of T-shirt slogans and bumper sticker gags. You know why? Because *they cannot be improved*. They. Are. Unable. To. Be Improved.

They're perfect as is.

They're simply perfect.

And *perfectly simple*.

The hardest jokes to write are the simple ones, just as the simplest melodies are the hardest to come up with.

Look at Einstein's equation E and then MC to the third. That's perfect! Why? I don't know but it works really well and it's short and easy to memorize.

The T-shirt joke is also amazing because not only is it true but it's also kind of sad. Getting old stinks. There's nothing really good about it.

But if you can make fun of yourself with a T-shirt about getting old, well, it doesn't get much better than that, right? That's why we're here on earth. To make fun of ourselves and old people.

So I thought that by making fun of old people, or at least trying to emphasize with what they were going through, I'd have a leg up when it came to ingratiating myself with Bruce and his fellow gang of older comedy writers. I arrived early and sat in the waiting room of Bruce's very large office.

A secretary asked who I was, I told her, and she phoned another secretary. I was told to wait. That was fine. *This was the big leagues.* I could wait as long as necessary. I had no dogs to walk here in California. I was my *own* boss.

Chris Rock has talked about this. Not to me but to others. That he waited for hours outside Lorne Michaels' office and that he'd have waited *another* five hours if he had had to. He'd have waited for as long as it *fucking took* to see Lorne.

Why?

Because it was worth it.

This would also hold true for my situation.

It was worth it. I wasn't going to leave, I wasn't going to complain.

After twenty minutes, I asked the secretary what was happening. She had no answer. I returned to my seat. I continued to wait. After another thirty minutes, I told the secretary that I'd give her five minutes to get me into a fucking meeting with Bruce or that there would be trouble. The look in her eyes told me that she *heard* what I had said.

Loud and fargin' clear.

There's only so long one can wait until they look like an asshole.

Within minutes, a new (younger secretary) came out and introduced herself. I'm forgetting her name. She was gracious and apologetic for keeping me waiting, and she was pretty goddamn slammin'. I do remember *that*.

I was humble but I also couldn't help but give a little smile and perhaps even an impish wink. *Ever the charmer!*

Looking back, it surprises me that I was so confident in my own abilities! I was young and naïve, sure, that goes without saying, and yet I wasn't going to *allow* the Hollywood machine to stop me!

There was no way that anything was going to prevent me from breaking into the ranks of the successful! I had a hunger emanating from a place that I can't describe and I'm not talking about from my armpits or groin area.

I'm not sure if this hunger originated with my teachers telling me I would never succeed, or from my father never thinking as much of me as he had of my brother, or any of my ex girlfriends thinking I was a "moron" or a "degenerate" or whatever they happened to call me out of anger at the time. (It's funny how friendly I remain with most of my exes. For all this talk about me not "loving" women, I seem to have more female friends than any other guy I know.)

I'm not sure where this confidence came from.

I really just don't know.

Part of it was not knowing any better and being too stupid to know otherwise. The rest of it came from knowing more than everybody else and being too smart to fuck it all up.

I was called into the room and there he sat, *the legend*. He was shorter than I expected but very gregarious and welcoming. Around him were a few women, whose names I'm forgetting. And a bunch of older comedy writers. And there was another guy there, a young comedy writer who was also working on his first Academy Awards show. His name was Tim McCalanson.

"So this is the infamous Skippy I've been hearing about!" Bruce exclaimed.

"Live and in person," I jested. Bruce laughed extremely hard. It seemed as if everyone joined in and it lasted for a good long while.

"Have a seat," he said. I saw that he was *also* wearing a funny T-shirt. I still remember it:

You're the Reason I'm Medicated

I could only laugh. I was also medicated but probably on different meds than Bruce's. I pointed to my shirt. And then I retorted "I know you're old, Bruce, but I also know that *everything* works!"

Bruce laughed for a very long time. His laugh was guttural and almost wet. In truth, it sort of disgusted me but I was thrilled that I was getting a laugh from a professional who'd been in the industry for so long. Getting someone like this to laugh was no minor feet.

He motioned for me to take a seat and I took it.

"So, we just wanted to meet the person we feel we know so much about!" Bruce said. "You're certainly *industrious*."

"I'll take that as a compliment," I said and then immediately grimaced. Probably the wrong thing to say, just reinforcing what he had just said, but it was better to err on the side of being nice than too clever.

"You've sent in so many jokes!" he chirped happily.

"Thank you. I like to keep busy. And I want to thank you for allowing me to write for the Academy Awards. This is a dream come true."

I meant it. I was now a professional writer.

"So we've looked over your jokes and we want to buy a few," Bruce said.

A few?! I thought.

"And while we appreciate your enthusiasm, we're wondering if we can convince you to attack by scalpel rather than cudgel."

What in the hell is a cudgel? I thought.

"What in the fuck is a cudgel?" I asked.

The entire room broke into laughter.

"Meaning," said Bruce, smiling widely, "that less is sometimes more."

I was beginning to get it. The jokes were amazing but too much of *anything*, no matter how *great*, isn't always a *positive* thing.

It was like the spiced rum cake that my Miss Benda used to make.

At first, I loved it. After eating the tenth bite, I wanted to kill myself.

"I get it," I said. "Less is sometimes more. It's cool."

Bruce nodded wisely. He'd been doing this a long time.

"Have you seen all the movies?" he asked.

"Yup," I said, a lie.

"Great. We could use more *Titanic* jokes. Especially in the opening."

"How so?" I asked, pleasantly intrigued and also happy he had picked the one movie I actually knew about.

"Billy's going to come out and sing his opening musical melody," Bruce said.

Translation: Billy Crystal was going to come out onto the stage and sing parody songs about each of the movies nominated for the big awards.

"Tell me more," I exclaimed, captivated.

"We're thinking we want to sing about *Titanic* but were kind of stuck on what to sing about. If you have any ideas, you can let us know, okay?"

With that he stood.

"But you don't have to send in so many. And email would be better than fax. You can send those to my assistant."

(I'm still forgetting her name.)

Was this a clue that they were so busy I should leave? That all they wanted was for me to come into the office just to get it out of my system? To tell me (without actually telling me) to calm down a little and to send fewer jokes?

"I have an idea," I blurted out.

In truth, I had nothing. But I didn't want to leave.

Bruce sat back down.

He spread his arms out wide as if to say, *What do you got?*

I still had nothing. But I had to think *fast*. I knew that my entire career could hinge on this very moment.

"*Gilligan's Island* ... song parody," I said quietly.

"What?" asked one of the women in the room, I'm forgetting her name. Regardless, she was incredibly spellbound by where I might be headed.

Which I found funny. I mean, even *I* didn't know where I was headed!

"Yes, *Gilligan's Island*," I said more forcefully, as if I had been thinking of it for years. "Billy comes out and sings a song about the making of the movie *Titanic*, but to the tune of *Gilligan's Island*."

I was getting goosebumps.

How did I come up with this? I still don't know. It was as if I was a vessel of God.

Bruce was perking up, and fast.

"I like this a tremendous amount," he said, or something similar. "I *like* this!"

I started singing the *Gilligan's Island* theme song and Bruce joined in. Soon, the entire room was also joining in, smiles spread wide across their faces.

"Would you be willing to work on this more?" Bruce asked.

Does the pope shit in a rabbi's mouth?

Yes!

"Sure," I said, all casual. "Yeah, I could do that."

"That's really wonderful," Bruce said, or something similar. "Email us what you have, when you have it!"

And that was it. My first professional meeting and I had already achieved *tremendous* success. Before I left, I turned around and asked, "Just out of curiosity, which few jokes of mine did you want to buy?"

Bruce said, "Now that I think about it, let's just have you work on something *bigger*. Send me what you have for this new idea and we'll go from there."

So he's not interested in any of the hundreds of jokes I sent? I wondered.

"So you're not interested in any of the jokes that I sent?" I asked.

"We'll talk," said Bruce, smiling, leaving it up in the air.

Looking back, I was being given a huge break. I was just too young to understand it at the time!

What I should have said was, "Thank you for this huge opportunity, sir!"

Instead I just walked out.

Regrets and all that.

But maybe that's what this book is for more than anything else: Bruce, if you're reading this, I apologize. I only appreciate what you did for me and if I didn't show it at the time, I *mucho apologizo*.

That's Spanish for *I was an idiot*.

I got to work immediately.

I headed back to Malibu and took a long walk on the beach. I had much to think about. What I was about to write would be heard by billions and possibly change comedy for the next generation. I was still in my funny T-shirt. A few others on the beach made an enthusiastic comment or gave me a hearty thumb's up, but my mind was elsewhere.

How to *tackle* this? Where was my "in"?

Okay, let's break this down, I thought. *This isn't rocket science.* (Some might say it's *harder*, actually. I haven't met too many *funny* neurospace engineers ... or brain surgeons, for that matter.)

How does the song go again?

Just sit right back and you will hear a tale, a tale of a fateful trip ...

Okay. It's a start.

Now how to meld the *existing* with the *new*?

For me, humor is a dash of cayenne pepper in a dish of leftover gumbo. It makes everything taste fresh. It makes it all *newer*.

But here's the thing: you have to *make* it your own. Each chef brings to the recipe their own definition of "dash."

I've been told many times that I have my own comedic style, my own specific humor signature. That when someone hears a joke that I wrote, they know instantly that it's me. I suppose it's no different from each of us having a different fingerprint. We're all unique and we all bring to the table something that is singularly *us*, different from anybody else. The same holds true for comedy. If you hear a joke by, say, Seinfeld, you know it's from him. Or if you hear a joke from George Carlin ... *that's George,* you think.

Same would hold true for Bill Cosby, although if you now hear a joke that the Coz tells, you'd probably be too scared to laugh for fear of being banished to PC Siberia. It's like detecting how different women have their own unique odor. All women have that special womanly scent. Some are more pleasant than others. But they *all* have it. *Trust me.* I've smelled more women than a working pig has unearthed truffles.

So I've been told that I have a very inimitable comic style. It's been described as a bit dark, very real, but with a slippery, greasy edge that could either spell danger or possibility.

With that in mind, this is what I came up with for the Gilligan's *Titanic* parody:

Just sit right back on that couch and eat some snacks,
Cause you'll hear a tale of a fateful film,
That's started from this very town,
Aboard a tremendously doomed ship.

From there, my mind was working in overdrive and I felt as if I was flying:

The director was a particular, creative man,
The producer with money brave and sure,
Thousands set sail on a crazy flick,
Something that would make them rich real quick.

By this time, I was singing to myself, quickly jotting down my ideas on a pad of paper before I—God forbid—forgot what was passing through me. Keep in mind I was still on the beach:

'Twas supposed to be a four month shoot,
A four month shoot … a four month shoot.

But the feeling in Hollywood starting getting rough,
All those huge egos were soon tossed,
If not for the courage of the fearless fans,
The project would soon be lost … the project would soon be lost.

A few people on the beach passed me smiling. They might have known what I was up to but I doubt it.
Writing jokes for a few billion people, was all. Making the entire world smile … No big deal.
Sure.
I continued, the ideas flowing:

The film set ground after funding b'came a prob,
Its mission no longer so sure.
Cameron wanted more effects, something that looked so pure.

With so many stars and Winslet, too.
He brought aboard DiCaprio,
The choice was not that hard
He once played a real good 'tard.

Leo drew Kate Winslow nude,
Or 'twas it the other way around?
They both looked just like girls to me,
Like two lesbians that you'd see downtown.

The shooting started getting rough.
Cameron bullied crew and cast!
He took way too long, he spent way too much,
His ego grew so vaaaaaaaast!

The studio was not happy,
With all those stupid overruns.
If not for the hissy fit that Cameron threw,
He would have lost all his funds.

The movie came out six months late.
It should have been a flop.
But thanks to the pre-teens and them gays,
Its box office won't stop!
Its box office won't stop ….

And, with that, my first professional assignment was done. *Swish, swash.* As *easy* as that. This one came *so* easily as most of the great ones always do. It had practically written itself.

My philosophy on comedy is this: If you have to strain in order to pinch out a project, it's not going to be as enjoyable as if you had just *scooched* that bitch right out.

It is always the easiest shits to produce that you enjoy the most.

Whereas, the ones where you have to sit on the throne and strain away, hoping for a Messy Marvin … well, those just ain't so fun.

And the audience can tell!

If what you're writing isn't fun for *you*, well, it certainly won't be fun for anyone *else*, right?

Shit gonna just stink.

I hurried to my house and wrote it all down on a pad of yellow paper. The last thing I needed was to come up with something this good again. I believe in the power of first go-rounds. If you capture magic once, why have to capture it again?

Once down on paper, I pecked it out on my 1990s computer and then emailed it in.

I waited.

And waited.

After not hearing anything for a few hours, I emailed it *again*. And then, a few hours after that, once again.

Nothing.

So I waited until the next morning and called the office.

The female assistant, whose name I'm still forgetting, answered. I asked if she had received the song parody. She said she had but sounded confused. I pressed her on it.

Are you sure you received it? I asked. *I mean, are you really sure?!*

She was a bit flippant. I asked to speak to Bruce directly. *You can't. Why not? He's busy. And what was I yesterday if not busy?* I asked. *I wrote an entire parody song to be sung at the fucking Academy Awards! Hold on,* she said. *Fine,* I said.

Bruce got on the line and he was a lot more pleasant than his assistant. He told me that my song parody *did* arrive and that he was a bit swamped at the moment but that he would definitely read it later that night.

Nice. Respectful. A class act.

I thanked him and hung up. And I re-read the song parody.

Shit.

One of my biggest hates on earth is turning in a joke and then re-reading it and realizing *too late* that it needs to be improved a little. I've been asked, *Well, if that's the case, why re-read them after you've already submitted?*

Because I'm a perfectionist, asshole. That's why.

Why does a surgeon make sure his stitches are secure after the patient returns a week later? Why does anyone do *anything*? Because they take *pride* in their work. I'm no different than that surgeon.

Before billions hear a joke, should I not be concerned that it's as good as I could ever make it?

I'm a perfection, as I said, and I have a keen eye to cast out anything I think is underperforming.

In the case of this particular song parody, what bothered me was this line:

If not for the courage of the fearless fans

It wasn't that the line was *bad* but it could have been *better*.

It wasn't what I had written. It was what I *should* have written.

A simple fix, in retrospect, and one that I was definitely kicking myself for not having included.

Where was my mind? as the Pixies once sang.

It's hard to explain to a layman but I'll try:

It's similar to looking at a complicated mathematics equation and seeing that the solution was there all along. I've heard that I have the reputation for being a "fixer." Meaning, someone who can just take a quick glance at a joke and immediately discern exactly what's wrong.

Sometimes this isn't so easy to do with one's *own* work. It's like smelling your own breath. Or tickling yourself.

But I've always found it *easy*. It's a just a talent.

So when I looked at the song parody again, it quickly became clear that the missing ingredient, the missing spice, was the word *tween*.

That's it.

Simple fix.

It would now read:

If not for the courage of the fearless tweens ...

See, back in 1998 or so, the word "tweens" was a word that was coming on strong, just as the word *teenage* had come on strong in the 1950s. Kids were maturing earlier and earlier and by the nineties, an 11-year-old was comparable to a 13-year-old decades before, at least physically. Because of that, tweens had crushes like any older normal teenager. And that particular year, all the girls seemed to have a crush on Leonardo DiCaprio. (I'm often asked if I've ever met Leonardo. I haven't. But a gorgeous model I once dated later slept with Leonardo's good friend from his "Pussy Posse," so there's *that*.)

A large part of *Titanic's* popularity was due in part to many (or most) of the fans being tweens or early teenage girls. The joke, really, had to have *that* detail in it.

I called the office back. The assistant answered and I hung up.

Fuck it.

I would just drive over with the new version.

I figured I'd make it easy for *all of us*.

I've always found that when it comes to success it is not only *talent* that's required. Also just as important—if not *more* important— is to be easy to work with.

To be someone that you'd want to hang out with in a small office for sixteen hour days.

Do you want to hang around with assholes?

You don't, I can *assure* you. When the workdays go late in the evening, and when people are hungry and in a foul mood, when the writing room is starting to smell and all you want to do is escape into the fresh air, these are your buddies you're stuck with down in the laugh trenches.

And you *better* like them!

I wasn't going to be rude about the indifference I was experiencing. I was just going to be firm but also respectful.

I had produced something good—*better* than good. *Really* good. I didn't mind waiting. Now all I wanted, really, was to know whether I was on the *right* path.

Stay on that path with the song parody? Or should I take a different route? Better to find out *before* taking a wrong turn and ending up hundred of miles away from where one *should* be!

"Hey," I said to the secretary. "Here to see Bruce."
Instead of waiting for an answer, I continued to walk back towards Bruce's office. There was really no other choice. I tell young comedy writers to do the same:

When in *doubt*, you gotta *FLOUT!*
One, two, three, four ... who's that knockin' on my door?

Why, that would be Skippy Battison ... *passin' on your goddamn right ... you like that, ya beyotch?! ...*

In I confidently walked. Bruce was alone. Actually, he was with a woman but I don't think she was important. I'm forgetting her name.

"Skippy!" said Bruce, excitedly. "What's the reason for such a pleasurable return?" (Or something like that, I can't remember exactly.)

"Want to talk to you about the *Gilligan's Island* song parody," I declared. "Have you read it yet? It's pretty great."

"I haven't, no," said Bruce. "But I plan to first thing later tonight."
"How about now?" I asked.

"I would love to," Bruce stated. (Or something similar.) "But really kind of swamped with material."

He pointed (a bit impotently) to a large pile of papers next to him. In response, I pulled out a fresh version that I just happened, "accidentally," to have brought with me.

I'd recommend doing this at *all* meetings. You'd be amazed at how many times I've walked into a meeting after hearing how great my material was, only to find that they had "lost" it or "misplaced it" or "never had it" to begin with. This is very common.

A smile lit up his face and Bruce happily stroked his big, bushy beard. "Wonderful!"

I handed over the song parody and stood above him as he read it.
He chuckled throughout, as I knew he would.
"This is *amazing*," he declared (or something similar).
"Thank you," I responded, modestly.
"This has a good shot of getting in."
"A good shot?" I asked, perplexed.
He then explained that for a three hour telecast, the writers might write enough material for *ten* hours. Bruce pulled out a huge, white binder.
"This is from last year's show," he said.

"It's *huge!*" I shouted.

And it was. Enough material to fill many Oscar episodes. I glanced through it. "These are all solid jokes," I said.

"Yes," he replied.

"But I don't recognize them," I responded.

"For *good* reason," he stated.

The reason was that maybe 15% of the jokes written for any particular Academy Awards ceremony end up getting used. They would rather have *more* material than *less* material.

One year Jerry Lewis literally clowned around for twenty minutes on stage because he had run out of material. Lewis was playing the trumpet, he was shouting, he was acting like a crazy person. *It was awful.* The Academy never wanted that to happen again. The sight of Lewis running around the stage, conducting an imaginary orchestra and blowing into a non-existent trumpet didn't exactly capture the nation's imagination.

"So what I'm saying," said Bruce, "is this will definitely go into the binder. Whether we use it or not, I don't know."

"I thank you for your honesty," I replied, and I meant it. I've always appreciated people who are honest.

Rejection doesn't bother me. What bothers me is being lied to in a manner that questions my intellectual ability. Now *that* drives me fucking crazy. Here was a man, at the top of his game, who was giving me the respect that I deserved. And I'll never forget it.

I decided to perform a move that I had once seen back in Maryland. I was having my hair cut by a new barber and he was obviously of the homosexual variety. A friend of his walked in. They chatted and giggled and before the friend left, he bowed to both me and the barber.

I thought that was really funny. He fucking bowed!

That always stuck with me: *I guess that's just how gays say goodbye.*

Interesting.

So I decided to try it in this situation. I bowed deeply to Bruce. His reaction was mixed, in a positive sense. He looked deeply touched but also surprised, as if to say, *How does this man know the code?*

I told him I'd be in touch with fresh jokes soon enough and I then left. It was a nice ride back to Malibu.

This was a little over a month before the March 24th Academy Awards broadcast. I got down to business. Each morning I'd wake up and take a walk along the Malibu beach and come up with ideas that I'd then put into written form when I returned back to my house.

Not sure if I pointed this out earlier, but when I told my father about moving out to California to write for the Academy Awards, he surprised me with a house just off the Malibu Beach.

I was finally coming into my own and I was still only in my mid twenties. It goes without saying that my pops was incredibly proud of his youngest son. My mother was also proud but she was too busy on the golf course to say as much, which is fine. *Whatever*.

I *still* love her and whoever her new husband is, her third.

Meanwhile, after I was done for the day, I'd head over to a local bar and shoot the shit with some of the local types. Some wrote comedy and I made it clear that I was now one of them. A few wrote for sitcoms and one for a late-night show.

We became a pack of sorts, commenting on the news of the day and adding our own delicious twists. All were super impressed that I had managed to score such a prestigious gig and I regaled them with stories about Bruce and the other writers in the office.

One night, about two or three weeks before the event, I met a woman at the bar, about my age, who had designs on getting into comedy herself. I took it upon myself to give her the ropes—and then, finally, "the rope."

We began sleeping with each other and after the tenth time or so, I asked her what she wanted to do in the business. "Anything," she replied. "I just love comedy so much!"

Before I knew what I was doing, I had already asked her to be my date to the Academy Awards, assuming that I would get a free ticket and then a plus one. She was thrilled and instantly called about six friends.

I was now *locked* into this date, which I didn't mind, I guess, but I always preferred to leave open the opportunity to be able to bring someone along who's way hotter. She was a real beauty—straight black hair, fair complexion, huge tiggasaurses—but this was Hollywood. There were *always* more beautiful women out there! In fact, Hollywood has more beautiful women per capita than any other city on earth. I would literally gasp any time I passed a woman who I felt deserved a "five" rating, which meant the very best. A "one" was the very worst. I'd find myself counting the numbers at the end of the day and it was not rare for me to reach over one hundred.

This happened *all* the time.

This particular woman, whose name I'm remembering as something like Cindy or Candy or Catherine, was very sweet but she was missing the genius spark. I could see her working her way up as, say, an agent's assistant and then moving on to maybe becoming a mid-level agent herself. I never envisioned that she'd ever become a *comedy writer*. She was nice but maybe *too* nice, if that makes sense.

The killer instinct was missing. That she later became quite successful writing for *Brooklyn Nine-Nine* and *The Good Place* and ended up winning multiple Emmy awards was a bit of a blow.

I reached out years later (I thought quite diplomatically) to congratulate her on all her success but she never got back to me. That's on her. I did the right thing.

That's life. *Relationships are complicated. Comedy is easy.* I should have that printed on packets of rubbers.

Anyway ...

I was writing a ton of great jokes, tweaking slightly different versions of my *Gilligan's* parody song, and also looking for places to rent a tux, when I received a call from Bruce's assistant:

"Hey."

"Hey."

"So we want to pay you for the *Gilligan's* song parody."

"Great!"

"I just need your social security number and address."

"Are you buying anything more?"

"Jokes?"

"Yes."

"Yeah, I think so."

"Which ones?"

"I don't have those in front of me."

"I'd like to know. I want to know what you really liked so I can concentrate on those areas for future jokes."

She said she'd call me back and did within moments.

"Bruce says he likes the joke about 'how you like them apples?' and the 'full monty.' Also the 'deconstructing Woody' joke and the 'if this is as good as it gets' joke."

"Four? Four jokes?"

She stumbled and bumbled. "Those are just the ones I know about."

This wasn't good. "Can I speak with Bruce?"

"He's ... busy."

"Is he really?"

"Yes."

"Will you have him call me when he has the chance?" I asked politely.

"Sure."

"And can you also say that I *bow* before him?"

"Okay ..."

"He'll get it."

I hung up and called a friend of mine in the business. I told him what had just happened.

"That's par for the course," he said.

"How so?"

"Because most of the writing for the Oscars is written on the fly, up on the stage, live."

"Really?"

"Yes."

"How do you know all this?"

"I just do."

He worked in a video store and knew more about Hollywood than so-called "Hollywood historians."

"So I'll be behind the stage, writing gags?" I asked, growing excited.

"You should be," he said. "That's where the best work is done."

This was an interesting twist.

To be at the show as it was happening *live*—scribbling down notes behind the scenes—would just be a *magical* experience.

I left a message with Bruce and waited a few hours. I then drove over to the office.

"Hey," I said to the secretary. "*HeretoseeBruce* ..."

And I walked right in.

"Bruce!" I declared, bowing.

He appeared busy. But no less friendly.

"How can I help you?" he asked, not taking his eyes off the yellow pad he was scribbling jokes on. He was in the *zone*. I knew better than to bother him too much. "Heard that the writers are there live at the broadcast, writing down jokes." He grunted. I took the grunt to mean *yes*. "And I assume I can be there behind the stage?" I asked. "Writing jokes for Billy?"

Bruce laughed very hard.

What I had said wasn't meant to be a joke but I've found over the course of my career, and life, that whatever I say, whether it was meant to be serious or not, typically ends up producing laughter.

I can't help it.

I remember being in a third grade Christmas play. I was playing the role of the owner of the inn where Jesus was born. I had one line and I received a huge laugh. I don't know why. The line was: "For which we are so thankful to welcome a newborn baby into this world!" It could have been the face I made due to me truly not understanding what I was saying. Or it could have been my lisp. Or my cut-off jean shorts. Or my "FUCK OFF DALLAS COWBOYS!" tank-top. Or any other reason. But it felt *great*. I suppose I've been chasing that feeling ever since. Bruce continued to smile very hard. He made a motion for me to leave, that he was swamped, he'd love to spend more time talking with me but that he had to get back to work. *Fine*. He was busy. I got it. And I was in a rush to get home and fuck my new girlfriend anyway. It all worked out. The next few weeks passed in a blur. It still bothered me slightly that I never received a definitive answer to my being needed at the Academy Awards ceremony but I chalked it up to everyone just being so damn busy. One morning I did manage to get through to someone in the office—a rarity, as everyone was incredibly reluctant to take even one minute away from their joke writing—and I spoke to Bruce's assistant, I'm still forgetting her name. This was two days before the big event. This is how the cal went:

"Can I be there or not?" I asked.

"There's a limited role for writers," she replied.

"Let me talk with Bruce," I said.

She came back with: "He's busy."

"Then I guess I'll just have to come on down," I announced.

"Hang on. Let me ask him," she said.

I was on hold for a few minutes and was just about to hang up and call back when she got back on the line and said, "Bruce says fine. Just meet at Door 7A at around 2:00 P.M."

I was in! I was in! I was in like motherfuckin' General Michael Flynn!

I drove home, quickly banged my new girlfriend, and then gently told her that there wouldn't be a ticket for her, as I now had to work backstage. We broke up a few days later, shortly after her grandmother died of a sudden heart attack. (What's ironic is that this young woman ended up going to the damn awards *anyway* as the date of one of the assholes up for the cinematography awards. Luckily, he lost. And they later divorced. So that's the good news.)

I rented myself a tux, emailed Bruce some last-minute jokes, and then, the night before, I did my best to earn much-needed rest before the biggest night of my life. It didn't work. I was too keyed up. At the bar at 2:00 A.M., everyone promised to be on the lookout for me off stage, furiously scribbling down gags for Billy to tell. I was modest but I was also super fucking proud of how far I'd come. A few asked if I'd be taking a limo. I thought about it for a moment and replied, *No, that's usually reserved for the celebs.* "But you *are* a celeb," said one very nice person, I can't remember her name. I thought about it some more.

Fuck it. Why not?

About twelve hours later I was sitting alone in a huge stretch limousine on my way, quite early, to the Dorothy Chandler Pavilion. Going stag to the Academy Awards was lame. But what was I *supposed* to do? The last thing I needed was to worry about some girl out in the audience not enjoying her experience or being bored or wanting me with her to hold her fucking hand. I had no time for that. (I *still* have no time for that shit. I will *never* bring a date to a show's taping or to my satellite radio or podcast sessions. I'd rather concentrate on pleasing the gods of comedy than the gods of pussy, who are *so* much more fickle—being *female* and all. Joking, joking!)

The limo stopped and idled in front of the theater. There was no media to bother me. Good. I hopped out and walked over to Door 7A. I knocked. And then again. The limo took off. After about ten minutes of knocking, a guard opened.

"Hi," I said. "I'm here."

"Congratulations."

"Thank you," I replied, even though I knew he was being sarcastic. *Whatever*. I was the guy who was *writing* for this event.

He was the guy *working* the fucking event for chump change.

"Skippy Battison," I announced proudly.

He checked his list of names.

There was no Skippy Battison.

"Try Skip E. Battison," I said. My name is often confused with this particular spelling.

"Nope, nothing," he eventually said.

"I'm here to see Bruce."

"Bruce?"

"Vilanch? The fucking writer of this evening's jokes?"

He shrugged.

I was obviously dealing with an idiot. A real flunky.

"Can I speak with your manager?"

"Manager?"

"Your *boss*."

"Sure."

Flunky limped away and here came Mr. Boss Man, in all honesty just another flunky who made a few more bucks an hour. I gave this moron my name, the different spellings, nothing. The door closed.

Hell was happening here?!

I walked around to the front door but was stopped by another guard.

Same routine. What's your name? Why are you here?

Zero reaction.

I've told this story a few times on my podcast and satellite radio show and each time I tell it a little bit differently. It's like a car crash you experience. You try your very best to block it all out. But you can't help but remember more and more details each time you think about it.

And you relive it differently each and every time.

Guess that's what makes it all so fresh.

Honestly, if you've heard this before—especially on the Judd Apatow episode of the Marc Maron podcast—just skip to the next chapter. I'm not going to be offended, I won't even know.

But just know that you're going to miss the *real deal*.

Here goes:

I've heard versions in which I was "outside the auditorium for ten hours." That's *impossible*. There's no way in hell that I would *ever* spend that long standing outside *anything* ... especially in a rented tux. I've also heard on another podcast run by a woman—I'm forgetting her name—that I was hanging out with Tom Hanks in his limo and we both were eating chili hot dogs. I'm not sure where *that* rumor came from. Sadly, it's not true. I fucking love Hanks.

By the way, my lawyers and agents are making me mention that I *did* reach out to Bruce for his side of the story, which is only fair, but just as he refused to come on my podcast and satellite radio show in the past, he's also now refusing to be quoted for this book. That's fine. Honestly, I still very much like Bruce. Beyond that, he's brilliant. So this isn't really about Bruce as much as his bitch of a former assistant who lied to me. I'm overly protective of my jokes and that's why I might have been annoying. My jokes are my babies, what can I say? Aren't most mothers and fathers protective of their babies? It is funny that Bruce's former assistant later became an Emmy award winning writer for various sitcoms including *30 Rock* and *Girls*. Maybe it was her bitchiness—sorry, her *drive*—that helped her achieve all of her success. I still forget her name but I wish her well. *Ahem.*

I ran around the corner to a pay phone and called Bruce's office. No answer. No surprise. They were probably already inside the auditorium.

I just *had* to get in.

If you check out the surveillance video footage from the evening— and I mean the *raw* footage, not the edited footage—one can clearly discern how I did so.

At around 2:45 P.M. you can see me pretending to be a correspondent for a local entertainment TV show, or so I was telling the passersby. That I wasn't even holding a microphone and that there was no camera anywhere around me didn't seem to bother anyone.

James Cameron was real nice and stopped to speak for a little while.

I made up some bullshit questions about the technical aspects of the *Titanic* film and he smiled. He seemed to know that I was more informed about the particulars than others might have been.

He walked over to the next interviewer. I put down my fake microphone and stood behind him. I was now part of his entourage.

It's pretty well stated among those with any inside Hollywood dope that Cameron has a huge ego. That's fine. I *also* have a big ego. Should this come as a surprise? For any major artist?

Anyone who thinks differently from other people—and then thinks differently from those who are already thinking differently—*should* have a huge ego. It goes with the territory. Fine. James Cameron has a huge ego.

Members of his real entourage—PR flacks, agents, idiot hangers-on—looked over to me, saw that I was wearing a tux and holding a paper pad and looking official.

It's like I said earlier.

HiheretoseeBruce.

You walk in. You don't look back. You keep moving forward. The world will open for you …

Into the auditorium I walked, just behind Cameron and his idiotic gang. I silently thanked all of them and then headed for backstage. The place was abuzz with activity. People were just starting to be seated. Up on the stage, meanwhile, people with headphones and clipboards ran around yelling instructions to each other. It was total chaos, every bit as wonderful as I had imagined. The biggest event of the year, the whole world watching, and I was a part of it all!

The orchestra was practicing and I could make out Billy up on stage, dressed casually, going through a huge notebook.

My jokes were *in* that notebook! It was fucking *magical*!

I listened carefully to what Billy was muttering. Was he practicing one of my jokes? I couldn't tell. I *had* to get closer.

When I talk about this on my podcast and satellite radio show, callers are always amazed that I got this far and that I could get within touching distance of Billy. But you have to remember that this was pre-9/11. People could do *all sorts* of things back then. And if you looked like you knew what you were doing, while wearing a rented tux, while holding a pad of paper … well, you could do practically *anything*. I'm always surprised that assassins don't just do this instead of hiding in the alcoves or behind trees for days at a time.

All you have to do is walk straight up, in a tux, talking to yourself as if you're important and busy, and then …*Whammo*!

"Hey, Billy," I said, all casual when I reached the stage. Surprisingly, he was alone. Just him and his huge folder of jokes.

He looked at me bleary-eyed. He was clearly exhausted.

"It's Skippy. Skippy Battison."

Still a bit confused.

"One of the writers," I patiently explained.

"Oh," he said, coming to pretty quickly. "Nice to finally meet you. Thank you ... for all the hard work."

"You got it," I said.

He went back to looking down at his huge white binder.

"I have three particular favorites," I blurted. "The deconstructing Woody joke and the 'if this is as good as it gets.' Both those are really solid."

"Wonderful," he said.

"But I have to say that I'm most proud of the *Gilligan's Island* song parody for *The Titanic*."

I knew this one would hit hard.

"You wrote that?" he asked.

"And came up with the idea," I announced.

"That's phenomenal," he said, or something similar. It's hard to remember.

"Yeah."

I waited about a minute. That might not seem like a long time, "a minute," but truthfully it felt endless up there on stage.

"Well, I can see you're busy. Nice to meet you."

"Real nice to meet you," he said, turning his back. He was in "the zone." I could tell because of my stand-up days. And when you're in that zone, it doesn't matter *who's* talking to you. It could be the goddamn pope.

I went off to find Bruce. It didn't take long. The look on his face was precious.

"I think you forgot to put my name by 7A," I said, mischievously. I bowed.

When I arose, he wasn't laughing. And he wasn't smiling.

He's in "the zone," too, I thought.

"How did you get in?" he asked.

"Walked," I said, impishly.

Someone came running up to him with a question. Eyes still on me, he answered. As with anyone at his level, he was a very good multi-tasker.

"And ... " He was stopped short by someone else asking a question.

He was busy. *That* much was clear.

"I'm here to work," I said. "Let me know if I can be of any help."

I retreated into the shadows. This was going to be fun.

I watched the people start filing into the theater. Here's a secret: for most of the ceremony, the stars aren't in their assigned seats. There's just a placard with their name on them. So it's their assistants who have to sit there while nothing exciting is happening. It was funny to see a fat schlump sitting in Brad Pitt's seat, and an ugly dame sitting in Julia Roberts' seat. It was surreal.

I thought back to my beginnings working as a stand-up comedian and then, later, all those packets I had written and everything I had gone through. I felt older than my years. But standing up on that stage felt … *right*.

There's no other way to describe it. It just felt like a solid fit. *This* was where I *belonged*. And I *never* intended to leave.

Sure, I was ultimately asked to leave and it came as a great shock and surprise–but that came later.

For now, though, the ceremony had started.

The uglies in the audience had been replaced with the beautiful people. I could see Jack Nicholson, front row. Meryl Streep, just behind him. Tom Hanks (he wasn't eating a chili dog). A woman actress whose name I'm forgetting. She was a big star back then. She was also there.

What I remember the most, however, is the *noise*.

Everything was so loud!

The music, the crowd, the announcer's voice over the speakers.

Everything *resonated*. I couldn't believe this was happening. I looked over to Billy and he was conferring with Bruce and a few other writers.

I wandered over but didn't say anything. There wasn't anything to say. By the looks of it, they had already worked out the opening and were just going over beats and such. I felt a glow of pride. The announcer mentioned Billy's name and he bounded out onto the stage.

It was show time!!!

In many ways, I have a ton of balls. I'm really not afraid of anything. But I have to say, just the thought of bounding onto a stage in front of five billion people … I almost pissed my pants. I remember turning to Bruce and saying, *This is incredible*.

I don't remember if there was a response. If there was, I couldn't hear it over the crowd noise.

My attention returned to the stage. It's a weird sensation to watch a production from the backstage. More accurately, to watch peoples' reactions in the audience as to what's taking place in front of them. I could see Billy, but only his back. For me, the performance was watching the laughter coming from the audience. What was also interesting was that some people laughed *before* others. They all heard the jokes at the same time but some people "got it" earlier. It's almost as if they understood a language more quickly than others in the audience. It was interesting. Their Humor IQs must have been a little higher.

Selfishly, what I was waiting for most was to hear one of my jokes and to see the visceral reaction, up close and live. It's one thing to watch comedy on a television but it's another thing to see it performed *live*. It's like sports. Okay on TV. Electrifying in person. This was the equivalent of having court side seats to an NBA game and the best in the business were bounding down the court!

Billy was introduced by "riding" onto the stage on a fake Titanic bow. The crowd went wild. I forgot if this was my idea or not but it was a good one.

It probably *was* my idea, actually.

"Good evening," he started. "And welcome to *The Titanic*."

Good joke, I guess, but not *great*. More importantly, *not* my line.

"We are just like that great ship. We are huge, we are expensive, and everyone wants us to go a lot faster."

Great joke. Not mine. But when a joke is great, it's great. And even if I didn't write it, I should still admit that it works, right?

"It's a wonderful night for Oscar, Oscar," he began to belt out. "Who will win?"

And then I heard the *Gilligan's Island* theme being played by the orchestra.

It was *happening*.

Holy shit, holy shit, holy shit!!!!

"Just ... sit right back and you'll hear a tale, a tale of a giant ship ..." sang Billy to the accompaniment of the orchestra.

So far so good.

This was going to *kill* ...

" *... that started many years ago with an over budget script ...*"

Huh?

" *... the boss was a loud director man who made accountants sick ...*"

What was happening here?

" *... two studios teamed up to pay for a three-hour flick ...*"

No.

No, no, no, no!

This was an *entirely different* version—*and it sucked!*

Billy sang on:

" *.. it's made a billion dollars now, I hope it springs some leaks, some other films deserve a break, like* 'My Giant' *in three weeks ...*"

What?! You're promoting your own fucking stupid movie over my amazing jokes, Billy?!

That ain't cool!
" ... *but* Titanic *is the story here, I've got to tip my hat ...*"
This was a disaster worse than the original Titanic disaster!
" ... *to Gilligan ...*"
They cut to a shot of Leonardo framed within a ship's steering wheel.
Gee, just *hilarious.*
" ... the Skipper, too ..."
A shot of James Cameron.
That's fucking it?!
" ... *the propeller guy ...*"
Some guy from the movie.
" ... *and the ice ...*"
A shot of an iceberg.
" ... the movie star ..."
A shot of Kate Winslet.
" ... the professor and Mary Ann ..."
A photo of the actual actress who *really did play* Mary Ann.
" ... *on Oscar's big night!!!!*"
And then Billy was off on another musical parody.
What in the fuck was that all about?! What just happened here?!
If someone had told me they were going to take my idea and turn it into something completely different, they could not have possibly done a better job.

It was a car crash. A train wreck. A nightmare, a travesty, a horrific tragedy. Why in the fuck would they change *anything* let alone *all* of it? I mean, *WHY?!* I was stunned. I couldn't move. I could barely hear the rest of Billy's opening performance—not that I wanted to. I thought about walking out of the theater, right then and there. But I thought against it: if I can't defend my own jokes, who the fuck will?

I asked a passersby for Bruce. She didn't know. I asked another. He knew and pointed me to an area of the backstage, sort of in a corner.

I marched right over.
"You fucking ruined it," I announced upon arriving.
"Fucking ruined what?"
"My song. My *Gilligan's* parody."
"How did we ruin it?"
"Where are all the *jokes?*"
"The jokes about retards?"
"That's one, yes. But there are also others."
Bruce smiled and walked away.

Again, I really can't say all my anger was (and still is) directed at Bruce. He's a *super* nice guy. But I will say this: that the entire broadcast would have been a hell of a lot funnier if my *original* parody of *Gilligan's Island* had been included and not merely shunted aside. Not to mention the hundreds of other jokes I had written for the show that were never used. Just to get it out of my system, here are a few:

"Gee, I wonder how Jack's character in As Good as It Gets *woulda done on the Titanic? 'Hey, don't mind me, I'm just wiping down this life vest before I awkwardly put it on."*

Welcome to the Oscars, or as it's known tonight, Scream.*"*

"Everyone wants an Oscar, but they're harder to get than a seat on a Titanic lifeboat."

"This truly was a year like no other. A year when a great, mighty vessel of hope and progress was tragically damaged by hubris, leading to an unavoidable disaster we will never forget. But Bill Clinton couldn't be here tonight..."

"But you know who is here? Newcomer Matt Damon. He's nominated for best actor alongside Nicholson, Fonda, Hoffman, and Duvall. I'm not saying Matt's competition is old, but he must feel like he's starring in the Jurassic Park *sequel."*

"By the way, tonight will be the second time Peter Fonda tries to survive The Titanic.*"*

"A lot of great comedies this year. In & Out *was a tremendous hit. Incidentally,* In & Out *was also the working title of the movie on the Lewinsky scandal."*

"Did you see The Full Monty? *Hilarious. It's about a well-meaning dad who takes a job that lets him expose himself to women— or as the President calls it, Tuesdays in the Oval Office."*

"You saw Face/Off, *right? Bill Clinton is currently starring in* Pants/Off.*"*

"Actually, a lot of recent movies from this year sound like they could have starred our president, including Liar, Liar, Mortal Kombat, and Fire Down Below.*"*

I can only think that if these, and all the other, jokes I had written were actually used, this particular year would now be looked at as being a classic Academy Awards ceremony.

As it stands on most lists, it comes in the middle, with a B average. Not terrible. But not *classic*.

After I was kicked out (by a very nice security guard named John Harmond whom Bruce Vilanch had summoned, I'm not sure why I still remember John's name, but he was sweet and apologetic about all of it), I made my way over to a bar not far from the auditorium. I had thought about hitting my own bar back in Malibu but just the image of walking inside with a rented tux and explaining the disaster that had occurred, was too much. I was looking for a place small and dark, with a TV bolted onto the wall, where I could drink my sorrows away, where no one knew my name.

Also, it was a long drive and I had no way to get back home. I couldn't afford a cab and the limo was long gone. I had always figured I'd catch a ride home with a celeb in *their* limo.

I found a local dive and walked in. Within minutes, I got to talking with the other lone customer, an alcoholic in his sixties or seventies. It's often hard to tell with alkies. I remember telling him that I had just come from the broadcast, where I had written a joke that Billy Crystal had earlier performed.

"Which one?" he asked.

"The *Gilligan's Island* song parody," I answered. "But they *fucked* it up."

He didn't remember it. I chalked it up to his dementia from too much drinking. But he *did* raise a glass in my honor. Or in someone's honor. Or someone else's glass.

The glass ended up slipping from his hands onto the ground and smashing. He then raised an imaginary glass.

I raised my glass back. It was a nice move on his part and I wanted to show him that I could be just as graceful, even under terrible conditions.

I suppose he, too, had been through some frustrations in life but I didn't think to even ask. Truthfully, I wasn't in the mood to hear any of it. I was too down on myself. Could I ever rise again to great comedic heights?

I could almost hear the live applause from the auditorium a mile or so away.

And it was mocking me.

I asked the bartender to turn down the volume on the TV. I couldn't bear watching even *one more minute* of my jokes being butchered.

By the time I finished my sixth drink (plus or minus a dozen), I had an idea.

And by the time I finished my fifteenth drink (give or take a lot)—and the 1998 Academy Awards were finally and mercifully over—I was well on my way to a new adventure—at least in my own mind.

Little did I know just how much it would end up changing my life forever—and in ways I could never have predicted ....

★ Chapter Eight ★

THE *WAYANS BROS.* INCIDENT

The *Academy Awards* event had been a disaster.

There's no use in denying that fact.

It's like a hitter his first time at bat in the major leagues. He bangs a hanging curve to deep left, *back, back, back*—and the fucking outfielder makes an amazing grab at the last second to prevent the goddamn home run.

Fuck!

I had come so far to only be blocked on the first-yard line.

So *goddamn* close!

Why was I stopped?

Why is *anyone* ever stopped who shows tremendous promise?

There's an ancient Japanese saying that goes something like: *Do not be the hammer that sticks out ... for you will only be nailed down.*

The same holds true for Hollywood.

The pure products of America are constantly being nailed down and I include myself in that category.

I'm not going to lie and tell you that murder never entered my mind. It did! Fixing the situation with a meat cleaver or a gun. It was an irresistible idea.

But Jesus!

I wasn't a fucking murderer!

What was I even thinking?!

I had been majorly fucked over by morons, but I was no killer of human beings!

I *did* want payback, though.

But I wasn't going to let this situation ruin my life!

Besides, I've never been a complainer.

I was always much more of a *fighter*.

I can tell you this:

I did *not* come from where I had come from (and gone through what I had gone through) to now fold at the slightest hint of any obstruction.

So murder was out of the question.

But I had to think of *another* way to get back at these fuckers.

I eventually (after a lot of walking on the beach) came up with the following plan:

I would take out numerous full-page ads in all the "trades" (as they're called in the biz) to complain about my treatment at the hands of the Academy and from all of the show's producers.

It was never my intention to go after Bruce or Billy in particular, or anyone else for that matter. My goal, more than anything, was to call attention to myself and to show the entire world that the Hollywood system as it currently stood was not the best system to produce the best jokes.

In a more selfish way, I suppose I was also hoping that advertisements like this would bring me some well-earned attention and future job opportunities.

I was *not* going to lay down and expose my belly like a *weak-ass dog*.

The first were in *Variety* and *Billboard*. This is how the ad read:

For Your Consideration!

A hearty thank you to Bruce Vilanch and to the Academy and Billy Crystal for the opportunity to write jokes for this year's broadcast!

As with every Oscars podcast, there are a lot of jokes written. Some are used. If I may be so bold, I would like to tell you a few that weren't chosen this year that I had a hand in writing. These jokes are below. Laughter is the best medicine, as they say. I hope these jokes will take you away from all of your troubles.

I then included a list of jokes, some of which you read earlier, and signed it:

Skippy Battison
Comedy Writer
SkipEBattison2@aol.com

Yes, I had an AOL address back then. Within hours of the missive being published, my In Box was already filled with congratulatory emails, or at least emails from people I never would have heard from otherwise.

In retrospect, I should have included my phone number, as that's how most business in Hollywood is conducted —or was back then. Now it's probably on Zoom or some other ridiculous program invented by a 24-year-old Harvard virgin.

God, how I hate people who've graduated from Harvard and the rest of those bullshit Ivey league schools!

I have to say that Harvard, in particular, *really* bothers me—or should

I say *Harv-nerd*?

I guess it comes down to petty jealousy. But more than that, it bugs me that if you have good enough grades to get into Harvard, you're basically then *set* in the comedy world.

Harvard has a humor magazine called *The Harvard Lampoon*, and it seems that *everyone* in TV and film from the past forty years has come from it. It's almost like a fraternity. You don't even have to have any damn talent! It's simple: if you come from the *Lampoon*, you're in.

That's always bugged me!

I didn't have that luxury.

I had to make it on my own damn terms.

I'm better off for it.

But, then again, it hasn't always been a fun ride.

Or an easy one, for that matter.

An express lane would have been *a lot* easier.

For me, the greatest comedy comes not from those who are terrific at school. It comes from the idiots *skipping* school.

Since when should comedy derive from the goody-goodies? It should always come from the bad asses, the rock and roll types. Not the nerds. Who wants to hear from the nerds about their love for sci-fi or fantasy or any of that shit? I want to hear about whores and hookers and muggings and *real-life* scenarios.

Comedy is not meant to be coddled like a precious baby. I've always pictured comedy as being more of a punching bag than a newborn. It needs to be taught a fucking lesson.

So I received a ton of emails from all sorts of people about these ads.

Some wanted things from me. Typical Hollywood! Those I had no time for.

What I was looking for was something from *others*: in particular, a job writing for a TV show and making a ton of money and then being able to write some comedic films.

Soon enough, I received an email from a producer for a sitcom called *The Wayans Bros*.

Now, I have to be honest: I had never even heard of *The Wayans Bros*. But it wasn't particularly aimed at my demographic: meaning a young white guy. I have no problem with black shows. In fact, I love *Martin*. I'm less a fan of other black shows that play up their blackness but I'm just being honest. I have nothing against "black comedy."

At the same time, it can be a little too "in your face." A bit too aggressive going after whitey and such.

I've gotten in some trouble on my satellite radio show talking about this. The topic was "what's the difference between white and black comedy?" We went round and round until one of my listeners called and said, "The difference is volume."

I thought that was interesting. There's no need to shout out jokes. A joke can be just as effective if it's said in a reasonable manner. I agreed with the caller and I was soon barraged with more callers disagreeing with *me*.

That's fine. I'm okay with disagreement. I think it's healthy for a discussion. But the problem arose a few days later when a Reddit thread was created to "put me in my place." From there, the local news in L.A. picked up the story, and then it went national — and, for all I know, international.

So let me try to explain where I was coming from without everyone fucking screaming at me from all directions at once ...

Richard Pryor was a genius but he never screamed. He didn't need to. He was telling the truth — *his* version of the truth, which is the only truth that matters — and doing it in a very funny way. In comparison, a lot of black comedians will amp up their material to such a degree that it becomes volume over personality.

But that's too specific. It's not just black comedians. It's also white comedians. So it's not a racial thing. It's just that whenever someone chooses to scream, except if it's me, it turns me off.

I feel as if I'm back in high school. It's like I need to be taught a lesson I don't really want to learn. It's aggressive. And it offends me.

Let me take this deeper:

Comedy is at its best when it's a stew that's not over seasoned.

Too much spice? No good.

Not enough spice? Also no good.

The seasoning has to be *just* right.

When it burns your tongue, it's *sad*.

130

When it's limp, it's *lame*.

When it's just right ... it's *rad*.

You want to ...fly, brother, fly off into that deep rad sky, way up high!

I've been asked numerous times to appear on the podcast *Comedy Bang! Bang!* to explain this but I've always said no.

I need a lot of time to explain my theories of comedy and I take these theories seriously. If someone starts joking midway through my explanation, then I want no part of any of it.

Which is another reason I chose to write this book.

Just shut the fuck up and listen to what I have to say.

End of story.

But beyond that, the hosts of that particular podcast (Scott Aukerman and Paul F Tompkins) have talked about me in the past and not always in a flattering way.

That's fine.

I understand that.

We're competitors in the same business. It's not unlike Montgomery Donuts competing with Dunkin' Donuts. (Montgomery Donuts was a chain of donut shops back in Maryland when I was growing up.) They were direct competitors but they worked in the same business. And they *hated* each other!

Or at least pretended to.

This is why I have not appeared on a lot of podcasts, such as Marc Maron's or any of the others. What's to talk about, exactly? I can do it all on my own podcast and satellite radio show, and now in this book.

All without anyone interrupting me.

Anyway, where was I? Before I interrupted myself—

Oh yes ... my relationship to black comedy. Which is to say that when a producer from the black sitcom *The Wayans Bros* got in touch with me by email and told me that she had read my *For Your Consideration* advertisements and that she wanted to meet with me to discuss a potential role as a writer on the show, my ears pricked up—as well as my prick.

Her voice was *that* hot.

We set up a date to meet at the show's office the following day. I immediately went out to look for a fun outfit to wear.

Hell, wearing a funny shirt got me the gig for the Oscars, why wouldn't it work this time?

Assuming this woman was black, I headed out to a T-shirt shop in Long Beach and I chose what I assumed would be the most appropriate outfit to land me this coveted gig.

The next morning, I arrived to the interview in Century City exactly five minutes early and was led into a meeting room where a group of writers and producers (and the woman I talked with) were already sitting around a large round table. The first thing I noticed was that there were very few white people in attendance.

That was cool. I've always had a solid relationship with people who are different colors and ethnicities than I am.

One of my best friends in junior high school was a kid named Wesley Jamison and he was black. Great guy. We'd trade baseball cards and comic books.

I'd make him pay more than they were worth but I did that to *everyone*, regardless of race.

Another great friend who was black was a kid named Ted Johnson. I knew him in fifth grade. We'd play soccer during recess and we both loved dirty puns. He later died. I forget how.

So I was no newbie when it came to dealing with black people.

Before I sat down, I took off my sports jacket and displayed my new T-shirt:

**I Will Wear Black
Until They Make
a Darker Color**

I took a seat and smiled to everyone sitting around me.

I noticed that the Wayans themselves were not there, which was fine. I just assumed I'd meet them later anyway.

"Great shirt," said a woman, whose name I'm forgetting. It could have been the woman who set up the meeting.

"Thank you," I replied. "I thought it might break the ice. The *black* ice."

"Very good," she replied.

It was clear these people were all business, and that was fine.

Sometimes the funniest, most clever people in the business are the most serious. I understood this fact even then.

"So, you're looking for a new writer?" I asked.

"We are," replied a woman whose name I can't mention for legal reasons. "We're staffing for next season. One of our writers is pregnant."

"Oh, that sucks," I said. "How long have you guys been on the air?"

"You haven't seen the show?" a woman asked.

"I haven't," I said. But then caught myself: "And yet I've heard it's hysterical."

132

"Well, let me give you some background," said Tom Harrode, one of the producers, as well as one of the writers. Tom was a great guy. He was also black. Again, it made no difference. "This show centers around two brothers who live together in an apartment in Harlem."

"Harlem," I repeated.

"Harlem," he said. "Yes. Harlem, New York."

"Got it," I lied.

"The two brothers own a newsstand in a fancy building," he went on. "Which used to be in Harlem. But moved downtown to a fancier building."

"Downtown," I repeated.

"And that's basically it," he said. "We saw the Oscars telecast. We thought it was funny. So we thought we'd call you in."

"What did you like in particular?" I asked.

He went to list some jokes, none of which were mine.

"Those were mine," I stated.

"And we were intrigued by your full-page ad in *Variety*," he continued. "I've been in the business a while; never seen *anything* like that before. It was funny. And *ballsy*."

"The jokes?" I asked.

"Yeah," he said. "But the *whole thing*. Clever. Very clever."

"Great," I said aloud. But inwardly: *And what was so funny about it?*

"Really sharp satire," said a writer at the table. I'm forgetting her name. She was black.

"It reminds me of a piece I did for the *Lampoon*," said another writer, also black. "Playing the role of aggrieved writer even though the jokes were not as good as they should have been. Very *clever*."

I didn't know what the fuck they were talking about.

But I wasn't going to argue. I mean, if they liked *any* of it, that was good enough for me.

"Gutsy," said another. This person was white. His name was Theodore McLellan and he worked as a writer's assistant. He later went on to write for *Malcolm in the Middle* and *Even Stevens*. Good man. I wish him well, wherever he is.

"And you're a member of WGA, of course," stated Tom. It wasn't a question so much as a statement. *How could I not be?*

"Are you repped?" asked someone else.

"Yup," I responded.

It was a total lie.

"By whom?" someone asked.

"CAA," I answered.

I knew nothing from CAA.

"And who's your agent?"

"CAA is in flux right now," I said. "My agent just left for UTA."

Was I a quick liar or what?!

"So you're with UTA and not CAA?" asked someone black.

"No," I answered, straight-faced. "My agent left CAA to work or UTA. But I'm still with CAA. I just don't yet know who the replacement at CAA will be."

They nodded. And the room grew quiet.

In a typical situation I love to fill silences with jokes or funny sayings or even burps and farts, if the need calls for such maneuvers.

But I wasn't taking a chance here. I had been in Hollywood long enough to know that sometimes silence is better than random noise and burps. Sometimes you just gotta know your audience. And, from what I was sensing, I needed to keep my honky ass silent—for now, at least.

"Are you staffed for the fall?" asked one.

"No," I said. "Everything really is in flux."

That seemed to do the trick. They had tested me.

I wasn't sure yet if I had passed. Blacks can sometimes be hard to read.

But I knew I hadn't *totally* bombed, which was good ...

I said, "Cool beans!"

I shook hands all around and was led to the front entrance and I had my parking ticket stamped and I headed back to Malibu.

That night I hit my favorite bar.

And got lucky.

And I'm not talking about getting laid either.

I met a white writer at the bar. Turns out, this guy was a writer for a few black shows in the past, including *What's Happening?,* and he gave me the lowdown of what to say and not to say if I ever did end up getting the job.

We spoke for a few hours and his advice was pretty damn solid.

He told me to keep my anger in check at any perceived slights.

He told me never to grab a plate of food that a black was eating.

He told me to always laugh at their jokes whether they were funny or not.

"You're going to be asked if you've ever dated or fucked a black chick," he said. "Always say no."

"What else?" I asked.

"Never get into a pissing contest. You *will* lose." He then laughed. It occurred to me that he was talking about the size of a stereotypical black man's penis.

It wasn't a good joke and I could see why this guy hadn't been staffed on a show in years. He was funny enough, I guess, but he didn't have *the spark.*

Have I explained what *the spark* is yet?

I've thought long and hard about *the spark*.

The spark is something you just *have* and that can't be taught.

The spark is that gleam in a person's smile.

The spark is the final lick on your cock after a dig ol' BJ.

The spark is a touch of gravy on your mound of curly french fries.

The spark is that little *something* extra that pushes you beyond the average and into the zone of the *above average* and, if you're really lucky, into the "cookie zone."

Have you I told you yet about the "cookie zone"?

The *cookie zone* is that secret hiding spot in your room where you keep your porno mags.

The *cookie zone* is smack dab in the fucking middle of a Hostess Cup Cake.

The *cookie zone* is a comedy routine that you go back and listen to over and over again, that you can never get enough of, the one you wrote to only please yourself.

You either have *the spark* or you don't.

You can either take people into *the cookie zone* with *this spark*, or you can't.

In 2017, I put out a DVD-ROM that had me talking about these and other comedic subjects.

If you can still find it, it's worth watching. I've seen it going for hundreds on eBay and I've seen it going for 25 cents in a flea market. It's called *Sparking That Cookie Zone* and it runs about 90 minutes. It's well worth watching and I won't get into it all of it here and now. It's complicated and hard to explain to those outside the business of comedy. But in layman's terms, only those with the spark will rise above anyone else. And only if you have the spark, will you be able to reside within the *cookie zone*, a place you very much want to take your audiences and fans.

When I went in for that *Wayans Bros* interview I was very young and I was very green. But I *knew* I had the spark and I knew I could take my craft easily into the *cookie zone*, even though I didn't have a name for all of this at the time.

The confidence must have been contagious. A few days later, I returned to my Malibu house to find a phone message waiting for me:

I had gotten the gig!

It started in a few weeks!

I was ecstatic. My first sitcom! But then it hit me: I had to find an agent! And fast! *Oh shit!*

And not only any agent, but an agent who worked at the very agency where I claimed I already had an agent!

More than that, I had to learn about black life and what they laugh at. But first: *an agent*.

I decided the best coarse of action would be to just show up at CAA and tell the receptionist that I was a working writer, I have a sitcom gig on a major network, and that I needed an agent please, thank you very much.

But the first thing I did was head out to buy a funny T-shirt. I found this gem at a Venice Beach store called She-Nag-Agains:

I'm a Writer!
To Save You Time
Let's Just Assume
I'm *Never* Wrong!

The T-shirt was incredibly funny but also a bit self-deprecating which I thought might work to my advantage. I bought a nice sports jacket to go over the new shirt, I ironed my jeans (yes, we did such things back in the 90s, teens!) and I drove over to the CAA office in Beverly Hills.

You walk in. You don't look back. You keep moving forward. The world will open for you …

"I'm here to see my agent," I said, as I walked right into the office.

"Who's your agent?" the secretary asked.

"Here to see my *future* agent," I said. "I just got a gig on a show called *The Wayans Bros* I have the job already. I just need an agent."

"So you *don't* have an agent?" she asked.

"I will in about ten minutes," I replied.

"But, as of now, you are not agented by anyone at CAA?"

"Nopers."

She told me to hang on.

She called a superior and told him or her the situation. She said "yup" a few times.

She hung up and looked over to me.

"Okay, you can go up to three now."

"Floor three?" I asked.

"Where else?" she said.

"Could be *room* three, right?"

"Could be. But you need to go to the third floor."

"And ask for who?"

"Mrs. Fitzgerald."

"She's an agent?"

"No. But she can point you in the right direction to one."

"Thank you for the help," I said, lingering. She was gorgeous. Hazel eyes, brown hair, an amazing set of pins, obviously someone who wanted to eventually get into modeling or acting.

I dropped my new business card in front of her. It read:

Skippy Battison
Comedy Writer
The Wayans Bros. **Sitcom**

"Heavy stock," she said, picking it up.

"The *heaviest*," I replied.

She smiled. I *had* her. "My number's on the back," I said. "And my AOL."

"Fantastic," she declared.

I returned her smile and made my way over to the elevators, which were just about the fanciest elevators I had ever seen in my entire life: gold paneling, mirrors all over, including on the elevator's ceiling, and beautifully lit buttons for all the floors.

Yes, this place would work out *very well*, indeed!

I reached the third floor and exited the elevator. There was a woman waiting for me. Instantly, I knew that I wouldn't like her immediately. She reminded me of every *woman* who would tell me "no" back in high school:

"No! You can't take off your clothes in the cafeteria!"

"No! You can't play strip poker in the library!"

"No! You can't fill out your SATs with a nude floaty pen!"

That type of asshole.

"Hi!" she chirped, all fake smiles. "I'm Ellen Fitzgerald. And I'm one of the agency's office managers."

"Hello!" I replied, sussing out what her deal was exactly.

"So, how can I assist you?"

"Can we talk inside the office, not next to the elevator bank?" I asked, quite reasonably.

"This will do for now," she said, still smiling.

You know what would do for now? I thought. *Me pitching a double fucking dookie right on your fat fucking face.*

"I understand you're looking for an agent?" she asked.

"I am, yes," I said. "I have a new gig writing for *Wayans Bros* starting in a few weeks."

"And you're looking for someone to rep you?"

I glared at her. Yes. *Why the fuck else would I be here now talking to you?*

"I'll tell you what: why don't you go ahead and leave your CV and I'll pass it around to those agents who might be the best fit?"

"What's a CV?" I asked.

"A resume. A list of where and whom you've written for."

"Don't have that," I said. "But I do have a business card. It has my AOL email on it."

"That would be perfect," she said. "I'll take that, *thank* you."

"Heavy stock," I said.

"Quite," she replied. "Have a wonderful day."

She turned on her cheap heels and walked over to the security pad, buzzed herself inside, and Mrs. Fitzgerald was gone for good.

Well, that was odd.

Are all successful writers treated like this? I thought.

I took the elevator back down to the main lobby. The secretary was smiling. Perhaps she thought I had already gotten an agent and was headed back out into the world, happy and content.

I wasn't going to tell her otherwise.

"Email me," I said, exiting. She nodded. I nodded. It was like a complicated dance.

I never did hear from her.

Back on the street, I replayed the meeting in my mind. Some things had gone well, others hadn't. What could I learn from what *hadn't* gone well? Should I have worn a different outfit? Should I have called ahead first?

Should I have reached out to a CAA writer who was already repped so that introductions could have been formally made?

It hurts me to even have to write this now because I'm so much more a veteran of the Hollywood "game." But I was a newbie then and I just didn't know. If I had to do it over, I would have emailed an agent first, sent them a script and some jokes and then waited until they called to meet with me. But that's 43-year-old Skippy talking, not 21-year-old Skippy. Sometimes I just want to hit that younger version of myself. Other times I want to hug him. But I can't do either. One can't reach across time to hug oneself. Or give oneself a hand job. At least not yet.

But I was young and naïve. And instead of marching right back into that office, I headed back home to Malibu and started researching black comedy.

What makes blacks laugh?

Does anything *not* make blacks laugh?

I had some work to do. I drove straight over to the Blockbuster in which I already belonged and rented a menagerie of black-themed comedies, including some movies by the Wayans brothers themselves.

It took a while—I wasn't at all familiar with this genre. When I was done, though, I had a big stack of black movies.

I honestly didn't know there were so many black comedies! This was what I rented:

White Men Can't Jump
I'm Gonna Git You Sucka
The complete episodes of *In Living Color*
Mo' Money
Blankman
Major Payne
Don't Be a Menace to South Central While Drinking Your Juice in the Hood
House Party

The first movie I slapped into the ol' VHS and watched was one called *Amistad*.

From the cover, it looked as if it might be funny, sort of like *Cabin Boy*, a great comedy starring Chris Elliott.

It wasn't.

Just the opposite.

This film probably couldn't be in any way labeled "a comedy." After fifty or so minutes, I stopped the tape.

Next up:

House Party.

Would it be good? Would it be *Heavyweights* good?

No.

I *hated* it.

In many ways, it was funny and I related to the characters even though they weren't my race. But it was just too noisy.

I slapped in another tape.

Blankman.

Didn't love it.

Didn't even *like* it.

What was *happening* here?

Was it me? Or *them*?

Confused, I placed a call to the Flammer back in Ocean City. The poor dickhead was *still* busting his tiny white ass as a house painter. He was happy to hear from me. He was complaining about lower back pain and an ankle he might have broken, or maybe only twisted. What made it worse, he said, was that he was working up on a tall building's roof without proper equipment or safety harnesses or *blah blah fucking blah*.

I was practically falling asleep listening to all of it ...

His mother was now in the hospital and there were a ton of other problems but I had too many more important matters on my mind. I felt, in some ways, that this dude owed me: I was *still* letting him stay at my father's apartment for cheap, except when I needed more dough.

I got right down to it:

What do you love about black movies? What is it about their comedy that appeals to you? What am I missing, exactly?

Out of all my friends, the Flammer had the most black friends and acquaintances—by far. He was never bothered or even thought about race or religion or anything else. I always admired him for that. Must not have been easy. Never a bad word to say about anyone or anything. That's what I'd find the most difficult. I can't keep my fucking mouth shut for two minutes if anybody annoys me, no matter their race, religion or ethnicity, except Christianity, which doesn't seem to bother me for some reason.

I guess you could say that, in that particular way, I'm very fair.

And I guess you could also say that it's gotten me into some PC heat over the last few years. (More on this later. I promise.)

Flammer gave me the low-down on why he found black movies funny.

Turns out he didn't know why specifically. He just did.

This was an important lesson for me.

Up to that point, I only thought *my* type of comedy was funny.

Everything else could suck my nutters.

I *still* believe this.

And yet I've also come to respect anyone who has a difference of "humor opinion" with me.

It's just too tiring to fight. If someone likes a certain movie or TV show that I don't like, god bless them. Let's just agree to disagree, okay? We can still be friends. Even though your favorite movies and TV shows suck shit.

I asked Flammer if he needed any money—he said he could *always* use more money.

I asked him if he could impersonate an agent from CAA. He didn't know what this meant but he did say that he could try, which was all I was really looking for.

Now *that's* a good friend!

If anyone at *The Wayans Bros* did ever want to call my agent for any reason, I now had one who worked for CAA—and who also worked as a house painter back in Ocean City, Maryland.

Let's just say he moonlighted.

I've admitted to all this before and I'm always surprised when anyone expresses shock that I lied in order to get a job.

I can only ask this question in return:

Have you never lied to get a job?

Never fudged on your CV?

Never asked a friend to act as a fake reference or representative?

Never hired a friend to take the SAT for you?

Never hired a poor dude to take your driver's test?

If you haven't, I might suggest that your career might be a lot further along if you had cheated, oh, just a *smidge*.

I learned this from my dad, a man who had been around the D.C. block for a number of years.

All men take basically the same path. But only a few take advantage of the *shortcuts* that are available to them.

The question is, Why? Why wouldn't you take a shortcut, even if it may not be deemed "appropriate" or "legal"?

And what *is* legal anyway?

Your illegal is no doubt different from *my* illegal.

I'll use a specific example.

When I was in high school, I would often take to work two main thoroughfares: Seven Locks Road and River Road. The problem was that both were very crowded and backed up, especially during rush hour. *What to do?*

Well, there was *one* alternate route available that would make my commute a whole lot faster—but it was a street that was closed every weekday from 7:00 A.M. to 10:00 A.M. and from 4:00 P.M. to 7:00 P.M. You know, the rush hours.

By taking this one particular route, though, you could save not only time but also an obnoxious reprimand from the boss who worked at the retail store in Montgomery Mall where you were making $8.25 an hour. I won't mention the store's name but it was Spencer's Gifts.

This particular boss was not too keen on me coming in even *one minute* late.

So, again, *What to do?*

So, while it was true that you couldn't take this particular road during certain hours, it was also true that you *could* take this route if you lived on neighboring streets. Cops would park themselves at both ends and pull over anyone who wasn't leaving or arriving home.

One more time, *What to do?*

How about paying someone you work with at Spencer's Gifts $100 to alter your license with an address that lists this particular street as your home address?

Was anyone hurt by me doing this? Did anyone die? Or was I just able to now get to work on time at a job that barely paid $8 an hour?

I think we know the answer to that one.

(By the way, I *still* have this driver's license and, for good luck, I keep it in my wallet. Who knows? Maybe it'll come in handy again. I couldn't even guess how ... but you never know. That'd be *kick* ass.)

What I'm saying is this: you just have to do what you have to do to not only survive—but *thrive*.

I've never been upset at anyone who wanted to excel.

So they cut corners. *Gives a shit?*

And as the date got closer and closer to my official start as a sitcom writer, I found myself watching not only black comedies but also black histories and black documentaries.

Truthfully, these documentaries also weren't my cup of tea.

But it did give me enough background for what I thought would be solid enough footing for when I started.

The Flammer called me one evening. Seems that the producer from *Wayans Bros* called him and the Flammer did his best to play act as a Hollywood writing agent. What's funny is that because the Flammer didn't know what the hell he was talking about, he didn't say much of anything. Which flummoxed the producer, who ended up giving me *more* money than I would have made otherwise.

Thanks, Flammer! Now get back to fetching my lunch, asshole!

So that was good. The contract was sent to me, I signed my name, I forged the Flammer's and that was that.

The day quickly arrived. And I have to admit that when I walked into that writers' room the first time, it was a *very* exciting feeling.

I had heard before about writers' rooms from friends.

But I had never actually *been* in one. The room itself was pretty awful, with low ceilings and bad lighting and only one window overlooking a sad parking lot, but there was definitely an *energy* in that room that I had never before felt.

I should also say that you are about to read some SPOILERS!

SPOILER ALERT!!!

SPOILER ALERT!!!

UH OH!!!!

If you haven't seen *The Wayans Bros* show and you don't want to learn how certain stories end or begin, skip ahead to the next chapter.

I'll also say that I'm officially giving you a TRIGGER WARNING! Some of the things you're about to read could very well trigger an attack of whatever happens to offend you for whatever reasons you become easily offended.

With that out of the way:

I show up for my first day at *The Wayans Bros* and everyone is quite friendly, if a bit standoffish, which doesn't surprise me: I was, after all, the "new guy."

Everything later turned to shit, I know that, but when the experience began, it was really nice. It took about a week to get into the swing of things, but I was soon joining meetings and contributing jokes and story ideas. I sensed *no* difficulty on the horizon.

True, my jokes never seemed to "land."

But still, not a bad place to work.

Now, keep in mind, this was the *fifth* season of a popular show that had already been broadcast for four seasons. The staff all knew each other really well and there hadn't been much turnover of writers through the years. So I was entering cold what was already a writing room that was brimming with friendship.

The staff was a very tight bunch and they could riff off each other very well. I did notice that whenever I said something, a few of them would look at the others almost as if they were waiting for or expecting some sort of reaction. They had smiles on their faces and I could see that they were enjoying the jokes and my comments, but there was technically never any laughter, or what someone might perceive to be "laughter."

When I arrived, the writing staff was already working on the very first episode for the upcoming season. It was called "Brother Can You Spare A Dime?" And it dealt with Shawn having to ask his brother Marlon for a loan of some money for some reason or another. I'm forgetting why exactly. This wasn't my script. My job was only to "punch it up" with better jokes.

Think of a sitcom script as a house. The house has to be built from the ground up *before* any furniture or wallpaper is applied. Think of the plot as the structure itself and the interior decoration as the sprinkling of jokes that every sitcom must contain by the bucketful. For me, the most fun of comedy writing is coming up with jokes. That's why I got into this crazy business to begin with. That's why I'm here, doing *my thing*. I guess you could say that I'm no different than an interior decorator, except that I make a shit-ton more money and I'm not gay.

It was the oddest feeling working for this show. I felt as if I was in a dream. Everyone was nice enough, the writers were talented, the Wayans brothers themselves could not have been nicer and more respectful, but if anything, there was a *disconnect*.

At least at the writing table.

Outside the writers' room, it was the opposite.

They never stopped laughing at what I said.

And I wasn't even *trying* to be funny!

It was almost *too* easy.

I'll give you one example:

It was lunchtime one day and I was in the kitchen brewing up a cup of coffee, talking with Nick, a black writer.

In walked a black woman (I'm forgetting her name). Just to make conversation, I motioned towards my coffee mug and I declared, "I'm up to fifteen cups a day. One more and I'll become that jittery dancing guy in the 'Thriller' video."

It's a fantastic joke but there was no laughter.

I then complimented her on her outfit:

"You look beautiful today," I said. "Really gorgeous." (It was true. She looked fantastic. She also smelled fantastic but I refrained from saying *anything* about that.)

"Thank you," she said, barely responding.

"No, I mean it," I said.

"I heard you," she said.

"It's bangin'," I replied.

"Bangin'?"

"It's tight! Slip it, *slap* it!"

She laughed really hard.

Finally!

That was it for that particular conversation but it stuck with me.

A few days later I was walking out to my car in the shitty parking lot.

I ran into Nick again.

I was *always* running into this guy.

"Where ya headed?" he asked.

"Gonna smoke a fat one and play some Nin Six," I replied.

"Nin Six?"

"Nintendo 64."

Nick burst out laughing.

"So you're going to get stoned and play video games?"

"Bowl and bang."

"Bowl and bang?"

"Smoke a bowl and bang a lovely lass."

Nick laughed even harder.

"And then what?" he asked.

"The five s's," I replied. "Smoking, shaving, showering, sleeping."

I waited for a response but none came.

So I then stated, "You're supposed to say 'that's only *four* s's.'"

"Okay. That's only four. So what's the fifth?" he asked.

"S if I know," I said.

Nick laughed really, really hard. A little *too* hard.

What is it with these people? I thought.

A week or so later we were handed the script that Nick had written for an upcoming episode. We were supposed to take it home and read it.

We'd all go over it together the next day in the writers' room.

What we liked.

What we *didn't* like.

And so on.

After we'd do that, we'd then hold a table read with the actors. And then a live shoot before an audience (but not taped) and then the *actual* taping of the show. This was a process the show had used for the previous four seasons and it seemed to have worked out really well. The plots were tight, the jokes were solid, the episodes were as good as they could be.

I took the script home. I read it. I arrived the next morning upset.

I mean, *really* fucking upset. I was seething. If this hadn't been a new job—or even if it *had* been a new job and I didn't want to keep it so badly—I would have come in screaming and yelling. But I said nothing. Not a thing. Which isn't easy.

At first.

There were some initial comments about the script:

"Loved it! "So funny!" "Yeah, great!"

I still said nothing.

The writer, Nick, began to read the script out loud and we were then supposed to shout out jokes.

Here is one of the jokes that Nick had written:

SHAWN: "What you up to tonight, White Mike?"

WHITE MIKE: "Smoke a fat one and play some Nin Six."

SHAWN: "Nin Six?"

WHITE MIKE: "Nintendo 64."

The entire room burst out laughing.

Sound familiar?

Here's another:

SHAWN: "You a big coffee drinker, White Mike?"

WHITE MIKE: "I guess you could say that."

SHAWN: "Why?"

WHITE MIKE: "I'm up to fifteen cups a day. One more and I'll become that jittery dancing guy in the 'Thriller video."

SHAWN (laughing): "That would be the 'Beat It' video, White Mike!"

WHITE MIKE: "Oh well. Tight! Slip it, *slap* it!"

That one also sound familiar? Or familiar *enough*?

Who the fuck was "White Mike"? Granted, I had never seen the show, or knew much about *any* of the characters, but it didn't take long to figure out what this particular character was all about.

After the reading, and still furious, I approached Nick.

"Wow, really a hell of a script you got there, Nick."

"Thanks, man."

"I really like the character of White Mike."

"Yeah, he's a trip."

"A trip to hell."

"Whatya mean?"

"I mean you stole the jokes I told the other day and used them for White Mike."

He looked at me as if I had lost my mind.

"Yeah," he said. "I did. So what? Everyone loved it."

"Those were *my* jokes. I know we're all working on the same show but how about some credit?"

"You do *have* a credit. You're on the writing staff. And those weren't your jokes. They were *my* jokes. You didn't say them to be funny. I wrote them to be funny. There's a damn difference."

He walked away. I continued to seethe.

What kind of show was this? Weren't we *all* supposed to be a team?

To work *together* to create a sitcom that made people happy?

The next day in the bathroom I ran into Shawn Wayans. I had been introduced to him at least once before and I'm absolutely certain that he knew my proper name. But when he saw me, he said, "'Sup, White Mike?'"

Now I was *livid*.

He was smiling and he walked out without saying another word.

I marched over to the kitchen area and confronted a woman writer, I'm forgetting her name. She was black.

"What can you tell me about White Mike?" I asked.

"What do you mean? You don't know who White Mike is?" she asked.

"He's a character on the show. Been on since the beginning."

"I think I do," I responded. "But I want to hear it from you."

"He's an idiot," she said. "Who tries to act black. But he's white."

"That's what I thought," I answered and walked away.

The next episode was called "Six Degrees of Marlon," and it had to do with Shawn arranging for Marlon to have a kissing scene in a show he was putting together for TV called "Everybody Loves Everybody."

But here was the twist: Marlon had to kiss a man.

Very clever premise and I was excited to sink my teeth into it.

The only problem was that no one was listening to what I had to say around that writers' table. I had a *ton* of great jokes for *all* the characters but they only cared what I had to say about White Mike.

And that would hold true for *every* episode I worked on that season, which was four.

Literally, the *only* jokes of mine that made the cut were for White Mike.

And I wasn't pitching them around the writers' table.

I just said them in the kitchen. Or parking lot. Or wherever. And they were never *meant* as jokes!

Here are some White Mike lines I supposedly helped with:

"You oughta slack back, Jack!"

"Bring it back and put a saddle on it."

"Ain't no thang-a-rooski."

"That's so whack!"

"Awesome sauce."

"Sincere props, yo."

"I just said that to break the ice. The black ice."

It was a miserable experience and I felt totally used.

This is why I was fucking hired?!

I mean, it didn't take a fucking Einstein to figure out that the show had only hired me to come up with ideas and jokes for the White Mike character.

One afternoon, I walked into Tim Harrode's office (he was the producer I had met with at the first job interview) and I just flat-out asked if he knew why I was hired. He expressed ignorance but I could tell that he was lying. I walked out.

I thought long and hard on what to do. I thought about calling my agent but he was, in reality, Flammer the house painter back in Ocean City, Maryland.

Little help he'd be.

I could stick it out. And I could accept the (very generous) paycheck.

Or I could sabotage the show altogether and then get out while the getting was easy.

But the more I thought about it, the more I wanted to be mature about the entire matter. No reason to be a jerk about it, right? I marched right back into Tim Harrode's office.

I thanked him for hiring me and for giving me this tremendous opportunity. *I was really very appreciative,* I said.

He said, *You're welcome.*

But did you think it was okay to hire me to only write for a moronic white character? Was there any reason I couldn't write for one of the, say, black characters? Was this not a bit of reverse racism? In fact, was this all not worse than the racism one might see in Hollywood that involved blacks?

He smiled. *No, he didn't feel that way.*

Really?

No.

You didn't hire me for any specific reason?

We felt you were funny. And if you were a good fit for the White Mike character, then so be it.

A good fit? You mean that you could take the things I said in life and turn them into a big joke on the show?

Why not?

Tim laughed. They were always laughing when I *wasn't* telling jokes. Yet *another* example …

No, man. Not at all. We thought you had a very funny comedic voice.

A white voice?

Tom shrugged. *A voice is a voice.*

Did you even like the jokes I wrote for the Academy Awards?

Not really, Tim said.

I'd been played, I thought. *Really fucking well played.*

I thanked him and walked out of his office and onto the street. I was more confused than angry. Is this how women felt to be hired just because they were women? Or ethnics?

To turn the situation around, let's just say that I was the producer of a very popular television sitcom and there was a black character on the show who would say some very silly things.

Would I only hire a black comedy writer to write for that character and for that character only?

It just seemed all so *unfair*.

Here's the saddest part about all of it:

If I *had* stayed on as a writer for *The Wayans Bros*, I'm confident that the show would have continued for many many *many* more seasons instead of going off the air after its fifth.

How do I know?

Well, I have the proof:

Remember that famous joke from the American version of *The Office* that they'd use over and over and over again?

"That's what she said!"?

And do you remember just how *popular* that line was?

And how often it was used on the show?

And how much it contributed to the success of *The Office*?

Well, guess who came up with *that* line first?

I was sitting in a writers' meeting at *The Wayans Bros* and we were going over a script—I forget which one, but it could have been the one where Shawn volunteers to hand out food at Thanksgiving. The dialogue went something like this (I don't have the script anymore, so this is purely from memory):

The character of Pops, played by the fantastic John Witherspoon, is sitting at a bench, eating a hot dog:

POPS: "This hot dog ain't *right*."

SHAWN: "What's wrong about it, Pops?"

POPS: "Don't taste right."

MARLON: "All hot dogs taste the same, Pops!"

POPS: "Why? Cause they all look the same?"

MARLON: "Some are bigger than others."

SHAWN: "Yeah. This one definitely don't taste *thin*."

It was a good joke but not *great* and I thought I could do better. It needed a capper of sorts. So this was my suggestion:

MARLON: "All hot dogs taste the same, Pops!"

POPS: "Why? Cause they the same size and thickness?"

SHAWN: "That's what *she* said!"

This was one of the few jokes I told inside the writers room that *did* receive a big laugh. It was never used in the final shoot but it was a *great* joke.

Dare I say, *a classic joke*.

The background to the joke is this:

When I was in high school, we had a friend named Jimmy. I spoke about him earlier in the book. He was a guy who rammed his sled into a fucking tree and was never quite the same. He was also fun as hell to drag around town and get into adventures with. One of the things we would say whenever Jimmy said practically anything at all was "That's what *she* said!"

This was an ongoing joke in our group. The origins are a bit murky. I can't lay claim to having *originally* come up with it but I was *definitely* in the same room when it was created. We'd use it constantly:

"This is way too salty!"
"That's what she said!"

"I hate the way this stinks!"
"That's what she said!"

"You asshole! You fuck! You're a misogynistic, selfish bastard!"
"That's what she said!"

So I can't remember specifically how or when we came up with this joke but we *definitely* did. I remember other guys in high school adopting it whenever they could and the phrase sort of becoming "a thing" back in the day.

This is where things get strange. I only learned about this recently: In school, there was a real dork no one liked. I don't remember his name. Not popular, not cool, not good looking, not athletic. For all I know, he read comic books on Saturday nights and watched movies no one else found funny, like Monty Python and all that Irish shit. He was basically a loser, although I never talked with him, just passed him in the hallways, as he skulked from class to class, miserable.

Lo and behold, I'm reading my high school Facebook page not long ago and I learned that this very dolt had become a "comedy writer."

And that he's won an Emmy. Or a few Emmys. And that's he's written for *The Office*.

He was interviewed by a local newspaper, *The Potomac Almanac*.

And he claimed that *he* was the one who first came up with the line "That's what she said."

Give me a fucking break!

There is *zero* way this loser would have ever known about this line back in high school if *we* hadn't invented it for him. I doubt he ever even had the opportunity to use it *once* in school, as he never talked to another living soul. From what I can gather from memory, he had a *terrible* sense of humor.

But guess what?

He attended Harvard and wrote for the *Harvard Lampoon*.

From there, it was a straight shot to writing for television in Los Angeles.

In essence, he had given himself an "express lane" to success.

Ain't that nice?

If I hadn't quit the *Wayans Bros,* that phrase would have become huge on the show. I could have copyrighted the damn thing and put it on shirts, beer koozies, kites, whatever the fuck I could have thought of putting it on, and I would have made a goddamn killing.

As it stands, there are a few people in the industry who know my background with the joke and know that it's mine, and that it was created years before *The Office* ever even existed.

But that doesn't bring in the money.

What can I say? Just another very frustrating element to my career—but one that I'm not going to cry over any time soon.

When I walked out of *The Wayans Bros* studio that day back in June 1999, I was more sad than angry.

I made my way over to a bar not far from the studio lot.

I had thought about hitting my own bar back in Malibu.

But just the thought of me walking inside and explaining why I had left a sitcom after only four episodes was just too damn depressing to even have to think about.

I stayed at this dive bar for hours, pretty much left alone, in front of a television with the sound off that played game shows over and over, with closed captioning helpfully provided. Just as I was about to leave, a man sidled up next to me. He seemed to be your average L.A. alcoholic, maybe late forties, early fifties.

At that time, he seemed ancient. We got to talking and he soon asked what I did for a living. I told him.

He asked if I still worked at the show. I told him I didn't. He asked why. I felt no reason *not* to tell him, so I did.

He said that he was a lawyer and that he might be able to help. *How so?* I asked.

Sue, he replied.

Over what? I asked.

He smiled.

Three hours later, after calling my father and asking for a loan, I had myself a lawyer.

As I write this chapter, the case is *still* wending its way through the court system. I hope it's resolved soon.

But cases involving discrimination against whites always take longer than those against blacks.

That's what my lawyer says anyway. And it's us versus a little company called "Warner Brothers."

This shit called *justice* ain't cheap, yo!

By the way, I suppose I should mention that I'm also suing that loser from high school who wrote for "The Office."

That particular case is also still wending its way through the court system. I'm asking for the amount I could have earned if he hadn't stolen the joke. I'm also suing for the millions that NBC *still* makes off the merchandise that reads "That's What She Said."

I have high hopes that it'll soon be resolved—very much in my favor.

One of the good things that came out of this entire situation is the full-page ad that I took out in *Variety*:

For Your Consideration!

A hearty thank you to _____ and _____ and the people at Warner Brothers for allowing me to become a major contributor to the hilarity of The Wayons Bros. show. I couldn't have asked for a better group of people to help bring this wonderful product to America's living rooms for four episodes!

As with every sitcom, there are going to be as many disagreements as agreements in the writers' room. That's acceptable.

What is not acceptable is the unfair use of stereotypes to bring about this humor.

Beyond that, what's completely unacceptable is to stereotype a writer with a certain type of comedic thinking: in my case, that of the ignorant white man who wants nothing more than to appear "black."

I write this letter not so much to attack as much as to ... educate.

I sincerely wish the entire staff of The Wayans Bros. the best of luck in all future endeavors. PEACE OUT YO!!!!!

Skippy Battison
Comedy Writer
SkipEBattison2@aol.com

It was short and, I thought, quite effective. The joke was on me, though.

Six or seven months later, I was watching an episode of *The Wayans Bros,* one of the last to ever broadcast.

The plot had to do with White Mike suing Shawn's character for not treating him with the sufficient amount of respect at a backyard barbecue.

Think about that: White Mike, *a white guy,* is suing Shawn, *a black guy.*

Sound familiar?

Guess where *that* came from?

Ain't that nice?!

I have to admit that it was a funny episode. I'd be lying if I said otherwise.

What can I say? People steal *all the time* in this business.

But it's not all bad. The *Variety* ad came out on a Tuesday.

The very next day, a Wednesday, I had already begun to receive a ton of emails from interested parties. A few were slightly negative:

"You weren't fired because of your race. You were probably fired cause you *sucked!*"

And so on. But ... I did receive some very interesting, *positive* emails. One was from an incredibly successful movie producer over in Israel. His name was Benjamin Globlan.

And it was this relationship that would soon come to change my life, not to mention my entire writing career.

In ways that I *never* could have predicted.

But that was yet to come.

And boy, did it ever ....

★ Chapter Nine ★

HE SHALL WHO BUT LIVE... OR SHALL HE?

It was around this time that I started to really get into the literature and philosophy of Ayn Rand.

To be honest, I knew very little about her work before.

But everything sort of came into focus at this moment in my life— I had more time to read, I had more time to think, I had more time to philosophize, I had more time do *everything*. For the first time in years, I had a moment to just relax and actually breathe.

I was out of work and was sort of going out of my mind.

I've mentioned this on my podcast and some listeners have found it ironic that I stole Ayn Rand's book from the library and never returned it. I don't find it ironic at all.

In fact, I had no intention of *ever* returning *Atlas Shrugged* or any of her other books that I borrowed and never returned.

After reading them, it was clear that this was the *only* course of action.

And if you've ever read her work, you'd agree that I *deserved* to keep them!

Why?

Because I *wanted* them. And sometimes that's just *enough*.

And because the library is run by the government. And the government should be eliminated from our society.

If you have ever read Rand's work, you're no doubt nodding your head in agreement.

If you have *not* read her work, let me try to sum it all up:
Worry about your own shit.

It doesn't matter what race or religion you are, it just matters who you are as a human being and how willing you are to pull yourself up by the ol' jockstraps.

I know a few comedy writers who got into Scientology.

And a few who blew their brains out.

And a few who became drug addicts and alcoholics.

When I was at my lowest point—without a gig, with no gigs on the horizon—I suppose I could have found myself falling into a much more dangerous and less savory vat than the one filled to the brim with the work of Ayn Rand.

But when I did finally read Rand's work, it was like hearing the Spin Doctors for the first time. I can't describe it.

It was like watching *Heavyweights* for the first time and not knowing *at all* what to expect.

It just hit the pleasure center of my brain and I wanted more, more and MORE. So within a few weeks, I had stolen and read every single one of Ayn's books from the local public library, sometimes twice. I still have these books to this day.

Ayn was from Poland or some such country. She believed in Abjectionism, which she defined as "the concept of man as a heroic being, with his own happiness as the moral purpose of his life, with productive achievement as his noblest activity, and reason as his only absolute."

I never understood that quote, so I had a friend translate it for me. (And if you have a really eagle eye, you'll have noticed that I've sprinkled some of Ayn's thoughts and quotes throughout this entire book like a jazz musician in a "boppy" song. If you can spot all of them, you win a free kick in the ass from yours truly!)

So, again:

Worry about your own shit. Take care of yourself. Put your goddamn head down and keep moving along that special path.

It hit me like a bombshell.

Fuck was I doing feeling sorry for myself those two weeks after I was fired from *The Wayans Bros*?

I did *nothing* wrong! It was the others who had fucked up for not appreciating a great writer! I didn't have to look any farther than my own damn self to know that it was on them who fucked up!

My confidence was quickly rebuilt and before long, I was back to where I had started.

Or close to it.

Man, I was *still* so young! I was *super* talented! There was *nothing* that was going to stop me!

I felt *great*.

And as soon as my mood turned from sour to positive, I was off and fucking sprinting into the next phase of my already successful writing career.

I received many emails after my *Variety* ad—maybe more than two hundred.

But the one that most caught my eye—besides the few from people who threatened to kill me or "teach me a lesson I'd never forget"—was from a producer in Israel named Benjamin Globlan.

At first, I thought that it was a goofy joke name but, no, it really was his true name and he was emailing me to congratulate me for my "chutzpah," which means *balls* in Israeli.

He was also asking if I might be willing to work on a film project that needed some "touching up."

The script had already been written.

It was about a huge, peaceful monster zapped by the Israeli military with a nuclear power beam in the desert and mistakenly turned into a creature of evil. It was written in English and it was called *He Shall Who But Live*.

That's all I learned from that first email.

We set up a call to talk on the phone, which wasn't so easy back then.

Especially when talking with someone who spoke with such a very heavy Jew accent. And lived in Israel.

"Skippy?"

"Yes."

"I am Benjamin Globlan. I am producer—"

"Okay, hold it right there," I interjected. "Let's go back to emails. I can't understand a fucking word you're saying."

He laughed very hard, thinking it a joke.

It wasn't.

After he stopped laughing, he agreed and we went back to the email.

This was his story: he had a script for a movie called *He Shall Who But Live* written by a screenwriter in Israel.

It was sci-fi and it was written in English to make it easier to sell across the world.

Benjamin sensed something in my *Variety* ad that told him I'd be the perfect writer to "punch up" this script, or to make it funnier.

So far there had just been one writer on the project. He had been paid and been told: "Thank you very much," and that was that.

It was time for a new writer to come aboard and make the script really "pop."

Benjamin would be willing to pay me $100,000 for the punch-up job. Could I start immediately?

Did the Pope just shit in a bear's mouth in the woods where no one could hear them both scream?

Yes, I could take on the job! I kissed my stolen library copy of *Atlas Shrugged*.

It's all about forging one's own destiny, baby!

And it's all about *capitalism*. If some other screenwriter wasn't up to the task, why shouldn't I then have the opportunity to step in and make success happen?

Why should it always be someone else who rapes the rewards?

I told him to send me the script (*in an actual mailbox. Remember those?*) and I started thinking about how in the world I could ever make a monster story set in an Israeli dessert *funnier*—especially when it concerned nuclear power? What in the hell did *I* know from Israel or nuclear power or desserts?

Then again, what did it matter? The dude was paying me $100,000. And in today's dollars that's a ... *whole fucking lot*.

The script finally arrived—smelling like cigarette smoke—and I read it quickly. There were a shitload of spelling and gramatical errors. There were parts that made me smile, but overall, I didn't see the purpose of a film like this one.

Was it sci-fi? Was it a comedy? Was it bad on *purpose*?

I read the script multiple times. And I even gave it to a few comedy writing friends, who also thought it was shit, but who were *super jealous* that I would be earning so much for this gig.

And a bit perplexed as to how I got it.

They all had managers and agents. I still didn't have one, not counting the Flammer acting as my fake manager back in Ocean City. (When I told the Flammer about this new job, he joked that he should receive the 10% he was due as my fake agent. I told him to fuck off and just be happy I was barely charging him to sublet my father's rent-free apartment.)

So how did I, without an agent, ever get such a plum gig?

And why were the other writers giving me shit about it?

I chalked it up to jealousy. The fact is, it definitely wasn't luck. I can assure you on that.

If I had not taken the initiative to spend the $25,000 for the ad in *Variety* like I had, I wouldn't have had the gig either.

I'd be a loser just like them. But I had bet that the $25,000 would accrue to a much higher sum, and that bet seemed to have paid off big time.

So yes, the script was garbage. That wasn't a surprise, I suppose. The question was: *How to break the news to Benjamin?* In a sense, he had to have known it needed *some* work if he reached out to me. On the other hand, if I said anything critical, I would risk fucking up the deal and then not make *any* money.

So I wasn't going to go *too* far out of my way to convince Benjamin to *not* make the movie.

I sat down before my Apple Imac 350—about as big as a fridge—and wrote the following:

Dear Benjamin:

What an honor to have read this screenplay! Thank you again for thinking of me as the go-to writer to punch up your script. Wow, there is so much to say for it! The monster character was my favorite. He was naïve but also, in the end, brave. When he left his cave that morning, there would have been no way he would have known that he'd be zapped by a nuclear weapon before the end of the day. And that his simpleness would turn into a frenzy of anger at the world around him and the state of political events. But he also had no way of knowing that by the end, he'd be zapped again and this time he'd turn <u>back</u> into his old self, but only wiser and more knowledgeable about the world around him. There was action and adventure and some humor but I can definitely see where you'd want it to be funnier and more entertaining. I have a few ideas we can talk about later but one would involve creating a girlfriend monster who could annoy him but then in the end save him from doing something stupid. Or he could save her from doing something stupid. Like marrying him in the first place! That's just a suggestion. We don't have to go with that. I can see the beauty in what's here already. But I can also see the beauty in what might exist. Does that make sense? If it doesn't, it might be a language issue. So thank you again and I hope to talk again real soon.

Yours, Skippy

The email was the perfect amount of humility and confidence. I hit SEND and waited. It wasn't more than an hour later that my IN box pinged in that early 21st century way, and there it was … a response from Benjamin! I took this to be a good sign. And I was even happier when I started reading:

Dearest Skippy

I am so happy for your email. The script needs help and I do know that. In the areas of the comedies would be the best to tackle. I am okay with plot that I think move along nice and to ultimate conclusion of showing we are all a like no matter race or religion. It is a good metaphor for the world situation. I ask that you begin to write to "punch up" script as soon as you are able. As discussed I can pay $100,000 upon completion. I look forward to see this finish product.

Yours,

Benjamin

Okay, so he wasn't the chattiest guy in the world. And he wasn't terrific with American grammer. But he was obviously rich and successful. If I had a real manager, I'd have asked him what to do. As it stood, I had no one except for Flammer. And he only knew house painting. And a few jokes about smoking dope on the boardwalk.

Fuck it, I thought. *Let's go all in.*

I got to work on the script right away, focusing on the areas that needed to be improved. I was going to take the tack that it wasn't poorly written on purpose—that the author wasn't *trying* to be bad.

And that all it needed was for someone, an expert like myself, to provide the audience with more laughs.

Simple!

The script opens with the backstory of how a huge monster (called in Jewish, the *Gadol*, or "the big one") is born inside of a huge egg and then grows up really peacefully and loving and is a big fan of eating grapes grown on a community Israeli farm. But when he's hit with a nuclear laser blast years later, he becomes uncontrollable. A Semantic professor talks to his classroom at an Israel college:

PROFESSOR: "In our young country's history we have never seen such potential for uninhabited violence. The potential is great for our total destruction. We must do everything we can to protect ourselves."

I wasn't a student of Hebrew history but I knew enough to know that this entire script was a metaphor. Which is fine. Metaphors are great for movies. But they're just not *funny*.

It was my job to make this piece of shit *funny*. So I got to work. The first change I made was that I felt the monster shouldn't just become evil.

That was too simple. I made him even more stupid. If he stood up too quickly, he'd rub his eyes all confused and fall to the ground.

That alone would be funny to an audience—and I don't care *where* they live. If they live in Israel, America, Australia or fucking Greenland, someone watching a monster rub his eyes and falling to the ground is going to be fucking *hysterical*.

So I started with that.

I then created the female monster to become, if anything, *more* human. She'd become a typical wife bitch. I had her wear giant hair curlers and she became a real ball buster. If the monster came home late from his "work" scaring the people in Israel, then she gave it to him real good.

It was hilarious.

I know this isn't PC to say nowadays ... but I created a few Arab villains who were more incompetent than dangerous. (You have to remember, this was one year *before* 9/11. We could still make fun of Arabs for being stupid and goofy.) The characters were named Ahmed and Raju and they were sweet and bumbling as they tried to steal the power of the monster to bring back to their own countries. In the end, they blow themselves up at a falafel stand. But they just shake it off and complain and walk off into the distance. That's the end of them.

It's very funny.

I put in a scene that takes place in a blimp. And I have the monster try to learn how to dance to the Macarena (kids, if you don't know this song, ask your parents. You were probably conceived to it).

There's a rap battle scene between the monsters. There are a ton of Jennifer Lopez ass jokes.

There are some references to *The Sixth Sense* (in one scene, the little Hebrew boy who befriends Gadol pretends he's a ghost and the monster believes him until the boy farts. *No* ghost farts).

And a few *Matrix* jokes, where everyone moves in slow motion but don't accomplish a damn thing. I did everything I could to keep the plot intact, while also adding the "spice" and the "filling" to make it one *tasty comedic offering*.

In short, it was still a piece of shit. But it was a *funny* piece of shit.

I mailed it back to Benjamin and waited. A week or so later, this email arrived:

Dear Skippy:

What can I say but I love it so much! It is so good and funny. This is why I hire you! So fantastically hilarious! You bring the characters to life in a very naturalistic way. Just one problem: the finance for film looks to have dried up. Hang and I will get back to you for more info.

Best,

Benjamin
Christ!

Just what I needed: to have my first script-credit struck down because of a financial issue over in Israel!

I didn't want to sound too bummed out but I also wanted to know what exactly was happening. And I wanted that $100,000!

Dear Benjamin:

Oh, that's a shame!! I think the script could really make a great film and I feel that it would bring in a lot of money! As the producer, aren't you in charge of the money issue? Or would that come from others? I hope you can get the money to finish and I really appreciate your nice words about my version of the script. I think it has a lot of "pop" and "sparkle." Did you like when the monster went doody in the Red Sea and it floated to the top? Hope to talk with you soon! If I can help in any way, please let me know!

Yours,

Skippy

In the back of my mind, I thought this email could very well be the end of the entire affair. But I wasn't too upset. I now had a script I could show agents and others. It's always good to have at least one script you're proud of "in the trunk," meaning a script that may not ever get made but that you are proud enough to put in a trunk.

I decided to treat myself to a night out. I thought I *deserved* it. I had worked really hard on the script for the past week, it turned out great, so why shouldn't I explore the city a little? My knowledge of Los Angeles pretty much consisted of the area surrounding my place in Malibu and the people who hung around at the Malibu bars I frequented every night.

Why not try a *new* bar? A new *scene*?

Cigar bars were sort of big back then, or at the tail-end of being hip. I've always loved smoking a good fat, thick one.

I've also always been really good at talking up women.

I know, I know.

On my podcast and satellite radio show, I portray myself as merely a humble servant unto thy intoxicating power of womanhood—I am merely putty to their pussy.

Not true.

I've also come across at times (purposely) as being too aloof to give a shit what a woman thinks about me.

Also not true.

In reality, I fall somewhere in the middle.

I love women, and they tend to love me.

I'm a nice guy, remember?

And I do *genuinely* love women.

Not feminists, maybe. Or the highfalutin' academic types. Or women with an attitude. Or who are "facially different."

But if you're a red-blooded American normal hetero female, I think we'll get along pretty damn well.

I have a fan club called the Peanutters Gallery. The club consists of women I've slept with or fooled around with and who I remain really good friends with to this day—at least on social media. The club is up to about 87 members.

I'd defy *anyone*—even the most "woke" men out there—to have as many members of such a club.

In fact, I doubt if most men would even have *one* member. (Maybe their ex wives? But who knows if even *that!*)

Dues are cheap to join—$199 a year. The members aren't told to say anything. I'm not out there dictating what they say when they call. They also receive free swag, including hats, bumper stickers and condoms, all with my name on them.

True, I'll hang up on *any* listener—man or woman—who disrespects me or lies to me but I have to say it's pretty clear that this is a club that *any* woman would love to belong to.

In May of 2015, two years and three months into my *Passing on the Right* podcast, I received a now infamous call from a woman who called herself "Mary from Maryland."

Excerpts from the call later ended up as a sample on A$AP Rocky's 2015 CD, *At. Long. Last.*

Listen to that CD carefully. It's between tracks six and seven, and I can be heard saying over and over again, "Tedious, man. Fucking tedious!"

Other excerpts from the call also ended up on a bootleg CD that (supposedly) went out on tour with a rapper named 2 Chainz, where he'd play a portion of the tape to begin the show, followed by: "Three, two, one ... here we go now!" The lights would then come up and people would go crazy. On this excerpt I can be heard saying "Don't know ya, don't wanna know ya, gonna know you gone now."

I'm not sure what in particular African-American artists found so fascinating about this particular taped call but I'm not complaining. I love rap music and I love black subculture and I was thrilled with any attention I could get at that time. So I never sued for copyright infringement or anything like that. (By the way, years later, in around 2019, just before Covid struck, I was at a party for my friend who owns the AntiHero skating clothing brand, and Travis Scott, the rapper, was there. We got to talking and he was blown away that I was the "guy who said all them cool things." We talked for a long while and really got along wonderfully. Ironically, he ended up sleeping with the girl I had brought to that party, but that's *another* story. I wish him no harm. He's a good looking dude ... and he likes my material!)

So when I received this particular phone call from a listener that was later used in rap songs, it was just another typical day at the Satellite Senter (what I call my broadcast studio, in which I talk to the world every afternoon from 2:30 to 5:00 P.M.).

I had just interviewed the actor and comedian Rob Schneider about his opinions on NATO.

I took the call. The voice sounded familiar but not a voice I could place right away.

"Is this Skippy?" I heard.

"Who else?" I said in return.

I hate when people ask if it's really me. I also hate it when they ask "how you doing?"

How the fuck do you think I'm doing? Here's a hint: exactly the same as I had been "doing" five minutes before when the *last* caller asked "how you doing?"

If it would make it any easier for the callers, just know this: as long as I'm in front of the mic, telling it like it is, calling a bird a bird, then I'm doing just fantastic.

After the small talk, she got right into it: "Do you remember me? I can give you a hint."

Here's another thing that I despise: *hints*.

Just give me the fucking answer already!

Who am I, Ken Jennings?

"Who is the girl I banged last New Year's?"

How in the fuck do I know who's on the line?

The caller then slipped into her "baby girl" voice which I actually love.

What can I say? I like my women to sound like infants.

Or to sound just like wounded baby animals.

I want them vulnerable and I want to take care of them. I'd never want an actual baby or any animal to be wounded, but a twenty-two-year old with huge fucking baby titties talking in a real high voice?

Well, I'm just fine with that. Act as wounded as you like!

"It's Maryyyyyy. From Maryyyyyyyyyyland."

Oh Christ.

I remembered this gem from around 1997, just after I graduated.

And I remembered her for a very good reason: she was wearing a baseball cap that read "MARY" when I fucked her. And she had a tattoo of MARY just above her pubic line.

In cursive.

I also remember that she was the first woman out of high school that I "shrimped." Ever heard of "shrimping"?

If not, I think I might just have invented it.

Take a dick. Place it on a girl's bicep. Have her make a muscle. Pump. Repeat.

It sounds ridiculous but I love it. I stumbled upon this maneuver back in high school when I was whoosh-zipping off cocaine and started to fuck a girl's forearm, thinking it was a vagina. It wasn't. She didn't seem to actually mind. No harm, no foul. But it also felt great and she didn't have to do a thing. I forgot all about it until the next day when her friends giggled when I walked back into the Georgetown bar.

Fuck is so funny? I remember thinking.

I was told that I had been responsible for taking Kerry's "arm cherry."

I started to remember what had happened but I wasn't too embarrassed. They could make fun of me all they wanted. I had gotten off, no one was pregnant, and it was actually a huge turn-on to fuck a girl's forearm area. It wasn't going to become a letter to *Penthouse* or anything , but I could only look forward to doing it again real soon.

Within no time, I was known as "Forearm Freaky" among a certain set. I always grinned when people called me that. There are a lot worse nicknames, let's face it. We all have our kinks. Mine just happens to be free and harmless and, as far as I know, pretty original. The trick—if there even is one—is to have the girl bend their arms at just that right angle in order for enough friction to be created between the front of the arm and the triceps of the upper arm.

Bang!

Instant vagina.

Or *faux*-gina, as I call it.

If you're lucky, she can even have some forearm hair which can simulate a woman's public hair.

For some reason that I can't remember, my friends and I called this "shrimping." Maybe because my dick smelled like freshly-shucked shrimp after I finished, I don't know. I've since heard that "shrimping" means something else entirely when it comes to sex but I can't remember what it is and I really don't care. The only "shrimping" that means anything to me is the forearm type. And if there's money to be made from trademarking the word on T-shirts and hats and beer cozies, I'm all in. In fact, I *am* in: check out my website for swag.

Here's a full transcript of the *entire* on-air call with Mary from Maryland, not just a few excerpts from rap CDs:

Mary from Maryland: "Hello?"

Me: "Hello."

Mary from Maryland: "Oh, I thought I was still on with the producer—or that I didn't go through—"

Me: "No, you're on. You're on the show. What's up?"

Mary from Maryland: "I'm passing on the right! Whoo-hoo!"

Me: "Great."

Mary from Maryland: "Is this Skippy?"

Me: "Who else? Who *else* would I be? Flammer in boxers?"

[Tremendous laugh from the Passing on the Right, POTR, crew]

Mary from Maryland: "No ... no, I figured it was you—Skippy from, from before."

Me: "Before what?"

Mary from Maryland: "I guess you got famous."

Flammer: "*Ha-bullshit*! I just sneezed."

Me: "More famous than your momma ever sucking me off, ba-yeetch!"

[Tremendous laughter from the POTR crew]

Mary from Maryland: "No, you are—"

Me: "Okay. Can you just tell me?"

Mary from Maryland: "Do you remember me? I can give you a *hint*."

Me: "Just fucking tell me already, Jesus ... The Flim-Flammery is looking at me like I'm the one holding all this up—"

[In baby girl voice]

Mary from Maryland: "It's Maryyyyyy. From Maryyyyyyyyyyland."

The Flammer: "You only dated people with speech impediments."

Me (in baby voice): "*Theems* that way."

[Tremendous laughter from everyone]

Mary from Maryland: "You still like shrimp?"

Me: "Excuse me?"

Mary from Maryland: "Do you still go shrimping?"

Flammer: "Shrimping?"

Me: "Shrimping?"

Mary from Maryland: "You know ...."

Me: "I *don't* know."

Mary from Maryland: "Your special move or thing that—"

Flammer: "*Special* move?!"

Jim Bucktooth Da Engineer: "Special as in *retarded*?"

Mary from Maryland: "Special as in *special*."

Me: "I don't know. There were a lot of people I met in Maryland. And this was, what—sixteen years ago or whatever—"

Mary from Maryland: "Seventeen, yeah."

Flammer: "Oh, you gotta describe this special sex act, oh you gotta—"

Jim Bucktooth Da Engineer: "Crazy, man—"

Me: "I think ... I think I do remember this, I ... I don't wanna even—"

Flammer: "Why not?"

Jim Bucktooth: "Yeah, why not?"

Mary from Maryland: "Yeah why not?"

Me: "Just cut it. Jim, cut the call. I'm not speaking to this stuttering bitch—"

Flammer: "Whoa! Easy, *Jesus*—"

Mary from Maryland: "He put his thing on my forearm—"

Me: "Three, two, one ... here we go now. Cut it, Jim, seriously—"

Jim Bucktooth: "No way."

Me: "I'm serious, dude. She's ... nuts, I remember her."

Mary from Maryland: "And then he has me fold—you know, make a muscle, like over his dick, like a hot dog and he goes back and forth—"

Jim Bucktooth: "And out pops some *man mustard*!"

Mary from Maryland: "Back and forth and he'd ... he called it shrimping. Said he even invented it."

Me: "Jesus. There it goes. There goes my career."

Flammer: "I think it's clever."

Me: "Well, thank you. I do, too—"

Mary from Maryland: "I didn't mind it. I just never forgot it. Thought I'd call—"

Me: "Yeah, that was super nice of you ... bitch."

Flammer: "Whoa, dude. Seriously."

Me: "All so ... tedious, man. Fucking tedious. So fucking tedious."

Flammer: "I think it's romantic."

Me: "Well, fuck you, too."

Flammer: "Jesus, what's up *your* shitter?"

Me: "Don't know ya, don't wanna know ya...."

Flammer: "Fuck are you talking about—"

Me: "I don't know, gonna know you gone now ..."

The call cuts off. The Flammer finally pulled the fucking plug. He told me later that he knew I was drunk and that I wasn't as nice as I would have been to the caller if I had been sober, which is all true.

This was years before I got sober. I've been sober now for four months and three days as I write this and I feel great.

I look like shit, but I feel GREAT ...

Then again, would I have acted any differently if I *hadn't* been drinking?

Probably not, no.

I'm just telling it like it is.

Well, it didn't take long for word to get out that I didn't like ALL women. Not true! I just didn't happen to like this *one* particular woman for telling the world something they had no business hearing. And the alcohol excuse wasn't cutting it.

I'm no longer ashamed of shrimping. But back then, I didn't at all know how people were going to react. I can also now tell you that I invented "jump humping," in which you enter a woman but don't move and a friend jumps on the bed and does all the work for you.

Anyway, I guess I overreacted on my *own* part with that phone call.

I mean, one of the reasons I wanted to write this memoir was to prove that I'm not the man I've been accused of being in the past.

I'm not a woman hater.

I'm not a black hater.

I'm not an Asian hater. I'm not a Hebrew hater. I'm not a hater of *anyone*.

I believe that if you're cool, I'll like you.

If you ain't, well … I won't.

It's a simple philosophy that's treated me well.

I have friends of all colors and nationalities and sexualities.

It honestly doesn't matter what you are.

I even have one friend who are a "them."

I like them. As long as them get my comedy, I'll love them forever.

And I'm not going to lie:

These days, I'm super proud of having invented the "shrimping" and "jump humping" maneuvers.

But when I was younger (and this was *years* ago now), I was a little squeamish about releasing details of my sex life. That's since gone out the fucking window and I'll talk about *anything*.

"Shrimping" has since become a *huge* craze among my Right-of-Wayers, who will even host events with shrimp, or they'll wear hats with an image of a shrimp on a forearm, or they'll throw shucked shrimp shells at me, which I don't even mind.

Whatever.

I'm living the life of a *Rocky Horror Picture Show*. I'm just glad I didn't call the sex act "the flounder stuffed with crab meat."

My point is that I, in no way, despise women.

I love and respect them.

I've brought this up on the show but never in print:

I loved women so much that as a single man, I created a system of hooking up that was later used by others who wrote books about this method.

Do you remember a guy from about 2012 who became a hit on television? He wore a top hat and goggles and he said he "invented" what he called his "guidelines for the process of seduction"?

He would tell the women he'd meet in bars these stories that were obviously fake but that he *knew* would receive a lot of attention: "I just saw a white horse running down the street!"

Lines like that.

He'd pull other tricks, as well. Like he'd control the conversation's beginning and end, and sometimes he'd cut women off mid-sentence and then just walk away.

So he'd be *in* their heads.

And they'd think:

What did he not like about me? Men don't do that! Hey, come back! You intrigue me!

It worked spectacularly!

Guess where he got it?

I can't prove this but I really do believe this guy (and others) were at the various bars I'd frequent around L.A. pulling off some *super* slick effin' moves.

But here's the difference: I *invented* this process of seduction for fun and not to earn money.

For me, and my friends, I called it "Scrumping for Sauce."

I know, I know. It's not politically correct but it's also not a *hurtful* name and it was never meant for outside consumption!

It was an entire process that I created.

And it fucking worked!

I should have named it *Pussy-Mandering*, but even I didn't know about "gerrymandering" back then!

I now kick myself for not trademarking this shit. But I was young and stupid and I was too hopped up off puss to care about any of the cash.

It was gash over cash. Now it'd probably be the opposite.

I broke my "Scrumping Style" down into a few different categories. If you combined everything, it spelled out the acronym OCR, or a word to be pronounced "*OCER*":

Obtaining

Completing

Remaining

In the "Obtaining" phase, it was my task to *obtain* a woman.

In the "Completing" phase, it was my task to *complete* the sexual congress.

In the "Remaining" phase, it was my task to decide whether or not I wanted to *continue* seeing this woman. If not, I went back to the bars and started over with the "Obtaining" phase.

And around and around it went.

Within each category, there were various sub-categories.

For instance, under "Obtaining", I had a few categories, one of which was "not telling the truth but also not lying."

I'll give you an example:

I've found that most women are tired of losers. And if you've achieved *anything* of any note in life, they're going to grab onto you.

Hungry like the wolf and all that.

Here's a standard pick-up line that I found worked quite well:

"Hi. My name is Skippy. And I'm a writer for television. Wrote *The Titanic* joke for the Oscars. And I'm up for an Emmy for *The Wayans Bros*."

Let's break that down. Some of it's true, some of it isn't, as you well know. I never did end up earning so much as an Emmy *nomination*, let alone *winning* an Emmy *award*. But this was before everyone had an iPhone and could check your lies instantly.

I found that it worked really well.

I would call a line such as this one "Skotching."

Not completely bullshit but also not completely true.

I *Skotched* all the time and it mostly worked—until I came across an actual Emmy winner who insisted I tell her how I had won an Emmy for *The Wayans Bros*. We didn't end up sleeping together. I wish her well.

I'd also end conversations even if I *was* interested in the woman. As I previously mentioned, this was later used by the person who wrote all those dating books. He called it "false-time constraints" and it'd be when a conversation ended too soon and the woman would want to know why exactly. She'd have already lost control, which is not a good place to be. It would seriously *bother* her.

I mean, like, this would *seriously* bother the fuck out of her! When I did it, I'd call it "The Ax." As in, "Gonna give the woman the *ax*." End of conversation, away I'd walk. A look of puzzlement on her part. Invariably, she'd approach to ask what the matter was.

Sometimes I'd say something and continue the conversation, and other times I'd just say nothing.

I'd also do something that I'd call "Mushrooming," which meant I would lift up the spirits or ego of a woman until the damn thing was mushrooming like a motherfucking nuclear cloud.

"God, I love your perfume!"

"You look so beautiful in that shawl!"

"You remind me of someone ... oh yeah! Julia Roberts!"

Sometimes I'd take that in the *opposite* direction. This was called "The Neg" by the idiot who wrote the dating guide. I called it the "God, You Smell Great ... for a Girl" move. I'd give the girl kind of a backhanded compliment so she'd at first say "thank you" but then wonder what my true intentions were. Here's an example:

"You look really beautiful! Like Liza Minnelli in *Arthur*. When she was drunk."

There would always be a quick "thank you" and then a confused look.

Another proven method to bag a babe was to wear a funny shirt. Here are some shirt slogans that worked really well for me:

"Simon says to fuck off."

"Ask me about my third ball."

"I'm a pepper, she's a pepper, she's a pepper too, it's a threesome!"

"Blow me, it's my birthday."

All incredibly funny and all incredibly effective.

I kick myself when I think about how much money I could have made if I had trademarked these very special seduction techniques!

Once again, ahead of my damn time!

And, again, while I can't prove it, I'm pretty sure the "inventor" of the dating system saw me at the various bars in L.A. over the years working my magic.

There's just way too much of my own material for him to ever claim he created all of this out of thin air!

But fuck it.

I got laid and it was well worth it.

The night that I heard back from Benjamin about the financing for *He Shall Who But Live,* I decided to hit a new part of town. I felt I deserved it. And as I mentioned earlier, cigar bars were big back then. I put on a funny T-shirt and hit a bar in downtown L.A. called The Buena Vista V-Cut, just off San Pedro Street.

I arrived commando, Rambo style, without my "Pussy Pack" (a group of friends I'd typically hit the town with to use as my co-pilots).

No, this time I just needed to fly alone, as I sometimes did.

The T-shirt I was wearing read:

Your Image Here

And then an arrow pointing down to my groin.

I thought it was very funny and would be super affective in bagging a chick.

And it was.

Within minutes of arriving, I met Caroline, who would become my girlfriend for the next few weeks.

Caroline was a *very* interesting person, as I've pointed out on my show. First of all, we're *still* really good Parler friends. She's married now and has an adorable daughter named Eve. Her husband's a good guy. He was in the military or something overseas or somewhere and was a hero for doing something or other that earned him a lot of medals or something.

Like I said, a good guy.

Caroline has since become a hit on my satellite radio show and podcast. I guess you could say she's become sort of the "butt" of my gags and pranks, but I don't really see it that way.

Just as I drive my sister-in-law nuts by calling her at, say, her weekly waxing session to tell her she's won a ton of money, I've also used Caroline on the shows as the recipient of many of my pranks.

Once I called her up at her shrink's office to pretend I was outside listening to all the shit she was saying about our relationship years ago. The listeners *loved* that one, especially when I told her that I could hear her talking about the size of my shling-shlong.

I have also called her at home pretending to be her backyard neighbor, asking her to move a little to the left so I could see her backside a little better.

Her husband hasn't always seen the humor in this, and neither has Caroline truthfully, but they seem to always eventually come around and we've remained terrific friends.

Going back to that night at Buena Vista V-Cut ... Caroline and I hit it right off. The conversation started slow but built up quickly when she told me that she was friends with a woman whose brother was a writer for *The Simpsons*.

Caroline suddenly became a *lot* better looking.

And *interesting*.

Funny how that works.

Seems that this guy had been a writer on *The Simpsons* for a few years and already had a few episodes under his belt.

Fascinating! Tell me more!

What were the fucking chances that a girl I'd be mackin' on at a cigar bar would know someone who could change my career forever?

This got me *very* wound up.

Caroline was a good-looking broad ... or attractive enough.

But the fact that she knew a *Simpsons* writer made her even *more* beautiful.

I just ain't gonna lie!

I launched into my own backstory, emphasizing the fact that I was a successful comedy writer, but not lying about having won an Emmy.

It was a good decision on my part. This could have later bit me in the ass. But my intuition was to play it *clean*. And it paid off.

More on my time at *The Simpsons* in the next chapter. Hold on to your hats. It's a doozy.

So I ended up sleeping with Caroline that night (sorry, hubby, but it's true) and it was pretty good. I was in a pleasant mood the next morning when I turned on the computer and, with Caroline still asleep on my futon, I read what the Israeli producer Benjamin Globlan had sent me the previous night:

Dear Skippy:

What can I say but that this business is frustrating one! I am the producer but I still need to collect money from investors! I wish I was rich. I need $100,000 USD to complete the film. And I hope to one day get it. In mean time are you working on other script ideas? Maybe you could send scripts for other's movies for me to see. Maybe we can partner?

Best,

Benjamin

Without even thinking, and with Caroline still snoring away in the background, I wrote him right back.
I think it was a very good email:

Dear Benjamin:

It's funny you should mention other scripts, because I have a trunk full! It's my biggest dream to write a comedic movie! Can I send you the ideas? Boy, if we could work together on these and other films, that would be a dream! Just me writing them and you producing them, popping them out, one, two, three!!! When you say $100,000, you mean american, right? Not israel money?

Best,

Skippy

Within minutes, my computer pinged and I received this email:

Dear Skippy:

Yes, US American dollars. $100,00 should do the trick. Please send ideas! I am always on the looking out for great movie ideas!

Best,

Benjamin

Well, *this* was a pleasant surprise! Someone who was actually interested in my work! *An actual fan.*

Shame about him needing more money for *He Shall Who But Live,* though.

Then again, if he *could* somehow find enough funds and if he *did* end up making *He Shall Who But Live,* I'd have my first movie credit under my belt.

It'd be an investment.

I called my father. I hadn't spoken to him in a few months since he learned that I was subletting his Ocean City apartment to the Flammer. I had hung up when he started giving me shit.

No one would have been in that apartment anyway, and he knew it.

Why not let a friend of mine stay there —especially after all he had done for me? Loyalty didn't mean much to my dad. I can understand why. When you hustle in the cutthroat world of D.C. politics, no one is really and truly a friend.

When I called my father this time, I had to keep my voice down. I didn't want to wake Caroline and have to explain why I was calling and all that shit. I had just met her. And now I'd have to tell her why I'm calling my father and requesting $100,000 to further my career?

Yeah. I don't think so.

It's funny but I'm not sure Caroline ever has heard this story before. If she's reading this book, she'll find out. Maybe she thought I was making a drug deal or something cool like that. Or had other secrets, which isn't always a bad thing for a woman to think.

By the time the call ended, and being the master manipulator and negotiator that he was, I had the $100,000 ... but ... I *also* had to promise that I'd fly back to Maryland at least three times in the next year, including for Thanksgiving and Christmas. Seems that my mom missed me. Who could blame her? I was a fun guy to have around.

Fair enough.

I wrote back to Benjamin immediately. I was excited but I didn't want to give *all* my cards away:

Dear Benjamin:

Say I know where to find $100,000. Then what? The movie gets made? Would there be any guarantee that I could then get at least one of my own scripts produced?

Best,

Skippy

I drove over to Dunkin' Donuts to pick up a nice breakfast for the still-sleeping Caroline. It was the least I could do. When I returned, there was already an email waiting for me:

Dear Skippy:

That is wonderful news. As for your question I would need to see the ideas first but I think that could definitely be possibility!

Cheers,

Benjamin

If that was the case, it was as good as done. How could it not be?
I was nothing if not a productive writer. I had a *ton* of ideas!
I knew what I had was gold. These were ideas I had been keeping around for years, honing and polishing until each one shone brighter than a goddamn shooting star.
No, I hadn't turned them into actual movie scripts yet but that was okay.
These were *weighty* ideas. If you held them in your palm, you'd practically feel the density and sense the brilliance.
Over the next few days I refined these ideas even more, making them truly *irresistible*.
How could anyone resist these? I mean, *c'mon!*
Along with the ones I told you about earlier, here's the entire list:

Young John Holmes – *A takeoff on "Young Abe Lincoln" and other such films. But this would be about the porn star with the biggest dick in the world when he was young. A sample joke might be the kid saying something like "I cannot tell a lie. I am hung like a fucking donkey" or something like that. Would be willing to work with you on the tone of this. I'm thinking funny but historical and accurate scientifically.*

James Blind – *A blind and deaf James Bond type character goes undercover and gets into adventures. It'll be a satire on adventure films but because James is also very handsome, he sleeps with a lot of women … many who aren't as attractive as they would have been had he been able to see and choose them correctly. A satire on incompetence at the highest levels of government and espionage.*

A Retarded Jason Bourne – *All there in the title.*

These ideas were amazing. I had little doubt that *any* of these wouldn't have made for a huge fucking hit.

When I heard back from Benjamin, he agreed:

Dear Skippy:

These amazing! I think with $50,000 more USD we could bundle one of these into monster idea and produce TWO movies. Just let me know but excited!

Yours,

Benjamin

I knew right away that $50,000 would not be an impossibility— just one more trip back to Maryland to visit the family ought to take care of *that* problem.

But I wasn't going to let Benjamin know that. I wasn't a fool.

Taking a tack from my father and his business acumen, I suggested $25,000.

Benjamin agreed.

And I immediately got to work on *Young John Holmes*. Truthfully, I wasn't sure if Benjamin even knew this very American porn hero but it didn't matter. John Holmes meant a lot to me as a kid growing up in

Maryland. He pulled himself up by his cockstraps and became a huge star based on his gigantic appendage. *God bless, right?* We all try to deal with the cards we're dealt.

In his case, he just happened to be given a full stack *down below* but not *up above*.

Luckily, I was blessed with *both* but I admired the gumption of this man born dirt poor down South.

I thought a lot could be done with this idea and I wasn't wrong.

It would be funny. It would be sad. It'd be hip. It'd be fresh. It'd be the perfect first original Skippy Battison movie script to be produced!

This idea had been out there for a while. I had talked about it for years with friends and I had even written a short story that I had submitted to *The New Yorker*. Sadly, it was rejected, which I thought was too bad. But fuck it. The stories in *The New Yorker* bore the shit out of me anyway. I only did it to impress my mom who loved the magazine for some reason.

What I didn't know was that the idea was *so* out there that it was eventually stolen and turned into the movie *Boogie Nights*.

I have no *specific* proof of this but it's all pretty obvious. For a few years I even thought about suing but what good would that have done?

And who would have believed me anyway?

No, this would be even more delicious: write a script that was even *better* than *Boogie Nights*. And shove that 12 inch cock right down the throats of Hollywood, bitches!

Young John Holmes takes place in the mid 20th century and opens with a baby being born and a doctor fainting at what he's seeing. It's astonishing, the size of this baby's dick. He's never seen anything like it and he's seen a *ton* of baby dick in his career.

But this little guy is *different*: it's almost as if he's the *chosen* one.

From there, I parody both *Young Abraham Lincoln* and *Young George Washington*. Young John Holmes gets into trouble, he apologizes, he becomes a better kid for it. He's picked on by his "lesser" schoolmates until he "rises" to the occasion and proves that he's more of a man than they'll ever be*come*.

When puberty hits, the movie really picks "up."

It's *Porky's* meets *American Pie* meets *Saving Private Ryan* (there's a shootout and a couple of deaths). Young John Holmes (or YJH as I call him in the script) faces off against a gang of dangerous cocaine dealers. While not "traditionally" smart, YJH uses his skin-sword-wangling moves to take care of not only this gang but also their unsatisfied wives and girlfriends.

And then things really "explode."

YJH heads to Washington to protest a Congressional Bill.

The bill (created by the Democrats) would arrest anyone with a cock that is bigger than eleven inches.

In front of stunned Senators and Congressmen, YJH stands before them, nude, and filibusters for hours, not saying a word.

He doesn't have to. (I should say here that when I wrote this script, it was *years* before filibustering became a huge deal and a household word. So, in that sense, and actually in many other senses, I was kind of ahead of my time.)

Like all geniuses, YJH is ahead of his time, too. When the script ends, it's clear that the world will eventually catch up to him—but on his *own* terms.

YJH
(Wistfully) I'm no different than anyone else. And I'm not talking about my shlong. I'm talking about my will to stand out and to take what already exists and to stand *proud*.

SENATOR SCHMIDT
Stand vertically?

YJH
Horizontally.

Senator Schmidt laughs very hard.

SENATOR SCHMIDT
You definitely bounce to your own rhythm, son.

YJH
Ever since birth, sir.

SENATOR SCHMIDT
Let's go, son. And see what the future brings.

YJH
Right behind ya!

SENATOR SCHMIDT
Not *too* close please!

Young John Holmes laughs very hard.

YJH
We all have our specialties. Mine just ... happens to come from
behind and end up ... *in front*.

At that, the script ends.

I was happy with it—*very happy with it*—and I showed it to
Caroline. She was critical. *Was this character realistic? Was he worth
writing about? Who was he exactly? She had never even heard of John
Holmes. Someone was willing to make a movie out of this?*

I spoke calmly: "Babe, we're talking Israel movies here. But it's
still a notch on my credits. I mean, how cool would it be to have *any*
movie made, let alone one so funny and cool and ultimately sad?"

She still wasn't buying it. But I didn't care. I sent it off to
Benjamin. I asked him that if I just "happened" to find the $125,000,
could we then make *both* this new YJH movie and *He Shall Who But
Live*?

I didn't dare tell him that I actually *already had* the $125,000
stacked and ready to go. I wanted to see if he liked this new script
before I gave away anything.

Again, I was no moron.

Once he received by mail the new script, he wrote back
immediately:

Dearest Skippy:

*Man this so good and funny. I remember watching John Holme when I
was younger. He was a BIG star even here in Israel! So funny in so
many ways!*

Yours,

Benjamin

Okay, now it was my time to *strike*.

I wrote Benjamin back that I was very happy that he liked the new script. That I knew he would like it even if my girlfriend didn't fully understand it. That he was a man with discerning comedic tastes. That I thought we could really work well together and I was excited about giving it a shot.

He, too, was excited. He had been waiting a long time to meet a writer who could "deliver goods." And now that he finally met him, he couldn't wait to get started. How best to send him the money so the process could begin? Could I perhaps send the funds to his Swiss bank account so as to avoid the very high Israeli tax rates?

Yeah, I could do that, I said. *I guess I could do that.*

Caroline was against the idea but I shooed her off for being naïve.

Off the money went. One day. Two days. Three days.

No word.

I emailed Benjamin:

Dear Benjamin:

Did you get the funds? It looked like they went through on my end. I was thinking: Maybe the John Holmes script isn't the best one to start with. Maybe the retarded Jason Bourne? Perhaps there's a bigger audience for that one? Let me know and I'll get to work on it immediately. Another option: instead of being retarded, Jason Bourne can be on the spectrum. That seems to be a big thing now. Hollywood is always into the new thing.

Best,

Skippy

An hour later, this email arrived:

Dearest Skippy:

Man this so good and funny. I remember watching John Holme when I was younger. He was a BIG star even here in Israel! So funny in so many ways! Benjamin!

What the fuck?! Was this a joke?
I wrote back:

Dear Benjamin:

There might have been a mistake on your part as you already sent me that last email. Anyway, I have SO many ideas, they're exploding out of me!

Yours,

Skippy

An hour later this email arrived:

Dearest Skippy:

Man this so good and funny. I remember watching John Holme when I was younger. He was a BIG star even here in Israel! So funny in so many ways!

Yours,
Benjamin

    Uh oh.
I tried calling. But I was sent straight to voice mail.
Hmmmm.
Interesting.
Not good but certainly ... interesting.
I never heard from "Benjamin" again.
You're not surprised. But I *was.*
Listen, I told you that this would be an *honest* memoir. I got conned and I'm willing to admit it.
    Am I ashamed? Not particularly. I was young. I still had so much to learn. I was eager for my chance, and I grabbed it but it was the wrong ring.
    I again tried calling Benjamin but the number would no longer go through. When I emailed, I'd never hear back. This was long before it was so easy to look up anyone's address from anywhere around the world. So I went to a local library and asked the librarian for the white pages for Israel, which she didn't have. I then called a friend from high school who knew someone who had an older sister who had

recently moved to Israel. She didn't know what I was talking about. I tried calling Israel's version of the operator. She also didn't know what I was talking about. I mean, she *really* didn't know what I was talking about.

I hired an L.A. detective who was a drunk and wouldn't have been able to find his own shadow. There went another $5,000.

Part of success is knowing when to give up. And I knew down deep in my bones, even though I didn't want to admit it: *I had been tricked and tricked but good.*

Nicely done, sir! You caught a live one!

Goddamnit! And the scripts were so fucking funny! *What a waste,* I remember thinking. *All I'm trying to fucking do here is to entertain people. I'm not trying to hurt anyone! And this fuckhead has the balls to break my goddamn dreams?!*

And to take my father's money?!

Fuck this goddamn show business shit!

No wonder so many people complain about it!

At this point, I seriously thought about quitting comedy altogether. It's true. I'm not even exaggerating.

I thought about heading back to D.C. to work with my dad as he attempted to convince politicians that soda wasn't as bad as most knew it to be. That wouldn't have been *such* a bad life, right?

Hello?

I was *that* low.

So low.

Lower than low!

After finally admitting that I had been conned by "Benjamin" (and after listening to Caroline say "I told you so!" a million times) I took to my bed and didn't leave it for a month.

Only to piss and shit.

Literally.

I only (barely) left my bed to piss and shit.

It was awful. And very unlike me.

When people say they're terribly depressed, I think: *You have no idea.*

It was only thanks to Caroline that I managed to muddle through and then achieve ... if not greatness, then hopefully *close* to greatness. I really do owe her my career.

Years later, long after we had broken up, I sent her a batch of flowers telling her as much. She was appreciative and told me that all of my success came from my own hard work, not from her. I half-believed her.

Another reason I love women: I was *saved* by one!

That and alcohol.

And junk food.

And very hard drugs. (I mean, not *that* hard. I was no 1970s punk rocker. But cocaine and I always did get along *very well*.)

My weight ballooned up to 255.

I consider this my "Fat Elvis" period. Or my "Fat Axl Rose" period. Or my "Fat Vince Neil" period." Or pick any heavy metal lead singer from the '90s and look at them these days and insert their name. It'll work, trust me. We've done this on our satellite radio show many times.)

It was a low point, a tail-spin that I never thought I'd escape out of.

For the first time ever—*and that's really no exaggeration*—I wasn't coming up with jokes and making others around me laugh.

Oh, it was *bleak*.

And when I *did* eventually leave the bed, with the encouragement of Caroline, I got into some *serious* mischief.

It felt like this was the only way to put the awful past behind me and to enter into a new phase. Almost like a sorbet cleanser between different courses.

I'm not proud of this time. TMZ found a ton of these old photos in August 2017 (I still don't know how but I have some ideas) from this booze-sloshed period. You've seen the photos, there's no doubt. You'd have to be living on Venus to not have seen them. Shit, even my mother's hen-clucking friends at the country club saw them. *Everyone* seemed to see them. Jimmy Fallon even showed a few on his show. Howard Stern supposedly talked about them (not that I listen to that asshole). Yeah, you've definitely seen the photos.

But I'll add a few *bonus* details just to make it that much more interesting! *(See?! This book is so much worth its price! I told you so!)*

Photo #1: Me stumbling out of a check cashing place on Ventura Boulevard around 2:30 A.M. and attacking a fire hydrant with a lacrosse stick **(Bonus info!** *I was receiving some necessary funds from back home and I played lacrosse as a kid. But I don't remember at all why I had the stick with me at 2:30 in the morning. Protection? I don't remember. But I do have to say I looked pretty cool in this photo.)*

Photo #2: Hugging Batman in front of the Grauman's Chinese Theater and then vomiting on Wonder Woman. **(Bonus info!** *I later actually dated this woman who played the faux Wonder Woman on the streets of Hollywood! Seriously! We would laugh about this event. She was later murdered. I'm forgetting her name.)*

Photo #3: Riding a stolen horse on the Malibu Beach on New Year's, waving a Confederate flag. (**Bonus info!** *I remember nothing of this event except riding past Barbra Streisand, or someone who looked like her. I'm most definitely not a fan. I gave the horse back to the stable.*)

Photo #4: Being arrested after emerging from out of Ben Stiller's garden hut I had been living for a month as he traveled to Cannes and other places. (**Bonus info!** *Okay, everyone knows this story. What they don't know is that I had done this for a very good reason. And the reason was so that Ben Stiller could read* Young John Holmes, *as I just knew he'd love it. I needed to recoup my money somehow! Guess what? He did! I think. I'm sure he did. I assume he did. I'm not positive but who cares. I definitely got his attention*).

Photo #5: Smashing my car into the kitchen at the Denny's on South Figueroa Street in downtown L.A. and mistakenly chopping off a busboy's pinkie. (**Bonus info!** *You haven't heard about this one as it was later settled very much out of court. But guess what? This being Hollywood, the kid later got in touch with me wanting to get into stand-up comedy! Part of his shtick was that he had no pinkie. I found this more sad than funny and I never got back to him. Got to admire the kid's fucking guts!*)

Things were bleak, I'm not going to lie. I had very *little* going on. I thought about quitting and I thought about suicide. I even thought about religion. There was a church near me in Malibu that accepted *everyone*. Seriously, you could literally be homeless and they still cared about you. *That's* how desperate they were! But I talked myself out of it.

No sense becoming that *one* religious asshole on every block!

No, I had to do this on my own and I intended to get my ass out of bed and face the new dawn and no one was going to do it but my own damn self. Back to Ayn Rand, right? I couldn't rely on anyone else. I needed to get my career back into high gear, where it *belonged*.

And I intended to do so quickly.

But how quickly I never could have predicted.

Not in a million years ….

★ *Chapter Ten* ★

I WILL NOT... HOLD A GRUDGE AGAINST *THE SIMPSONS*

(WRITTEN 50 TIMES ON A BLACKBOARD)

What follows is the infamous *Simpsons* situation.

I'll try to make this brief.

The Simpsons has never been one of my favorite shows but I liked parts of it. I've always felt closest to the character of Bart Simpson. He hated rules, always did his own damn thing, never got the highest of grades, but he always had a ton of fun.

That was me.

I also liked Homer. Drinks a ton, eats a shitload, grows fat as hell but he doesn't give a flying shit.

The women characters have always bothered me, I don't know why: I find Marge to be overly dramatic and too much of a ball buster. Lisa is a show off and a know-it-all and she plays jazz, which I fucking despise. What's the baby called? I can't remember. I don't feel one way or another about her. The twin sisters are disgusting. And Miss Crabapple the teacher is fuckable, I guess, but she's also a big fat mess, like most women her age.

To write an episode of *The Simpsons* is about as high up the ladder as one can get in the comedy writing business. It's the crème de la crème. The top of the top. The heap of the jeep. The scrunch of my munch. Again, I'm not the biggest fan but even I have to admit as much.

I guess it would be like playing for the Orioles versus playing for the minor league Bowie Bay Sox. Once you get to "the show," there ain't no going back.

My relationship with Caroline wasn't doing so hot. She had some solid elements—like her eyes and her crotch—but she really wasn't my "type." She'd say the same thing about me. None of this is new. We've talked about this on my show—or I've talked about this a lot. Our attraction was really more of a very bright flame. Very intense and then *nothing*—or not much.

But I wasn't yet ready to extinguish that flame.

I first wanted to meet the *Simpsons* writing brother of Caroline's good friend, Stacey.

I'll call the guy "Alex." That's not his name.

Since Alex and I haven't exactly been pals over these past fifteen years due to him being jealous of my success and his lack thereof, I'll just call the dude "Alex." It's a simple, boring name for a somewhat simple, boring man who never achieved much beyond writing a few episodes of *The Simpsons*.

Granted, yes, he did reach "the show."

Then again, a lot of major leaguers have themselves a few hits and then never play again. I'd lump Alex in with this level of player. A few hits, maybe a few extra bases, no home runs, one or two seasons, then ... *see ya!*

Off to coach high school ball!

No hall-of-famer to see here, folks!

And then there are others, like myself, who work on a show like *The Simpsons* ... and then reach levels even *beyond* what *that* show offered.

But that's in the future. Back to the story:

Caroline was getting on my nerves. She was a nice girl but, like I said, not particularly my style. She also had a medium sense of humor and wouldn't always laugh at my jokes. Even worse, she never made *me* laugh. That's important in a relationship. If a woman isn't a ten, then her sense of humor *has* to be tip-top. If both are missing, forget it.

You might be asking: what did I like about her in the first place?

Well, she was sweet. And willing to talk to me. And she was interested in my career. And cute enough, I guess. And willing to introduce me to her best friend's brother who wrote for *The Simpsons*.

This might sound callous. But this is how Los Angeles works. Or is *supposed* to work. I know people outside showbiz who don't—or won't allow themselves to—understand this.

It's brutal. It's a snake pit.

And one has to do what one has to do in order to achieve success. Period. End of story.

So while our relationship wasn't hot, I figured I'd get at least *one* good thing out of it: a contact.

Caroline wanted to move in with me. I kept hemming and hawing that the time wasn't right, which was true. But she was only going to put up with my nonsense for so long before she took off and never returned.

This was my last chance. The clock was ticking …

I suggested, very casually, that we double date — me, Caroline, her best friend and her best friend's brother.

"Why would we want to do that?" Caroline asked. "She's looking for a boyfriend. Why would she want to have dinner with us along with her brother? Can't you fix her up with anyone?"

"I could … after I meet her brother," I said. "I have an amazing guy I could introduce her to. *Seriously.* They'd be *perfect* together!"

"You're incredible," she replied sarcastically.

I think she knew my plan to meet this *Simpsons* writer from the get go.

"I am, yes," I said. "I am *super* incredible!"

She rolled her eyes.

She was annoying but what could I do?

We ended up at a nice restaurant by the water in Venice. I think the brother of her friend was at first a little confused as to why he was there, as he was only told that there was a "like-minded dude" he might get along with.

But we quickly it off.

It's funny.

I often compare two comedy geeks finding each other to two dogs sniffing each other's assholes.

Like-minded always ends up with like-minded.

We immediately shared a comedic patois that we launched into: jokes, impersonations, cartoon characters, TV music themes, high-pitched clown voices, we did it all. It's almost as if we could read each others' minds.

All of this fooling around just drew stares from Caroline and her friend. That's fine. I was in my element and really liked Alex. We were like a pair of twins who spoke the same language that no one else could understand.

And if the girls didn't like what we were doing, fuck 'em.

The night was grand. We made plans to meet up again soon. *Without the girls.*

This was going well. *Really well.*

Within no time, we were *best* pals.

It was at this point that I broke up with Caroline. Things just weren't working out and I had other matters on my mind: such as how to get a freelance script accepted at *The Simpsons*.

I'd drop hints when I was out with Alex that I'd like nothing more than to write for *The Simpsons*. He seemed to ignore these hints. Or perhaps he was so used to hearing people wanting to write for the show that it was all he could do to just tune out.

Even though Caroline and I had broken up, we remained friends.

And oddly, she *still* wanted to hold me to my promise. She *still* wanted me to find the perfect guy to fix her friend up with.

Well, I did.

Me.

I started going out with Alex's sister, Stacey, and, again, it wasn't a perfect match. I thought she was okay looking and smart enough, I suppose, in her own academic way, but there was no *zip* to my *zap*, no *yin* to my *pang*, no *slang* to my *rang*, no *slick* to my *dick*.

Whatever. She was the sister of the guy who wrote for *The Simpsons!*

And for now, that would be enough.

It would be *more* than enough.

The three of us became the best of friends and would travel to Palm Springs on the weekends (their grandfather owned a small house), and I'd be invited to their parents' place in Thousand Oaks for really great dinners.

We'd hit the beaches and swim until dusk. It was magic.

When the dame wasn't around, Alex and I would watch old comedies from the 1980s, some of which I liked, some of which I hated. I turned him on to the genius of *Heavyweights*—or tried to. He never came fully around, much to my chagrin.

He tried to turn me on to the comedies of Albert Brooks and Woody Allen and Fellini, all of which I despised. Too much *thinking*. Too clever for their own good. And, I have to be honest, maybe more "ethnic" than I was used to or even wanted in my comedy.

We smoked a ton of dope and took a lot of car rides.

After a few weeks, I knew it was time to just come right out and ask: Is *The Simpsons* hiring or not? *And why do I even need to ask? You know I'm a comedy writer who loves* The Simpsons, *right? And that I'd love nothing more than to be a staff writer on the show, yes? And if not, then to at least sell them a freelance script that I can put on my resume to impress other shows, correct?*

The more I thought about this, the angrier I became. What were friends for anyway? Hollywood was such a viper's nest *without* friends.

Wasn't it friends who were supposed to help you succeed? Why would it be on *me* to have to even bring this shit up? *Hello? Over here? You're best pal of nearly a month? A little help please?*

I told Alex about getting conned out of all the money by the "Israeli producer." He found it shocking but also a bit *too* entertaining, asking me to repeat it a few times, and then a few more times for friends of his, some of whom wrote for *The Simpsons*.

Soon, word got around town that I had been a sucker for a con man. A few journalists reached out and asked if they could write about it. I said not a chance in hell. I was also a bit upset that Alex would have spread this story without asking my permission first. I only told him because we were best buds. It really wasn't his for the taking. Granted, I would have found it hilarious if it had happened to *someone else...*

But it didn't. It happened to *me*. And that shit wasn't funny.

Meanwhile, because of the stupid promise I was forced to make with my father, I'd have to soon head back home to Maryland, leaving my career unattended back in Los Angeles.

That wasn't something I was looking forward to.

I didn't need it. I didn't ask for it. But I *had* to do it. Because I had been conned. Was it my fault? Maybe. I don't know. The guy was good, really good. It could have happened to anyone. I just happened to be the victim. So why was I the butt of this particular joke?

I have to be honest here: I wasn't in love with most of the other *Simpsons* writers. Truthfully, I wasn't even in love with Alex as a friend. But I could deal with him. The others seemed to be nothing more than nerds with an attitude. Harvard Lampooners "made good." Brainy without any street smarts or spark.

This was the "best of the best"?!

And yet I still wanted in. I wanted to strut my own damn stuff.

So one night, when Alex and I were alone, watching some shitty foreign movie he had found funny, I just came right out and asked: "Listen, I hate to come right out and ask but I was wondering—"

"If you could write for *The Simpsons*," he finished.

"Yeah, actually. Yes."

"Sorry. Everyone asks me that. But it's impossible."

Impossible? How impossible could it possibly be if *he* was doing it?!

"I'm sorry?" I asked, slightly annoyed. "How would that be *impossible*?"

"Listen, I know we're friends but it's just an impossibility. I'm constantly being asked and you just don't know what I had to go through to get on the show myself."

"What did you have to go through?"

"I submitted about thirty ideas for episodes. I wrote five or so full drafts of spec scripts. Only then was I allowed to actually submit real ideas. My friend wrote for the show, although he's since left. When he did, I took his place. I busted my ass to get in that door."

"So there's no way in?"

"Well, I guess you could pitch a ton of ideas for a few years or something. It's just really—"

"What type of ideas? For episodes? Jokes?"

"Episodes first."

"And I'd pitch them to you?"

"I guess ... but I'm low on the ladder. There's really not much I can do besides pass them on."

"And you'd do that for me?"

He looked at me for a long time. Maybe too long. *Were we friends or weren't we?* If yes, why did I go out of my way to befriend him to begin with?

Because he liked stupid "brainy" comedies?

"I suppose," he finally said, without as much enthusiasm as he perhaps could have as a "friend."

"Great," I said, changing the subject. "Let's walk on the beach and fling pebbles at seagulls."

Which we did. We were still pals. But after that conversation, I noticed a slight chill between us. I tried warming up the friendship by buying him things, like expensive LPs (he collected old soundtracks to movies, some of which were quite rare), and old toys still in their boxes. Shit like that bores me to tears but he was a friend.

Or was *supposed* to be.

Soon, we were back to where we had been from the get go: just hangin' and bangin'.

Now was the time to strike. I typed up the episode ideas I had been gathering for the past few days and printed them all out for him. I slid the page under the front door to his house and took off.

I didn't want to put any added pressure on him to read the ideas in front of me.

I wanted an *honest* evaluation.

A day passed. And then two. And then a few more days.

Nothing.

But I didn't mention a thing. Instead, I printed out another copy, with a few *added* episode ideas, and then slid *this* version under his door.

Again, nothing.

Now I was *really* determined.

I came up with even *more* ideas and then dropped *that* list off.

Meanwhile, we were getting together most days to just hang.

Was he not going to say anything? Should *I* be the one saying something? *This was becoming uncomfortable.*

And then fortune smiled upon me.

Alex was offered a producing role on a new animated show called *Clerks*, based on the movie with the same name by Kevin Smith. He was leaving *The Simpsons*. (Smith once pitched a show about me but it never got picked up. Whatever. Next time, ask permission first.)

This was exciting news. Sure, for him (although the show bombed and he was soon out of work) but *also* for me: there was now an opening at the show for a writer!

And yet I *still* hadn't heard from Alex about any of the ideas that I had passed along to him.

We were playing *Half-Life* on Xbox one night. I couldn't take it any longer. I just blurted it out:

"Dude, did you read my episode ideas or what already?"

"Yeah," he replied, eyes on the TV screen.

"And ...?" I asked.

"Some good, some not," he said.

"Okay. So which ones did you like?"

"I can't say I really liked any of them all that much. But some were better than others."

Gee, thanks ... *friend.*

"Like what?" I asked.

"I liked the one where Bart mistakenly joins the Marines."

"Okay. Any others?"

"The one where Homer gets upset with Marge for buying organic food."

"Yeah. I thought it'd be cool to have an episode or two in which Homer isn't the one who's the dickhead."

"Not realistic but it was a funny idea."

"So?"

"So?" he asked, looking at me.

"Now what?"

"What do you mean?"

"Now what? How can I move into your position? On the show?"

Alex wasn't really a laugher. Most professional people in comedy aren't. Some will just say "that's funny," oftentimes in a dry voice. Others will only nod. I know one who will give the thumb's up. And if he's *really* excited, a real *high* thumb's up. He's an idiot.

But after I asked "how can I move into your position," Alex laughed hard.

Very hard.

And for a very long time.

To the point where I thought he was suffering from a fucking fit.

He finished laughing. "It's already filled," he said. "It was filled even before I walked out that door."

"You're shitting me."

"No."

"Who is it? What's his name?"

"It's a *her*."

"You gotta be *double* shitting me! You hired a *woman*?!"

"Sure. Why not?"

"It's a dude's show!"

"It's very much not. Women love it. So why shouldn't a woman write for it?"

I knew as soon as he said this that our friendship was over.

I mean, listen: I *love* women. I *adore* them. And they adore me! I'm a nice guy. I think they're funny in their own peculiar ways. And it wasn't even a question of sex, to be honest. It was more a question of loyalty. *I was his friend. Why* would he *not* have hired me? Or at least put in a good word? How hard is it to do *that*? I'm *always* putting in a good word for someone if I like his work.

We hung around for the rest of the evening but I never saw Alex again. Our friendship was over. He'd call and I'd ignore him until he didn't bother anymore. Mentally, I wished him the best of luck on the animated *Clerks*, even though I sensed the show wasn't long for this world.

Luckily, Alex mistakenly left behind his laptop. *Wa-woopsy!*

I returned it ... but not after copying all of the email addresses for the *Simpsons* writers.

I'm not sure Alex ever learned about this.

If he's now reading this book, first of all, I apologize for calling you "Alex." Your real name is much cooler. Also, I want to say that I could have stolen *all* of your credit cards and social security number and everything else related to your finances, for that matter—but I *didn't*. So there's that.

One has to do what one has to do in order to climb that ladder ...

If that sounds mean or ruthless, so be it. It's nice up here. The view is terrific. Much better than wherever Alex happens to be living and working at the moment. (Actually, I *know* where he is. He's writing for *Call Your Mother* on ABC. By the time you get around to reading this best-selling book, his show will most likely have already been cancelled.)

After I broke up with Alex's sister by fax, I thought long and hard about how to reach that *next* stage of my career. It was close, I could smell it—I could smell the hot and stanky Duff beer's smell on Barney Gumble's breath ...

So damn close!

I even *liked* this smell!

Allow me to digress and really slip into the comedic weeds here. If you're not a comedy nerd, you can skip this section:

Barney Gumble, to me, is what *The Simpsons* is all about. All the feel-good family stories bore me terribly. As much as I love Bart and Homer, the show isn't about them. And certainly it isn't about Marge or the twins or the kids.

I guess you could say *The Simpsons* started off about Bart. But as the show progressed, at least to me, it became so much *more* about Barney than anyone.

Why do I think this?

I'll tell you why: the heart of the show is *sadness*. The saddest character on *The Simpsons* is Barney. He started off bright and smart and well put-together but crumpled into the disaster he eventually became: he's *America*.

Once proud and handsome, Barney is now skimming the bottom of the beer barrel, struggling to survive.

Just like America.

I mean, Barney is a very *American* character.

Why?

Because he's allowed to do whatever the fuck he wants. No one's telling him otherwise. He wants to drink, so he drinks. End of story. He's allowed. He's a grown man. No nanny state is bearing down on him. If he wants to become a disaster, let him. He has no wife to harp on him, which makes his life that much easier.

I once talked about all of this with Matt Groening, the creator of *The Simpsons*. He very much disagreed with me. But that's okay. I know I'm right. I also told him my theory about who *really* shot Mr. Burns. The show portrays the baby girl as the shooter after Burns tried to steal her lollipop. But I always felt the *real* shooter was the dog, Santa's Little Helper. It's just a hunch.

But again: I'm pretty sure I'm right.

Groening disagreed strongly about that as well, and we kind of got into it, back and forth, back and forth. I thought he was mad at me, but I've since heard he doesn't even remember the incident. He's a nice guy and I'm happy to have worked for him—*whoops, I'm getting ahead of myself a bit!* (I've asked Groening a few times to be on my satellite radio show and he's always graciously refused. He just has a very low ego. Or maybe he feels bad he stole my date when we first met at that party and were talking about who *really* shot Mr. Burns. Whatever. That's *long* in the past. He's a good dude.)

Anyway ... with the precious *Simpsons* email addresses in hand (most of them were of the clever variety, like RUtalkin2me@aol.com) I thought about what I should do with them. The gun was loaded. Where and how should I pull the trigger?

I could sell them to the highest bidder for a tremendous amount of money.

I could publish them as an ad in *Variety*. Or I could be smart about all of this and use them to my advantage.

I took a long walk on the Malibu beach. I had much to think about. My career so far had been impressive enough—but I wanted *more*. I *always* wanted more. I *still* want more! I'm voracious. You might be asking: more of *what* exactly? Just *more*. I want it *all*. And I'm an American. *I deserve it all.*

Especially if I *earn* it. Why should I be denied *anything*? I'm not a mope. I adore life and I *think* life adores me—but I haven't asked it recently.

Walking on the beach cleared my head. There were a few ways I could handle what I was about to do but I only had *one* chance. By the time I had walked the length of the beach, I had my answer.

I raced back to my house and sent off an email "blast," a term that probably did not then exist. I very well could have invented it. The email was sent to every *Simpsons* writer whose email I had. And the email read:

Ahoy there, fellow participants in this bizarre game of trying to make people laugh for a living!! Allow me to introduce myself: My name is Skippy Battison and you might have heard about me from my work on the Oscars and other high-end, quality projects. I'm someone who's achieved much in the short time that he's entered the comedy writing business but there's so much more that I'd like to achieve! One of these would be to write at least one episode for The Simpsons. It goes without saying that there are few more hilarious shows out there. This is well understood in the industry. The show is the "gold standard" for what's funny. With that in mind, I'd love to write for the show. I know it's probably not as easy as just saying "I'd love to write for the show," but I've found that sometimes it's easier and quicker to avoid bureaucracy and go straight for the juice. With that in mind, I also know that you don't know me (personally). But you might know my work. In fact, I'm pretty sure you do. I'd love to meet all of you. Drinks on me! Let's consider it a "coming out" party as I step into a brand new world!

Love, Skippy Battison

I listed the bar's location and the time and the date.

Now, this event has been written about *extensively*. There have been at least four oral histories about it, one for *Vulture* and one for *Vice* and two others.

But do you know who has never been interviewed about it for *any* article?

Me.

And I'm here to tell you for the first time what happened at that event.

Everything else you've heard or read is just bullshit.

Here's the *real* deal.

Just as it happened.

And happened to *me.*

Let's start at the beginning:

According to the oral history that was published on *The Onion's AV Club* in 2009 by a certain Nathan Rabin, "it was an unmitigated disaster from start to finish. And one of the saddest examples in showbiz of someone punching above their weight."

Clever. But what the hell does that even mean? I wouldn't call an event that led to a writing gig on *The Simpsons* as being "an unmitigated disaster."

There was *some* truth to the piece, I have to admit.

Out of the seventeen writers I invited, three showed up.

And then they quickly left.

But do you really think I expected *anyone* to show up?

Do you take me for a fool?

Years later, when I was emailing the producer on Marc Maron's podcast to audition as a guest, I told him the real reason for me hosting this get-together. But I never made it onto Marc's show. And so I could never tell the world.

I guess I could have told the world on my *own* show and podcast.

But I just haven't.

Yet another delicious little tidbit I was leaving for my memoir when the time arrived!

And the time has finally arrived!

So here it is.

When I was a kid, maybe seven or eight, a loser in my class invited about ten other boys to his party at a McDonald's off Rockville Pike.

Zero showed up.

Zero.

As in ... *not a single one.*

His mom complained to someone, who knew someone else, who worked for a local paper. This (female) reporter wrote up the story.

And within days, a party was rescheduled with so many kids that they had to hire out an entire bowling alley in Frederick!

I never forgot the lesson in this.

It's not how cool you are.

It's how cool you *aren't* that can help.

It's a party.

But a *pity* party.

And is there anything *wrong* with pitying someone?

In this particular kid's case, yes, people pitied him. And that's why they showed up at the second party. But he earned a ton of *new* friends out of this experience, or so I'm imagining.

It's not as if I kept in touch with the kid.

I mean, shit. I never came to *either* of his parties even though I was invited to both.

So, years later, when I planned my own party with the *Simpsons* writers, I figured I couldn't lose: either the writers for *The Simpsons* would show and I'd get to make a ton of new connections or …

They *wouldn't* show. Which would *also* be fine.

In my case, they *didn't* show.

So I took a full-page out in *Variety* that I created to look as close to an actual *Variety* article as possible.

I wrote it myself. There was a photo of me alone at a bar, posing, head down, looking all mopey.

The headline read: NO SHOWS FOR SHOWBIZ SOIRAY!

A few readers knew right away that it was a paid ad.

Probably because of the "PAID AD" label at the bottom.

Others knew because of the misspelling of "soiree."

The *Vulture* oral history (the first one, anyway, from 2010) quoted an unnamed *Simpsons* writer as saying "it was like a children's birthday party that you'd walk in on and just start to cry. No one there. Banners hanging from the ceiling. Half limp balloons. We left, we couldn't take it. I gasped when I saw it. I *still* think about it."

This was one of the three writers who showed.

I think I know who said this but I won't mention his name even though he didn't have the balls to mention his *own* name when talking to *Vulture*.

But let me say this: if it's who I'm thinking it might be, he was on *The Simpsons* for a total of two and a half years and later wrote for less than one season of *The Boondocks*. And then that's it. End of career.

So there's *that* guy.

Another of the unnamed writers wrote for *The Simpsons* for about three more episodes and then switched over to writing "humor" pieces for *The New Yorker*.

So there's *that* guy.

Finally, the last of these unnamed writers who actually *did* show up at my party claimed that he saw me wearing a rented tux.

This is true.

I'm an aristocrat, what can I say? An aristocrat who doesn't want to spend money on a fucking expensive tux that won't fit him in two years time!

To me, that just sounds *smart*.

Also, was I *really* going to pay full money for a tuxedo when half the purpose of this party was for *no one* to show up?

Seriously?

Three people showed, they left, the photographer took photos, and that was it.

At least for the *first half* of my plan.

The second half was to write the fake article I just told you about, which I did under the byline "Quincy McGillicutty."

Great name, right?

Without bragging, I have to admit that the fake *Variety* article really played up on the sadness of the entire (planned) event.

Here was the gist:

Skippy Battison was a new(ish) writer to Hollywood. He had had some success, perhaps he was a little naïve but he also thought that throwing a really cool party and inviting *Simpsons* writers would help him achieve *more* success.

What's interesting is that the attention that came from this Pity Party came not from the *Variety* ad that I spent $25,000 on but from the *free Onion AV Club* article that was written *about* the *Variety* ad.

Now *that* got attention. Especially with the writer pointing out (correctly) that I had paid for the *Variety* ad myself.

The mystery of why anyone would have done this delighted the entirety of Hollywood. There were mentions on practically every radio and television show and program. Literally, for one week, the story appeared within every crevice of Hollywood, including Harvey Weinstein's own backass (as opposed to his front ass).

People asked:

Why did he do it exactly? On purpose? Has this ever happened before?

Quite honestly, I'm not sure if it had *ever* happened in Hollywood before me.

But I knew it would work. Because I saw it work back when I was a kid in Maryland.

And in recent years, it's become fucking *huge*!

You know the routine: no one shows up at some suburban kid's party, they put up a really sad photo on the web, the clucking hents tweet about it, it goes viral, and now the kid is a millionaire and getting a ton of presents.

Nicely done, parents!

You knew damn well your kid was a loser *before* you threw that party. You knew no one was going to show up because no one RSVP'ed! But you go ahead and have the party *anyway*. Why?

People think I'm joking when I talk about this on my radio show or podcast. But I'm not.

I began this craze. Or I at least made it really popular.

When *The Onion AV Club* article came out there was a tremendous amount of noise within the industry—but, more specifically, within the comedy community.

I received hundreds of emails from people telling me how much they felt sorry for me and wished me well. Some felt sorry that I'd spend $25,000 to get hired.

Whatever.

All I was doing was trying to earn enough pity from the *Simpsons* writers to get my fucking scripts looked at!

Real simple!

Nothing more complicated than that, I promise you!

The odds were in my favor no matter *what* happened that day.

If people showed, great!

If they didn't, *even better!*

I swear to you this is true!

The very day after the *Onion AV Club* article appeared, I received an email from a *Simpsons* writer.

I won't use his name.

But he said he and some other writers wanted to meet with me.

Well that was easy!

The meeting was set at a bar not far from the Fox lot, where the *Simpsons* writers' room was located. When I walked in, a group of writers was already sitting around a large circular table. A few of them tittered, almost as if they couldn't help themselves.

As I said before, there are people I've found over the years who induce laughter just by existing. And I seem to be one of those people. Which is fine.

I'd rather have a stranger laugh at me than cry or gag!

I took a seat and everyone was very welcoming. The questions began immediately: Was I the guy who got conned by an Israeli fake producer? Was the party for real? Did I write the *Variety* ad? Why did I write the *Variety* ad? Did I write the earlier *Variety* ads? Was I genuinely upset at Billy Crystal for not using my original parody

Gilligan's Island song lyrics? Did I really know that the ads would be so funny? Was this all an act? And if it was, did I really spend close to $75,000 on the ads in the various trades?

Etc.

Their curiosity intrigued me. They were almost looking at me as if I was some type of exotic creature.

Seems that I had already made a name for myself in the industry!

A woman writer asked, "Is this all a prank? Like an Andy Kaufman thing?"

I knew nothing about Andy Kaufman at the time but I played along and I said that Andy was a *huge* influence on me and my work. This seemed to make them happy, which made *me* happy.

I later learned this was the very woman writer who replaced my friend Alex! I still don't know her name.

"Yeah, Andy Kaufman," I said.

"What do you like about him?" asked the woman writer.

I then said something that might or might not have gone over well. I really didn't know a thing about him. There was a look exchanged between the writers. Trying to change the subject, I said, "And as far as the Israeli guy, I did get conned. $125,000. Yeah."

Everyone started talking at once.

They were laughing and nodding and I felt now would be a great time to pitch them my episode ideas. I started off with the strong ones (Homer accuses Marge of stealing his paycheck to buy organic food, Bart meets the inventor of Adobe Photoshop, Lisa quits playing jazz and learns the sax licks for Spin Doctors songs ...)

The ideas all seemed to go over well, with a lot of shared looks that they gave one another, as if to say *"This* guy, he's *definitely* one of us!"

Then there were more questions about the *Variety* ads and the Israeli producer and how much I lost.

Jesus. *Didn't I already go over all this?*

One of the bar's waiters, a guy in his early twenties, not much younger than I was, overheard some of the conversation and asked if we were writers for *The Simpsons.* When he heard that we were, he became very excited—down right ... *animated.*

(Sorry! *Had to do it.*)

"I've *always* wanted to write for that show! It's been a dream of mine forever! How could I make it happen? What would I have to do?!"

I looked over at the others. We gave each other a look, as if to imply: *Sorry, pal! It doesn't just happen that way. You have to* make *it happen. And even then, you have to get really lucky and pay your dues.*

One of the writers was nice enough to tell the waiter that it was impossible but that he should keep trying, and the waiter happily left, perhaps even thinking he had a chance.

Poor bastard.

I had been in the game for far too long to not realize that he actually *didn't* have a chance. But I didn't say a word. Let the kid have his dreams. What else does he have? Besides a shitty job in a crappy bar near the Fox lot? I mentally wished the kid my best.

The evening ended really well. I offered to pay for everyone's drinks and sliders, and we hugged outside the bar.

"So we can meet again?" I asked.

"Sure," said one of them.

"Yeah," said another.

"And *my* ideas?" I asked. "About episodes?"

"How much again did you lose?" asked one.

Around this time, I have to admit, I was pretty exhausted and probably a bit too whiffled from drink to even *try* to pretend that I was interested in repeating this story.

"Jesus, enough with that shit already! How about me just writing for you guys?"

Silence.

What was their game here?

If they weren't a fan of my comedic stylings, why even meet with me?

They said goodbye, we all shook hands, I hugged the one woman writer (I'm still forgetting her name), and they took off, leaving me behind. Confused—and a bit angry.

I just spent over $100 on drinks and sliders and fried pickles ... *and for what exactly?*

Was I a joke to them?

Here's the thing about me: I don't like being the butt of a joke. I don't like being the butt of *anything*.

It was nice of them to want to meet with me, to hook up with a like-minded comedic talent.

But I was now angry. And when I get angry I become *very* determined.

I was going to write a *Simpsons* episode that would eventually air—*at least one episode*—or I was going to die trying. There's a look I get in my eyes when I want something. It's hard to describe. Primitive, maybe. I just know that there's an obstacle in front of me and I need to get *past* that obstacle.

This look has been described to me over the years as a steely gaze that can cut through anything in its path. The person who described this look was a state prosecutor I had to deal with when I was arrested in high school for stealing radios out of expensive cars in Bethesda. He also said some other things—none of which was very nice—but I don't really give a shit what he said. It was the "steely gaze" description that I've always remembered.

Basically, *stand the fuck back! Skippy coming through, yo!*

It was interesting: a day earlier I would have thought that writing for *The Simpsons* would have been the biggest deal to me.

Now that I saw, for my own eyes, how stuck-up these assholes were and how much they didn't understand who I really was, I couldn't have cared less about working *full time* on the show. I just wanted *one* episode under my belt for bragging rights.

I sent them an email the night after we met:

"Could we maybe meet again to talk more about me writing for the show? Or contributing jokes?"

Crickets.

Yeah. I thought so. Now I know *so. Pricks!*

Is this the way they treated a fellow comedy writer?!

I mean, c'mon, man!

How hard would it be for them to just let it fucking happen?!

I really did feel—perhaps naively—that I was going to walk out of the bar that night with an episode under my belt. That didn't happen.

But that didn't mean that it *couldn't* happen.

I called my father back in D.C. Of course, he wanted to know when I was next coming home. Getting that shit out of the way, I told him my predicament. I asked if he knew any Fox executives. He told me that of course he did. He knew a few from back when he used to lobby for the repeal of the "Fairness Doctrine" for the GOP in the late 1980s, whatever the fuck that meant.

"In plain English," I said to him. "Can you talk in plain fucking English? Can you help me get on *The Simpsons* or not?!"

My father, of course, knew nothing about the show—or barely knew anything. "Is that the sitcom with the character who drinks all that beer and soda?" he asked.

I rolled my eyes.

Of course he'd know *that*.

"Yes," I said. "But he's not real. He's animated."

"Animated is just as good," he answered. "Maybe even *better* than real."

Whatever. Do you know someone who could help or not?

I'll see what I can do.

Fine.

Are you coming to visit—

See ya, pops!

The first thing I did after getting off the line with my father was to again email the group I had just met, thanking them for meeting with me. I told them that I hoped they had a terrific time and I trusted that they liked all of my ideas for episodes, I really did!

What I didn't write was this:

What was I? A fucking slob off the street? A fucking creature in a zoo they just wanted to goggle at?

Was that all I was good for?!

So I decided to play them like I had played the single women in the bars whenever I wanted to get laid in years past.

Do you remember when I talked earlier about my move with women that I called "The Ax"?

As in, "I'm going to give the woman the ax"?

This was when I'd just end the conversation and not talk with the woman and they're wondering what exactly happened?

I decided to give this a try with the *Simpsons* writers.

I didn't write another email to any of the writers for nearly two weeks. It was my hope that they'd wonder *why* I wasn't interested in them and that they'd *then* get back to me to find out why.

When this didn't work, I switched to the "God, You Smell Great … for a Girl" approach.

I'd compliment them on their show but in a backhanded way. By doing this, I was hoping they'd inevitably ask what I felt wasn't working and then perhaps ask me to help fix it.

So I sent a group email to the gang that basically said, *Listen, I like this season of the show but it's not as solid as previous seasons. There's* one *thing in particular that's bothering me. But I'd rather tell you guys in person.*

When this didn't work as planned, I launched into my "Mushrooming" act, in which I'd lift the spirits or ego of the group until their egos were mushrooming like a nuclear cloud.

"That last episode was incredible! We're so overdue for a drink!"

When *this* didn't work, I knew I was dealing with one tough dame.

If anything, it only made me *more* determined.

And when I'm determined … well, the look in my eyes would make the look in Rosie O'Donnell's eyes as she heads to the fridge at 2:00 A.M. look like child's play.

I talk about this on my podcast all the time and you're probably quite familiar with all of this already. For those who don't listen to either my podcast or satellite radio show (and if you don't, honestly, fuck off), I'll just tell you that, quite simply, I *did* end up writing a *Simpsons* episode and I am very proud of it. My "Right-of-Wayers" will sometimes call to tell me that they agree that it's the best episode ever. One even told me that he and his girlfriend were watching it when their son was conceived. That's pretty cool. I wonder if the kid's name is Bart or Lisa?

Kabing. *Kaboom*! Ka-*Shwing*!

Here's what went down: there was a big wig at Fox my father had known for years.

My father called in a favor—a *big* one. God knows what *kompromat* my father had over this Fox exec—the rumors were either photos or a sex video—but it *worked*. "Sure! I can help your son! No problem!"

I sent this guy all of my ideas for the show, as well as my ideas for jokes.

I will not mention this guy's name as he's still, shockingly, married.

But he did me a *major*.

If you're a fan of *The Simpsons,* you no doubt have seen the episode that I was ultimately responsible for. It was yet another example of *The Simpsons* predicting the future. Have you heard about this?

In so many cases—and there have been at least fifteen to twenty instances—the writers for *The Simpsons* have somehow predicted the future, whether it's with specific events or with detailed inventions. In my case, the episode that I wrote predicted that Trump would one day become the President of the United States. Keep in mind that this episode aired in March of 2000, a full *sixteen years* before Trump actually *did* become President. It was called "Bart to the Future."

When I turned in the script, it was titled "Rezzies for Four." It's a pretty simple premise: The entire family, including that dopey granddad, takes a vacation to an Indian reservation. While there, Bart smokes a "peace pipe" and hallucinates what happens to his family in the future. The idea was straightforward but it allowed me to *really* dig deep into a lot of ideas and jokes.

Sadly, the version that you ended up seeing and the version that I had turned in weren't at all similar. My draft was quite different from the finished, animated version that ended up being broadcast on Fox.

But I am here to tell you that my first version was *funnier*.

Far fucking funnier.

But funny doesn't matter much in Hollywood.

That's pretty typical.

Do you know what's also typical?

To be shunted out of the process completely and to not be allowed to so much as participate at a table read.

I wasn't allowed to do *anything*.

I wasn't allowed to give my two cents while others yelled out jokes to replace mine. I wasn't allowed to be at the recording sessions to suggest last minute fixes.

I wasn't allowed to do fucking *anything* ... except send this executive my script and then wait.

And wait.

And wait.

And fucking ... *wait*.

For two fucking years.

Two.

Fucking.

Years.

Even worse, I just knew my script would be ruined by these assholes.

And they very clearly *were* assholes.

Fuck the script you ended up seeing.

Take a gander at *my* original script:

It opens with the family deciding to head to an Indian reservation so Homer can bet at their casino and buy cheap and tax-free booze and cigarettes. Once there, an Indian chief takes a liking to Bart, recognizing in him a likeness to a friend from the Indian's past life. The Indian's name is Horny Bull, which cracks Bart up. After smoking, Bart hallucinates that he's a rock and roll star (very similar to one of my all-time favorite rockers and very good friend, Ted Nugent) and that he's surrounded by much wealth and gorgeous ladies.

Immediately, Bart loves it.

Why wouldn't he? Being a rock star kicks fucking ass! Especially if you look like Ted Nugent!

(Hey, Ted!)

In her particular dream, Lisa becomes the first female president of the United States, taking over from Donald Trump. In the final version, Lisa is shown to be competent and Donald Trump just the opposite. In my version, it's the opposite of *that*—Donald is one of the *best* fucking presidents since Lincoln, and Lisa is an asshole goody-goody.

Mine was *realistic* and *funny*.

What eventually aired was *bullshit* and *not-so-funny*.

Mine was fresh and cutting edge.

Theirs was *limp* and *pathetic*.

In *his* dream, Homer, also a fan of the Donald's, ends up living in Trump Plaza with Marge, and becomes the condo president, which at first annoys Donald, until he finds that Homer is fun as hell to have around and markets a beer named after him called *Trump's Liquid Homer*.

The script is hilarious and it's not just me saying that. There's a bootleg version of it available online and I highly recommend that you seek it out and read it.

Some assholes have claimed that I never had *anything* to do with this episode, as my IMDB page lists nothing about having written for *The Simpsons*.

Fuck off.

They took my name off out of spite. And for no other reason.

And if you don't believe that I originally wrote this *Simpsons* script, I have a copy of a deposit check from Fox to prove otherwise.

I want you to read my script and to *then* watch the finished version of the episode. Please tell me that the final version is funnier. Seriously. Compare the two. And if you *still* think my script isn't much funnier, then you're as mentally challenged as the current Democratic President of the United States.

I was one and done at *The Simpsons*. I pitched them additional script ideas (like Homer becoming an acrobat. Sound familiar?) and more jokes, and I asked them multiple times if they wanted to hit another bar to celebrate the success of my episode, but I never heard back. To be fair, they may not have been allowed to talk to me for legal reasons.

I hold no grudge. They were geeky and dorky and I hated everything about them from the get-go but they *have* produced okay work over the years and I'm happy to be able to tell the world that I'm also a *Simpsons* writer.

How many writers can claim that honor? Not many, I'm imagining.

So the episode was all set to air in March of 2000.

I flew back home, if only to shut my parents up. I landed and immediately hit a few bars to meet old friends. It was interesting: I felt that I had lived a million lives since I had seen them last. They had mostly gone off to colleges and didn't seem to have grown much. They were still naïve about the real world, it seemed. They were innocent. Giggling and doing beer bongs.

Oooooh! Adults!

I likened myself to a kid who headed off to join the carnival at a young age.

It ages you *quickly*. A week on the streets is equivalent to a year anywhere else, especially if it's ivy covered. I had zero interest in their fraternity stories. Their relationships to women seemed no different than they had been back in high school. They seemed protected and innocent and not yet ready to graduate and enter the real world and all of the madness that it so often contains.

I felt for them. And silently wished them the best.

I *still* feel for them.

Lambs to the slaughter.

I did tell them about all of my adventures, and invited them to join me at my parents' house for a party to celebrate the airing of my *Simpsons* episode. They eagerly agreed. They were super thrilled for me.

For them, it was nice to see someone from the group "make it" in the real world. It gave them true hope that they could also become a success. The difference was that I never had the patience to wait. I *always* went for it.

But that's just how I operate. It's the difference between, say, a leopard and a sloth. I'm on the plains of Africa taking down prey. Others are sitting in trees, fiddling with their animal anuses. (I'm not against a nice *anus fiddle* every now and again, but I don't ever want to make it a goddamn career!)

My childhood house was packed that night. All my friends were there. Some knew each other, others didn't. My nearly brain-dead friend Jimmy (remember the guy with the scar on his forehead?) had never met the Flammer but everyone got along really well. I ordered square pizza from Lido's, a couple of kegs of Natty Boh, and we were off and flying.

My parents were standing in the back, taking it all in. I could tell they were super proud. My father had spent a ton of money to get me to this point. It hadn't been easy on him or on my mother (or on *me*, for that matter) but it seemed now to all be worth it.

Truthfully, although my mother was proud, she *still* didn't seem to *totally* comprehend what was going on.

But that's okay. I now consider my mom one of my biggest fans and I can guarantee you that every day at 2:30 P.M. when my satellite radio show is broadcast live, and every Friday afternoon when my podcast is released, she is most definitely in her golf cart at the Chevy Chase Country Club, listening to me on her iPhone with her new husband.

I'm still forgetting his name.

People started arriving at my parents' house around 4:30 or so. By the 7:00, air time, everyone was super zoop-whished and ready to let loose and laugh and have just an amazing fucking time.

This is why I was put on earth. *To make people laugh.*

The episode began with the famous theme song that everyone already knows and loves. The room erupted. My high school friend Leigh stood up and applauded and spilled half of his drink on my mother's rug, which she has *still* not forgiven him for. It's okay, mom! He's now the vice president of Potomac Utility and remains my biggest fan. He's even told me that he *forces* his drivers to listen to my radio show every day!

The credits started to roll and someone "shushed" everyone else up and yelled "Wait for Skippy's name!"

The room quieted down ... and everyone was waiting ... and still waiting ... and then there were the "Written By" credits ... and where was my name?!

I heard a friend of mine say, "What in the fuck?"

A few friends turned to me, as if to say, *Are you okay?* and a few as if to say, *Are you shitting with us?*

I played it real cool even though I was dying inside: "It's all normal, guys! I wrote the episode but had some help from other writers. It's a political thing!"

That quieted things down a bit and the episode began after the commercial and the party went crazy with laughter and it never stopped.

Which was great.

Except that I wasn't responsible for any of it.

The script I had turned in was *completely different*, as I already pointed out.

In fact, it was *totally* different.

It might be the only case of a *Simpsons* writer turning in a script in which zero percent of the jokes made it to air.

I should take that back.

The show that I watched had *two* of my jokes from the original script, both names of fake stores in a shopping mall.

One joke was about a restaurant that only served venison: *Deer John*.

The other was a joke about a children's toy store that was named *Everything Plastic Crap*.

After the episode ended, there was applause and a lot of noise and someone yelled, "Look for Skippy's name!" I knew it was useless but pretended we'd be able to see it in the end credits, and that it wasn't going to be too fast to read.

Later, I bought this episode, and others, on DVD and I rewatched it, slowing down the end credits to where I could actually read the names and titles.

And there it was, at the very end, or close to the very end: *Special Thank You to Skippy Battison*.

But if you were watching the episode in real time, live, and you were watching it with a crowd that was too drunk to see and incredibly loyal to an old friend from your schooldays, you'd *easily* miss it.

Which they did.

The room became very quiet.

And although we had a great rest of the evening, with plenty of food and booze and even a rendition from The Flammer of "Piano Man" on the spoons, the night was sort of a bummer for me.

I received a ton of congratulations but it was hard to convince all of these people that I really *had* been responsible for what they had just seen—or two of the jokes, anyway.

I was *not* about to stand there and patiently explain how my version would have been so much better. Doing something like that would only have been too inside baseball for a group of suburbanites in Maryland.

A few guests patted me on the shoulder on their way out: *Great job! We're so fucking proud!*

Others didn't even care that they hadn't seen my name. They trusted me complicity that I *had* written the episode and that was *enough* for them.

My parents hugged me before heading upstairs and leaving the cleanup to Miss Benda.

I didn't know *what* to think. Yes, I had written a script that became a *Simpsons* episode. And that's pretty damn cool!

Shit, I can live with that!

I would say 99.9% of the world won't ever have one joke in *The Simpsons*, let alone *two*.

It's like a baseball player with two hits.

Hell, at least the guy made it to the major leagues! How many people can claim *that*?!

But when I think about it now, it kind of bugs me. It must have been jealousy on the writers' parts. Or anger for being "forced" to take on this project. This has been written about in a ton of *Simpsons* books, and in a book of interviews with comedy writers called *Killing a Dead Horse,* which I haven't read, as I wasn't asked to participate.

A *Simpsons* writer whose name I won't mention claimed in his own book that my name sort of became a joke around the office. As in "You're acting Skippy" or "You're pulling a Skippy" or "You just wrote a Skippy" or "Somebody just Skippied!"

As in, "I can't stand the way you're acting/writing right now" or "that joke is a stinker." It's become shorthand for a type of person who really wants to succeed but doesn't have the ability. Whether that's true or not, I *do* take offense to it.

To begin, they don't really *know* me. Maybe they *think* they know me, but they don't truly know me or really understand what I'm capable of achieving in a comedic sense.

Second, I've found that some of the worst bullies in life are those who were *themselves* bullied when they were young. I don't know each of the backstories to every *Simpsons* writer, but I can assure you that they weren't the popular class clowns in school. They were more likely skipping class to read geeky graphic novels in the library. And I can guarantee you that they weren't out pulling pranks with the best of them!

I wouldn't trade the success I had in high school for the world!

I wouldn't have *wanted* to have been a member of the *Harvard Lampoon* for anything or anyone! (I did have my father take a look at me attending Harvard about eighteen years ago just to be able to say that I worked on the *Lampoon* for a year and maybe to improve my chances in Hollywood but thankfully that didn't work out. Looking back, it seems kind of a naïve thing to have done.)

I'm happy with who I've become. I came *from* nothing and I achieved everything I've achieved *by myself*. If the dorks at *The Simpsons* want to make fun of me, then fine. I'll just weep to myself about feeling like an outsider—*and to a million other listeners to my podcast and satellite radio show*.

There are people out there who love me.

A lot of them!

And I find myself lucky that I found them.

So that was *The Simpsons* situation.

For the year after that *Simpsons* episode aired, I concentrated on writing TV spec scripts for other shows, both animated and not.

I also wrote a ton of movie scripts, including one of my favorites. It was about a talking car that hated its driver. They would bicker in a very funny manner. At one point, the guy buys a foreign car but he can't understand it because of its obnoxious foreign accent. The guy then goes back to the American car and they do eventually become friendly and bond over their love of long drives and full-grain leather.

It was called "B.U.R.T."

Or "Better Unbuckle youR seatbelT."

I visited my family a few more times because I had promised my father.

I got into a fight with my brother and sister-in-law over a lawn ornament.

(Listen to my satellite radio show from 3/5/18 in the "Batty Barchives" for that one.)

I got laid a few times—okay, *more* than a few times.

I "Obtained" and "Completed" and "Remained."

I "Mushroomed" and "Skotched" and "Axed."

I became addicted to a new drink I invented called the SlingShoT.

(Want to know the recipe? It's delicious! Half Crystal Pepsi and half SKYY vodka with just a twist of fresh lime. Check out my website for specific details on how to make it!)

I got rid of my AOL email and started an even cooler one over at Hotmail.

And I soon got rid of that Hotmail account and started an *even cooler one* over at Gmail!

I relied a bit on rent from the Flammer, *still* working as a goddamn house painter in Ocean City, Maryland!

Before I knew it, it was the summer of 2001, around mid August.

What happened next would change my life forever.

But not in ways that might be considered for "the best."

In fact, I had *no idea* as to how *bad* things would get. Not just for my career but for me as a human being.

But all that was yet to come … and boy, did it ever! ….

★ **Chapter Eleven** ★

THE NIGHTMARE OF 9/11

I have to be perfectly honest: I really wasn't affected too much by 9/11.

But I can *certainly* understand those who *were* affected by it.

★ Chapter Twelve ★
A + B = COMEDY

The *real* nightmare for me began in October 2001.

I was feeling a bit … adrift after the *Simpsons* situation, to be perfectly candid.

My career so far had been pretty goddamn impressive. But I just felt that there was somehow *more* that I could accomplish. *So much more!*

I didn't know *what*, though. That's the funny thing about life.

Sometimes you just feel that you want *more*. But you don't even know *where* to look or *what* to look for.

And I had been fucked over but good by those *Simpsons* assholes.

I was tired.

I was dragging a bit.

But Skippy Battison is not one to feel sorry for himself.

No, sir!

Remember his love for Ayn Rand?

No, all this moping just wouldn't do.

It was time to discover a new path.

In October 2001, I discovered the Learning Annex.

If you're not familiar with the Learning Annex, and if you weren't around in the early 2000s to have taken at least one of their courses, which I'm imaging you wouldn't have been, as they sucked, let me explain: the company set up a system by which you could take courses on all different subjects, be it writing, acting, or dancing, painting, business, or hanging your hairy nuts outside the window to dry just for the hell of it.

Literally, there were *hundreds* of classes for anyone to take, all taught by "experts" in their fields.

I use the quotes around the word *experts* for a good reason.

Remember when I said earlier that my advice for a young comedy fan is to take advice by those who have *made* it? And to ignore advice from those who can't make a living at what they're teaching?

If you had taken a look at a Los Angeles Learning Annex catalog back in 2001, you would have seen a few things.

One: there would have been a lot of courses about how to "make it" in showbiz.

And two: none of these courses would have been taught by people actually *making a living* in showbiz.

There was a class about acting, taught by a guy whose name I won't mention, but who hadn't acted in years. There was a class on movie directing taught by a guy who had directed commercials for pet food.

And then there was writing.

So many writing courses. *Oodles* of writing courses. All taught by writers who hadn't made a successful career at writing. One wrote a few spec scripts for *Golden Girls*. Another had a "Story By ..." credit on *Boiler Room*.

Not exactly the *aristocrecy* of Hollywood scriptwriters.

I was at an outdoor café in Malibu one afternoon reading over a Learning Annex catalog, beautiful women walking past me, the sun shining, the sound of the ocean barely off in the distance ... when I hit upon my next venture:

I'd start my *own* fucking Learning Annex.

For writers only.

Taught by someone at the *pinnacle* of his profession. Me!

Why not, right?

I could use something to take up my time until my next writing gig peeked its furry little head up over the horizon.

I could also use some extra spending money and it'd be a terrific way to meet women.

Always another boner! Er, *bonus*!

And I could meet a ton of young writers who might be able to help *me* down the road.

Does that sound selfish?

It isn't.

Let me explain to the neophyte:

In Hollywood, everyone (no matter at what level) is looking to take advantage of others, be they *below* you or *above* you. Tomorrow's stars are today's students.

It took me years to figure the following out: *it's not how good you are*.

It's who you *know*.

Simple as that.

Let me repeat that:

It does not matter how good you are. It does not matter how many books you have read or written. It does not matter how much you practice.

It's really quite simple and it comes down to this one sentence:

It. Is. Who. You. Know.

Memorize that.

Write it out in fucking calligraphy and place it on your goddamn fridge.

I don't care what you do with it. Just know that this is the ultimate truth about success in Hollywood.

Or, for that matter, for comedy.

Okay. Let's break this down:

Say someone submits a packet to a writing show and it's *incredible*. Say another writer submits a packet and it's just *okay*. The producer knows the latter but not the former.

Who gets hired?

Showbiz isn't the NFL where if someone ain't cutting it in the 30-yard dash, he gets fired, no questions asked. In sports, it's all about numbers and speed and strength and all the rest of it.

Showbiz is *entirely* different.

It's high school with plentiful pussy.

That's all it is.

Knowing people and them knowing you.

And them *liking* you.

No one wants to be stuck with an asshole in an office all day!

So *know* someone.

But also have them *like* you.

Over the years, I've done many things to get people to hire me.

Things like sending them gifts or even just giving them a "loan" that I later conveniently forgot all about.

It's important to be known.

And it's important to be *liked*!

As for me, I had no problem with networking with students just starting out.

So they were younger.

So what?

What does it—or *why* should it?—matter as to how many spins around the ol' sun I've taken compared with others?

For me to network with those who were younger than I was, well, that was a damn *smart* thing to do.

This has been talked about in various Hollywood circles and on certain "real life" documentaries about me.

But at first, it really was just a way to make some small change and to spread the gospel of comedy, and to make some connections. That's it.

When I tell you that this wasn't a Trump University endeavor, I'm telling the truth.

All of the accusations that came later, whether having to do with pyramid schemes or sexual harassment or micro- or macro-aggressions, were all based on the fallacy that my intentions were *not* good.

Wrong!

They *were*.

How can I prove this?

I can't. But it's the truth.

So let's back up and start at the beginning:

In October 2001, I was between writing gigs. I'd wander the beach during the day, hit the cigar bars at night, sometimes I'd get lucky, sometimes I wouldn't, but I was just trying to keep busy. I'd speak with the Flammer back in Ocean City to see how he was doing. The answer was always the same: he was hungover and he was painting houses. And his knees and his back hurt. *Blah blah blah*. That's it.

In a way, this was an X-ray version of my life. The exact *opposite* of where I was but could easily end up if I didn't pay attention to where I was headed.

There's nothing wrong with painting houses for a living in Ocean City, Maryland. It just wasn't—and isn't—for me. It's for people like Flammer who (and how do I put this delicately?) might not have been born to become a success on his own.

Flammer, like a lot of people, is just a guy who needs a helping hand to reach a position he might not have been able to reach all by his lonesome.

Someone without a ton of dreams or fantasies. Someone who heads straight home after work and plays video games while eating Doritos.

And god bless.

I admire people like that.

Without many cares, it must be a hell of an easy way to live.

I wish I were so simple in my needs and desires.

But I'm not. I need to *achieve*. And it's a hunger. And it never ends. And once you catch it, it's like Herpes Simplex one or two. (I always forget which is which, but they both suck. My luck, I'll one day catch Herpes Simplex *three*.)

You can *never* get rid of it.

The first order of business was to find an office in which I could teach.

A friend of mine from one of my favorite bars told me about a friend of his who was leasing a small space for the cheap in the San Fernando Valley.

While not an area I liked or had ever been to, I decided that this would be the *perfect* location for my enterprise.

I next had to come up with a name. I made a short list:

The Learning Alcove

The Learning Center

The Learning School for Adults

Comedy University

Laff U Silly

They were all amazing names. In the end, I went with The Learning Alcove. I trademarked the name, fixed up the office as it was a bit untidy and still filled with items left over from the last inhabitant (a low-level porn company called Spread Productions), and I got down to the difficult work of trying to figure out what exactly I'd be teaching.

There were a few ways I could go with this. I could concentrate only on TV writing. I could concentrate only on movie writing, or I could teach writing comedy for print.

I went with all three. It'd be more work for me but why not hit every topic and gain the *widest* audience available?

It seemed like a no brainer.

Before long I had my choice of offerings for students:

Television Writing 101

Movie Writing 101

Writing Comedy for Print 101

The last class was a bit of a misnomer, to be perfectly honest. While I had achieved a ton of success with the television and some for movies, I hadn't really written anything for *print*.

Except for one major thing.

A few months previous, I had discovered a parody newspaper out of Madison, Wisconsin, called *The Onion*.

I thought it was okay. Nothing great.

Just on a lark, I thought I'd try to pitch them some headline ideas.

I got the name of an editor from another writer who'd already sold them some jokes, and I sent a pitch with my headline suggestions.

Here are a few of the headlines:

Hendrix, Lennon Come to Blows in Rock and Roll Heaven

Zimbabwe's F.C.C. Cracks Down on Seven Dirty Clicks

Executioner Closes Eyes, Imagines Applause Solely for Him

*Axl Rose Changes Name to "Fifer Junks Jot,"
Anagram for "Just Jerkin' Off"*

Area Man Tired of Female Bullshit

"Pussy Patrol" Certificate Professionally Framed

*Local Drummer Still Intimidated by Tommy Lee's
1994 Upside-Down-Solo*

*Op-Ed: "So Maybe the Rape Whistle Wasn't the
Best Chrismukkah Gift"*

Scientists: High Levels Of Lead Found In Lead

Friends Saw Hack Screenwriter's Suicide Coming

I showed the headlines to all my comedy friends and they really loved them. One accused me of stealing a few of his headlines. Actually, all but one of his headlines. But, overall, they told me that for someone who had never before submitted to *The Onion,* this was a *brilliant* set of headlines.

I readily agreed.

I emailed the heds and waited. And waited. And waited.

After a week or so, I called up the *Onion* office in Madison. Turns out they had just moved to New York a year or so before. I called *that* number. I talked with an intern, I'm forgetting her name, who told me that it could sometimes take a long time to hear back about a submission—if at all.

If at all?!

Who were these people? The fucking editors of *The Wall Street Journal?!*

Let me talk with a superior, I said.

The main editor? she asked.

Don't give a shit who it is, I said. Just get me someone with some pull.

She said someone would call back.

No one ever did.

Later that afternoon I called back. Same intern. I gave her the same request. But I wasn't taking no for an answer this go round.

An editor finally came on the line. I asked if he was the top editor. He said he was. Whether this was true or not, I don't know. But I felt that this was maybe the best I could do.

I asked about the status for my headlines. He said he didn't know. Furthermore, he said, he didn't care.

Are you fucking kidding me? I asked. Why would you not care that a professional comedy writer just sent you a really solid batch of headlines?

For fucking free!!!

Do you know how many headlines we receive a day? he said.

Playing along, I said, Ten?

Hundreds, he answered.

Great, I replied. But what does that have to do with *my* batch?

It has to do with the fact that we receive loads. And we'll get to yours. Or we won't. Have you sold to us before?

No, I replied.

We'll get to them, he replied. Or maybe we won't.

I hung up on the bastard.

Is this how they treated talent? If so, fuck them and the Wisconsin boat they sailed to New York on. Bunch of assholes!

I put it out of my mind. I was above them and I could always find a place for these jokes in future projects—they were *that* good, I felt.

A month or two goes by and I received a call from a friend: "Hey! Did you see this week's *Onion?*"

No. Why?

Your headline is in it!

What?! Why wouldn't they have told me?!

That's not how they work! Go check it out!

I drove to where I typically picked up a copy of *The Onion* but they were out. Or they hadn't been delivered yet. I then spent the rest of the morning driving around Los Angeles looking for the current issue. By sunset, I had found it. And my friend had been right. There, staring right back at me, was the headline I had submitted:

"Drunk Driving Certificate Professionally Framed"

They had tweaked my joke, made it their own, which was fine with me. But where the fuck was my money?

I called the office in New York. No answer. I called back. Still no answer. Hell was going on?

Granted, there had been a terrorist attack in New York the morning before.

But what did that have to do with them? As far as I understood, their office was nowhere near ground zero.

The next day, I called again. And again. And again.

Nothing.

About a week later I finally got through. Same intern. I told her the situation and asked to speak to a superior.

He's busy.

Why?

He just is. It's been a busy time.

Huh?!

We went back and forth for a bit and then she hung up on me. I called back but no one answered.

At this point, I thought, *Fuck it.* Who cares if I don't get paid? I'm officially now an *Onion* writer, whatever that's worth, and probably worth very little.

Cut ahead a month or so ... and guess what?

It seems that being an *Onion* writer was, indeed, worth a lot.

(Side note: Years later, after I had *truly* made it, I talked with potential Saudi investors about a conservative version of *The Onion* to be called *The Shallot*. It never got off the ground but I'm still into the idea. Why should all headlines, even supposedly funny ones, lean left? Why can't a funny headline pass you on your fucking *right*? There's no reason why not. Let's make it *happen*.)

Shockingly, when I put out the advertisements for *The Learning Alcove,* the thing most people responded to was that I had been published in *The Onion!*

I know. It's insane. More so than writing for TV and coming close to writing for cinema! And all because I had written a stupid joke for a fake newspaper originally out of Wisconsin, now out of New York!

The full advertisement I took out in various trade newspapers (including *Variety*) read like this:

Simpsons and Onion Writer Teaches the Secret to Making a Living at Comedy!

Three Different Courses!

TV!

MOVIE!

PRINT!

Simple. To the point. Accurate. Eye-catching. *Irresistible*.
I inserted my new Gmail email address at the bottom and waited.
Literally within a few hours, the emails started rolling in.
I'm 55 and always wanted to write comedy but never knew how! I'm interested! How much?
Simpsons my favorite shit! How much?
I might be interested how much?
Clearly, most people were more interested in how much this was going to cost than in what I was going to teach.
That was interesting.
I hadn't even thought about the cost, to be honest. How much would be fair based on all my experience and expertise? The Learning Annex typically charged between $250 and $350 for a five week course, one night a week.
That seemed a bit low for me.
Fuck it.
I doubled those figures and decided to charge $500 for a five week course in PRINT (one night a week) and $750 for my TV and MOVIE classes (also five weeks, one night a week).
The emails kept arriving, and within a few days, I had more than thirty students for all of the classes.
But I knew this wasn't enough.
Have you heard about the dipshit who used to teach his three-act Hollywood script structure to thousands of students across the country, selling out huge halls, giving the same shit speech over and over again about how each story should have three acts and that there should be *this* in the first act, *that* in the second act—

And I'm falling asleep just typing it out.

I forget his name. But he was an asshole. And yet he'd give the same spiel night after night, day after day, year after year. And he made a goddamn *fortune* doing it!

The more that I thought about it, the more I wanted to do something bigger than just stand in a shit classroom a few nights a week, teaching losers the art of comedy.

Why not combine teaching with some of my comedic stylings? Make it a fun night, as well as an informative night? Talk to *hundreds* of people in different cities across the country?

Shit, at the very least it'd be fun as hell!

I've always loved to travel. And if I were to be paid really well do to so, all the better!

I took out advertisements in various national writing magazines and I contacted writing centers across the country to post an ad on their bulletin boards. Obviously, if I were to do this today, which I wouldn't ever need to do, as I have *more* than enough money, thank you very much, I would just shoot a video, put it online, and watch the cash flow in.

Couldn't do that back in 2001. Wasn't even an option.

This was the best I could do.

I put my head down, reached out to a million places (typically through fax at the local library) and drummed up some magic. Within a week, I had fifteen events set up throughout the country. On average, twenty or thirty students were signing up for each event.

My PO Box became filled with checks and cash.

It was as easy as that!

Holy crap! Why hadn't I thought of this earlier?!

I contacted the person I knew who owned the Spread Productions office and told him to fuck off. I didn't need it anymore.

Why take a bus to heaven when you can take a goddamn plane?

(He didn't understand this metaphor but it didn't matter. I hadn't paid him anything, I hadn't signed anything, and I was obligated for *nothing*. Funnily enough, I ran across him a few years later at my lawyer's office. We were both suing different people. Not sure he recognized me but I definitely recognized him. He was ugly.)

I mapped out my itinerary, booked hotel rooms, did all this myself, no assistant, just put my head down and did what needed to be done.

It never really occurred to me that I actually needed to come up with material that I'd be talking about. Comedy for me has always come so easily that teaching it to those who don't find it easy ... well, that might not be so easy. But with the number of students adding up, I decided to get to work on what I'd actually be talking about.

I took a long walk on the Malibu beach. I had much to think about.
Comedy.

God, what a broad topic!

Where to even begin? Where's my "in"?

I kept walking. And walking.

All I could think of was that comedy has to come from *within*.

The truth of the matter is you can't really teach it. But how would I teach *that* aspect of it?

Hey, assholes?! You shouldn't be here! You can't actually learn comedy! Teach yourselves! You're wasting your time and money!

Yeah. Smart move, that would be.

No, sir.

I had to come up with a course that would encourage a younger writer to get into comedy, while also being realistic about the lack of chances in comedy, while also encouraging them about how much money they could eventually make, but all without letting them know that they would be struggling when they started, but without discouraging them from helping me if they ever *did* eventually make it.

It was complicated.

Beyond all that shit, I had to teach them to actually write funny!

Me. Imagine. The idiot who nearly flunked out of all English classes in high school!

If only my old writing teacher Miss Bailey could picture me now! If she were only alive! Which she isn't!

This drink's on me, Miss Bailey! A martini glass filled to the brim with Surge soda! I can drink it to your memory in a steaming backyard hot tub!

But seriously, how to teach someone how to write funny?! I mean, it's like writing a song, I suppose. How do you teach someone to write a beautiful melody? Either they can *recognize* a good melody or they *can't*. To write a great joke—actually, to even write just a *good* joke—one has to have perfect comedic taste.

And how do you teach taste?

You don't.

You can't.

It's impossible.

Shit. What had I done? What had I gotten myself into here?!

Maybe this hadn't been such a great idea after all.

Meanwhile, more and more students were signing up.

This led me to another idea: how about teaching the first course down at a resort somewhere really beautiful, say Sandals in Jamaica?

This was getting *interesting*.

Why not?

Within a matter of hours, I had the marketing director for Sandals on the phone with an exciting offer: two hundred students of comedy, partying their asses off, learning about the craft but also having the time of their lives on the sandy beaches of Jamaica!

She loved it! (I'm forgetting her name.)

Things were coming together.

This led me to yet another idea:

Why would it have to be *me* who was the schmuck who had to travel around the country teaching at seminars? Why would it have to be *me* who had to deal with the hassles of post 9/11 travel? Waiting in lines forever? Taking off my belt? Taking off my shoes? Who the fuck needed it?!

Also, there was the very real risk that the terrorist acts weren't yet over. The last thing I wanted was to end my life flying to a seminar on how to teach comedy writing!

Let some other asshole teach it. And, while they were at it, they could also find themselves the students!

I would call these teachers the "Smile Vessels."

Pretty good, huh?

Let the Smile Vessels do everything!

I'd just sit back and relax and watch the money *flow* in! I came up with a very specific plan:

So it'd go like this: Someone would pay *me* for the opportunity to teach my "Secrets to Achieving Comedy Success," or SACS for short. They then would get half of the proceeds from ticket sales, which I thought (and still do) to be more than fair. It's *my name* going on the title, after all! Why shouldn't I get half? All they had to do was find enough people to pay off their own costs.

The course load that I would come up with would be called the "Treasure Box," and it would contain my copyrighted secrets for making it in the comedy world.

And then it would be up to *them* to teach others.

The entire enterprise would be a runaway train chugging down the tracks.

The more people I had under me teaching, the more money I'd eventually earn. I could sit back on the beach, relax and watch the cash just come streaming through!

I got to work immediately, putting up an advertisement in various writing trade magazines across the country asking for teachers willing to teach a very highly-regarded, ultra-specific and detailed course (already written for their benefit). Much money to be made! Travel across the country (on your own dime!). Stay in fancy hotels (on your own dime!).

Who could resist?

It turns out, *very few*.

Within days, my email was *filled* with hundreds of people asking for more information about how they could get involved.

I sent out a form email explaining the premise.

If they asked for details, such as what in particular they would be teaching, I told them that all this would be sent their way once they signed up and paid the $1550 application fee. If they *still* asked, I blocked them.

Trouble.

Who THE FUCK needed 'em?

But it did bring up an interesting point: what *was* I going to teach exactly? And *how*?

That could come later.

In the meantime, I got down to creating instructions for finding more students for those who signed up as teachers.

I called this aspect "Pushing the Comedy."

So here's how it would work: someone would say, "Yes, I want to do this. It sounds super interesting and very different. I would like to teach this new approach to comedy." I'd then say, "Fine. Send me this amount of money. When you do, you'll then be obligated to find your own 'Comedic Truth Tellers' to teach to *their* own students. I get *half* of your money from ticket sales. You then get half of the money from *your* own team. I take only a *quarter* of that."

Simple.

Everyone would be a winner. Students are taught, teachers make a shitload of money and my brand of comedy spreads throughout the world—or at least throughout this country.

More and more "Laugh Teachers" were signing up every day and quickly getting to work finding their own "Subset of Laugh Teachers."

Each subset would have *another* subset but there would be a tier system.

I would be "Tier A."

Beneath me (otherwise known as the Laugh Leader) would be those who signed up right away (this was one of the incentives for doing so), and they would be known as Tier B or the Trusted Sidekicks.

Beneath that, Tier C, D, E and so on.

Once it reached Tier Z, it would then start over, but with double letters:

Tier AA. BB. CC.

I tried selling this concept.

It took very little effort for it to work.

Surprisingly well.

Within no time, I had about thirty "Comedic Truth Tellers."

Beneath these CTTs, there soon existed about eighty "Pushers of Comedy" or PACs. Beneath the PACS were about 250 "Giggle Merchants" (or GMs) and beneath *them* were about 500 "Yellow Shirts," teachers who had yet to prove themselves by finding even more students than the Giggle Merchants and the Pushers of Comedy and the Comedy Truth Tellers. I called these teachers the YS's.

Intermingling amongst all of the Pushers would be SwaTN's, which stood for "Stop With All That Negativity."

These would be Roamers who would put the Big Kibosh on anyone who so much as uttered one single negative thought about this course.

I pictured that the SwaTN's could even be fierce dogs, like rottweilers or something.

I also envisioned the HOT SEAT, in which a comedy wannabe would sit in the midst of a circle and tell jokes and pitch ideas.

If those around the circle did not like what they heard, they could throw something at the HOT SEAT person.

Nothing that would hurt them, of course, and maybe even be sort of fun: like a foam brick or an unsharpened pencil.

But people were becoming antsy to begin.

Quite a few Comedic Truth Tellers started to harass me for details about the course load they would soon be giving: what would they be teaching exactly?

How to acquire a literary agent?

How to land a spot on a sitcom?

How to get yourself a job on a late-night show?

All reasonable questions.

But first I wanted to really dig deep into the business matrix of my plan.

The first course for Receiving the Comedy (or RTC) would be FREE.

After that first course, which would last for ten hours, without a bathroom break that would take them out of the Comedy Zone, the Smile Vessels would be given an option: to retreat back into the cold, cruel world to make it on their own ... or to sign up for a follow-up class in which they *truly* learned the secrets of achieving great success within the comedic field.

If they chose the correct option, each Smile Vessel (or Purveyor of Humor, or POHs) would then be required to purchase a set of audiotapes with my comedic bits of wisdom and advice for them: that would be ten cassettes total, each costing $150.

That's $150 for each cassette. Not for all ten.

Once the POHs purchased these cassettes (and they were encouraged to purchase *all of them*), they would then be required to purchase 10 VHS tapes, with me lecturing about comedy in front of a green screen.

Once they completed the first course level (or the Borscht Courst), they could then sign up for the five other levels:

Silver Chuckles

Golden Giggles

Tittering for a Livin'

Standing O(s)gasms

Purely Heavenly Delight ENLIGHTMENT!

Everything was coming together nicely.

I thought it was now time to come up with the course load.

But before I did, I had to put together the cassettes and VHS tapes I was going to sell.

After much thought, I decided to just record a few of my favorite scenes from sitcoms onto *one* VHS tape.

I wouldn't be talking in front of a green screen. I'd just tell the student why each of the scenes worked.

A problem soon arose … I couldn't figure out how to technically *do* this: how to narrate over a clip. So I then decided on including a script that the student could read along to while watching the tape. He could look to the screen and then back to the script, back and forth, back and forth. Or just pause the VHS tape while reading.

For instance, in one of my favorite episodes of *The Simpsons*, Homer gets high from a very spicy habanero given to him by a dog voiced by Willy Nelson. So this is what the student would read:

The dog in this particular scene is voiced by a country singer to give it gravitas. In a sense, this dog stands in for the devil. Homer is sweet but stupid. What he isn't is evil. He's also not a drug taker. To watch him get "high" from the power of the habanero is to experience, along with this innocent guy, what it's like to get high for the first time. He's not used to it. You're probably not used to it. This makes it double as funny which makes it double as effective. Watch closely as Homer begins to hallucinate: most normal characters would envision something that would be close to god. But not Homer. By doing this, the writers stick with the character being funny and not themselves being funny. In a sense, the writers are in the background, pulling your funny strings. Notice also how no time is wasted. Homer isn't bumbling around looking for a bathroom. Every other line is a joke. And each joke works. Don't waste your time on jokes that don't work. We can also make fun of Homer because he's a gentle idiot. If he were mean, it might not work as well. I worked as a writer for The Simpsons. And I wrote an episode in which the whole family gets high and hallucinates from a peace pipe. Did they steal my idea? Probably. But it still really works. Trust me on this.

And so on.

Short. To the point. Most helpful.

I then created the cassettes that the POHs would be selling. Feeling lazy I just made them all duplicate copies of *Dice Rules*.

It was now November 2001.

The first *Laughter Session* was set to drop in two months.

I had yet to come up with the real nuts and bolts for what exactly the students would be taught, but that was okay. I felt I had more time.

So I decided to give myself a rest. I was exhausted. It was true that the train was about to explode down those tracks—but I was the schmuck placing that heavy train *on* the tracks! And I was beat.

I decided to take a quick "practice" trip down to Sandals Jamaica. I got the marketing director on the phone—the same one who had set up the upcoming group learning trip for March, when two hundred students of comedy would come down to party their asses off, learning all about the craft.

The trip had already sold out and this marketing director, needless to say, was a fan of mine.

So when I broached coming down on a practice run with a few friends, she offered up a few rooms for free.

I'd thank her right here and now in this book ... but I'm still forgetting her name.

The first person I called was the Flammer. I told him to get his fat ass in gear and to meet me down in Jamaica in precisely one week. Bring a girl, bring a boy, bring a goat, just get ready to party really fucking *hard*, son!

I added one additional room for him. I'd occupy the other. But I didn't want to go alone.

I placed a fresh ad in *Variety*:

Learn Comedy from a Pro!

On the Beautiful Beaches of Jamaica!

Win a FREE Trip!

All I Ask if That You SPREAD THE GOOD WORD
about this COMEDY COURSE!!

Looking back at this ad now, it's clear that I invented the idea and the term "Social Influencer."

I was giving away a free trip. This was years before the Fyre Festival.

All I asked in return was that they tell their friends that this course on comedy was a *must* for anyone who wanted to "make it." Really, this is the best type of advertising. "Word of mouth."

At the bottom of the ad, I asked for passport photos. This is what later tripped me up in court. Why, the prosecutors asked, would you need passport photos of potential comedy students?

To see if they were legal, I'd reply. And to see if they were funny.

Could you have asked for their driver's licenses? they responded. *And what does their looks have to do with being funny as a writer?*

I shrugged. I didn't want to say as much but photos on driver's licenses aren't always as clear as you'd like them to be. They're similar to the photos that you'd see on dating sites of women who look fantastic and then you meet them and ... well, *not so fantastic*.

So I didn't say anything—*wisely*.

Passport photos were better representative. And that's just the truth.

The two women who ended up suing me, Mary and BethAnne (not their real names), claimed that I had asked them for nudie shots. Not true—at least then. I did later but that was a different story and not brought up in court.

Here, for the first time, is the *real* story. I probably even shouldn't be telling you about *any* of this.

The lawyers and I "settled" out of court.

But fuck it.

Innocent as a bump in a rump with just the tiniest hint of a *hump*.

This is what *really* happened:

I received an email from two women, Mary and BethAnne. Again, not their real names. I received a lot more emails from others but I threw all those out. Both Mary and BethAnne always dreamed of getting into comedy writing. Both said they loved the beach and couldn't imagine a better setting to learn the difficult craft of making others laugh. Both were friends and they were a "comedy writing team." They had no professional experience to speak of but they wanted to learn from someone who had written for *The Simpsons,* one of their favorite shows.

I immediately asked to see passport photos. Instead, they sent me photos of them posing in front of what looked at first like a post office. I later discovered that it was their high school. But when I first saw it, I just assumed they were young postal workers who wanted to get into comedy writing. So I didn't even ask about their ages.

I'm not going to lie: the fact that they were both gorgeous definitely did not at all hurt about taking that chance.

I also figured that having two beautiful dames in the program, who would later spread—among other things—the good word, could only be a good thing, right?

Did I ask to see their birth certificates?

No.

Did I conduct DNA testing to determine genetic background?

No. Because that didn't yet exist.

Although taking oral swabs doesn't sound like *too* difficult a task. *That's right, ladies. New device. It's no longer a Q-tip but a … tongue. Step right up for this delightful new swab!!!!*

This was also years before Zoom and Face Time. When I tell you I never knew they were 15, I am telling you the god's honest truth. When I tell you that I never knew they did not have their parents' permission to take a week off from their tenth grade courses and hit the party scene down in Jamaica without telling anyone where they were going, I tell you the 100% god's honest truth. I don't believe in god but I do believe in the truth. That these two girls disappeared and that the FBI were called in to find them and that a notice was posted on Interpol … I knew *none* of this at the time.

This was years before everyone had a cell phone. No one had shit at this time. To go onto the Internet, I would have had to pay the Sandals resort a couple bucks a minute. And I didn't want to do that.

All I knew then was that these two very mature young women wanted to learn comedy and that they won the valuable opportunity to do so through my contest. I met them at the Jamaica airport, we all took a van to the resort, and I know we spent five blissful nights together.

Honestly, it was heavenly.

We got high, we got drunk, we talked all things comedy. I taught them what I knew about the business, about the art of creating laughs and yes … we made love.

All three of us. Yes, together.

And then we all went home.

Or *they* went home—on the same flight as the Flammer and his date, who also turned out to be fifteen.

I stayed on in Jamaica, and it was a good thing I did. Turns out the Jamaicans weren't nearly as high-strung about sexuality as Americans. The D.A. down in Kingston—or at least the equivalent of an American district attorney—couldn't have cared less.

He was a way cool dude who always had a blunt in his mouth. My type of bro.

In an interview with a Jamaican paper he later said that he blamed the parents for letting these two tasty yum-yums out of their sight.

I'd have to agree with him. *What type of parent would do that?!* I mean, where the fuck were they when these two were applying for the free trip, and then packing, and then taking a cab to the goddamn airport to fly them to motherfucking Jamaica?!

Screwing fifteen-year-olds in Jamaica was a godsend for me. If I had done it in New York or Washington or Los Angeles, game fucking over.

Again, I'm just being honest.

Please show me a twenty-something man who *wouldn't* want to bang a fifteen-year-old.

I'm waiting.

I'm *still* waiting.

The fact I got to do it at all and get away with it … I've never apologized.

And I never will.

What do I have to apologize for?

What I find particularly funny is that both these women (I can assure you they're no longer fifteen) eventually did go into comedy, with one now writing for *Big Mouth* on Netflix and the other for Hulu's *Shrill*.

So how great is *that*?

Maybe their week with me was worth something after all?

Which makes it all the more upsetting that The Learning Alcove never happened.

With all that work I put into it, with all that time, with all that money I could have earned, for it to have all gone bust because two sets of parents were angry with me for sleeping with their daughters … well, I find that tragic.

I often think about how many future students would have entered into the comedy lifestyle and how much we all missed out on with what these future students could have provided to the world.

I once heard a philosopher, or maybe it was an actor, talking about all of the talent extinguished because of the Holocaust. That millions of future doctors, philosophers, artists, heroes to a generation would never get to become doctors, artists, philosophers, heroes.

We'd never got to know *any* of them.

Obviously, I'm not comparing the shut down of the Learning Alcove to the Holocaust but there are similarities.

I do believe that if I had put my mind to it, I would have come up with an incredible itinerary and course load for those young students seeking to make a successful career as a comedy writer. And I do feel that many, if not most, would have contributed in some way to change comedy forever.

But we'll never know.

Because two sets of parents lost their minds.

Years later I ran into Mary and BethAnne at a party for a writer at *Brooklyn Nine One One*. They were still close pals. I asked if they remembered me. They both laughed. *Of course they remembered me!* I asked if they had any regrets over the entire incident. They were stoned and just kept laughing and glancing at each other. I considered that a win. I want to emphasize that it was never them who sued—it was their parents, most likely without their permission.

We had fun, we now have our memories, and they have an amazing career in comedy. I don't remember what I told them at the party or what they said back, but life seems to have worked out well for them.

As for me, the Learning Alcove just sat on the tracks. It never did officially take off.

Even better, I never had to pay back the tuition to all of the students. It fell under some sort of technicality.

So I now had $455,000 to do as I wished.

What I decided to do next changed the course of my life.

And it changed me in ways that I *never* would have expected.

Or needed.

Or even wanted.

Nor ever asked for.

But it happened just the same ... boy, did it ever ....

★ Chapter Thirteen ★

JUDD APATOW AND THE "ME HIDING IN HIS OFFICE FOR A MONTH WITHOUT HIS KNOWLEDGE" SITUATION

My lawyer begged me to not include this chapter and I won't.
But it ain't easy.
I never could hold my tongue.
My cock, certainly, but not my tongue.
It's supposedly a fact that Judd is litigious. Listen to my podcast or my satellite radio program if you want to know what happened. Or just email me and I'll tell you. It's a good story:
battybattison@gmail.com

★ **Chapter Fourteen** ★
LAST COMIC REELING

I want you to put on your time-traveling helmet, maybe the one you see crazy homeless people wear, and I want you to go back to another world, another place.

To *before* the so-called January 6th "coup" at the Capitol.

To before Trump's presidency, before Bruce Jenner became an ugly chick. To before Harvey Weinstein got raped in Riker's. To before an asshole in Vegas opened fire on a ton of people because they happened to be fans of patriotism and country music.

I want you to imagine a world in which there were no Apple iPhones, Jeff Bezos was not yet the world's richest man, and avocado toast wasn't yet a hipster brunch necessity. Kosher food wasn't yet an option for prisoners, everyone on earth didn't yet have their own podcast, and dickheads weren't wearing frameless sunglasses with faded lenses.

I talk, of course, about 2002, when men were men, women were women, and Joe Biden was young enough to know who he was.

Before *The Apprentice,* before *Game of Thrones,* and even before the best show ever to air in the history of mankind, *Entourage.*

Do you remember this time?

I'm talking about a time before *Last Comic Standing.*

In fact, I'm talking *about Last Comic Standing.*

If you're a fan of comedy, and I'm assuming you are if you're reading or listening to this book, and if you're of a certain age, which I'm not so certain about as many of my fans seem to have been born *after* 2002, then you'll be familiar with *Last Comic Standing.*

Around the winter of 2001, I started to hear murmurings amongst the comedy crowd about a new reality show that was set to run on NBC. I had been hanging out in a few L.A. comedy clubs as a fan of stand-up, networking with like-minded comedic minds, and enjoying myself after the hardship of the previous few months.

To be honest, I was exhausted and almost totally emotionally depleted. It had not been an easy year for me. The litigation was piling up, as were the accusations, most of them unfair, and I needed nothing more than a break. I thought about heading back to Jamaica's Sandals but thought better of it. My paranoia kicked in and I was afraid that the U.S. government would pay someone there to arrest or even kill me.

Does that sound *too* paranoid?

If so, let me tell you a story about a friend of mine who went to the Dominican Republic and never returned. The government claimed he got drunk or high and drowned. The truth of the matter was that he hadn't paid his U.S. taxes in ten years. From what I've heard, the U.S. government wasn't going to take such nonsense and they put a hit out on my friend.

A handful of people who witnessed the event told me that my friend was dragged out of a pool during daylight, shoved into a car, and was never seen again.

There were some rumors that he hadn't paid off a drug debt but I don't believe that. My friend was many things. But he wasn't an idiot. I have no doubt that the Deep State killed my friend for remaining a libertarian and not wanting to pay taxes. Now this was years before I, too, didn't want to pay taxes. But I still could sense that the highest levels of government weren't exactly thrilled with this type of attitude.

And who the hell knows? Who's to say that the parents of the girls I slept with down there didn't have friends in high places? Who's to say they hadn't themselves slept with a few Supreme Court judges? Or FBI agents? Or fucking Mossad spies from Israel?

I might have been born yesterday ... *but I stayed up all night.*

So I wasn't going anywhere. I was sticking close to home and mapping out my next move up the ladder of success. The stand-up scene in L.A. around 2002 was pretty strong. I'd see Louis CK, Todd Barry, H. Jon Benjamin, Greg Giraldo, Patton Oswalt, a woman whose name I'm forgetting, Mike Birbiglia, Marc Maron, Dave Chappelle, Jim Norton, another woman whose name I'm forgetting, and others. I'd typically be at the bar at either The Comedy Store or the Laugh Factory drinking my Tequila and soaking it all in. Often, the performers would stop by before or after and talk to me and the bartender. There was a *simpatico* among us. People in comedy can sniff each other out. It's like two animals at a petting zoo. There's no anal smelling going on in comedy, except on Louis CK's part, but there *is* a metaphorical sussing out of anyone else: *Are they in the club? Or outside the club?*

I don't mean the individual comedy clubs.

I mean the world that the comedy *inhabits*.

Comedy is like a carnival. Either you're a carnie or you aren't. Either you're in the life or you ain't.

And if you're outside the life, those inside will *know* it.

There was always a recognition on the part of stand-ups and comedy writers when they saw me sitting at the bar, drinking the day away.

He's one of us.

He knows about this world.

He's seen the ups, the downs, the madness.

Now, it could be said that some of these people recognized me from the local TV news reports about the Learning Alcove, but I doubt it. Comedy writers don't tend to be newsies, at least the ones I hung out with. If I was on a sitcom or my voice was on an animated series, I'd be recognized faster than having Larry McCormick call me a "shyster" on KTLA local news. Which he did. Many times.

I'd be at the bar at a number of clubs and I'd always get a nod.

Sometimes even a wink. Sit back and watch me work, fellow practitioner of the dark arts of earning that mysterious, elusive laugh!

I saw a lot of great stuff.

I saw a lot of shit.

And it occurred to me that it just might be the time to jump back into performing some stand-up myself. I always felt I was given short thrift the last go-round. Now that I was more established, I figured it'd be easy. I called Tim-Tam-Flimm-Flammery back in Ocean City where the poor bastard was *still* working as a house painter. We swapped some ideas back and forth. I was looking for a new and fresh on-stage character to take on. We came up with a few ideas:

#1. Jaded comedy writer

#2. Wise comedy writer.

#3. Blue-collar guy who just says dumb shit all the time and is surprised when the audience laughs (he may not even get the joke himself).

All three were fucking solid but I went with the first. I would be the comedy writer who'd been out in L.A. for a few years and liked to talk shit about the industry and about all the crazy shenanigans I'd seen in the business.

I got to work on my routine. I started to jot down notes in my special journal to later use on stage.

I ran through these ideas and jokes over the phone with the Flammer and they did really well. I now had to perform them before a live audience and needed to get a "spot" on stage.

I talked with the manager at the Comedy Store, a guy I knew from just sitting at the bar and drinking all day. He liked me and I liked him and I thought it'd be a given that he'd let me have a spot up on stage, say at 10:00 P.M. on a weekend, a prime position for any comedy club.

"Hey, man," I said one night.

"Hey," he said back.

"You know, I started off my career as a stand-up."

"Oh yeah? Where?"

"Ocean City, Maryland."

"Interesting."

"Yeah. Thinking about getting back in the game."

"Great."

"Think I can lock in a spot for this Friday or Saturday night?"

"Like open mic?"

I laughed. "No. Like a spot. I was a headliner back in Ocean City."

"What was the club?"

"The Sand Bar and Grille."

"Never heard of it."

"It was big."

"Yeah but never heard of it."

"That surprises me."

"Does it?"

"Yeah."

"All right."

"So ... a spot?"

"I don't think so. I need to see you on stage first."

"You're a dick."

"What?"

"Joking."

"Is that the type of material you do?"

I smiled. He was trying to egg me on.

But I didn't take the bait. I slowed things down.

"Listen, I get that you find me funny in real life but don't know yet how I'd do up on stage. But I'm telling you that I'm funny as shit on stage. Just let me prove it to you. You won't be disappointed."

He sighed as if he was doing me a huge fucking favor. "Fine. Wednesday night, a week from tomorrow. You can perform the opening slot."

"Thanks, duder. I appreciate it."

I meant it, too.

Beyond spending thousands on Tequila at his bar, I genuinely liked the guy and appreciated that he was taking a chance on me.

"You won't be disappointed," I said.

"We'll see," he said, walking away.

I let it go. I was above petty squabbles. The guy had given me a fucking spot at the L.A. Comedy Store! This was a big deal. Letterman had performed here years ago. Leno had performed here. The Hispanic *vato* who had his own show and then later shot himself in the head, I'm forgetting his name, used to perform here. Chico or something?

This place was major!

I got right to work. Here are some notes from out of my special joke notebook:

I'm only up here now because I want to get on Last Comic Standing. *Typically, the last comic standing is the asshole who's the designated driver.*

People back home think that Hollywood is about running into Meg Ryan on the street or at the grocery. In reality it's running into the Diff'rent Strokes *actors at the methadone clinic.*

I felt as if I had tapped into a character that would provide hours of material.

And, most importantly, for both the audience and for me, everything was true!

As I earlier mentioned, the best comedy comes from being tethered to some sort of *truth*.

If it's connected to nothingness, there might be a few laughs, but they won't be meaningful laughs.

It's the difference between a penny and a quarter. They're both considered currency. But one is better. And you'll be richer with a dime than you would with a penny.

If it *penetrates*, it's funny.

If it *ricochets*, it's not.

I once tried telling this to Gilbert Gottfried at a party being thrown for a reality show producer years later. Gilbert looked at me as if I was insane. He's a funny guy but I think he missed the point. Maybe he'd be a funnier comic up on the stage if he understood this. (By the way, I arrived at the party with an actress who you'd know from a little show called *The Old Christine*. She played Julia Louise-Dreyfuss's best friend from college who was visiting because she had broken up with her husband. You know the actress I'm talking about. Gorgeous. Tall.

Blond. Funny as hell. I adored her. Anyway, she left with Gilbert that night, which is fine. He's a good guy and he had a way with women, even though it was a *strange* way. I don't think she necessarily found him funnier than I was, just more *unique*. They went out for a few dates and then she dated Matt Dillon, which is cool. I love his acting. Gilbert and Matt, come on my podcast please, *all is forgiven*!)

A few days before the big event, I went clothes shopping. I needed that *perfect* T-shirt, a piece of clothing that would show that I was hip but not from L.A.

But I also wanted the T-shirt to prove that I was *aware* that I wasn't from L.A. It was a complicated shopping goal and I set out early to the Venice Beach T-shirt shops.

I was lucky. It only took me five minutes to find the *ideal* shirt, at the very first shop I stopped at.

This is how it read:

She *So* Wants the D

The D was in the shape of the Los Angeles Dodgers baseball logo.

So the joke worked in *multiple* ways: one, this supposed "she" wanted dick. And two, and maybe more important, she was a baseball fan who also wanted dick.

It was very funny and appropriate for my appearance up on the Comedy Store's stage.

If anyone claimed that it was offensive, they could kiss my asshole.

With that out of the way, I basically just got stoned and drunk for the entire length of time before my performance. It was six days.

Listen: I have to get this out of the way. I only do pot now and I don't drink. I think alcohol is a *real* problem in this country. If you want to drink, I'm not going to stop you. But I say this as a recovering alcoholic: the most insidious drug out there is not marijuana. It's Tequila and gin and whisky and any other "legal" shit you want to ruin your life with.

For seventeen years, give or take a few short periods in which I quit, I was a drinker, a juicer.

It took me until four and a half months ago to finally come to the realization that I had a problem. I woke up hung-over on a Jet Blue jitney at JFK airport I had been riding throughout the night. The bus driver was kind enough to just let me sleep it off and I repaid him for his graciousness with a $200 tip. But the thought of families with children sitting next to me for that short ride throughout the evening and into the early morning hours just makes me feel very embarrassed now. Especially because I was shirtless and holding a mop.

I would never lecture *anyone* on not drinking. I'm not into the whole AA bullshit (although it has worked for friends). I just decided that enough was enough, and I quit. I'm not proud of the drinking I did, but I'm also not ashamed of it. I did what I had to do to survive my climb up the ladder out of the snake pit that's show business. We all have our medicines. Whether it's valium or alcohol or sex or cosmetic surgery, all of us in this crazy business rely on *something* that helps us get through the long and lonely days and nights we must face.

So what I'm saying is that I'm not excusing my behavior on the evening of my Comedy Store performance. I'm not blaming it on the tons of Tequila I had drunk the previous week and right up until I was supposed to step on to that stage. I'm not blaming *anyone* but myself.

My career contains highs and it contains lows like any career and I'm scarred forever, literally, by what I chose to do on that Comic Store's stage.

I'm not complaining.

I'm a big boy. I take *full* responsibility. I'm not one of those who blame my childhood or those in power or religious figures for all of my problems.

They were *my* problems. And I know that.

But what I *am* saying is that I had a disability and that, like anyone with a disability, I wasn't operating at full capacity.

I later apologized to the manager of the club, as well as to all of the comedians involved.

Some were nice enough to write back with their own tales of addiction woes.

Some weren't as happy and I'll leave their names out of this, although it might be semi-obvious who they are after you read what happened that night.

What *really* happened.

Not what journalists and comics have talked about on podcasts or written about in their own shitty memoirs.

But what *truly* happened.

You might be asking: *if you were so fucked up, Skippy, how could you remember exactly what happened to the nth degree?*

There's a simple answer: I have a bootleg tape of the entire night that it took years to force myself to listen to. And when I did, it corrected a lot of the bullshit that's been bandied about by people in comedy who don't know what the *fuck* they're talking about, excuse my English.

The night of the performance I arrived at least three hours early. Sadly, I put that time into not honing my act but imbibing more Tequila. By the time I was set to hit the stage, I was fully whoof-whiffing off the silly sauce.

Even for me.

And my tolerance was *high*.

The order of performers that evening was supposed to be me, Craig Shoemaker as the middle comedian, and then Dana Gould as the headliner. Dana is a great guy and a terrific writer, one of the funniest people I know. He's a very sweet man and we've always really gotten along. Just a nice dude, which in this business is rare.

I was looking forward to giving a kick-ass set and then watching Craig and Dana perform their magic.

The hostess of the evening (I'm forgetting her name) was about to announce that I should take the stage. I straightened my T-shirt, smoothed down my hair, took a last shot of Tequila and started to make my way to the mic—

When a huge noise—it was almost an explosion, I can *still* feel it— resounded behind me. I thought at first that the applause and clapping was for me and it felt good, so good, as if I was born for this feeling, I had worked years for this feeling—

But the clapping and laughter seemed to be aimed *behind* me. When I reached the stage and waited for my name, there was only the thunder of applause.

I squinted through the lights.

It was Jerry Seinfeld. Making a "surprise" appearance at the club to hone some fresh material. With his sitcom off the air for five years now, he decided it was time to get back into what made him famous to begin with: standup.

And *this* was the night he chose to return to his roots. Not only the night, but the *exact* time that I was about to step onto the stage. The roar was truly deafening, a returning hero coming back to gloat in all his smarmy glory.

As I mentioned earlier, I hate *Seinfeld*. I hate the whininess. I hate the outfits that Jerry wore on his show. Everything was pleated. I'm sure even his condoms were pleated. I loved Elaine, I always thought she was hot as shit, but hated the ethnicity of George and the bizarreness of Kramer. I never found Kramer funny. I found him mentally unstable. If someone kept barging into my apartment when I was gone, I would have shot his head off. No joke. I hated the anxiety of it all and, quite honestly, I found it to be way too New Yorky Jewy.

Sorry. Just being honest. Again, my great-grandfather was one-quarter Jewish.

One of my favorite sitcoms, *The Odd Couple,* had nothing to do with Jewishness even though half the writers were probably Jews. I just don't like religion. And I'm an equal opportunity hater: I hate Muslims as much as I hate Jews as much as I hate Buddhists as much as I hate Hindus. I hate them all, except probably Christians.

It's all nonsense.

If you listen closely to the bootleg tape, you can hear a gasp from the host for the evening (I'm still forgetting her name) and you can actually hear me mumble: "You have got to fucking be kidding me!"

You can also hear me try to grab the mic and begin my set—but the audience was definitely not having it. They were shocked to see Seinfeld appear out of nowhere like a magician's ethnic rabbit and they weren't going to abide by anything else. The night was shot. "Fuck it" I can be heard saying. At that point, I blacked out. That's the last I remember.

So let's go to the audiotape for what happened next:

The applause dies down and Seinfeld asks, "Didn't expect me to be here tonight?"

The applause picks up again.

"Faggot!" someone screams from the audience.

Seinfeld ignores him: "I was in the neighborhood getting my car waxed and thought I'd stop in."

"Asshole!"

Mumblings from the crowd.

"I see that *all* my friends showed tonight."

Laughter.

"Fucking faggot asshole *cocksucker*!"

A hush over the crowd. A scuffle in the back.

Seinfeld to the hostess: "I can just wait till he gets out of—"

"Fuck off, don't touch me!"

Seinfeld to the crowd: "We'll wait for Whisky Pete to be escorted out and we'll begin."

Laughter.

"Fucking pathetic assholes! Fags!"

Chairs scraping and the audience members can be heard:

"Finally!"

"Good!"

"Was he supposed to perform?!"

"He's fucking trashed!"

"Just put him out. I'll call a cab."

"Jesus!"

Seinfeld from the stage: "Wow, I forgot what this was like! Can't say I missed it. She's over there thinking, *I didn't pay for that part!* [LAUGHTER] All right—has anyone here traveled recently? …"

Do I blame Seinfeld for ignoring me and not coming to my aid? No, I really don't.

He was attempting to return to stand-up after having been out of it for years. He was rusty. He was off his game.

Now if I had yelled all this out years before, he would have come to my aid. He was a fellow comedian, albeit totally sober.

About a decade later, I had a friend who wrote for Colbert. Seinfeld appeared on the show one night and my friend asked him if he remembered this incident, me drunkenly razzing him.

Seinfeld claimed not to remember at all and gave that look that he gives, half smug, half disinterested. Maybe he remembered, maybe he didn't. I'll never know. I've asked him to appear on my podcast and satellite radio show a few times, but his sister, who's his manager, always gives me a polite no.

Listen, I'll once again admit it: I'm no fan of the guy's sitcom. I thought it was cheap and lousy and filled with annoying bass licks. But he did have some skills as a stand-up, I can't deny it. So I'm giving him a pass here. A soft pass but a pass all the same.

Then again, he knew the scene and knew that comedians sometimes drank. Instead of having me thrown out, maybe he should have just seen to it that I was okay and maybe could sleep off my booze in the green room?

I don't know. It's hard to second guess someone like Seinfeld. I'm not him, he's not me, and that's it.

Sadly, the owner of the Comedy Store sent out word that I'd be banished forever, which was just fine with me. I hated their watered-down drinks anyway and the bar never even had a television, which always used to annoy the shit out of me. One of my favorite activities, or one that I used to love, would be to sit at a bar all day, drinking, watching game shows without the sound but reading the closed captions. It was a fun way to pass the day away. So the fact that the Comedy Store had no television was only yet *another* reason for me to never return.

Fuck that place!

I had better things to be doing.

So many better things!

Like trying to hunt down Jay Moor to ask if I could try out for *Last Comic Standing*.

I figured that I didn't really need to get up on stage to *prove* I was funny.

If anything, it'd just hurt my chances. Why rely on others to decide if you're funny? I could prove it myself.

I knew Jay a bit from the scene. He was a nice enough guy but never seemed to recognize me from one meeting to the next. Just a nod or a quick smile. I find it annoying to have to remind people who you are every time you meet. It's like a dog I once knew named Rufus. His nickname was *Toothless* because he was so old. He'd bark when he first met you. He'd then warm up to you. But then he'd leave the room and come back, and *forget* he had ever fucking met you! He'd bark once again. I found that exhausting. *Who the fuck wants to put up with such shit?*

Same thing, in a way, with Jay Moor. "Dude, we already met! How many *times* do I have to *introduce* myself?!"

I knew where he used to hang out, at a bar in Silver Lake that was hip, but not too hip. So it was actually even *more* hip, if that makes any sense. It was a big comedy hangout.

I knew Jay would stop by after a performance.

I went one night and waited.

He never showed.

I arrived another night. He never showed again but I did get to meet Kaley Cuoco from the show *8 Simple Rules*. She asked me for a light and I gave it to her. Seemed nice enough.

On the third night, I arrived to find Jay already there, regaling a crowd of people with a story about Lorne Michaels. As soon as he took a break to hit the bathroom, I wasted no time.

"Hey."

"Hey."

"It's Skippy Battison. I used to watch your pets."

"Okay."

"I'm back in stand-up. You might have heard."

"Right."

"Well, I know you're hosting a new reality show. Would love to be on it."

"Would you?"

"Yeah."

He walked away.

I found that rude.

I followed him.

"Hey."

"Yeah?"

"I'm not asking for a favor, yo. I just want to have a shot trying out for the show. I don't think that's too much to ask."

He sighed as if he was doing me a *huge* fucking favor.

He handed me a card.

"Here's the producer. Call her."

I looked at the card. It was a female's name, I'm forgetting what exactly. But it did say "Last Comic Standing, Executive Producer."

Now I've been in situations where people have handed me fake business cards just to get me out of their hair. In one case, I was asking a television executive about being put on his writing staff. He handed me a card, I thanked him, and only when I got home did I see that it was for the "Mino Hair Salon."

I won't tell you his name but I will say that he later worked for Jeffery Katzenberg's short-lived streaming platform, Quibi. So it goes without saying that the asshole is now out of a job.

With that in mind, I have to give Jay props for actually handing me an *authentic* business card.

I thanked him, handed him a $20 bill, and winked.

He looked confused.

"What's this for?"

"Greasing the wheels," I said.

He handed the $20 back and walked away.

To his back, I offered to buy his next drink but he said nothing in return.

But I already *had* what I wanted.

When I got home, I immediately called. (Again, for you younger *Passing on the Righters*, please remember this was *before* everyone in the entire world had their own iPhone and you would actually have to *wait* until you were *home* to call someone. *Prehistoric*!)

I left a message (executives never used to pick up their phones, at least when I called), and I went about my day, walking on the Malibu beach and hitting my favorite coffee shop for a nice espresso beneath the California sun.

When I returned home, I found a message waiting for me.

It told me to call so that I could set up an audition.

Bingo!

This is how life works, I thought. You gotta just fucking *make* things happen!

If you *wait* for things to happen, you'll be waiting *forever*.

That's just a sad fact.

Type A's receive Oscar awards.

Type B's work as office temps in Rockville, Maryland.

You know the difference between a Star and a Never Was?

Balls.

Now I don't mean you literally have to *have* testicles, although I do think it helps. I mean that one has to take a *chance* in life.

Grip and rip and slip and dip!

You want to be an average asshole? Then get into your 2008 Ford Taurus every morning and make your way to your shit job at an office park on I-270.

You want to hang out with the stars? Then get on that goddamn rocket ship, holmie!

The audition was the next morning and I, probably quite rightly, assumed this executive producer was doing Jay Moor a favor. But ask me how much I give a shit. I was going to take *whatever* I could get.

If she only wanted to see me because she liked Jay, and if she had no idea who I was, that was fine. Who cares? I wasn't in this business to make friends.

I re-thought my stand-up character.

Was this the right persona to slip into for an international television audience?

The more I sat in my outdoor hot tub, sipping Tequila, the more I felt that maybe it wasn't.

Why should I do the same shtick every other comedian was probably doing? I mean, even if a third of the comedians were doing something similar, that was way too many.

I wanted to do something different.

And it was here where I first stumbled upon my "I'm Not Like the Rest of the Liberal Assholes in This Town" persona.

I have to admit—and I *have* admitted this on my podcast and satellite radio show many times—that when I first sunk into this role, it wasn't a totally comfortable fit. It was a bit loose and not entirely natural. It was only after perfecting the role over the years that I found that it actually *did* fit perfectly. I just didn't know it at first.

I've talked about this at various conferences and gigs I've performed for think tanks and associations in Washington over the years, including the Heritage Foundation.

I've said that when I first began with this character, it was just that: *a character*.

But that character eventually *became* me.

And I became *him*.

I started to re-think my philosophy of life, politics, social issues, global events and other important topics, all through the prism of this character. And I found out something interesting: I believed in what he believed!

Remember when I was telling you earlier that comedy is all about the truth? And that comedy can only fly when tethered to reality and honesty?

When I think about it, I believe the following:

It was only after adopting a character that I *believed in*, that my career began to truly take off. It seems so obvious now. But I assure you: I could very easily *still* be struggling through showbiz, faking my way to the middle, under the guise of every other loser out there.

I think of it as being an epiphany of sorts but not in the religious sense.

In the comedic and monetary sense. Which is even better.

Prepping for that audition for *Last Comic Standing*, I thought: What joke would a comedian *never* say?

What joke would be incredibly hilarious and true but a subject that *none* of the other auditioners would ever have the go-nadz to say?

And if I could combine something funny with something that truly pissed me off, something I *really* and *truly* believed, would it hit that much *harder*?

I'd never seen anyone do this before. I'd only heard mumblings behind the scenes about comics doing this. But I had never actually *seen* anyone up on that stage speaking the *absolute* truth.

Within hours, after I left the hot tub and retreated into my house to jot down ideas in my special jokes journal, my act was completely finished. Typically it'll take a stand-up *months* to come up with an hour's worth of solid material. But I felt as if I had tapped into a very deep and pure source, like a mountain man dowsing for a water well.

I've heard artists talking about becoming a sort of vessel for God. Ideas flow through them as if they can't control them. I had never before truly understood this concept. I could listen to Paul McCartney talking about dreaming up the melody to "Yesterday" but it wasn't really something I could digest.

Now I could understand it.

It was like I had entered into a trance, only to emerge hours later with something that was brand new, that had never before been done, that was entirely fresh for the world to see.

I slept well that night. I had no reason not to. And I arrived the next morning about thirty minutes before the 9:00 A.M. audition time. I sat in the waiting area with my thermos of black coffee and watched the rest of the stand-up wannabes arriving. They all looked nervous. I didn't. Confidence is a funny thing.

People could *sense* my confidence; they could *feel* it. And I think it scared them. There was zero fear in my eyes. I was like a Navy SEAL about to parachute out of a copter and into a war zone. I was actually *looking forward* to what was about to happen.

I saw a few people I knew from the scene. I saw Rich Vos, a comedian I always loved. We shared a mutual friend and we had talked for a few minutes some months earlier while we were both waiting to have our tires changed. I nodded to him and he nodded back but we didn't get into any small talk. We were both professionals and we both knew that we should never—not even for the slightest moment—take our eyes off the ball. I saw Geoff Brown, another really funny comic who once stole my girlfriend at a party, but that's fine: she was boring. I saw Rob Cantrell, someone I once loaned some money to. He was another great comic. Rob paid me back in drinks. Not cash, but that's cool.

I didn't recognize anyone else.

A young woman stepped out of the audition room and called my name. Everyone turned to look as if they sensed that I was someone special. Why else would my name be called first? I strolled into the room as if I owned it. I had a good feeling about this audition. Maybe Jay Moor *had* called in a favor?

I stood in front of a group of producers and waited for the "go signal." There were about six sitting around a half-circle table. The lights were in my eyes. Someone said "you can start" and I then peeled off:

"I would like to thank you for allowing me to audition here this morning. My name is Skippy Battison, I'm a comedy writer and stand-up comedian and all-around life artist. You might notice me slurring some words. No, I don't have cerebral palsy—I have *urinal salty*. Do I have a drinking problem? Define 'problem.' You telling me to stop, well, that's kind of a *problem*. Me eating peanuts at a bar and drinking all day while the rest of the world works, well, I don't consider that much of a *problem*. I like to get drunk. Sue me. I like to smoke and drink and eat fatty foods and I'm tired of people telling me what to do. Notice it's always the fatsos who give you the most dieting advice. Or the ugliest who are always giving you the most personal grooming advice? It's like Big Foot telling me I need to shave my neck more often. 'Maybe you shouldn't eat that,' says the woman who weighs three hundred, munching on a caramelized ball of pure lard. 'Gee, thanks, expert. But I couldn't hear you over the crack of your neck waddle breaking the sound barrier.' I hate nonsense. This town is *filled* with nonsense. You're white. You can't write for a black sitcom. Any reason why? You're a man. You can't write for a woman's show. Any reason *why*? I've been so confused on some days that I've literally suffered the bends. Maybe *that's* why I'm slurring. 'Oh, you look beautiful!' they say in public. In private, you're mocked harder than a 'tard at Spring Break. This town is built on the silt of B.S. Every time you practically move, the truth beneath your feet shifts. 'You're brilliant!' they say in the morning. 'You're fired,' they say in the afternoon. It's like dealing with a schizophrenic ... but one with money. You deal with street crazy and there's no reputation involved. You deal with Hollywood crazy, you're out on your ass. I've noticed a few things: honesty isn't admired; ignorance is respected; up can be down and down can be up. Everyone's beautiful until they're not. Everyone's hilarious until they're not. And maybe never were. Is anything funny out here? Is that even *allowed*? You may appreciate my honesty. Or maybe you won't. But at least I had the balls to tell the truth. My name is Skippy Battison and I'd love to be on this show. To prove to the world what being *truly* funny means."

I finished and waited for applause which never arrived. I was surprised at first but then I remembered that *no one* claps or laughs during auditions. I shielded my eyes and tried to see the people I just performed for but was led out and that was that. People outside in the waiting area looked up. I think they could sense that I had killed it. Perhaps there was even a look of fear in their eyes—it's hard to remember. My mind was elsewhere. And I was drunk.

I had just *popped* that fucking audition! I was vibrating. I was flying.

Better, I had done the material that *I* had wanted to do. And I felt as if I had hit it out of the park. It was a terrific feeling. Even if I *didn't* end up getting the gig, I had opened myself up for others to either like me or not. That was up to them.

I liked *me*.

Audiences can sense that.

I can admit that this early version of my new comedic persona was a bit raw. But even with that rawness, the power shone right on through.

Would I perform a better set if I had to do it again today?

Sure. But I was young then. And experimenting with this magic potion. A little bit of *this*. A little bit of *that*.

The first few times never taste right for any formula or recipe.

But at least I was on the right track.

And even if this show was not yet ready to include a truth teller, then at least *I* was ready to tell the world.

I drove back to Malibu and waited.

Nothing.

After a few hours, I called a producer whose name I received from another comic.

I called him at home, around 10:00 P.M. Again, this was pretty much before everyone had their own iPhone. He answered immediately, thinking I was his daughter's physician. I guess she had a very high fever. When I explained I wasn't, he was less than thrilled. He asked me my name and then said he'd get back to me.

He never did.

Which I found ironic: did my act not deal with *just* this type of Hollywood behavior?

I had *already* won.

When I didn't hear a definitive answer on the second day, I knew I had to take action. I drove over to the production offices and saw that they were *still* auditioning comics.

I wanted to say to the comics, "Leave. *Now*. These people won't respect your ability or your talents. Get the fuck out. These people don't have your best interests at heart."

I did the right thing, though, and didn't say a word to any of these suckers.

I marched into the audition room itself. No one was performing but the semi-half table of executives was filled.

"Can I help you," some woman flunky asked.

"You can shut up and listen," I replied, surprised by my own anger. In all honesty, I didn't know what I had planned. I just *knew* I had to get it out.

I stood before them and launched into an improv that I still consider to be one of the best I've ever delivered:

"Some of you may have been here when I performed my set yesterday; some of you might not have been. I won't repeat it. I wouldn't do you the honor. I thought I had to be honest. And that honesty would be what you were looking for. I was wrong. I can now see that you're no better than any of the other shit production companies in Hollywood. You're all fakes. I'll perform my truth for those who *want* to hear it. Good luck finding comics who tell it like it *isn't*. I'm sure they'll be capable of a ton of fake laughs. Fuck all of ya! The show is going to bomb anyway!"

I did a little bow and walked out.

From out of the corner of my eye I could see that a woman perhaps had tears on her cheeks but I admit that this could have also been caused by a trick of the light. Or my own friendly-fire spittle.

Regardless, I was happy that I had pulled *that* off.

It really was something I had to do.

I emerged back into the harsh sunlight of Los Angeles a happier man.

I truly believe that you have to honor your inner spirit animal. Mine's a tiger. Yours might be a beaver or a flamingo or something even more complacent. If you're not true to what's inside of you–and I mean, what's *really* inside of you–then you won't accomplish jack shit.

Do you want to accomplish jack shit?

Or do you want to fulfill *all* of your dreams?

Then print out what I'm about to write and pin it to your bathroom mirror so you can look at it every morning:

TAKE. FUCKING. CONTROL. NOW.

And I swear to you–as sure as I'm sitting in my fifteen bedroom mansion in Great Falls, Virginia–that if you do this, your life will go from the shit fire it currently is to something so so *so* much better.

That's what I did. And my life changed forever.

But what happened next, I never could have predicted.

Even if I had wanted to ....

★ **Chapter Fifteen** ★

HITTING THAT LONG AND DUSTY ROAD

I began to take many, many walks on the Malibu beach. I had *much* to think about. I had been flying high, *so* high—but I guess you could say that I had just hit a speed bump.

But at least I was on the *right* path.

Around this time, I began to see a twenty-two-year-old named Charlotte Kay. She originated from Kansas and had literally stepped off the bus in Hollywood to see if she could "make it" as a … well, I'm not sure.

Actress?

Model?

Who the fuck knows?

The first person she met just happened to be me.

What a coincidence!

What were the chances!

It'd been my habit to hang around the bus depot to meet fresh young meat. I had been told it was a great place to greet those from the sticks, especially those who were beautiful, who tended to be a little dumber than the *authentic* actresses who weren't as attractive and who just arrived like everyone else: by fucking airplane.

I met a number of girlfriends this way. Karen Ann (from Rhode Island), Beth Anne (Idaho), Bets (short for Betsy, from Illinois), Anna Bell (a ton of these women had *two* first names), Rene (from Toronto), Beatrice (she went to high school with Jon Hamm), and a chick named just "Z." Never did find out where she was from but, wow. Z was saucy in dat der *zack*!

This time, it was a gorgeous brunette from Alabama named Kaitlyn. She had just graduated from University of Alabama and was told she was beautiful (she was), talented (she was *not*), and would have no trouble getting an acting job in Hollywood (she would have plenty of trouble). She was a wreck, a girl-woman who literally didn't know how to fill out a check or how to calculate the tax on a store purchase or how to solve the mind-numbingly difficult task of coming up with the 5% for a restaurant tip. Her college major had been art history but the most she knew about art was posing nude for a bunch of artistic bums for a free bed and a hot meal.

A true art lover.

In the midst of all this, my father called from D.C. My mother was sick, could I come home? It was a woman's problem, I'm forgetting what exactly, maybe a removal of something or other. I said to him that I wasn't able to, I was working on a new project and that it was important, but I'd be home soon enough.

Then my brother called and gave me shit for not immediately returning.

"Is she dying, doc?" I asked.

"No," he said.

"Then ... maybe you could *handle* it?" I responded.

We didn't end up talking for another eight years.

The next time we saw each other was at my father's death bed. The irony was that my mother was still living and my father wasn't.

Like all brother relationships it was (and still is) complicated but I do love him. I later used this relationship in a movie script that I wrote for Jim Belushi called *Deep Dish Dose of Love*.

It was never made but I still hope to one day get it produced.

Jim would have played a character named Burt who owns a taxi stand in Chicago and is starting to suffer from dementia and wants to learn how to surf. It's always been a dream of his. He calls everyone "pally" and, for the first time in years, he reaches out to his family who has always despised him and treated him like dog shit.

I fashioned Burt after me.

I created his asshole brother, Stan, after my *own* asshole brother.

When I sent the script to Jim Belushi, his agent returned it. I wouldn't have minded a "no." But to just have an actor return it without a response is kind of low-rent.

Maybe Jim Belushi was more like Stan than I thought. Maybe he really *was* an asshole like his brother in the movie.

Hollywood. *Frustrating.*

Kaitlyn and I would have sex all day, every day, and then hit the clubs at night. One evening we were out at a favorite cigar bar when a man approached and sat down next to Kaitlyn. I thought at first he was coming on to her. But, instead, he turned to me and said, "You look familiar."

"Yeah?"

"Yeah."

"Familiar how?"

"Like I've seen you some place before."

"I've been *many* places."

He laughed very, very hard. I could tell he had a terrific sense of humor. And that we'd soon be terrific friends.

"No, I meant professionally. Are you an actor?"

"I act. I write. I perform stand-up," I said. "So yeah, an actor. Mostly a comedy *jack-off* of all trades."

He laughed very hard again, this time even harder than he had the last time. I thought food was going to fly out of his mouth. Or would have, if he had been chewing.

"*That's* where I've see you! At the *Last Comic Standing* auditions!"

"Yup," I said, all cool. "I 'twas there."

He looked thrilled. He eagerly continued: "You went in first! Did you have an in or something?"

I smiled. "You could say that."

"Wow. That's so impressive. Who's your connection? Jay Moohr?"

I nodded. "Yeah. We know each other."

"Incredible. So ... how'd you do? You know, with your bit?"

"Me? I did amazing"—I could feel Kaitlyn's proud eyes on me (I had already told her how well I had done)—"but those jackasses wouldn't know funny if it bit them on their fat asses."

This time he *did* spit out food (he had begun to eat some chicken wings). Typically this would have bothered me but not so much this time. He was a fan and I liked that.

"How did *you* do?" I asked, pretending to give a flying shit.

"Amazing," he said. "I kicked ass. But I won't ever get the gig."

"Why?"

"Cause I'm white."

I looked over to Kaitlyn, who flinched a bit.

"What does that have to do with anything?" she asked.

He looked at her as if she were retarded.

"I'm also not fat or gay or handicapped. I'm a normal white. So ... *ain't gonna happen.*"

I want to stop right here and remind you of something: this was in 2002.

This was a *full seven years* or so before the Tea Party came into existence.

This was nearly *two decades* before the backlash to the MeToo movement.

This was at least thirteen years before an army of *Passing on the Righters* would call on-air to complain that they were not getting jobs because they weren't *this* or *that* or the *other*.

This was *years* before being cis or Miss or Shim or Sham.

What I'm saying is this:

This man I was talking with, this man you might now know as The Rim Rambler, or Da Executioner, my faithful pal and fellow member of my Passing Posse, was someone back then known merely as "Kevin Reynolds," a person *way* ahead of his damn time.

Something went off in my head. Kaitlyn was still looking at Kevin in a funny way. I was also looking at him in a funny way. But for me, it was an entirely different reaction. The reaction was: *Lord, what he just said is the truth!*

I was not going to get this *Last Comic Standing* gig. That much was now quite clear. And there was one reason:

I was a White Norm.

Kaitlyn started to say something but I gave her the sign to shut the fuck up. I wanted to hear more of what this guy had to say. But I had to know his name first.

"What's your name?" I asked.

"Kevin Reynolds," he answered.

"You speak the truth," I said.

"I do," he replied.

This guy wasn't messing around. I liked him *a lot*.

I broke up with Kaitlyn that night. You could say that Da Executioner and I have been together ever since—or mostly.

I can't stress enough how this conversation changed my life. It was like that scene in *Wizard of Oz* when Dotty opens her front door and walks from a black and white world into one of color and gay midgets.

It was like seeing *Heavyweights* for the very first time.

Or the first time I ever fingered a girl (back booth of the Rockville Pike Bob's Big Boy, while eating a tuna fish sandwich on toasted white and reading the restaurant's awesome comic book that they would give out for free).

Kevin and I became instant friends and bonded over the fact that it was Hollywood's problem that we weren't blowing up. Kevin was about my age, only a few months younger, and from outside Detroit. He worked in retail for a few years after high school and then felt he wanted something *more* out of life. He took off for Hollywood with the idea that he'd either act in funny films or perform stand up.

Like me, he was a huge fan of when *SNL* was actually funny. When men could dress as fat women and still get laughs. And he wanted something more out of life than to go to work every day, earn a living, and then return home to a wife each evening and be told what to do around the yard, just like his schmuck of a dad, a world-famous surgeon of some kind.

One night, we were getting stoned in my apartment when the subject of *The Kings of Comedy* came up. *The Kings of Comedy* was a documentary about a group of black comics who toured together and filmed the results.

As a joke, I said to Kevin, "We should gather the rest of the comics who didn't make *Last Comic Standing* and head out on tour."

He dropped his red plastic party cup. "Wait. That's actually an *amazing* idea!"

I was used to Kevin really digging what I came up with but I thought this time he was joking.

He wasn't.

"Really?" I wasn't just pretending to be modest. I honestly thought it was only a joke.

A great joke but a joke nonetheless.

"No, man! We gather everyone together who's funny as shit but who's too raw for Hollywood, dude!"

I laughed but thought about this more after I kicked him out when my new girlfriend, fresh off the bus, arrived to fuck my brains out.

I hadn't seen *The Kings of Comedy* but heard it was funny enough. And I assumed it was doing well in theaters.

The next day I put an ad in *Variety*:

> Did you try out for a role on the new reality show
> *The Last Comic Standing?*
> But didn't make the final cut for reasons
> That had nothing to do with the
> Strength of Your performance or Jokes?
> Are you too *Raw* to Play Ball with the Law?
> If So, Contact Me at
> battybattison@gmail.com

Within hours, my box was flooded with emails from hundreds of stand-ups who hadn't made the show, or at least just assumed that they *wouldn't* make the show. Their desperation was palpable:

"I told a joke that I really loved but I could tell it wasn't 'appropriate' for them. Didn't get into comedy for this nonsense."

"Total bullshit. I killed it. They know it, I know it. Fuck that place."

"Just a symptom of what's gong wrong with this country. Whatever happened to truth in comedy? It's gone, gone for fuckingever."

Most of the comedians sent me links to their work. I was blown away by how great they were. It confused me as to what *Last Comic Standing* was going for exactly. Was it more important for them to check off all the boxes rather than producing the *funniest* show they could have been produced?

To me, the answer was clear: they didn't care about funny.

They cared about *other* matters.

Like appeasing everybody.

But the audience only wants to laugh.

Why don't TV executives *know* this?

When I eventually brought my civil lawsuit against the show, and NBC, I made this quite clear in the complaint. The suit is still dragging on all these years later but that's Hollywood for ya!

All I'm asking for is $1 more than what I've paid for legal fees. I only want NBC to admit that they weren't after laughs so much as appeasing some mythical god of diversity. (By the way, I wonder what a god of diversity would look like? Woman? Man? Transvestite? One arm? No arms? *Something to think about*.)

Within a week I had picked out my favorite five fellow comedians, not counting Kevin who was already included in the mix.

In the end, there would be seven, myself included. It's the lord's honest truth that I would have picked women or minorities if they had made me laugh. In fact, I was *desperately* searching for women or minorities just to cut off the inevitable criticism that was sure to arrive. "White men only! We *knew* it!"

Please.

You have the crankies with Skippy?

I was only doing what the rest of Hollywood didn't have the balls to pull off: and that was to pick the funniest group out there regardless of sex or religion or race.

That I ended up picking six white men was a coincidence.

It all came down to these six being the *funniest*.

There were a few minorities and woman comedians who got in touch with me and who were angry they weren't chosen for *Last Comic Standing*.

But I watched their work online. And I just ... did not laugh. That's it.

Is that so wrong, really?

In those cases, the producers of *Last Comic Standing* had been right not to select them.

Am I breaking laws? God's or otherwise?

I look back—this was nearly twenty years ago now—and I just can't help but think how ahead of the times I was.

Telling the truth but getting in trouble for it.

Organizing a touring comedy ensemble that I thought would be the most capable of making the most people laugh.

Who else was doing this back then?

Well, there was Jeff Foxworthy who had just started his "Blue Collar Tour" with a group of Southern comedians doing their red-neck shtick. And then, of course, there was the tour of black comedians, "The Kings of Comedy."

And that was about it.

Once again, there I was—at the forefront.

Or fore*skin*.

Which isn't always a nice place to be.

When you're *that* ahead of the game, sometimes you're *so* ahead that you're *behind*.

Does that make sense?

I also knew that besides laughs, a lot of my tour's success would come down to marketing.

The black comedians had their "The Kings of Comedy," which was great. They also had amazing outfits that would have looked silly on me but looked really cool on them. These outfits weren't cheap! We're talking $5,000 suits and $500 ties. I mean, they looked incredible. I have to admit that.

The members of the "Blue Collar Tour" wore outfits that went with their "redneck" characters, like jeans and bandanas and cowboy hats and all the rest of that honky shit.

I wanted to look really good but I also wanted a killer name for our group and tour. Something we could brand on beer koozies and T-shirts and CDs and all the rest of it. Some ideas I jotted down:

Calling a Spade a Spade Tour

The Don't Brook No BS Tour

To the Right of Nonsense and to the Left of Center Tour

The Too Hot 2 Handle Tour

The Kicked Out of Hollywood 4Ever Tour

The Magnificent Funny 7

The Last of the First Comics Still Standing

In the end, I went with what I thought was the most affective, as well as the punchiest:

Comin' At Ya *Hard* Tour!

As for outfits, I eventually decided on something simple. But something that was also funny. And cool to look at.

I went with baseball T-shirts, three-quarter length sleeves, all with "Comin' At Ya *Hard* Tour!" on the front, and numbers, from one to seven, on the back.

I took number one. I'd let the others fight over two through seven.

I trademarked the tour name with a friend of my father's who worked as a lawyer at the Washington D.C. patent office.

I then asked the six other members of this new touring team to meet me at a Hollywood bar to discuss what was about to happen. Besides me and besides Da Executioner, there was Todd Rogers, Dennis McKallahon, Randal Dreher, Seve Green, and Robby Holdstick.

We sat around a table and talked about who we were exactly and what we wanted to accomplish in our careers and with our lives.

We learned there was a lot of overlap. Dennis had worked for nearly a decade at an automobile parts warehouse in Louisville, Kentucky, but had always dreamed of making it big in comedy. His father managed the warehouse. He told Dennis that he'd give him two years to make it. If he didn't, he'd have to come back and work for him.

A pretty shitty thing to say but there you go.

Dennis was under the gun.

Dennis performed at local shows in Louisville but then hit the road with his '88 Grand Am for Hollywood. Kicking around for a few years (yes, he went over the two year mark), he finally built up an act (for some comics, it takes a long time to come up with an hour's worth of material. For me, it was always easier), and he started to perform around town with varying degrees of success. Throwing his hat in the ring, he thought, *Why the hell should I not try out for this new reality show called Last Comic Standing?* He received a polite thank you at the audition but never heard back. He felt some of that had to do with his routine about retarded circus clowns. Shit, at least he got a "thank you"! I got a nothing!

But now, without his father's financial help and struggling, he had made the cut for what was sure to become a successful comedy tour!

So no heading back to the warehouse!

For the time being, at least.

Todd was a goofball from the sticks of Georgia who had always amused his friends with his impersonations, mostly of the handicapped kids in his schools (I guess there were a *lot* down there). He was just an amiable guy who slid from bad job to bad job and hoped to one day make it on "the television set." That's what he'd call show business: "the television set." Not a smart guy in the traditional sense, but he was supremely likable and was incredibly loyal. Audiences loved him even though you could never say that his bit was "high brow." Maybe "high unibrow." In fact, a reviewer in Ohio once called him "about as smart as a Big Foot and as handsome to boot." Todd didn't care. He sent the clipping back to his parents outside Macon. As well as money. Both his parents were on worker's comp after sawing off their own limbs at a slaughter house (on different days, the father's hand, the mother's right foot).

Poor Todd was the outcast of the family. He was the only one out there *earning*. And with all limbs.

Seve was a mixed bag. Funny at times, he could also be a little *too* serious for his own good. He would tend to make rambling pronouncements up on stage about politics or global events that you wanted to fall asleep listening to. He always had his eye on the greater prize, whatever that happened to be. I'm not sure he ever found it. I always liked Seve and we got along well but last I heard, he was working as a media rep for a tech company out in the San Fernando Valley. It could even be Twitter or Yahoo. I wish him well. I really did like the guy. And I really did laugh at some of his jokes. It's a shame how he came to eventually leave the group but he's doing just fine for himself.

Robby and Randal were actually a stand-up comedy team before they decided to go their separate ways up on the stage. Their original act was that one was liberal (Randal) and the other was far-right and conservative (Robby). The joke in real life was that they were *both* pretty conservative and Randal was only pretending *not* to be. It got harder and harder for Randal to pretend. When Randal tired of acting the liberal stooge, they became a team of conservative comics, but the act no longer worked. Every comedy duo needs a straight man and a dummy. With no one to feed liberal softballs to hit out of the park, the duo fizzled. So they both went solo up on stage. I liked Robby more than Randal, truthfully. They're out of the business altogether these days. Randal became a Buddhist monk and Robby owns a iPad repair store in Dayton, Ohio.

That left me and Kevin Reynolds to round out this new pack of laugh producers.

My style you already know about. Kevin's style, I soon came to learn, was quite impressive. He was just a normal guy who was sick of the nonsense.

Tired of all the bullshit.

He was a frustrated everyman in Hollywood who was exhausted of silly and just wanted to start getting *busy*.

Someone who wanted a fair break and for all the world to recognize his talent, of which he had a lot. I'll give you some examples of Kevin's "pure joke" style. Not jokes necessarily tied to his character but just jokes that are made to get laughs, which they always did:

"I met my alter ego last night. We both had nothing to say."

"Do you think the Indians a hundred years ago had dental floss? I mean, all that fucking *corn* ..."

"When I was a kid I tried playing doctor with the neighbor girl. My luck ... she didn't accept the insurance."

"You might have read my recent autobiography: *Men Who Fart Too Much and the Women Who Live With Them*."

"I worked a few years as a comedian at a leper colony. The audience would literally laugh their asses off."

As you can see, Kevin was (and still is) a brilliant jokester. Just pure, unadulterated, no filler jokes that could make just about anyone laugh, no matter the age or political inclination. But, like the rest of us, he had had enough with the bullshit of Hollywood and decided it was now or never to take control over his own destiny. His mother was begging him to return to Detroit to work in the bank her grandfather founded. Kevin would have been set for life. But he had a hunger to just see what he could accomplish if he did things his way and not *their* way.

Not only his parents'. But Hollywood's.

It was what we *all* were after with this tour. To show the world that we were talented but maybe not in the traditional Hollywood PC way.

All we wanted was a *chance*. If it didn't work out, then we'd just move on.

No complaints. No whining. We'd walk away like the men we were and try something else.

I started contacting concert halls throughout the country. Surprisingly, not a single one was interested in taking a chance on us. To me, it seemed like a *guaranteed* hit, but not to these jokers.

Whatever. I wasn't going to allow that to stop me.

Next up were comedy clubs around the country.

Guess what?

They *also* had no interest. They wanted to do their *own* bookings of individual comedians, not *sets* of comedians.

Did people realize what they *had* here? And what they were missing out on?

I had to guess that they did not.

But I also had to be a little patient, not always easy for me in the best of circumstances.

When something is *too* new, it's often misunderstood.

Our big break came when my father told me about a large event that his best friend had told him about that was set to take place in a week.

It seems that the Independent Petroleum Association of America would be holding their yearly celebration at the Washington D.C. Hyatt.

(This hotel might not sound familiar to you but just hang on a sec and I *guarantee* that you'll recall it: remember when Ronald Reagan was nearly fatally shot to death by John Hinckley? Remember seeing footage of it? That shooting took place just outside the entrance to the D.C. Hyatt.)

This was a *huge* event in D.C. and those in Hollywood might look down upon it, but I assure you that it's considered one of the largest parties in all of Washington and perhaps the country.

My father was a childhood pal of the President and CEO of operations for the Petroleum Association, had been for years. The CEO's name was Archibald Hendrix and he was a good guy. I've had my differences with my father but I'll give him this: *he could be loyal.* My dad suggested that I'd be the *perfect* choice for that year's annual entertainment. Archibald agreed.

The year before, the association had hired a well-known comedian who shall go unnamed but who had been *way* too left for their tastes.

For all you newbies who don't know a thing about the strange, mysterious world of Washington, D.C. politics and government, allow me to explain everything you need to know about *associations*:

Every product that's sold or purchased in this world has an association that represents it.

Basically, associations are just lobbyists for whatever products they're paid enough to shill. They make legislation fall in their company's favor.

For instance, do you like potato chips?

Well there's an *association* for that. I'm not fucking around: the Snack Food Association, located in Alexandria, Virginia, located just outside Washington.

Love to go to amusement parks? Guess what? There's a fucking association that represents the best interests of amusement parks throughout the country: the Global Association for the Attractions Industry.

Again, I ain't fucking kidding.

Does your kitchen have cabinets? Or are you a contractor who builds cabinets? Well, either way, you *also* have an association (I fuck you not): the Kitchen Cabinet Manufacturers Association in Reston, Virginia.

Literally. *Anything.*

As for the Petroleum Association, they handled (and still handle) the best interests for, yes, petroleum, but also for many other important products, such as plastics.

Every bottle of soda you purchase (right, the industry that my father lobbied for), every toy you buy for your nephew, literally anything you buy that has any plastic in it is controlled by this association.

These guys were the big time.

All of this outside of the D.C. area might be considered somewhat of a joke and maybe even provincial, but trust me when I tell you that it's huge in Washington.

HUGE.

This particular bash for the Independent Petroleum Association of America—at least in D.C. terms—was going to be the Oscars, the Emmys, the Grammys all rolled into one.

With better food.

And booze.

But with less attractive women.

But I did tell you about the ... free booze?

Many famous comedians have performed at these events over the years, often for a *ton* of money. They're not bragging about it on their Instagrams but it's the damn honest truth that they love it.

Flown in for free, put up in nice hotels, they perform for about 45 minutes and earn up to $250,000.

Who *wouldn't* love that?

For our group, we'd each earn $1,000 and we'd have to pay our own way to D.C. But I considered it worth it, as the promotional possibilities were *endless*.

I booked a flight out east, first class, and told the fellas they were on their own. A few had no money, so it looked like they'd have to take a bus cross country, meaning they'd have to leave immediately. They gave me some blowback for this. I looked at them as if they were crazy. They, too, had no idea how big this event was going to be.

Get your asses on the bus, dickheads. Who am I, your fucking daddy?

On the flight over, I began to hone my particular act. The rest would do their own acts, seven of us, about seven minutes each.

My own seven-minute act was good to go—meaning that it was all ready—but I thought I'd throw some local D.C. references into the mix.

For instance:

"I was crossing the Key Bridge this morning into the city ..."

"When I arrived yesterday at Dulles International Airport ..."

"Had an interesting thing happen to me yesterday at the Roy Roger's on Tuckerman Road ..."

I also figured that my complaining about Hollywood wouldn't work so well in Washington. So instead of bitching about my time in Hollywood, I changed it to my bitching about having to deal with liberals.

Again, let me re-emphasize that this was in 2002, *way* before it became a hip thing to do. This was before Obama. This was before Benghazi. This was before the supposed insurrection.

As I started working on the act, it all came together very quickly. I found that it was easy to substitute Hollywood for the nation as a whole. Instead of producers who wouldn't hire me, I had fun writing jokes about idiots who complained about what gas supposedly was doing to the environment.

I had fun writing jokes about how without plastics, we'd all still be, literally, in the stone age.

These were ideas and concepts I hadn't even really thought about before, to be totally honest.

But when I *did* start thinking about them, they made a lot of sense.

I wasn't what one would call overly "political" when I was growing up. To me, and from where I grew up, politics was everywhere. I was always more about pranks and having fun and messing shit up. Plus, my father was into politics. Aren't kids supposed to differ in opinion from what their parents think about the state of the world?

But the more I began to read, the more I began to think that I had better get *more* involved before it was too late.

I remember buying a few books at the L.A. Airport before I took off for Washington. One was the memoir of G. Gordon Liddy. Another was a book by a dude named Barry Goldwater. I was already into Ayn Rand, as I mentioned previously, and I did truly agree with her about what she had to say about the government staying the fuck out of our business. But I bought a book of Rand's I hadn't yet read. And the last book I bought for the trip was one called *How to Talk to a Liberal (If You Must): The World According to Ann Coulter*.

You're rolling your eyes.

Or maybe you're not.

But *if* you are:

Stop.

Look.

And take a *listen*.

I've spoken about this on my satellite radio show, as well as on my podcast.

I will read *any* book by anybody.

I'm a reading addict.

Per year, I read on average twelve to fifteen books.

All the way through.

I think the average for a typical American is three.

Some books I agree with.

Some I don't.

Some books I love.

Some books I don't.

Some books I forget instantly.

Others I remember forever.

How to Talk to a Liberal (If You Must): The World According to Ann Coulter would be one of those books that I'll remember forever.

As I sat in first-class on my flight from L.A. to Washington D.C., I practically *ingested* and *digested* this book.

Thankfully, I didn't then *excrete* it.

Everything Coulter was saying to me was dead on.

Everything she was writing about was exactly what I had just experienced back in Hollywood for the past few years.

The world was about *do-ers* and the world was about *take-ers*.

The world was about the *strong* and the world was about the *weak*.

This following sentence struck particularly hard:

"The liberals have an absolute conviction that there is one set of rules for you, and another, completely different set of rules for everyone else."

Sound familiar?

Sound like Hollywood?

This person is funny but *that* person isn't?

I can make all the rules because *I* know more about funny than *you* know about funny?

I kept reading. And by the time I landed at Dulles, I was a fan for life.

(Hi, Ann!)

It was a bolt of lightning not only for my personal philosophy but for my *comedic philosophy*.

After my father picked me up from the airport and took me home, I hit my old bedroom and honed my act even farther.

Before I knew it, I was ready. It was the night before the big performance.

Problem was … where were the rest of the Comin' At Ya Harders?

Turns out, they were stuck on a Greyhound in Pennsylvania! Their bus had crapped out a few miles west of Pittsburgh.

Dennis called me from a pay phone. He wanted to know if I could spring for plane tickets for him.

Actually, for *all of them*.

Greyhound was requesting a new bus but that wasn't expected until late that night. The best the boys could do was to arrive the next morning and have to then head straight over to the Hilton.

But they were complaining.

You flew and we have to take a bus! This is crazy! Why are we being treated like second-class citizens! This sucks!

I responded: *Do you know what touring entails? And the troubles and aggravation and hassles that so often crop up?*

Were they really and truly ready for what they were about to experience over the next year or so, assuming we could book dates based on word-of-mouth after this first show?

If they weren't, maybe they should just take a Greyhound back to Los Angeles!

There was silence on the other end. Dennis mumbled something and said he'd talk with the rest of the guys and then get back to me.

He called a few hours later while I was poolside, drinking a refreshing cocktail that my Miss Benda had whipped up. It was my favorite: a Moscow Mule in a copper mug.

In some ways, it felt real good to be home.

Miss Benda walked out and handed the cordless phone to me.

So it was Todd calling this time. His voice was quivering, out of fear or anger I don't know. I asked where Dennis was and why he wasn't the one calling back? He said Dennis was too upset to talk.

"If you don't send us a plane ticket, we're gone," is what Todd then said.

Now Todd will tell you differently, as he has over the years to anyone who'll listen. According to Todd, I offered to buy them plane tickets but then rescinded. The fact is that I *never* offered to buy them *anything*. High on what I had just read in Ann Coulter's book, I was in no mood for being at all generous.

Fuck this guy.

I found the irony then (and still) very funny. Here we were about to launch a tour of "conservative comedy." And here were six pricks, flouting every belief that we supposedly held!

The world was about do-ers and the world was about take-ers.

The world was about the strong and the world was all about the weak.

These words kept reverberating through my mind as I was listening to Todd scream at me from a pay phone somewhere west of Pittsburgh.

Was he being strong?

Were the rest being strong?

Our first major gig was the *next day*. They were insisting that I send them airplane tickets, tickets they claimed they themselves couldn't afford.

Or they wouldn't come at all.

Does this sound like a bunch of do-ers?

Or does this sound like a bunch of take-ers?

Todd has claimed in various interviews on podcasts (and it seems as if there's not one podcast he *isn't* willing to be on, except mine) that I told him to "shut the fuck up, grow a pair, and get on the next goddamn bus."

I did say that.

Wouldn't you have done the same?

I mean, who *were* these guys? Ten-year-olds? Just get on the fucking bus like an adult and ride into town like a man and perform the goddamn show that you had promised to perform!

Robby was next on the call and then Randal. And then Sev. And then Kevin. All shouting the same nonsense. "We were a *team*." "We can't afford to fly but we'll *pay* you back." "Sev is deathly sick with the flu." "Todd is complaining of appendix pains."

All bullshit.

I wasn't their daddy.

And I was tired of hearing all the crap. The tour hadn't even started! And I was *already* too tired to deal with this lack of ambition. Here we were as a group of so-called conservative comedians about to spread the gospel of what we believed in, and yet here they were malingering their way across the country!

I fired 'em right then and there, me still in the pool, sipping on my Moscow Mule, these six dolts on a shared grimy pay phone just west of Pittsburgh.

I never talked to any of them again — except for Kevin, who later (like thirteen years later, after I already had started my satellite radio show but not yet the podcast) called to apologize and to ask if we could somehow become friends again. As any listener to my podcast and satellite radio show, you'll know that Kevin is now called Da Executioner for getting a certain type of caller off the line more quickly than they'd ever wish. His shtick is to play the sound of a crying baby and then canned laughter from *Married with Children* and then the sound of a guillotine dropping ... and the audience just fucking *loves* it.

As for the rest ... see ya, assholes.

I had no time to waste on children. I still don't.

But now I was in a bit of a pickle. How was I going to fill nearly *seventy minutes* of performance time with just my own act, which only lasted (with *every* joke I practically had) about forty minutes, at the very most?

I went for a walk on my parents' property.

I had much to think about.

I walked for hours, from one end of the property and then back, over and over and over again.

Miss Benda kept running out with food and snacks. She was worried about me.

She was, and still is, like a member of the family. But I had no time to eat.

All I could think about was how exactly I was going to fill all that time.

Not for one minute, though, did I ever think about calling and cancelling.

I didn't work that way then. And I don't work that way now.

In the 25 years or so I've been in this business, I've only cancelled once.

And that was for pussy.

But that's for another book.

Never have I cancelled for illness or being in any way weak.

So it never even occurred to me to cancel.

What an embarrassment that would have been for my father who went out of his way to get me this amazing gig!

No, I didn't get into showbiz to *cancel*.

Then again, I also didn't get into it to bomb on stage without enough material.

Around hour three of thinking and walking, an idea hit.

Who was I going to be performing for exactly?

Members of the Petroleum Association.

And what did they do every day?

They spread the good word on petroleum and plastic products, for which this country was practically founded.

Okay, so there was *that*. Not let's take this farther:

Who was trying to stop them in their goal?

Liberal assholes.

Not to mention ... a very *specific* group of liberal assholes that I had *just* read about in a copy of the *Wall Street Journal* that my father had in the shitter. It was fresh on my mind.

An idea began to form.

Like a speck of sand in a baby oyster.

By the time I finished my pacing an hour or so later, my act was fully planned out.

My act would be character-based and would consist of two different elements.

I shivered.

This was going to be *good*.

Now I was ready to eat again. The first thing I did after eating the late-night snack made by our Miss Benda was to give the Flammer a call. I asked if he was free the next day. And if he could find three or four other people who could come along to help in the production of what I had planned.

"Do you mean stand-ups?" he asked.

"I really don't give a shit," I replied. "They could even be your idiot painter friends. Just get their assholes and your asshole down here."

I gave him the information and he promised he'd be there.

That's the thing about the Flammer. And one of the reasons I've kept him around all these years as a gofer: fucker is *loyal*.

I arrived early the next night at the Washington Hilton and spoke to the woman in charge of that night's festivities (I'm forgetting her name).

I explained to her the situation and she was okay with me performing alone.

Actually, I take that back.

I lied and said that all of my former partners had died in a horrific car crash. This was before anyone could easily check out such a fact on the internet. She was stunned and even cried. I'd apologize now but I'm still forgetting her name.

But I was clear: I was *not* going to cancel on her, the show would be amazing, I would fill the entire amount of time I had promised. I told her I was a professional and this is what professionals do. I wasn't going to kick this opportunity in the groin and then roll it into a gutter and take a leak on it.

No, sir.

My father wasn't able to attend the show, which would have been nice, as he had never seen me perform, only listened to cassette tapes of my shows in his car on the way to and from work. But his best friend from childhood, the President and CEO of operations for the Petroleum Association, would *definitely* be there watching.

I'm not sure if mother even knew about it. Shit, I'm not sure she even knew I was back in town. Looking back, she was probably already fucking the assistant golf pro at the country club.

Whatever.

I shook hands with this woman in charge. As I did, I thought back on the occasion years earlier when my father had told me that he could get me a job at this association if I ever wanted. *Now* look at me! I still didn't want a job with them but here I was entertaining them at their biggest event of the year! There were probably more millionaires in this crowd than anywhere else in D.C.!

Who knows *where* this might lead!

I headed back to the "green room" (really just a converted storage area) until my start time kicked off.

It's funny: this was, without a doubt, the *biggest* goddamn gig I ever had to perform, but I wasn't nervous. It was as if I had studied for a test and was now ready to take it, not that that ever happened in real life! I just felt super comfortable and calm. Buddhists call this something or other, and I think they're right. You just feel ... okay. All will be well. There will be no problems. You're on the right path. *Keep going, rittle glasshoppah ...*

I could hear a jazz band playing American standards like "God Bless America," "Battle Hymn of the Republic," "Sweet Home Alabama," "America" by Neil Diamond, and, believe it or not, the Beatles' "Taxman."

The band stopped playing. There were going to be a few speeches and then the first course would be served and then the second and then I'd come out and perform my act while they ate their desserts.

I glanced at my watch:

It was getting close to start time.

Where the fuck was Flammer and the guys I had requested?

If they didn't show, I'd truly be *screwed*.

One portion of the act I could pull off by myself.

The other ... well, not so much.

It was a delicious feeling. I imagine pilots feel this way when they wait until the very *last* moment to put down their landing gear. It could all end in a disastrous crash.

Or it could work out *perfectly*.

I looked at my watch again. The speeches, I could hear from onstage, had already begun. This would give me about fifteen or twenty minutes until the first course arrived. It'd be another fifteen minutes until the second course arrived. Give them thirty minutes after that and it'd be go time.

Fuck!

Where were these jokers!

I guess if they didn't show at all I could perform my original act that I had planned and then launch into a half hour of pure improv but—

I heard a crash behind me.

It was the Flammer!

With four of his idiot friends!

"So sorry," said the Flammer. "Took us a while to find the spears."

I laughed. Flammer and the rest were dressed as indigenous people from the Tapauá River in the Amazonian area in Brazil!

They looked absurd. Nude from the waste up, wearing loin-cloth type shorts, holding spears, skin painted brown, hair cut into bowl shapes, holding wooden bowls in their free hands. I laughed so hard I cried!

One of the guys I knew from Ocean City. I think he worked at a T-shirt shop on the boardwalk. He had coated his entire body with shit that I could only assume had to be brown shoe polish. He was so in character he just primitively grunted when I nodded at him.

The rest of the guys I didn't know but they were all straight-faced. I'm not sure what Flammer was paying them, beyond beer, but they were taking this shit *seriously*.

Even Flammer remained in his role until he, too, started to laugh.

Before long, we were all on the floor, laughing.

This was the funniest thing I had seen in years.

After I stopped laughing, I said, "You can put down the wooden bowls. And the spears for now."

"What you got planned, brother?" asked Flammer.

I loved it! The moron didn't even know what the fuck I had asked him here for! He just did as he was told and showed up, dressed as a fucking Amazon native!

I then told him what I had planned for the show. He laughed incredibly hard. When he stopped, I walked over to the woman in charge (shit, I'm still forgetting her name), and told her that she should notify me a few minutes before I was to go on. I wanted to read something over the sound system.

I hurried to change into my own costume as Flammer and I caught up. He asked why he was dressed the way he was. I told him about the original plan with the rest of the comedians and the three-quarter T-shirts and how I had to fire them, and how I came up with a *fresh* plan for the evening. The rest of the natives drank their free beer and nibbled on some appetizers I had managed to find for them, and before long, it was T minus five minutes.

I was handed the mic and I read the introduction I had jotted down the night before:

"Ladies and gentlemen! I'd like to welcome you to this year's annual Independent Petroleum Association of America's 'Gas Bash' at the Washington, D.C. Hilton!"

I waited for the applause. When it finished, I continued:

"Tonight, we have for you a *special* evening of entertainment by comedian Skippy Battison!"

Applause.

"And we also have something *extra* special for you! Joining Skippy on stage ... five members of the Suruwaha Indian tribe of the Brazilian Amazon!"

A hush.

It was pretty clear from the audience's reaction that they were not expecting *these* types of guests.

I continued reading into the mic: "There have been many stories, as you all know, about the Petroleum Association's relationship with these and other uncontacted tribes who'd rather *not* sell their land to oil producers and exploratory gas giants."

Murmurings in the audience.

"Tonight, we *all* come together to celebrate another amazing and productive year for IPAA. Tonight, we are *one*!"

At this, I motioned for Flammer and the others to approach and to lift me on top of their shoulders. When I was safely up, I said to them, "Hit it, fellas!" and we emerged from out of the backstage and into the lights.

Quiet at first—

And then—

A fucking explosion of laughter and applause.

Did the crowd *really* think I had flown these primitive assholes they'd been fighting with for the past year up to the Washington D.C. Hilton to appear at a yearly bash for the Petroleum Association?

Does the Pope have wings and jerk off into Sinead O'Connor's huge, yawning mouth?

The boys were moving quickly, carrying me onto the stage. I told them to slow down. I wanted to really squeeze the juice out of this one and I wanted to improvise my way from the stage to the tables.

The laughter and applause kept growing. People were pointing. Taking photos. Standing and clapping.

I was making mincemeat of those assholes who lived in the jungles who wanted to prevent this association from getting what they and the rest of the world wanted ... and these people were *loving* it!

Now, to be honest, I really didn't care one way or another if these natives were right or if this association was right.

But I did know one thing: the natives weren't paying me $7,000 to perform my comedy tonight.

I also knew, in the deepest part of my bones, that the adulation I was feeling was something I wanted to feel for the rest of my career, as long as that might possibly last. I was locked and loaded and solidly in muse control, just cruising without a thought in the world, effortlessly gliding above the heads of all of earth's sadly landlubbing creatures.

It was heaven.

I wished my father could have been there and not at a Washington Capitals game.

He would have loved it.

But I knew that my father's friend, the head of the Petroleum Association, would certainly tell my pops how his son had done!

I had hundreds to entertain for the next forty minutes or so.

As I passed each table, each of the "natives" holding me would cluck and bark out a fake language. I hadn't even told them to do that but these four morons from Ocean City were taking their roles *very* seriously!

The audience members, all seated around tables, having just finished their meals, reached out to try to touch these natives' bodies. The women in the audience, in particular, tried to grab a nice piece of flesh for themselves. Some would say their own names, like "Elizabeth," and the "Brazilian tribe" would then repeat it, nonsensically, grunting and clucking out the name so mangled that one could only laugh.

Around the entire party ballroom I was carried, to the absolute delight of everyone in the room, including most of the wait staff.

There are *always* a few jerk offs who can't take a joke and I did notice that a handful of the workers at the Hilton weren't laughing or even grinning. Some were downright stone-faced. But I wasn't going to let these Sour Steves and Negative Nancys ruin the evening for me!

Eventually, maybe after fifteen minutes, we circled back to the stage and I was lifted straight up onto it, just next to the dais with the microphone. "Now what?" asked the Flammer.

"Just stand behind me, partnah!" I said. "And accentuate any jokes that I tell."

"Got it, partner!" he answered excitedly. It was evident that he had missed performing desperately.

Who wouldn't?

What idiot would rather paint fucking houses than earn laughs up on a stage?

This was the turning point for the Flammer. And even though he struggled for years afterwards to earn as much in comedy as he did painting, he stuck with it and achieved great notoriety. Not to mention money. But that was still years down the road, *after* he joined my satellite radio show and became my sidekick.

When I hit the stage, the entire audience could see my outfit for the first time.

And the laughs came even bigger and harder.

This is what I was wearing:

Flannel jeans.

A T-shirt that read, in large red letters, "ACLU".

Cheap brown loafers.

A WETA PBS tote-bag.

A baseball hat that had "DANNY THE DO-GOODER" written on it.

I launched right into it:

"It's great to be here tonight! My name is Danny. And I'm a do-gooder."

[Tremendous laugh]

"I would have come today in a gas-powered automobile but I don't *believe* in the importance of gas."

[Huge laugh]

"How do you like the Indians I brought? Only two months late. They also don't believe in the power of gas. Just arm strength."

[I made a rowing motion]

[Explosive laugh]

"You might have heard about a little problem down in South America..."

[Very knowing laugh] ...

For the next forty minutes, I tore through this new character, a jerk who didn't believe in gas but who wanted to fly to every tree-hugging event in the world. A hypocrite who complained about plastic but who had no trouble drinking throughout the performance from a plastic water bottle. And then, not wanting to use a plastic cup along with his plastic bottle, pores the water directly into his stupid cupped hands.

A lefty-liberal who "hears" on NPR that the Independent Petroleum Association of America wants to burn down the jungle at Disney World to look for petroleum. A moron who thinks that the Petroleum Association handles the Vaseline industry. A young do-gooder on a dinghy who attempts to stop a gas tanker from reaching its destination. A seagull choking on a six-pack plastic ring holder.

Enunciating each stupid statement would be the Brazilian "natives" behind me, dancing and shaking their spears and wood buckets. For a moment, I was afraid they'd soon be wandering into the audience, using the buckets to collect *actual* money. But I then remembered these were not *real* natives.

When it was time for me to leave the stage and for the audience members to dig into their slices of vanilla cake with raspberry filling, the Flammer and the others lifted me onto their shoulders and led me off the stage.

The entire place was in hysterics. I received a standing ovation. Honestly, they were going bananas. Downright haywire, practically losing themselves with the ecstasy of their own laughter.

Afterwards, my father's friend, the head of the association, came running up to me backstage.

He was crying.

Literally.

We hugged. It felt wonderful.

"Thank you," I thought I heard him say, over all of the noise. "*So* much fun. This was *perfect*."

God, that felt so special!

Skippy Battison wasn't a local loser.

Skippy Battison was a fucking *returning hero* made good.

No ... make that ... *great*!

Meanwhile, out of desperation, I had found a new comedic niche and I intended to use it!

There were so many characters I could play, for so many associations, for so many think tanks, for so many foundations. My brain was already buzzing with ideas. The free alcohol didn't hurt.

The world of performing for conservative agencies in Washington D.C. was all mine.

All mine!

(Insert evil laugh here, *bwaaaaa-haaaaaa-haaaaa*!)

And *nothing* was going to stop me.

I had *finally* found my calling!

It felt so damn *goooooooood.*

I spent the rest of this magical evening with the natives eating the association's free food (Jesus, they even had fucking free Maryland crab cakes. How *well* was this association doing?!) and quaffing free soda (thanks to my dad), as well as plenty of high-shelf free liquor.

At one point, one of Flammer's friends pretended to barf into his wood bucket and everyone surrounding him, mostly men in suits, laughed.

I swear to you, these natives were like celebs.

It was very funny.

It was a beautiful evening and I never wanted it to end. But I was also excited about the future.

Things were *finally* going my way. It was like having the answers to a test.

Why be nervous, when I knew how it would all end?

I could do *anything*!

Christ, it felt so damn right!

Everything had been leading up to this point.

It was *my* future for the goddamn, motherfucking *taking.*

One that could bring in riches and adulation and laughs ... and respect.

I'd show everyone I had grown up with that they were *wrong* to assume I'd only become a loser.

I was back in my home town and I was loving it!

What came next, though, was something I never could have predicted.

Or wanted. Or needed. Or even asked for.

But, unfortunately, was very much *going* to receive ... whether I wanted to receive it or not.

I didn't.

But it happened anyway.

Boy, did it ever ....

★ **Chapter Sixteen** ★

WASHINGTON D.C. ... A TOWN SO LAME THEY NAMED IT ONCE!

In the summer of 2004, while you might have been lining up to be gay-married in Massachusetts or were going door-to-door handing out *John Kerry for President* pamphlets, I was working hard at becoming the toast of this swampy, humid settlement called the "Columbia of the District of the Washington of the D.C."

I was the "it" guy.

Granted, summers in D.C. can be sort of ... *sleepy*. But I would take whatever I could get.

When I say the "it" guy, I don't mean in politics or in law or even in governance. I mean in comedy.

Now, let's be honest here, D.C. wasn't known for its comedy scene.

There was Mark Russell, the bow-tied git who supposedly wrote 3,000 songs for the piano, all sounding exactly the same.

There was the Capitol Steps, a group of government workers by day and "hilarious song satirists" by night. Here's a sample of one of their parodies, "How Do You Solve a Problem Like Korea?" sung to the tune of "How Do You Solve a Problem Like Maria?" :

How do you solve a problem like Korea?
I have got nukes in case you haven't heard
Respect from U.S. could be a panacea
But your Evil Axis always lists us third ....

And that was about it.

Washington wasn't exactly known as a "funny" town.

Now it's a bit different. Things have definitely changed.

To begin, *I'm* known to come from here. So there's *that*.

Not counting me, Dave Chapelle and Patton Oswalt—two adequate enough talents—are also from this Slippery Swamp.

I once met Dave at a tire-rotation place in Rockville. He was there alone with his incredibly beautiful car. Honestly, it must have cost a million. I nodded to him and he nodded back. There was a silent simpatico happening. I knew him, he knew me (I assumed), and then we went our separate ways.

Patton's run-in years later was more a little more complicated.

What happened was this:

Around 2015, I played a practical joke on Patton on my satellite radio show. I called his cell and told him that I was a representative from the IRS and that he was in big, big trouble.

Me: Is this (stumbling over name) Patwon Oswalt?

Patton: Yes. Who's this?

Me: This is Richard Yahayhlee. I'm calling from the IRS in Washington D.C.

Patton: Okay …

Me: I'm calling specifically about your 1099 form.

Patton: What about it?

Me: We've found that you've purposely miscalculated lines 17 through 24.

Patton: I don't know what that means.

Me: What it means is that you're in violation of HRH-3929.

Patton: Meaning?

Me: You're in *big* trouble.

Patton: Have you talked to my accountant, Jim _____?

Me: Yup.

Patton: And he gave you my number?

Me: He sure did.

Patton: Why would he … I mean, I don't—

Me: When's the quickest you can come down to IRS headquarters?

Patton: In *Washington*?!

Me: Yeah.

Patton: I … I'm on tour now. Maybe next month? I'd have to check—

Me: This is *very* serious.

Patton: Can you give me your number? I'll have my attorney or accountant call you—

Me (sighing): I guess so. You ready? 202-328-2818.

Patton: 202-328-2188.

Me (very impatient): No. 202-328-2818.

Patton: 2818. Okay. I'll have someone call.

Me: 202-328-*2188*.

Patton: Wait. 2818? Or 2188?

Me: Either works.

Patton: Well, what is it?

Me: 2188.

Patton: 2188. I'll have someone call.

Me: You better! You're in big, big trouble!

Patton: What?—

I hung up.
But I wasn't yet finished.
Far from it.
I then had a friend of my father's who actually *did* work at the IRS give Patton a call from a *real* IRS phone number. My friend's father used a phone in a meeting room so he wouldn't be traced. On Patton's phone was an incoming number from the "IRS, Washington."

He did this because he owed me a favor. The previous year, I had set him up on a "date" with a high class call girl I knew back from high school. She was from Holton-Arms. I think her nickname had been "Hairy Arms." But god, she was *beautiful.*

IRS: Is this Mr. Patton Oswalt?

Patton: Yes?

IRS: I am following up on Mr. Richard Yahayhlee's phone call with you just a moment ago?
Patton: Yeah. I told him that I'd have my lawyer and accountant—

IRS: I'm afraid it's too late for that.

Patton: Too late for *what*? I was just told about this!

IRS: You're in big trouble.

Patton: With what?!

IRS: HRH-3929.

Patton: Listen … let me just have my lawyer—

IRS: *Big* trouble!

Patton: Jesus! I get it already!

IRS: Oh no you don't! But you will! Big, *big* trouble!

Patton: Okay!

IRS: Oh so big, such big trouble. Wow! *What* trouble!

Patton: Jesus fuck, okay already!

What happened next was not what I had planned and I take full credit. In retrospect, I should have called Patton back immediately and told him that it was just a gag for the benefit of my satellite radio audience, most of whom were already huge fans of his.

But I didn't.

Maybe I was too busy that day? Maybe I had other comedy bits to be doing?

In all honesty, I truly can't remember.

Regrettably, Patton *did* end up calling his lawyer and then his accountant and both called the IRS, who had no idea as to what these two were raving on and on about.

But ... now suspicious that something really *was* up, the IRS delved deeply into Patton's past tax documents, something they might not have done otherwise, I'd be the first to admit.

What followed was a three year battle between Patton and the IRS: depositions, more depositions, court battles, countersuits, everything.

Happily, Patton in the end was absolved of any tax wrongdoing. In fact, it turned out he had actually *overpaid* on his taxes for all those years. But it was an ordeal. And an expensive one at that.

As of last year, Patton *still* didn't know that I had been behind it all.

And that it was only a harmless radio gag.

So I decided to pull yet *another* gag on him one afternoon while live on the air:

Me: Mr. Patton?

Patton: Yes?

Me: This may sound strange but my name is also Patton Oswalt—

Patton: Okay—

Me: And we're always being confused for each other! I thought I'd call and let you know as much!

Patton: Um—

Me: Yeah, it's funny. I hadn't paid my taxes for years and then I heard through the grapevine that they went after *you*. So I wanted to apologize—

Patton: That was *you*?

Me: Patton Oswalt. In Boulder, Colorado.

Patton: Jesus! That was a three-year fucking thing for me—!

Me: Sorry! I'm not the smartest when it comes to money.

Patton: Jesus. Who—where are you? Why would—

Me: I don't know.

Patton: So I got confused for you? And you're just—you're just finding this out—

Me: I guess.

Patton: Christ, I mean—

Me: Okay. I have to go to the dog track and bet a lot of money and not report the earnings. Bye bye!

It was *hilarious*!

I had gotten away with some *really* good pranks in my career (more on this to come!) and, in fact, I'd say I was a *master* of the prank.

That's what I call myself: *Skippy Battison, Master of the Prank.*

Or just Skippy Battison, MP.

My *Passing on the Righters* know what this means.

So *here* was yet another prank that was seamless and had gone off flawlessly.

It was only a few hours later that someone—I still don't know who exactly—called Patton and told him he had been "got."

Thanks, asshole!

When Patton found out, let's just say he wasn't at first *amused.*

In fact, he was really fucking upset. Can't say I blame him.

But I was *pissed*. Why would someone give up such a perfect prank as this? Can't anyone be tricked anymore without them finding out who the perpetrator is?

Since I figured I was caught and there wasn't anything I could do about it, I called Patton right away to explain.

But he blocked the call. I then tried to go through his lawyer and accountant. No luck there either. I finally wrote him a letter that I sent to his manager. I heard that he received it and that he was very happy I had sent it. In the letter, I talked about the D.C. area and all of the things we had in common, since he also grew up just outside D.C.

One commonality was that we both worked at the same record chain in Northern Virginia, Waxie Maxies, although not the same particular store and not at the same time.

But it was still pretty cool.

A few months ago, I was eating at a restaurant in Fairfax, Virginia called The Three Chefs. I had just finished my satellite radio show interview with a lobbyist for the pesticide industry and I was jazzed. It had gone really well and I was seriously pumped.

I'm eating my crab cakes when in walks ... Patton Oswalt. Straight into the fucking restaurant. He must have been visiting family and was just taking a break to get himself some lunch.

He walked right past me.

"Hey, Patton," I said, putting down my crab cake sandwich.

"Hey," he said.

"It's me. Skippy. Battison."

He stopped. He glared at me.

There existed an unspoken communication that took me, I have to be honest, a few days to digest.

What I finally came to understand was that his look seemed to imply: *We're both professionals but I got pranked bad! Nicely done, sir! I can admit that I'm not happy about it, but I can also really respect the shit out of what you managed to pull off! Maybe you did go too far ... but in the comedic life, you simply must take chances! I totally understand that urge! I get it! We're in the same world, bro!*

I have to give it to him. He was pretty cool about the whole thing, all things considered.

I tried to call him a few times afterwards to invite him on to my satellite radio show and podcast but his number was still blocked, out of either spite or by mistake, I don't know. I'm not sure why he wouldn't have thought that any publicity would have been *good* publicity. Seems pretty basic.

In fact, if he had just played along, maybe today he'd be even *bigger* than he would now be otherwise.

There are always at least two ways of looking at something.

Anyway, Patton is also from D.C.

That would make it: me, Patton and Dave Chapelle.

I might be forgetting some others.

But *three* is better than *none*.

It's *not* a fun city, Washington.

It just *ain't*.

The purpose of this city is to govern and that's pretty much it.

But Washingtonians are like anyone else, right?

They love to laugh.

Who can blame them after working at such dry jobs all day, every goddamn day?

They let their (short) hair down like anyone else.

As I launched the next phase of my skyrocketing career, upwards, ever *upwards*, I contemplated a few directions where I could head.

One idea was to create a *conservative* version of The Capitol Steps.

I figured I would call the group The Confederate Monuments and sing altered "classics" with Ayn Rand lyrics.

Or just lyrics about issues that conservatives cared about and not libs.

It was a terrific idea but I thought it might be too difficult to find enough like-minded performers at my comedic level to pull it off.

Some song parody titles I thought of, though:

Twisted Sister's "We're Not Gonna Take It (this Liberal Bullshit)"

Led Zeppelin's "Handicapped Ramp to Heaven"

Blue Oyster Cult's "Don't Fear the Reaper (But Especially If He's with the CDC!)"

Queen's "You're My Best Friend (But I Despise Your Stupid-Ass Liberal Policies)"

I *still* want to do this project!

It'd be fucking hilarious and it would be a true riot.

But I'm just slammed.

However ... I *would* be willing to franchise this.

So reach out if interested ... 60% for me, 40% for you ... and that's a damn good fair deal ... battybattison@gmail.com ...

Anyway, the city of Washington was mine for the comedic taking and I got right to work.

I hired a secretary through a temp agency who I immediately started to bang. She was a recent graduate of George Mason University, with a major in communications, and I can assure you that she could communicate very well with just grunts and moans. I'm forgetting her name but she gave terrific phone ... and sounded professional when speaking to people who reached out to me.

Within a week or so, I had six or seven gigs already set up.

I kept a diary for six months at this time because I felt my career was exploding and I was going to one day write a book and it'd be easy to take the information and then rewrite it into beautiful prose that everyone would love reading.

I did end up writing a book (what you're now reading) but I'm not going to *rewrite* what I wrote back then. I'm too lazy to do that.

I probably would be unable to improve upon what I *already* wrote in my diary and why should I? *I already wrote the damn thing!*

So what follows are excerpts from various entries in my diary from that period. Nothing has been changed except the occasional last name. I'm just tired of being sued, people!

Actually, before I get to the diary, I want to give you some background on my living arrangements: I was still at my parents' house. My mom was barely around ("golfing") and neither was my father (working). I loved our pool, I adored our Miss Benda, and I loved having old high school friends over to play video games and get baked. I had already sold the house that I had owned back in Malibu and I gave the money to my father, which I figured was the right thing to do, as he had paid for it.

I would spend the mornings by the pool working on the new material I'd be performing later that night. That is, if I had a show. If not, I'd just read books on politics that my father had in his own private library. I vacuumed through practically every Tom Clancy book, as well as the works of Kurt Schlichter, and the columns of Charles Krauthammer, which was ironic because I would typically read Krauthammer in the pool. And the reason he was paralyzed was that as a kid he dove into a pool with shallow water. So that was ironic.

I read all of the autobiographies that Trump wrote.

And I even read the New Testament, page to page, from start to finish.

Actually, it was the *Cliffs Notes* version to the New Testament but even *that* version was fucking never ending and tough to untangle.

What I really came to love the most, though, were the comic strips of Scott Adams' *Dilbert*.

Scott Adams has gotten into a lot of heat in the past few years for supporting Trump and conservative causes. I happen to agree with him on all of that. But what I really think separates Adams from everyone else is that he's a comedic genius.

Seriously.

You're looking at me funny.

But hear me out: Is there any other newspaper comic out there that's as true to life and as fucking funny as *Dilbert*?

Name one ...

I'm still waiting.

Sure, there's *Zits*, which I still love. And a few others, including *Pickles*, about a kindly grandfather and his inquisitive grandson. I find *Pickles* kinda cute and the grandmother reminds me of my dead granny, although the cartoon version is a *lot* nicer and more patient with kids who pull pranks and do "bad" things, like light food on fire.

But *Dilbert* ... it just astonishes me the quality of this strip day after day, week after week, year after year.

As someone who prides himself on his ability to produce a ton of great material quickly, I sort of feel inferior to Scott Adams.

I've told Scott this a few times on my satellite radio show when I've interviewed him and he's always been very humble and modest, but I truly believe that Scott has created a fucking entire world out of the character of Dilbert and his friends that in many ways seem *more* realistic than *our* world.

Think about that. It's almost as if Scott *invented* virtual reality.

Sometimes when I dream, I'll dream about the *Dilbert* characters as if they're real people!

Or I'll dream that I actually work with them! *How the fuck does he pull it off?* He claims that it's just a talent he was born with, which I can understand as a fellow artist. But I don't see other cartoonists pulling off this magic trick.

I once masturbated to an image of Alice.

Alice is a character in *Dilbert*.

That was pretty cool.

I never looked at *Dilbert* as being "conservative."

I've always looked at *Dilbert* as being "realistic." As in "no bullshit."

I can't tell you how much I hate newspaper comics that deal with the workplace in a fake manner. *Hate it!* Life doesn't work like that!

Or it *shouldn't*!

The office life depicted in *Dilbert* is exactly the life that I experienced when I worked as a temp in Rockville for a few weeks in the summer of 1995 going into my senior year of high school.

Exactly!

Fuck *The Office*.

Fuck every show *about* the office.

This is what office life was like for me and I defy anyone else to show me *anything* that comes close to capturing that life as accurately.

So what I'm saying is that I was educating myself around this time with conservative ideals from *all* aspects of society: both the high and the supposed low.

To me there's very little difference: *wherever* you learn is just fine!

Whether it's from a *Cliffs Notes* to the bible or to a newspaper comic you find in the back of the *Style* section of the *Washington Compost*.

What difference does it make in the end?!

It's like how millions of listeners learn from *me*.

Or millions of readers are learning from *this* book.

Is my knowledge any worse than the bullshit articles in *The New Yorker*?

So with learning and performing, I was keeping very busy, except on days when I wasn't performing. On those days, I would just relax and soak up all that life had to offer.

Back to my diary from this period. Some excerpts:

June 9, 2003

D.C. pretty empty this time of year. That's the bad news. Good news: tons of associations throwing picnics. After my write-up in the *Post* (the Compost?) getting a lot of emails and requests. The article was nasty and based on an "unnamed source" who was at the Petroleum show and who didn't like what she saw. How do I know it was a *she*? I just do. It had to be. But any publicity is good publicity and this has proved no different. It was all word-of-mouth after that initial show but now kicked into a different level. Calls went from two a day to more than ten a day. Gigs set up through the summer and into the fall. Excited!!

June 14, 2003

Huge gig yesterday at a Poolesville farm with the American Conservative Union doing their annual "Conservative Political Action Conference." Beer, wine, crab cakes, all manner of beautiful ass women in pretty hats. A Skynyrd cover band called "Free Byrd" opened the show with some kick-ass jams, priming me for the crowd. Walked out in my ACLU shirt and "Danny the Do-Gooder" cap. Crowd goes berserk. Launch into character. Some bits: I couldn't find the farm because I just assumed it'd be an "organic" farm. Volvo was running on solar power and hit a "cloudy patch." Munching on vegan corn dog. Called it a "Not Dog." Boy this sun is *strong*! I hope I don't get cancer! Uh oh! What should I do? Remove baseball hat, slap on very wide-brimmed "Danny the Do-Gooder" sun hat. End performance by bringing cow onto the stage and begging for its life. Are summer burgers *that* important? Crowd goes *bonkers*.

June 23, 2003

Birthday party at very famous conservative lobbyists' backyard in
Potomac. My name is getting out there! Danny the Do-Gooder asks
Ginni Thomas to dance. But Danny insists she do so with his
cardboard image. Afraid of being accused of overstepping his
"boundaries." Huge laugh. Even from Ginni! New bit: "Charlie the
Chastiser." "Put down that can of Coke! It's *offensive*! Contains too
much *sugar*!" Walk around crowd with can, collecting for "America's
student debt." It's all an act. People are in hysterics. After gig I talk
with one of the Supreme Court justices. Forgetting his name. Not one
of the more famous ones that everyone knows.

July 4, 2003

National prayer breakfast. Lots of prayers and then I come on. Huge
laugh when I come out as "Vince Foster." I wasn't killed by Hillary
Clinton after all. I was forced to work as a river guide at their
Whitewater property. I turn around and the back of my head is bloody.
Huge laugh. I'm dead and am just a ghost, but a *liberal* ghost. I don't
feel that it's my right to knock objects of dressers. It's too "hurtful." I
also don't believe in "scaring" people. My job as a ghost is to make
people feel better about themselves. End performance by getting into
the Danny the Do-Gooder outfit and taking a nap on stage. I heard this
was important on "All Things Considered." The crowd goes wild. I'm
"asleep" for ten minutes.

July 8, 2003

Picnic for a secretive group called "The Family." I pretend to pull my
pants down and then pretend to use my behind as a ventriloquist
dummy. My ass is a liberal character. Then do some jokes about Jesus
being Jewish. Did he have a bar mitzvah? What was the theme of his
party? Did they serve water that he then turned into kosher wine? Was
he too cheap to pay for it? Then Danny the Do-Gooder chastised the
group for not accepting any women. Big laugh. Ended the
performance with my "free market" bit, in which Danny refuses to
leave the stage until he's paid more money. Ends with: "Off to the
market!" Huge laugh. Gave card to head of NRA.

July 10, 2003

Federalist Society in the basement of Bullfeathers on the Hill. Plenty of interns. So young! One sat before me and laughed the entire time. Talked with her after the show. She's 21 from Nebraska. Forgetting name. Didn't get her number as I wanted to be professional. Regretting it. She had large breasts and an innocent look that all interns have: *Wow! DC! Magical! Professional*!! What a load! She'll learn. Oh, will she learn! God her cans were fucking huge! Would have been hot as a fucking crack pipe in the hay. Tomorrow: the Koch brothers' Americans for Prosperity annual picnic. But they supposedly won't be there. Will start off with my "no dark meat allowed on the grills" gag.

July 15, 2003

Heritage Foundation. Interns smokin' fuckin' hot. If I don't unleash my load I'm-a gonna *explode*! Hard to concentrate on act when so backed up. Performance of Danny the Do-Gooder almost becoming rote. And frustrating that audience might even confuse me with the character? I hope not! Fun though.

August 1, 2003

Rare day off! Finally watched the first episode of my TIVO'ed *Last Comic Standing*. I can tell you already who's going to win: the Asian dude. Or the fat dude. It's pretty clear that the Chinese guy is going to win. Or the really fat dude. That's my prediction. Final in four days. Won't bother to watch the rest. Guarantee it! So glad I didn't make the cut for that shit. Everyone sucks.

August 5, 2003

I was right. The Asian dude. So clear. SO fucking happy I decided not to do this shit show. What a joke! Some funny people on it, or funny enough, but nothing of the highest caliber–no "top notch" here. And the Asian dude stinks!! Just a lot of hand gestures, which he'd be doing anyway, even off the stage. SO happy I steered cleared of this disaster! It would have only harmed my career and what I'm trying to comedically create. Tomorrow is the NRA picnic which is a *huge* gig. All networking has paid off! And *handsomely*!

August 6, 2003

Walked onto the NRA stage, pretending to have just been shot but then blamed it on gas pains. The audience went berserk. Was wearing a trench coat. When I removed it, people could see that I was hiding books. I explained that in case of an emergency, like if I was ever mugged, these were copies of the *Diagnostic Manual of Mental Disorders*. I was going to *analyze* whoever was attacking me. The crowd again went nuts. The Flammer flew onto the stage and went to "tackle" me. He screamed, *"Give me all your money!!!"* I pulled out one of the books and started to read out loud: "Did you have issues with your mother when you were reaching adolescence? Does that perhaps have something to do with your aggression towards me?" The "mugger" is so confused that he walks away. The book saved the day! Afterwards, head of the NRA, some guy named Wayne, came up and hugged me. Said it was the funniest show he'd ever seen. I'm telling you, this character is only getting bigger!! Rumor has it that Charlton Heston was in the audience but didn't understand a thing. That's okay. Interns hot as shit but a bit stuck-up. Or *stick*-up! Ha! Thinking about purchasing a gun just for grins. Asked to return next year! Hard to believe I could still be doing this … but why not!

This is where the diary ends.
And with good reason.
Okay, so what I'm about to write has never fully been written about.
Anywhere.
Forget all the articles, forget all the podcast episodes, forget all of those stupid comments on Reddit, just forget *all* of it.
And open your mind to the mother-*fudgin'* truth:
Women are complicated. Men are too, I guess.
Combine them: you have definite problems.
So my own specific problem started when I received an email from an association I wasn't at all familiar with: The Arc of the United States.
Strange name.
Turns out this group helped people with disabilities, both mental and physical. At first, I thought it was a joke but when my secretary told me they had called to ask if I could perform, I knew this shit was real.

I said yes … but only because I assumed they were a conservative organization that helped people with disabilities (why else would they name themselves after Noah's Arc?).

I gave them a call and talked with a woman whose name I'm forgetting.

She said she had heard good things about me from a few of the social directors at other associations and was wondering if I would perhaps be free to work an evening of entertainment for the association's donors.

I asked if they were conservative.

The woman said that they were neither conservative nor liberal. Just a group who wanted to help those in need.

Then she asked if I could work for free.

At first, I was furious.

Why the fuck would I ever work for free? This is my job!

It was offensive that she would even fucking ask!

Why would she ever even *assume* that I would?!

But I held my tongue.

I told her I'd get back to her and I did some research. She wasn't lying: the group definitely had no political affiliations. They just wanted to help those in need, which I was fine with.

I believe people should get off their asses and do their own work but let's be fair: if they can't even stand and get off their asses, maybe they *do* need a little help.

Also, and more importantly, doing charitable work could actually help *me* and my career with future gigs.

And one of my best friends growing up, please remember, had slammed his damn sled into a tree and was very much "special."

So yes, I guess I could perform for free. As long as they made an announcement after my performance that I was wonderful and loved everyone no matter how they looked, and then drum up even more interest in my act ….

The problem was this:

What, in particular, was I supposed to perform?

Come out on stage as Danny the Do-Gooder?

Sure, that'd go over *real* well.

The audience would already be *filled to the brim* with do-gooders.

Another issue: besides the crips, who else would be in the audience?

Caretakers? Regular people who could understand my jokes? Or people too afraid to laugh at *anything*?

And most importantly: were the specials capable of *truly* appreciating my jokes?

If not, then I'd have to re-think the entire act, which wouldn't have been a bad thing anyway.

I had been contemplating that perhaps I could also create a *conservative* stupid character. Not that I believed in that shit but it would double my chances of getting a gig every weekend.

I knew very little about liberals (only that I didn't particularly like them) but let's admit it: the color of their money is, and always will be, the same no matter the political affiliation.

I thought about it.

And then quickly ruled it out: it could only have ruined my chances with the hundreds of conservative think tanks and associations in D.C.

I mean, once word got out about that, I was *fucked*.

But again: What in the world should I perform before a crowd of cripples and their caretakers?

I took a long dip in my pool, I had much to think about. Miss Benda brought out my favorite drink and also dinner, which she had cooked. Chicken with white rice. I asked her opinion. She had none. I called the Flammer. He said I should do it, take the money and run, which was something the audience would never be able to pull off.

He's a funny guy, that Flammer. A real funny guy ...

I was no closer to a decision when Miss Benda brought me my favorite dessert: her cheesecake with fresh raspberries on top. Eating that cheesecake before a setting sun over the Potomac, I came to the decision to say yes.

Why not?

What's the *worst* that could happen?

If I had to just do my old act, but toned down, then I'd just do *that*. I was a professional performer and *this* is what the pros did: no matter the gig, no matter the audience, they took the money and they killed and then they went on to the next event.

And if I had to work for free to get some good street cred, so be it.

I called from the pool and told the woman I was in. I asked her how long I needed to be on stage and she said twenty-five minutes. I asked her about the audience and what type of people it would consist of: she said it'd be a mix between those who benefited from the group (cripples) and those who *ran* the group (caretakers and secretaries). She asked if I was sure I could work clean. I assured her that I could definitely work clean.

And that was that.

I downed the last drink and I toweled off and then I went up to my bedroom to prepare.

By early morning, I had come up with a new character.

Ain't that nice?

The gig was on a Friday night at Wolf Trap but not on the huge stage. Rather, it was on one of the smaller stages on the property.

A few hours before the gig, I hit the mall and bought just the right shirt. Something that would be fun to look at for the specially-abled but also a shirt that would be poignant enough to wear on such an important night. Driving over into Virginia from Bethesda, I thought about how far I had come from my beginnings in this town.

It had only been a few years but, quite honestly, it felt like a lifetime.

It's strange. Driving to this gig felt surreal. People don't believe me now, but it felt as if it would be my last gig for a very long time.

I don't know *why* I felt this way.

I wasn't scared. I was pretty confident this new character would do great.

But I felt an air of sadness surrounding it all. Perhaps it had to do with the retarded kids I was about to meet. Or with me having diarrhea from Miss Benda's fish dish a few hours prior. Whatever the reason, things felt a bit weird. Almost as if I was driving to my own hanging. I mean, I was doing a charity event for free.

What could possibly go wrong?

Little did I know.

I arrived at the site and introduced myself to a few of the charity workers. There were some specials and they seemed nice enough, if not necessarily overexcited about my upcoming performance. I also met a few of the donors, some of whom I knew from my previous performances.

That's the thing about conservatives. We get a bad reputation in a charitable sense but we probably end up giving more money to charities than anyone!

We just don't fucking brag about it!

The woman in charge (I'm still forgetting her name) came over and we began to chat. I assured her that the act would be clean and that I'd make everyone laugh.

There would be three acts that night. There would be a comedian (me), a magician (a guy named Magic Matt), and a bluegrass band (The Soothsayers), and then speeches thanking the donors and workers, and then that would be that. Show over.

I'd be up first.

The lights came down, the audience filled the remaining seats (or tried to) and I stepped onstage wearing a T-shirt that read:

I LOVE U!

Next to the U was a giant heart.

It wasn't a funny T-shirt, but it made a very solid point: I was nice, I was kind, and I was here to make *everyone* laugh, no matter their political leanings or ability to walk.

I said a few nice things, I thanked them for having me, and then I made some jokes about the Washington D.C. heat and humidity, which got some laughs. I then made a few cracks about the traffic, which *always* earned laughs, even from those without a "traditional" sense of humor.

I guess my mistake, in retrospect, was to do "crowd work," hitting the audience to ask questions and to then play off their responses. In the best of circumstances, a comedian needs some really chatty responses to play against. But if the audience's reactions are weak … well, it'd be like Roger Federer playing against a much worse opponent: he'll still play well but maybe not *as well* if he played someone really slamming the balls back at him with great force and top-spin.

I approached an audience member who looked entirely normal but was anything but.

"What brings you here today?" I asked.

"What?" he responded.

"Why are you here," I asked again, smiling at the crowd, really wanting them on my side.

"I was invited," he said. "Yeah."

Whoo boy.

This lemon didn't have a visible dent.

I went on to the next person, trying my luck once again. Thankfully, this one was a bit sharper.

"You having a good time?" I asked.

"I am, yes!" she said.

"Is this your date?" I asked.

"No," she said, quite seriously. "This is my daddy!"

Ooofa.

I went on to the next person in the crowd.

"How old are you, sweetheart?"

"Sixteen." But she said it with a speech impediment: "Thix-theen."

"Soon you'll be old enough for *this* guy!" I said pointing to the other "daddy." Actually, he *was* her daddy.

There was a laugh.

Not a *huge* laugh, though.

Just a laugh.

Hmmmm.

I moved on to a middle-aged woman.

"Hi!"

"Hi," she responded.

"Do you work for ARC?" I asked.

"I do," she said. "I work in accounting."

Thank fucking Christ! I thought. *Finally! Someone who can think!*

"Is there good money to be paid in non-profits?" I asked.

"No," she said. "Not at all. It stinks."

There was a hush.

If you take care of the retarded, I guess it makes sense that it won't bring in much dough. But I guess one isn't supposed to *admit* to that publicly.

In retrospect, it might have been a mistake to keep going with the crowd work and not then taking the opportunity to jump *back* on stage and launch sooner into my "I'm a Good Guy" character.

"Where ya from?" I asked another special.

This apple was very *clearly* bruised.

"Rockville!" she mumbled.

"Hey! I'm from Rockville," I said. "Wait, no. I'm from Bethesda. It's fancier. Even the cherry blossoms have their own lawyers!"

She didn't laugh. She didn't get it. Her Humor IQ was *very* low.

Uh oh.

On to the next person, a woman who looked to be in her twenties: "Whatya do?"

"What do I do?" she repeated slowly.

"Yeah? What do you do? Like all day and stuff? How do you earn your living?"

"I work at the Giant," she said.

"Oh, I shop at the Giant!" I replied, pretending to be super excited. "What do you do at the Giant? Are you a manager? Do you stock the grocery shelves?"

"I take bags to cars," she says. "I help."

"That's wonderful," I retorted.

"Yup," she said.

I was then going to say something obnoxious but it hit me.

I couldn't.

I couldn't go after these people.

Even if I desperately needed a laugh.

Why in the fuck didn't I think of that *before* I stepped off that stage to do crowd work?

Skippy! Jesus! Fuck are you thinking, moron!

These weren't the type of people to be razzed, they really weren't!

These were not audience members I could mock about their clothing.

Or their hair. Or their dates.

Or *anything* else, for that matter!

"Well, you do good work," I eventually replied, trying desperately to get everyone back on my side. "Honestly, the world needs grocery bag carriers. I don't know how much you're paid but that there is a job I wouldn't do for all the money in the world. It's very, *very* important. But just not for me."

She nodded.

The crowd was silent.

Where was I going with this?

Shit. I had *no* fucking idea! Where *could* I go?

"Well, keep it up," I eventually said. "It's really important work and we're so blessed to have you doing it."

Okay, that's enough, I thought. Back up to the stage where I was in full control.

I hopped back up and started with my official "I'm a Good Guy" set.

Jokes about how retarded people are our "beacon of light." Jokes about how I wouldn't know how to knit a place mat for all the money in the world. A few jokes about retarded people who have Baltimore accents and how strange that must sound to people outside the area. A joke about once attending a Redskins game and a retarded guy ran onto the field and was tackled.

I did my bit about the famous Nazi director, Leni something, I'm forgetting her name. She was the movie director who filmed the 1936 Munich Olympics in beautiful black and white.

But what people might not have known was that she *also* shot the 1938 *Special* Olympics for film. There were long, endless scenes of thousands of wheelchairs moving in unison.

Before I knew it, the set was over and I received a nice, if not amazing, round of applause. Maybe it was a physical issue as a few didn't have full use of their extremities.

So, contrary to reports, the performance, itself, really wasn't a disaster. Honestly, it really wasn't.

I wouldn't grade it an A.

But I also wouldn't grade it a C.

Maybe a B. Perhaps a B plus.

There's no audio of this gig, so I'm not sure how critics are so confident that it was "historically bad," as one asshole wrote on Reddit.

Was it my *best* performance ever?

Hardly.

Was it my worst?

No, not even close. I'd put a few others up there for that particular award:

The NAACP Awards in 2017, the B'nai B'rith Award Ceremony at the Rockville JCC in 2014, and the group of gay First Iraqi War vets in San Francisco, 2016.

Those were *bad*.

Maybe even "historically" bad.

Listen, I'm all for honesty, I really am.

If you want to say I'm not attractive, which probably isn't true, you're more than free to say that.

Or if you want to say that I grew up in Maryland, well, that *is* true.

But to just make shit up about me? I have *no* patience for that nonsense.

And I *hate* nonsense.

I was there that night.

I *saw* what happened. I *heard* what happened. I fucking *lived* what happened.

Yes, I know NBC local TV news personality Arch Campbell was there and he hated the performance. I know a few (liberal) politicians who were also there and despised what I did. I know that the owner of the Redskins was there and that he *did* like the show.

So the problem was not with my comedy or with my performance or with my new character or fresh material.

No, the problem was everything that came *after*.

And it was something I never, not in a million years, could have ever, ever have imagined.

But it *did* happen.

And I'm finally willing to talk about it.

What came next was something I could *never* forget.

But it would be something that I would be forced to deal with for many years to come.

Even though I didn't particularly want to.

But I had to.

And it would change the course of my life and my career forever.

And there was nothing I could do about it ....

★ Chapter Seventeen ★
PLAYING BALL WITH THE LAW

In truth, Washington D.C. is not so much a city as it is a *small town*.

Everyone who matters—whether they're lawyers, lobbyists, or comedians—tend to know each other.

(To be fair, I guess everyone who does *not* matter—whether they're retail workers, blue collars types, capitol policemen, crab shuckers—*also* tend to know each other, but whatever.)

So when word got out about what had happened *after* the show ... well, your boy was in a bit of a pickle, amongst those who *mattered*.

I didn't much care about those who didn't.

As I said earlier, I'm a man of truth, so I'm going to lay it all out for you here ... *truthfully*.

The problems for me started *after* the show.

Not before.

Understood? Good.

Not *during* the show.

But only *after* my performance.

With that out of the way:

I look back and wonder what the hell I was thinking.

Did I really need to ask out one of the audience members?

Did it really need to be the girl who was mentally challenged?

Did it really need to be with a girl who was fifteen (but *very* close to becoming sixteen)?

Did it really need to be with the girl who worked at the Giant grocery as a bagger?

Yeah, I have a lot of questions. What a dummy. Me. Not her.

Although she wasn't the brightest. In fact, she was a real dummy.

Another question: Did I have to fuck her at the foot of the steps to the Lincoln Monument?

Honestly, and this is the god's honest truth, I had no idea she was fifteen (but *very* close to sixteen). With specials, they can age faster.

Beyond that, I had no fucking idea that Maryland even *allowed* fifteen-year-olds to work!

Zero idea!

I never worked at fifteen! My friends didn't either!

Who works at fifteen? Especially if you're not quite "right" in the ol' coconut?

You have to bring in money to feed the family? Or are you just doing all this shit for the spare change to buy your bubble gum?

I stand before you and I now fucking admit it:

I fucked an underage specially-abled chick in front of the Lincoln Memorial while wearing only my I LOVE U t-shirt and gym socks.

Okay?

That's the truth.

The god's honest truth.

But do you know what's *not* the truth?

That she *looked* fifteen.

That she was so brain damaged that she didn't know what she was doing.

That I did it for the free grocery food.

That I fucked her more than once.

That I pregnated her.

I could go on and on and on, like god knows others have and still do, but I won't.

I paid the price.

I did wrong.

I *admit* that.

I was backed up and horny and my "man snake" desperately needed to be milked.

I blame all the normal women of "legal age" who had said *no* to me over the past few weeks that summer. The Georgetown interns, the Gaithersburg secretaries, the haughty women lawyers in their white stockings and tennis shoes on their way to the Metro and to downtown Washington.

Would I do it again?

Probably.

Let's not beat around the "bush" … this chick may not have been the brightest, but from the neck down, she was smarter than fucking Einstein.

She was fifteen (almost sixteen) going on thirty-five.

An idiotic thirty-five-year-old but still …

And guess what? We're *still* friends to this day and keep in touch! No hard feelings, at least on her part.

What does that tell you?!

She's now a mother of two (believe it or not!) and her kids are supposedly fine. Not sure who her husband is or if he has any major problems himself.

But he must have the patience of a fucking saint.

Yeah, all of it was definitely a most *uncomfortable* situation.

But it was made all the worse for a number of reasons.

For one, the late-night tourists at the Lincoln memorial were taking *a lot* of photos and videos that night. (By the way, who *does* that? I'm from D.C. and have *never* been to a monument at night. I mean, who in the fuck *does* that?! There's nothing better to do at night in D.C. than visit a fucking stupid monument?)

There was also the president of Ecuador and his wife and their two young daughters who were visiting the monument that night. The girls were "traumatized." *And what was he doing there?! He had nothing better to be doing as the president of Ecuador than visit the fucking Lincoln Memorial?*

With his kids?!

And then there was *another* issue.

And that would be the issue of this girl's difficult father.

[Clearing of the throat. A sip of water. An "ahem." A nod of the head. Okay! Now let's *hit* this! …]

The bastard was one of the goddamn heads of the motherfuckin' ACLU.

Yeah.

Let me say that again but slower, for all you idiots:

This girl's father was one of the heads of the goddamn ACLU … a group I didn't love in the *best* of times and grew to love even less, if that was possible, in the upcoming *worst* of times.

At least for a while.

If I had known then the ups and downs my life would soon take, specifically my experiences involving the ACLU, I would have … well, I don't know what I would have.

There was so much to come for me, both good and bad. But I had lived through so much already—like a war veteran—that I truly thought of myself as ancient.

Little did I know.

Of course, I was still only in my twenties.

So just a baby. But that's the way it is right? No matter the age, you always *feel* older. I imagine five-month-old babies feel ancient and pine for their younger days. That could make for a good Pixar movie.

The true problem for me began as soon as my father reached out to the father of the woman I slept with.

My father was doing a good thing. He was proposing a peace offering. My father actually *knew* this guy through a friend of a friend. Like I say, D.C. is a small town, and everyone who matters tends to know each other.

The offer was rudely rebuffed through a lawyer for the other side. This is when things got ugly.

My father didn't like to be pushed around, god love his soul.

I didn't either but I was not as strong willed.

This father we were dealing with was a block of steel.

But I was still pretty confident everything would work itself out.

I really didn't feel that I was totally in the wrong here.

True, she was fifteen (but very close to being sixteen).

But I can swear to you that, as they say, the patio was in and the pool was already wet.

All systems go!

It was like a rocket with a fully capable engine. Why just sit on the launchpad for another few years?

She was ready to explode.

Obviously her father did not think of his daughter as being similar to a rocket ready to explode.

I guess to him, this rocket was still a baby rocket and still being "built."

Which is understandable.

My father, sensing trouble, then kicked into high gear.

This was really his specialty.

Mine was making people laugh. My dad's was protecting his interests, whether it was soda or his son. We had a lot of differences. But I'll give him this: the dude was loyal.

My pops then moved into full operational mode. I'd seen him do this a few times.

Once (I think it was 1996 or so) poison was found in a certain very popular soda brand.

Have you heard about this?

No?

Really?

Why not?

Oh, I *know* why.

Because my father quashed it.

I *did* hear about it and I am here to tell you that if *you* had heard about it, the company would no longer exist.

My father was a fixer. He had his problems and could be selfish but the motherjumper could fix *anything*. He was a magician. Have a situation that needed fixing? Hire my dad and watch it disappear.

Typically, this wouldn't have been cheap. But for me, it cost nothing. He did it out of true love. And I can only thank him wherever he might now reside, which I'm guessing is a comped room up in the big H.

My pops generously offered the other side a very nice settlement offer.

They refused it.

Outright.

So he launched into the next phase:

D.C. has PR firms like other cities have methadone clinics. Or Starbucks. Literally, in Washington public relations firms sit on every corner. Some are good. Some are okay. A few are *amazing*.

One is the *best*.

My dad just happened to have gone to Georgetown Prep with the CEO of this particular firm. Let's call it Rubicon & Woebegone.

I went in one afternoon and sat down at a huge conference table, surrounded by the best and the brightest in the PR field. Young men just out of Harvard, young women just out of Yale, here they were, the top in their very field.

I wasn't used to school smarts.

I was used to *street* smarts.

But when you get into certain fights, street smarts can only get you so far.

When you're in such trouble, you want on your side *wonkies*.

Not *honkies*.

And I *got* 'em. The intellectual energy inside this meeting room could have lit a thousand moons. These people were fucking *smokin'* smart. They wouldn't have been the people I'd want to grab a drink with at a bar, necessarily, but I wasn't there to drink. I was here to save my career. And possibly prevent myself from headed off to fucking lockup.

This was no joke. I knew it at the time but it really hit home when my father's lawyer told me that I could be facing up to 25 years in a federal prison!

25 fucking years!

For what?! Beyond that, I'd be branded a sex criminal, not allowed to look at the internet (let alone internet porn), not be anywhere near children, forced to register as a sex offender every time I moved, forced to notify comedy club owners, producers, executives … *fucking nightmare*.

I did *not* want that.

I *really* did not want that.

I soon heard that the other side wanted to head to trial.

Good Lord, really?!

Here we were, offering a ton of money to fix the situation and you just want to make this public?

Putting your supposedly precious daughter in the public eye? Why?!

I could only think it was purely for retribution.

Why else?

So, yeah, there might now be a goddamn trial.

It hurt to even say the word "trial."

But whether that happened or not, the trial for my *reputation* had already started.

And this I needed to *win*.

The PR team (which I nicknamed the "Batty Down the Hatches Club") got right on it. They were going to prop up two elements of my brand:

Me as a human being (personal life).

Me as a comedic performer and comedy writer (professional life).

In the past, when, say, this firm represented politicians who had gotten into a bit of a ticklish situation, they had come out swinging.

This seemed to work for their clients, whether they were caught in a public bathroom doing something they shouldn't have been doing or whether they were seen on video accepting something they shouldn't have been accepting.

And this is what they did for me.

Came out fucking *swinging*.

This was a good team. And they were on my side.

It felt good.

Advertisements were taken out in the *Washington Compost* and even the *Washington Times*, as well as *Washingtonian* magazine. The ads had a photo of me and the tag-line: "Rumors aren't *always* true."

The team then attempted to put me on various local TV news programs, not so much as to dispute any particular accusation made against me but to show that I was a local guy who made real good.

When that didn't work (it seems at this point in my career I wasn't well known enough), they took out thirty-minute chunks of pre-paid programming on local TV channels.

These ads typically aired very early in the morning on weekdays. They hired an interviewer (really a local actor, Tony W.____) who lobbed softball questions at me about my career and my common decency.

It was all a good start but the trial was starting to get ramped up. And the ACLU father was pulling in some big guns, lawyers who had very successful careers putting famous (and not so famous) people away for a long time. They weren't asking for money here. They wanted my goddamn *blood*.

The next phase was for me to visit various children's hospitals, old-age centers, animal kill shelters and other annoying places that I'd typically avoid for some top-shelf goodwill maneuvering.

A photographer followed me around at each and took what seemed like a million photos of me hugging kids, old people, old dogs and cats that no one wanted or needed any longer.

A webpage was created at SkippyBattison.com (don't bother looking, it's long since been removed) with photos taken at these places. There was also a long bio and a list of all of my accomplishments on this webpage. I wanted to put up some performing dates but I was talked out of it.

Seems that this would have looked bad … although I still don't know exactly why.

A man has to earn a living, right?

I was sent to high schools to talk about my career choice.

I traveled to the Voice of America to talk to Europeans about my experience in the comedy industry.

I taught some free comedy classes for the underprivileged, all the while being photographed for my good work.

If anyone asked about my case or the upcoming trial, I'd claim that I wasn't allowed to talk about it, although very few people did. They just thought I was another successful comedy guy making the rounds. What they didn't know was that in a few weeks I was going to go on public trial for something that could have looked bad.

I was getting the jump on what these assholes could end up doing to my reputation.

A few weeks before the trial was set to begin, I was already plum-fucking exhausted from running around, telling everyone how great I was. Did I believe it? Even *half* of it? I believed I wanted to stay out of lockup, so, yes, I believed *all* of it. And why not? I really wasn't a bad guy. I just had needs like every other red-white-and-blue-blooded American male.

That's not an excuse. That's just *reality*.

And I bring it up because of what happened next:

The CEO of Rubicon & Woebegone was my father's good friend. He was someone I knew all throughout my years growing up. He was almost like an uncle to me. He had two daughters, one of whom was my age. Her name was Robyn. He also had a younger daughter, this one seventeen. Her name was Lynda. A lot of names with "y"s in this family. Why they couldn't just spell names normally always confused me. But who was I to complain? I'm surprised they never called me Skyppy.

I never really talked much to Lynda growing up. She was just a kid. She was good looking enough, I suppose, but I just wasn't interested.

Well, all that changed when she approached me one night, a few days before the trial was supposed to begin, to say that she had been watching me on the TV shows and reading about me on my webpage and in other publications. And she apologized: "I had no idea you were this successful."

One might say that Lynda fell for her own father's spin.

But one could also say that she was falling in love with me, *the real me*.

I was in a tight spot here.

This young, now quite attractive young woman (almost eighteen) wanted me as her boyfriend.

My higher conscience told me to run.

But my lower libido made that impossible.

So when her father caught us fucking in the gazebo behind his Potomac house ... well, that's when things became even *more* messy.

My father quickly stepped in and had a long chat with his friend but it did no good. This guy didn't even want any money.

He wanted *nothing*.

Nothing, that is, except to no longer have *anything* to do with my case.

What he *would* do, however, was to keep what had happened between me and Lynda under wraps, until at least the trial was over.

So that was cool of him. There was no talk of this chick being mentally challenged. Not this one. She was a smart girl who ended up attending Harvard. There was definitely no bruising on *this* lemon. We still keep in touch and we're still really great friends on Facebook. I have no ill will towards her. I wish her the very best.

The PR team was no longer behind me, though.

That was the bad news.

The good news was that most of their work had already been completed.

And it had worked. People I knew from high school were emailing and telling me how proud they were of my career success. Teachers were writing to tell me that my talks to the kids about my life in comedy really helped quite a lot of them, mostly those who weren't the brightest. I received a *lot* of emails asking if I'd run for some sort of office.

I very humbly said no.

My purpose on this big, blue, wobbly ol' marble is to make others laugh and smile. Not to pass laws. But I appreciated the sentiment nonetheless.

If D.C. has no shortage of people in PR, then it also has no shortage of people in another profession:

High-priced hookers.

Sorry. Joking. Too easy.

No seriously:

I'm talking about the *legal* profession. It's very much a lawyer town, with one lawyer for every fifteen citizens. Or something like that. There are *a lot* of lawyers.

A ton of people I graduated with at Georgetown Prep later became lawyers and judges.

The defender my father had found for me was the best. But he didn't come cheap. We're talking $300 an hour. And this was in 2004! Imagine how much he'd be today! I'm not going to use his name as we didn't end on the best of terms. But I will say that he represented Ted Kennedy a few times, to varying degrees of success.

He was a player.

My father knew him from when they both attended Georgetown Prep in the '70s.

He was a partier then, and a partier now.

But he had an *amazing* legal mind.

(And no, I'm not talking about Kavanaugh here. He did *not* represent me in this case, as much as people now seem to have *wanted* him to.)

Anyway, my lawyer's first task was to attempt to have the case settled out of court.

Didn't work.

He then went into the long game of delaying each of the trial dates. That *did* work.

Before we knew it, it was 2005. The supposed criminal action had taken place back in 2003. I had been living at home all this time. I call this my "lost period." My fierce hunger to achieve success was put aside for the time being. I did all of the things I had missed out on the first go-round: went out to bars with friends, fraternity parties at the University of Maryland, spring break down in Florida, sorority dances, everything that others my age had already done when not shunting aside their lives to make it big in comedy.

I felt rejuvenated.

This felt great!

So this *is what it felt like not to be driven to success!*

It felt good. And it was fun. There were moments when I honestly wondered why I hadn't partied more after high school and refused to have all the fun that most teens and early twenty-somethings are entitled to experience.

And then, before I knew it (or wanted it), the trial date finally arrived.

The judge could not be persuaded to settle for lesser charges. The family could not be persuaded to settle with money. There was only one thing to do: suffer the indignity of going through a public trial in my hometown of Rockville. Actually, I was from Bethesda, but close enough. (The girl lived in Rockville with her family and they decided that a jury of Marylanders would be *a lot* more on their side than a jury would have been in D.C., where the "incident" took place. They probably weren't wrong.)

What came next you've probably read about in either of the two books written and published about the case.

I suppose it's a famous trial now at law schools. I know every comic on earth has talked about it on their podcasts. I know Tenacious D has written a song about it. I know *Brooklyn Nine-Nine* did an episode based on it. I know Bob and Dave did a parody of the trial during a live concert of *Mr. Show* at New York's Beacon Theatre. I know that even the fucking *Mendendez twins* watched this trial from their jail cells and later wrote about it to their wives, which later "leaked" to TMZ. (Yes, the Mendendez twins are fucking married!)

It was *big* news.

Maybe not *O.J. murder big* but definitely big news.

The trial date finally arrived.

There was no way to avoid it any longer.

But there was one thing I could do to improve my chances:

And that was fire my idiot of a $300-per-hour lawyer and to take on the case myself.

The lawyer was useless and expensive.

And it occurred to me that I didn't *need* him.

I was an entertainer. That's what I *did*. I entertained audiences.

Whether they were in comedy clubs or at Wolf Trap or whether they were court juries.

People liked me! I made them laugh! So why couldn't I work this very same magic on this particular group of twelve of my peers?

The answer was so startlingly obvious that I laughed when I first came to the conclusion.

Shit, why not?!

I can *save* money. Or my father's money.

And also my own *damn life!*

Who do I trust more with saving my life than me?!

No one!

My father didn't find it so funny and begged me to keep on his expensive friend.

No dice.

I was a glorious bird and I floated alone.

It was just the way it had to be.

Some humans fly in packs.

Other fly alone.

I was a solitary human flyer.

The point I'm trying to make is that I *wanted* the trial to go the way it did. I did everything on purpose. It was not due to any other reason than that I wanted to be in *full control* of my own destiny.

I kept a diary around the time of the trial and I'm now going to share selected excerpts from those two weeks in February 2005. This is the first time anyone is reading this, beyond myself and some dame I slept with in 2009. I'm forgetting her name.

The entire performance—and, yes, it was a *performance*—was an "optics" choice. Influence the narrative and you influence the future.

Looking back, this could have been the greatest performance I've ever given. Why people refuse to see it as a *performance* perplexes me. But I was *always* in full control.

I was the pilot.

And this plane was headed straight into uncharted territory. Just where I *wanted* it.

My diary, complete with coffee stains:

Day #1

Showed up shirtless in a fake executioner's mask. Jury consists of seven women and five men. The men range in age from twenty-three to some dude in his fifties. The women are all below the age of forty, which is awesome. I have them in the palm of my hand. A few laughed when they saw me. Always a good sign.

Day #2

A few laughs today that only I could discern. It's like the "Real Feel" weather. I think some jurists don't want to piss off the judge by laughing too hard. Initial instructions from judge are over. Tomorrow begins the trial. Excited.

Day #3

First witnesses arrived. I started the day by demanding that the court supply me with a "hemorrhoid donut." Real Laugh Count: 7 jurors or more. Hoping they forget why they're here and just concentrate on my <u>jokes</u>. The president of Ecuador took the stand and looking none too pleased. I guess it's a long flight from Ecuador to describe watching two people fucking at the foot of the Lincoln Memorial. Accent strong and thankfully jury couldn't understand. Got a few laughs by looking over at them as he mispronounced "furiously." I couldn't help but also giggle.

Day #4

The girl herself showed and looked supremely confused. Sat in the crowd. She appeared very happy to see me. I was wearing a funny T-shirt that read STOP SNITCHING. She laughed but not sure understood the joke. At break, I very calmly sat at the defense desk and thought about lighting a cigar with a $100 bill like De Niro did in Cape Fear. Didn't.

Day #5

D.C. officer on the stand. I asked him if he could get me free tickets to the July 4th event at the White House. He smirked.

Day #6

Asked the judge real loud: "Who we stickin' it to today, boss, huh?!" When he banged his gavel, I launched into a short Stomp-style percussion beat with my feet.

Day #7

I showed taped testimony from the girl's friend to prove that girl actually enjoyed the love-making. Prosecution having a hissy fit. To lighten things, I pretended I had a funny limp. Hobbled around and told the jury, "It's an old war injury." I then whispered: "Drug war."

Day #8

I asked, "Wait, is this a <u>Sharia</u> court?" Judge not pleased. I asked if he could be replaced with "Dancing Itos." When he kept chastising me, I slapped on a pair of night vision goggles I had brought for just this type of thing and insisted that I needed them to see <u>the truth.</u>

Day #9

Cross-examination today by the prosecution on yet another witness to the Lincoln Memorial incident. When the lawyer finished, I made the Law & Order "chung chung" tone. This time the entire place burst into laughter, especially a real cute and tasty kumquat in the jury.

Day #10 (part one)

Returned from bathroom break and told judge I had been "looking for clues." Father is begging me to hire back his lawyer friend. I got this.

Day #10 (part two)

Gave my final thoughts or whatever it's called. Jury looked pleased. To thank them for all their hard work, I made each a T-shirt with their names on them. Judge chastised me. I mumbled, "Do you want to be banged with my meat gavel?" When he still chastised me, I shouted "<u>Odor</u> in the court!" Real Laugh Meter: ten to twelve.

Day #11

No decision. Passed the time by practicing my autograph.

Day #12

Still waiting. No jury to amuse. Thought about asking the judge if he had time to talk to "Mr. Ben Franklin." I would then hand over a few $100s. But thought better of it. He doesn't have the best sense of humor and could take it all wrong. Also I don't have a few hundreds. Overall, I think it went well. Truth is, I don't have much of a case. I took a chance. Hoping it'll pay off.

Day #13

Well that didn't go well. When the verdict was first read, I thought at first they were joking. They weren't. I checked their faces for the Real Laugh calculation but saw nothing. The judge gave me some crap about how this wasn't a comedy club but a courtroom and none of it was any laughing matter. He then handed down his sentence: I was headed to prison from what I understood to be 18 – 24 months and I was "lucky" that I was getting only that much time and not more. And the only reason I wasn't getting more had to do with the girl putting in a good word for me. I guess it could have been worse. I don't have to register as a sex offender. But, then again, I'll never be elected to high office. Some cheered and other looked pained. I could hear my mother cry. My father mouthed "it'll be okay." I motioned over to the jury as if to say, "C'mon, guys." No one returned my look. A real solid group of people, this jury. They weren't my true peers after all.

End of diary.
I will say this:
It ain't like it is on television. Or in the movies.
Or *My Cousin Vinny*.
God how I love that movie.
But in real life, the American trial system mostly consists of waiting and filling out papers and approaching the bench and meeting in the judge's quarters and having to cross-examine the president of a Latin American country with two "damaged" daughters.
And then me trying my very hardest to provide some levity and jokes.
The verdict was read.
One of the sheriffs cuffed me and I was led out. It was a very surreal feeling. The only thing that helped was that I began to imagine that it was a skit that I had written and that it would all end with a giant laugh and then applause.

This is strange but it's true: a scene from *Heavyweights* came to mind. It was the scene in which one of the fat kids was being picked on and having food thrown at him. It was hilarious. But the audience was supposed to feel bad. He was fat and he was having food thrown at him. I felt like the same type of victim. I knew I'd make it through but I really did feel awful.

I looked over to the girl. She was also crying. I didn't blame her then and I don't blame her now. It was her father I had a problem with. I didn't dare look at his smug-ass face.

Fuck him.

Honestly, this was a *nothing* incident.

The girl loved it, I thought it was okay and the tourists found it oddly amusing. Welcome to the *real* D.C., assholes!

But the jury didn't see it that way.

No, they definitely did not.

And I was then led off to the next chapter of my life.

To a world I never knew existed.

But that I would soon very much be a part of.

To say that I had no idea of what was coming next would be an understatement.

What came next changed the course of my life forever.

In ways I never would have predicted ....

★ Chapter Eighteen ★
DOING HARD TIME IN A HARD, HARD WORLD

I'd never known anyone who had been to prison.

It wasn't in my worldview.

My father knew criminals, just harmless white-collar stuff. And I think he almost had to go himself but he got out of it. We never really talked about it.

I *had* known friends who had gotten into trouble for nonsense like not paying taxes or bilking employees or trying to kill their ex-wife's current boyfriend.

But this was new territory for me.

My first stop was a prison in Bethesda called the Montgomery County Detention Center, which is off Seven Locks Road.

It's basically a way station until a prisoner has been properly entered into the system and then sent to a real prison.

I had passed the place a thousand times but had never really thought twice about what happened inside.

From the courtroom in Rockville, I was taken by van by a couple of moron fake cops (otherwise known as "prison guards") on I-270 to the jail. Passing all my familiar haunts in this white van was weird.

How the fuck did I end up here?

Was it my fault?

Or was it the fault of the fuck-face father who had brought this down on me?

Again, I don't blame in any way the girl. Her brain engine wasn't exactly a V-8. Her attic wasn't exactly lit with fluorescent lighting. Her penthouse wasn't exactly staged for buyers.

No, it wasn't her fault.

But I knew that my life was about to change forever.

There was a *before* and now there would be an *after*.

Would I survive it?

More importantly, could I *thrive* it?

Could I come out of all this shit stronger, with my career *more* intact and headed in the right direction than it had been?

I had been doing so well!

Goddamnit!

And then the rug was pulled out from under me!

And here I now sat, in a shitty white van, cruising at the speed limit west on I-270.

I'd be lying if I were to tell you that I wasn't nervous.

Who wouldn't be?

I was a tough guy in a lot of ways, but I was not "prison tough."

Who was I going to meet? Would I be able to handle the prison politics? The craziness? The violence? How about the godawful food? I *loved* good food! And I had to eat *this* shit for up to two years??!

No boardwalk fried clams in *this* place!

The first thing I noticed when walking into the facility was the smell.

And the noise.

God, that *awful* noise!

What a racket!

It was like being thrown into a rock polishing machine.

A machine that stunk worse than death itself.

Screaming. Yelling. Crying. Laughing. People being sick. Bars clanging. Screeches. Whooping. Hollering. Even *more* screaming.

You name it, you heard it.

You heard it, you *smelled* it.

I can only compare the smell to once visiting a friend's fraternity at University of Maryland. Old socks, body odor, vomit, rotting food, piss, shit. Anything you ever stepped on by accident. Anything you ever stepped in *on purpose*. Your grandmother as she lay dying. The breath on that one kid in school with the orthodontic wrap-around headgear.

I had no idea people could *live* like this.

I was being put through all this hell because I banged a chick? I was now stuck with rapists and murderers and bank robbers and muggers and all the rest of society's scumbags?

Me?

Any *reason* for this?

I was taken to the R&R (Receiving and Release) and was forced to strip, bend over, and spread my ass cheeks.

The last time I had done this was prom night.

I was handed pants, shorts, a shirt, boxers and a jacket. Everything was orange. I was sent to GP (or "general population"), which is a nice way of saying "a large room with a bunch of fucking monsters."

I'd never seen people like this in my life. It was like the bar scene in *Total Recall*. All that was missing was a midget chick with three tits.

These people were goddamn *freaks*!

To think that I'd lived around these creatures for the past twenty-seven years ... and never noticed them before!

How?!

I had seen my share of beasts on the Ocean City boardwalk, but that was *nothing* compared with this sterling crew.

Perhaps I felt sorry for myself.

And, as much as I hate to admit this, maybe I even began to cry.

I didn't belong here! I belonged up on stage, entertaining. Or writing jokes for billions of people to enjoy!

Fuck! I was the same guy who had written the Titanic parody song at the fucking Academy Awards!

That counts for *something*, right?

Maybe a little *more* than something?

I had fucking written for *Wayans Bros* on network television!

That counts for a little something, too, *right*?

I mean, how many people have written professionally for television?

Especially in the D.C. area?

I wasn't exactly Prisoner Zero here.

I had fucking *accomplished* something!

And *this* is where I ended up?

Did I *deserve* this shit?

For making love?

People were awarded fucking medals in the 1960s for making love and not war!!!!

The irony, I guess, is that people *now* were being handed awards for making war and *not* love!

(You can use this quote if you want. It's a good one.)

I arrived at the prison.

I became prisoner 64684-947. (I wanted to ask the intake guards if they took vanity requests, like they would with license plates. I thought *DNT RPE ME* might be a good one to have. But I didn't ask.)

No, this place definitely wasn't the Four Seasons.

The entire prison was a mess, with one huge holding cell where people could hang all day watching television and playing cards or checkers, and then another room that held a lot of bunks where we'd be sleeping.

The bad news was that the bunks were right on top of each other.

The good news was that I wouldn't be in this particular facility any longer than 72 hours before I was eventually transferred.

I'd be given a bunk later. But for now I was just told to "hang" until things were sorted.

Great. Just hang out. Anyone wanna play cribbage? Talk about Judd Apatow's *Heavyweights*? Maybe gossip about Billy Crystal?

I sat down at a round metallic table surrounded by round metallic seats. No one seemed to pay me any mind.

There was a pack of cards.

Fuck it. I was playing solitaire.

Nothing wrong with me playing alone in prison.

I figured I'd better get used to it.

A guy sidled over.

Uh oh.

Was this trouble?

He asked my name. He then asked what I was in for.

Jesus, already? That didn't take long!

I told him "bank robbery."

He nodded.

"Same. Nice to meet you. You look like one of the normals."

Phew. This guy wasn't after my ass. He just wanted to pick my *brain*. And maybe he was lonely.

We shook hands.

And began to talk.

And talk.

And talk.

Before I knew it, hours had passed and it was finally time for "chow," which meant a bologna sandwich and chips.

We talked some more and then we said goodbye.

It was time to hit my new bunk.

I followed a guard to a bottom cot in the corner of the huge room. He handed me a towel, a bed sheet and a case for the pillow.

"Who's on the top?" I asked.

"Depends on who's the boss," he said.

A real jokester.

"I meant the bunk," I replied. "Not *me.*"

He shrugged and scuffled away.

Loser.

I turned around and started fumbling with the sheets. Making a bed was *never* my specialty in the best of circumstances, let alone in prison. Typically Miss Benda would make mine when I was growing up. When I got older, I'd hire a cleaning woman once a week to take care of such shit. And then when I moved back home, Miss Benda would continue to make my bed. It was convenient.

The sheets felt like sandpaper. God knows who had slept on these already. Could I request Washington Redskins sheets like the ones I had as a kid?—

I heard someone approach behind me.

Now what?

Before I could turn, I heard, "Let me help."

Oh shit.

Just what I need! A Helpful Henry! Who'll want "things"!

I turned.

Guess who?

The same guy I had been earlier talking with!

And it looked like he was now my bunkmate!

I'd tell you his real name but you wouldn't recognize it anyway.

But you would recognize his *Passin' on the Right* moniker: Doctor Feelgood, Lifelong Intern Extraordinaire!

That's right. The guy I first met and bunked with inside the dreaded Seven Locks Correctional Facility was none other than Doctor Feelgood, the world's oldest radio intern.

Never heard this story before?

There's a good reason.

I've never told *anyone* this story. I'm only telling you now because I have the good doctor's permission. I *still* won't give you his real name. There's a solid reason he's never been photographed or interviewed. Let's just say he has a "past." But he's a loyal pal and that's good enough for me.

We ended up really bonding over those three days at the Seven Locks facility, talking all day and sometimes even into the night, until we were told to shut our fucking honky yappers.

The good doctor has an interesting backstory: born in Hagerstown, in Western Maryland, he was raised by a single mother in Germantown who worked at Lakeforest Mall as a sales girl at one of the department stores. I think it was Hechinger's. She worked a second job at night doing the books for a crab restaurant on Rockville Pike. It was all she could do to support her family. There were no complaints, no requests to feed off the government teat. She died at age 45 driving to work, her car veering off the road and crashing into a ditch on Route 28. The poor woman had fallen asleep.

The good doctor was then on his own, living with relatives and friends, working the odd job, smoking a ton of reefer, listening to music, seeing live shows, just having a grand ol' time.

Then he got into a stitch of trouble.

And here he now was.

The three days flew past. We talked all the time and played cards. And when it came time to eat those delicious prison meals, we also ate together.

At the end of our stretch at the temporarily lock-up, it was announced that a group would be leaving in a van for their new permanent (or semi-permanent) homes.

I said goodbye to the good doctor, told him we'd be in touch after we both got out, and I then made my way to the van ... *which was the same goddamn van the good doctor was being taken to!*

I couldn't get away from this fucker!

We were both headed to the same shit hole: the Maryland Correctional Institution in Hagerstown, the same town where he was born. We laughed when I entered the back of the van all chained, only to see him already seated. He, too, was chained from head to toe.

Coincidences are a funny thing.

I've experienced a few in my life. I'm not talking about having the same birthday as a celebrity.

No, I'm talking times when a higher power, or whatever the hell is up or down there, makes it known that you're *meant* to be with someone.

This happened with the Flammer when we met on the Ocean City boardwalk over our mutual love for Stephen King's *Needful Things*.

And it was happening right here in prison with the good doc.

Two Maryland guys finding each other in the worst of circumstances and going through all of it together—*and beyond.*

I love stories like that.

There have been articles written about my time in prison. And I've spoken a little about it but never at length.

Many assume that it was the worst years of my life.

Just the opposite.

I hesitate to even write this because I can only imagine the callers from future shows giving me shit.

You *liked* prison?

How could you enjoy fucking prison?!

No, assholes. I didn't exactly *like* it.

But in the end, it was *good* for me.

I *still* don't think I necessarily belonged in prison for what I had done. I'd be lying if I said otherwise.

But a few good things came out of my time there:
I matured into the person I am today.
I came up with the idea for this book and started working on it.
I met a lot of cool people I *still* keep in touch with.
And the stories.
So many stories …
The good doctor and I arrived at Hagerstown and were interviewed, screened, given a fresh set of cardboard-stiff clothing and sent to our separate cells, his a few down from mine.
And yes, we each had to bend over and spread our cheeks again.
Fun times!
I met my cellie. This was a guy I'd remain friends with for the rest of my life. He, too, shall remain unnamed. But he's someone who *still* sends me a dirty digital Christmas card every year much to my absolute delight.
(Check out my homepage to see cards from years' past. My very favorite might be the one in which Santa is bent over a log and Mrs. Claus is holding a rolling pin and an elf is saying, "Shit gets weirder and weirder by the year!!")
My cellie was in for robbing a convenience store for $17 and a bottle of generic orange soda.
Hey. We *all* do stupid shit.
These days, he's working for a lawn-care company in Gaithersburg, Maryland.
I love the guy.
Loyal bastard.
And he's also a frequent caller to our show under the moniker "Ruff Stuff."
Anyway, this is when I like to think that my *real* education began.
I think of it as earning a Prison PhD.
The lessons for my Prison PhD began immediately. *What to do. What not to do. What to say. What not to say.* I was in fresh territory here. I was on my own. Keep your head down, mind your own business, don't bother no one.
That worked for a few days. And then I was approached by the jail's "main man", a monster who weighed more than three hundred pounds and had to be six feet, six inches tall. He was a badass motherfucker and he was in for bank robbery.
"Heard you're also in for robbery," he said to me in the yard one afternoon.
"Heard right," I said, toughly.
"Hmmm hmmm," he said. He gave me a long look as if he knew something.

"Could use some things," he said, mysteriously.

"Like what?" I asked.

"Flaming Hot Cheetos. Cigarettes. Other shit."

Fuck was he talking about?

"Okay," I said, while also thinking: *So why not just buy them your own damn self? Who am I, your daddy?*

"I want them quick. Be seeing you."

He walked away. Guy was fucking *huge*. And, I have to admit, a tad menacing.

I walked over to the good doctor who was playing horseshoes and told him about the encounter.

"Yeah," he said, barely looking at me. "He wants something. And he *knows* something."

"Knows what exactly?"

"Why you're in here."

"Bank robbery—" I started.

"You ain't in for bank robbery. You ain't in for bank robbery like I ain't in for bank robbery."

"Then what are you in for?" I asked.

"Same as you. Banging an underage."

"But—"

"No *but*," he said. "Everyone knows. Drop the pretense. And give him what he wants."

I burst out laughing. So the good doctor was in for what *I* was in for? And he also lied? No wonder we became so friendly. *Great minds ...*

He started to laugh, too. "I told you 'bank robbery' because I didn't know what else to say. But everyone *knows* it. That's just how things work here. Give the fucker what he wants and be done with it."

"He literally wants Cheetos? And cigarettes?"

The good doctor nodded. "And maybe a radio?"

He went back to playing horseshoes. I retreated back to my cell. I had much to think about. I began to pace.

On the one hand ... giving another prisoner whatever he wanted showed weakness on my part.

But on the *other* hand ... how much would it cost me to purchase a bunch of cigarettes and Cheetos and maybe even a radio?

I mean, not *that* much, right?

We're not talking about a six bedroom house in Potomac here.

We were allowed to use the prison phones once every other day.

At the very next opportunity, I called my father and told him to deposit $10,000 into my prison account. He asked why and I told him to just to do it.

Did I really have time for small talk? Did I really have to explain myself? Especially inside a prison fighting for my damn life?

Didn't think so.

I thought more on the subject: it's well known that a prison is a microcosm of life on the outside. And what did I believe on the outside? That free capitalism was the best way for a society to proceed. I take that back: that free capitalism was the *only* way for a society to flourish. You leave everything to the whims of the market, whether it's medical insurance, or minimum wage, or real estate prices, or the cost of hiring a divorce attorney (something I've been lucky enough to have been spared as I've never been dumb enough to get married).

It's *all* market driven.

Everything!

Or it *should* be!

So why couldn't the same be said for life *inside* a prison?

I wasn't paying rent.

I wasn't paying for food.

I wasn't paying for clothing.

I wasn't paying for entertainment.

I wasn't paying for a cleaning woman (not that I was paying for Miss Benda on the outside either).

I was not paying for *anything*.

I had plenty of money to spare!

That's just a fact.

So if I wanted to flourish, why couldn't I abide by my own damn philosophy and just treat the prison as my own personal fiefdom?

I was going to get the shit beaten out of me for ... what exactly?

Because I didn't want to pay for a huge asshole to have his hot Cheetos?

If I paid for his hot Cheetos, would that would make me any *less* of a man?

If I paid for a fancy suite at a four-star hotel, would *that* have made me any less of a man?

Do you see my point?

I may not have been the richest person on earth.

But I can assure you that inside *that* particular prison, I was the richest inmate by fucking *far*.

Within no time, I was like a fucking Medaci or whoever was rich back in 13th century Australia, controlling the entire fucking town with his wealth and his purchased wisdom.

I'll give you but one example: the head of the Aryan White Power gang, a guy who called himself Steele, put out word that he wanted to *shank* me, meaning knife me to death. He thought of me as a "cho-mo." A child molester. (Like *he* never fucked a 15 year old.)

I sent word back that I was not in the mood to be shanked, I was too young, too handsome, and too funny. And I didn't exactly sleep with an infant. She was fifteen (nearly sixteen) and she kept her motor clean, if you know what I mean.

How about we compromise?

Can we agree to disagree?

Word quickly came back through the prison internet (basically the guys in their cells throwing out little notes attached to something heavier, a process known as "kiting" or "fishing") that Steele was a huge fan of Whole Shebang potato chips from the commissary.

For those who've never been to prison, let me explain the power of Whole Shabang potato chips. To begin, they aren't available in the "real" world. They're called "jail chips" because they're only available *inside* prisons. Fights have broken out over these chips. *Killings* have occurred because of these potato chips! Fan pages are devoted to these chips, as are hundreds of message boards! The chips sell on eBay for more than a hundred dollars a fucking packet! Inmates become like animals, raving and rabid dogs after they taste that peculiar combination of vinegar and salt and barbecue seasoning.

I, personally, hated them. To me, they tasted *way* too much of the ghetto. But others liked them. So who was I to judge?

I sent word back that if Steele wanted his Whole Shebang chips, then he could have them. Even if he wanted *two* a day, that would be fine.

I mean, who cares?

Let's see: getting my face punched in and getting a shank to my heart ... or spending the $7.50 a day on two bags of Whole Shabang chips for Steele?

The answer was simple.

Whole Shabang chips ...

Priceless.

Before I knew it, I was supplying the *entire* fucking prison, including the red beards, as we called the moronic guards, with *anything* they needed.

And when I tell you that I was treated like fucking royalty ... well, that would be exaggerating things a tad.

I would *still* be yelled at for being a "honky" and I would still have shit thrown on me (not *real* shit, although that happens in prison, too). But word came down from all of the leaders of all the gangs: *Do not mess with Skippy Battison.*

He's a good dude.

With money.

A weird dude who paces in his cell every fucking day, talking to himself, but that's okay. We'll just give him a prison nickname. (And that, ladies and gentlemen of this book, is how I earned the name Batty, as in Batty Battison.)

That dude so batty he pace ten hours a day! ...

Little did *they* know that there was a reason for my madness: I was pacing around my cell because it helped to come up with new ideas for movies and jokes and scripts once I was eventually released from this shit hole.

Sorry, but I just was *not* going to allow this time to go to waste.

Just the opposite, in fact: I wanted to take advantage of *every second* in this dump.

Hitler did it.

Why couldn't I?

(I can hear you gasp. *Wow! Did he just write something positive about Hitler?! Holy fuck! Call the PC police! I can already hear the siren: "Do gooder, do gooder, do goooooooooooooooder, coming through ..."* Yeah, I did.)

Allow me to explain, although I've dealt with this many times in the past.

I'm no Nazi sympathizer.

My time in prison was your time in college. Or grad school. Or clown school. Or wherever the hell you went to do some higher learnin'.

I never had that opportunity. I went straight from high school, where I barely graduated, straight into the big old mean world.

Sure, I taught myself plenty but there was also a shit ton of traditional learning I never had the luxury to ingest.

When I tell you that I read two hundred books in prison, I am not exaggerating.

Most of these books were history and philosophy and general knowledge.

I read books on the stars. I read books by Plato and Socrates. I read books about math, science, religion and mythology.

I read books on politics, *so* many books on politics!

I read books written by Henry Kissinger on why the Vietnam War wasn't his fault (I believe him).

I read books about Ronald Reagan and why he hated big government (I *definitely* agree with him).

I read books about Jesus and his teachings that have nothing to do with religion (love the guy).

I read books by Newt Gingrich, Bill O'Reilly, Dinesh D'Souza, a young Tucker Carlson, Sean Hannity, Rush Limbaugh (god rest his soul), David Horowitz, Mark Levin, Alan Dershowitz, and other Jewish authors. Books by the finest minds in all the land.

I read *everything* the library had.

And yes, I read *Mein Kampf* by Hitler.

And this is what got me into trouble. Not that I read these books, I guess, but me later talking about them.

Listen, I'm not an idiot. I know Hitler was bad. He killed thousands. For all I know, he killed my Irish relatives but I doubt it. They were too poor to have been killed. They just were forced to move to the 19th century south end of Boston.

And I know it's not politically correct to say that *Mein Kampf* influenced anyone. But I will say this: reading that book *did* give me the idea for *this* book. So, for that alone, you have the ol' mustachioed dickhead to thank.

He was a monster. He was a maniac.

But not at first.

He was like the rock group Boston. He started off okay. It was only later in his career that his work wasn't so hot.

Steele the neo-Nazi had loaned me his copy, which had been highlighted with a golf pencil. I have to admit it took a long time to get into it. Let's just say it was written a little differently than Stephen King's books, which I was more used to. But something struck me right away: this guy really believed in what he was saying and he wanted to get the word out.

Also, he was taking advantage of his bad situation in jail by *producing*.

He wasn't whining.

He wasn't bellyaching.

He wasn't asking for a free hand out.

He just sat down and wrote a goddamn book that was later read and enjoyed by millions.

Again, is what Hitler produced a great book? Do I agree with everything in it?

No! Maybe 25%.

But at the very least, I admired his *gumption*. And, again, let me remind you that my great-great-grandfather is a quarter Jewish.

With that in mind, I gave the copy back to Steele, thanked him with a few sleeves of double stuffed Oreos and got to work immediately on my *own* memoir.

Even though Steele left me alone, as did the rest of his Aryan gang, I wouldn't call our relationship "friendly." At least then. It was a relationship born out of a mutual respect.

I gave them something they wanted: free snacks. Or radios. Or televisions. Or whatever the hell they wanted from me.

And, in return, they gave me something that *I* wanted: not to die at their hands.

And the freedom to work on this very book you're reading.

That's a fair deal.

Here's an interesting fact that just might blow your mind:

The first couple chapters of this book, not including the introduction, were written in the Hagerstown Correctional Facility.

Want your mind to be farther blown?

I didn't write them.

Sure, these are my words, but I didn't put them down onto paper. That's a pain in the ass.

I paid an Aryan gang member a carton of Asian spiced Chi Chi Raman Swolls and an adult diaper box filled with Little Debbie Honey-Buns to take down what I was saying aloud and put it down on paper. (Adult diaper boxes are common in prisons and are often used to transport large amounts of commissary snacks. I know, strange but ... TRUE!)

I won't mention the Aryan gang member's name but I will say that it wasn't Steele, who was pretty much incapable of not only writing but also of reading or really talking (his tongue had been cut badly during a prison brawl and he communicated with finger and hand gestures unrelated to official sign language).

No, it wasn't Steele. But it *was* a man who was surprisingly gifted with the written word and who was willing to sit there, in my cell, day after day, hour after hour, and write down what I was saying with a tiny stubby pencil and maybe even improve on some things he felt could be punched up.

True, he also wrote down a lot of other things that I *didn't* say but I'm not including those excerpts. All those are *gone*.

He was a scary dude. But loyal.

I can't stress this enough.

Once in prison, I saw him drop a barbell on someone's trachea.

Granted, the other guy had been asking for it but, I have to tell you ... that sound, it's something I'll never forget.

Like a honeydew being smashed by a fire extinguisher.

Which is *also* something I once saw in prison.

And yet this was the same guy who would argue with me if a sentence needed to have a different word.

Or whether a chapter needed to end differently.

In another reality, he would have been a very successful editor or writer. I'm pretty sure of that.

In *this* life, though, he's doing fifty for stabbing to death a cashier at a rural gas station for $4.74.

Anyway, I would sit on my top bunk while this nameless Aryan gang member would sit on the bottom bunk, and I would just talk. Every so often I'd hear a grunt, as if he didn't understand what I was saying. It was only later that it occurred to me that our upbringings were so different that when he heard certain details (like, for instance, that my family had a tennis court and a pool) he would audibly gasp.

That was what he was grunting about!

I mean, this is a neo-Nazi! This guy had *seen* shit! *And this is what surprises him?!*

When I got to the part about my experience with improv, he perked up.

Tell me *more*, he said.

I proceeded to tell him what I knew (which was considerable) and how much fun improv could be with a receptive audience.

Even though I only performed improv twice, I *still* felt that I had fun with it.

A few days later, this Nazi returned to our cell demanding ten garlic pickles and twenty-five pepperoni sticks (which he'd slice with a flattened canned-corn aluminum lid). After we visited the commissary, and after he was fully satiated, he asked me more about improv and whether it was something that could be done in prison.

I was kind of blown away by his hunger for comedy.

I hadn't even thought about performing comedy in prison.

At first glance, he didn't appear to be the funniest guy in the world, although he *did* have a very dry sense of humor.

But how cool was this? A neo-Nazi wanting to do improv?

How great would it be for him to explore his *real* inner self while also producing laughs? How amazing would it be for *all* of the different gangs within this shit hole of a prison to lay down their weapons, for at least an hour a week, to come together to produce guffaws for fellow prisoners?

Pretty damn *awesome*.

I could also see this becoming a story that the media would pick up on. It couldn't hurt my reputation when I finally did leave this prison.

One afternoon, I walked up to a screw in the yard and asked to see the warden.

"I want to see the warden now," I said. "Like immediately."

"You've got to fucking be kidding?" he said.

"That's my job. To make people laugh. But right now I'm being totally serious. As fucking serious as a snake up your ol' wazoo. I want to talk with the warden."

338

He didn't laugh. Guards did *not* have a sense of humor. *Not one.* I have *never* met a guard who had a sharp funny bone. *Never. Ever!* You know why? Because you need *intelligence* to be funny. And if you choose to fucking spend your entire fucking life inside a prison, and you're not a fucking prisoner, how smart can you be?!

Not smart.

He asked what I wanted to tell the warden. I told him that that was between me and my warden.

He scoffed.

I smiled. Okay.

You wanna play ball?

Fine. *Let's play ball, asshole.*

I made my way over to the phones. There was a long line of people waiting for the three pay phones.

Fuck this.

So I announced really loud, "Who wants free pork rinds?"

Hands shot into the air.

"Then let me at a fucking phone," I announced.

One phone soon became all mine. I dialed my father. He accepted the call (*"... we are calling from a Maryland correctional facility. Do you accept the call? ..."*) and I immediately told dad the plan. He loved it. He said he'd contact the warden immediately and would let me know what he said when I called the *next* time.

From there, I hit the library and the *one* prison computer.

Steele had just told me something very interesting.

The guy hated Jews. And blacks. And everyone else who wasn't what he considered to be *purely white*.

But the fucker was *smart*.

He loved eating kosher prison food.

Why? Because it was *good*. It was delicious. And the rest of the prison food was utter garbage.

So what Steele would do was this:

Steele would contact the ACLU prison authorities and *demand* that he be provided with daily meals that were deemed "kosher" by the appropriate rabbinical authorities.

I shit you not. Steele was pretending that he had converted to becoming an Orthodox Jew.

Because he *loved* the kosher food.

And it became so popular that now half of the Aryan Nation gang members were eating kosher food!

Because it was their "right."

This fascinated me. And gave me an idea.

I sat down and wrote a quick email to the ACLU that Steele had provided for me. I told them my predicament, that I was in jail for reasons that had nothing to do with me, that I was converting to Judaism and could they possibly provide me with three daily kosher meals a day?

When I tell you that it took only two hours for them to get back to me, I'm not exaggerating. They said they would help.

Which was incredible, especially considering that I was in prison for sleeping with the daughter of one of the heads of the ACLU! Maybe they didn't know this. And I wasn't about to tell them.

I was a bit shocked, to be honest.

I hadn't expected this. I had *never* expected a liberal organization to step forward and help me in any way. Meanwhile, all of the conservative organizations I knew and had been emailing, never got back to me.

Gee, thanks, assholes. A real loyal bunch here.

Think about that: I had entertained countless conservative clubs and organizations and associations and think tanks for the past few months. I *knew* these people. They knew me. And when I emailed them for their support, for some help, for some free legal actions, they roundly ignored my plea.

And here was the fucking ACLU, an organization I always looked down on, getting back to me pretty much immediately!

I was stunned.

The email they sent back very carefully laid out what I needed to do in order to receive the specific brand of food that I now deserved as an "observant Jew." They even included applications that I needed to fill out that would help me in my quest.

Once filled, they would then submit these for me.

I quickly took care of the applications and sent them back.

Within days the prison system had accepted my Kosher requests.

Flushed with success, I put in more requests to the ACLU, this time for benefits involving homosexuals, Muslims, the Church of Satan and a host of other affiliations and religious organizations.

All went through.

This was incredible!

Soon enough, my cell (already filled with *everything* I was allowed to buy, such as a small color television, a fancy alarm clock, a small fridge, a three-way mirror for grooming, and other privileged goodies) was soon packed with *all* manner of food, kosher or not. My roommate fucking loved me. Without a doubt, our cell became the *best* place to hang. If other prisoners wanted to eat my food, fine.

I just didn't want to be shanked or raped.

Shit, dudes! Have as many orange porkies and mock cheesecakes as you want! Fuck do I care?!

Now with this reputation for being, let's say, a *generous* prisoner with my money, the requests from other prisoners only went up.

And yet I factored that into the equation.

First chance I got, I called my father and requested *another* $10,000 be inserted into my commissary fund—immediately.

I didn't have time to waste.

The heat was soon off.

Which gave me even *more* time to spend on my own, which I craved. If I wanted everyone out of the cell at any time, I'd hand out food and even styrofoam cups of toilet wine (or pruno) that my Nazi roomie was making with all of our new ingredients. (Ever try toilet wine? It's actually *a lot* better than you might think. It's easy to make: take some apples or a fruit cocktail or even just hard candy, *any flavor*, and place into a plastic bag. Add in some bread bits to provide the yeast. Let it ferment in the toilet or any other hidden little alcove that you can find or create. Then strain through a gym sock, preferably unused and your *own*. The more sugar involved, the higher the motor or "kick." Serve to cellies and watch them become bewildered and bedazzled. Leave before anything violent happens. This last step is *key*.)

The good doctor was in charge of selling the cups of toilet wine.

All of the funds went directly to pay off all of the Aryan gang leaders who could have killed me but weren't. Money *very well* spent.

There was a white prisoner named Huff N' Puff (not his real name) who came strutting up to me one day, all confident and cool. He had a question for me:

"You think I got a helmet or a hose?"

Huh?

"My cock. Helmet or a hose? Cut or god given?"

"Um ... a hose?"

"Right. And I want it sucked. Tonight in the laundry. Make it happen, Chomo."

Lord. Just what I fucking needed! Blowing a guy named Huff N' Puff in the laundry room!

I ended up paying off Huff N' Puff with fifteen six-packs of Cool Off drink (think really cheap Kool Aid). *Problem solved!*

Basically, I was buying my life.

And time.

Time to do all the things I wanted.

Like to write to the goddamn warden to attempt to get this prison improv thing off the ground.

I was really missing writing and performing comedy. Entertaining an audience live. Making them laugh. Making them smile.

Making them feel just a *little* better about themselves and their current situation. It was why I was put on this here earth.

And it occurred to me ... had there *ever* been a prison humor column?

I mean, how effin' *cool* would that be?!

Why not?

I *love* to be first.

At *anything*.

With the ACLU now helping me "pray to Mecca" three times a day, I'd have even *more* free time to spend at the library computer that I'd bribe the other prisoners to never use with commissary snacks.

A win/win/win.

(It's funny. I started receiving requests from other prison gangs for things as harmless as peanut butter cookie filling. And for *less* silly items, such as heroin and cocaine and marijuana, then still pretty much illegal. There were a few gangs in the prison system in Maryland including the Flying Dragons, the Snakeheads, the Ghost Shadows and the Bamboo Union. But I was known to be a "part" of the Aryan Nation and was thus considered off limits. I was an honorary "made guy" and it would be best to leave me alone. So the blowjob requests died down *real* quick, although I would do an occasional favor, such as when the leader of the Ghost Shadows got married and I conducted his wedding ceremony and did some shtick for free.)

I contacted the editor of the prison newsletter, which was called *The Shank Redemption*.

It came out once a month. It ran about thirty or so pages and it was Xeroxed in the prison library and handed out free to anyone who wanted it, which, surprisingly, were quite a few prisoners.

It was dishy and funny (in an amateurish way) and it also contained tons of legal advice for those wanting to bring their cases up for appeal. The editor was a guy named Jamal and he was in prison for murdering his mother-in-law, which became the source of many jokes among the married prisoners. He was a black dude with dreadlocks and, quite honestly, he scared the shit out of me. But he turned out to be a pussycat.

Jamal always wanted to be a writer and editor but couldn't afford college fees. So he got into detailing cars outside Laurel, married his high school sweetheart, and then killed his mother-in-law when she wanted to watch *That's So Raven* and he wanted to watch the Redskins play the New York Giants.

Who could blame the dude?

Joking.

Actually, no, I'm not. The Skins actually won that game, a rare win made even more impressive as they had already lost the first game they had played that season against the Giants. In overtime, no less.

Anyway, Jamal was a good dude and his job wasn't an easy one, especially since he never graduated high school. I approached him one day in the cafeteria and told him who I was. He was pretty impressed, to be honest, and asked if I had any interest in contributing. I asked him if he knew Dave Barry, the syndicated newspaper humorist. He hadn't heard of him but he sounded intrigued. I asked if he'd be interested in a weekly column that would sort of poke holes at the silliness of most prison rules without going so far as to piss off the authorities in charge. It would be similar to Dave Barry, but inside a prison.

He said he'd think about it. *Think about what?,* I thought. I'm a professional fucking writer. And I'd be doing this for *free.*

What's there to even think about?!

Confused, I headed back to my cell and handed out snacks to hungry Nazis.

Later that night, Jamal sent out a fishing message to me that read "Okai!"

Not the best speller but he wasn't exactly the editor in chief of *The Wall Street Journal.*

I got right to work, not even heading back to sleep, spinning off idea after idea after idea and writing them all down on a roll of toilet paper with my golf pencil. Isn't this how Hemingway wrote *The Sun Also Rises*?

By morning, I had enough ideas to fill columns for the next ten years, which I prayed I would never have the opportunity to do.

And thus began my prison humor column "Welcome 2 Da Jungle!" which ran on the last page of the newsletter every week.

It was a *huge* hit. Before I knew it, everyone (and I mean *everyone* from *every* gang, white, black, Hispanic or otherwise) were repeating lines back to me in the rec yard or inside the cafeteria. Even guards started yelling out lines, for crying out loud! *Everyone.* Secretaries, jail nurses, every goddamn person in that jail started reading my column! Fuck, I think even *the warden* was reading it!

If you look around hard enough on the internet, you can find rare copies of the book compilation of these columns I self-published in 2007 and sold on Amazon and on some other sites.

It's called *Best of "Welcome 2 Da Jungle."* The last time I checked, prices were in the $250 range, and these were *used* copies!

And *really* well used! Whoo boy!

If you can't find a copy, no worries. What follows are some of the best bits and pieces from the fifteen columns I pinched out of my ass before Jamal the editor was shanked in the weight room for something I wrote.

But it was really his fault.

Seems that Jamal could have easily paid off the killer but he was too cheap to do so. Not me. I paid the fucker anything he wanted. I'd mention the attacker's name but Jamal's family and I settled out of court in 2013 and, sadly, I'm not allowed to.

I'm not going to excerpt that particular "offensive" column here.

Suffice it to say that I put some words in Jamal's mouth (in a humorous, *fictional* way) and that these words offended a certain weightlifter who wasn't thrilled about being referred to as short and ineffective as a fighter and as a man.

Anyway:

"Meat Mondays Ain't For the Weak"

... growing up in Bethesda, there used to be a popular restaurant called Steak in the Sack, and it only served questionable beef inserted into a hot-pocket type confection of pita, slathered with a mysterious white sauce and served steaming hot. My friends and I used to call the place 'The Shit in the Sack' but we'd hunger for their food like a lion would for blood. We yearned for it. We dreamt about it. Did we feel good after eating it? Never. I remember once sitting on the toilet for an entire weekend. I kind of feel the same about Meat Mondays here at Hagerstown C.I. I always look forward to it but I never really feel too great after consuming it. And what is it exactly? Once when I was around fifteen, my parents took me to the Amalfi Coast area of Italy. Pretty enough. But what I remember most is the raw horse meat I saw another tourist eating. The next morning, he looked a bit green under the gills. I asked him how he felt. He neighed and stomped his front right foot. Consuming whatever I ate this past Monday, even assuming it had once been a living "thing," I know that feeling oh so (neeiiiigh) well ....

"Daydreaming the Hard Time Away"

... when I was a kid in Bethesda, I'd often float in my backyard pool, daydreaming the day away. I'd daydream about all of the amazing things I wanted to accomplish in the future, usually involving making

people laugh and getting to kiss girls. And nowadays, as I lay in my cot within my cell in Wing D, I find myself daydreaming but in a different way: I'm not being yelled at by mom to get out of the pool. But there's also another major difference: I now daydream about the past. What could I have done differently? Did I have to end up in this dump? Did my cellie have to shit himself and me awake at 2:30? If I'm being honest, and I am, and I'm going to be, I'd have to say that I have no regrets about being sent here to Hagerstown C.I. But I do have plenty of other regrets: never having had the chance to hike the Alps; never visiting Athens when I had the chance; not taking a year abroad in Italy; not going to The Palm in Dupont Circle on prom night and instead going to The Magic Pan; not seeing the Doobie Brothers and Foreigner on August 31, 1994 at Merriweather Post Pavilion. What are your major regrets? We all have them! Tell me in the yard or just send me a fishing line to my cell and I'll publish right here! ...

"A Suggestion Box Would Be Beneficial For All Of Us"

You've seen them in shopping malls. You've seen them in the offices where you've worked. And you've probably even seen them at the summer camps you attended for many years as teenagers. They're everywhere. I'm talking, of course, about Suggestion Boxes. And they should be here *in Hagerstown Correctional Institute! I mean, why not? We have plenty of suggestions! So with that in mind, last week I placed my own Suggestion Box outside my cell. Here are a few of the helpful comments I found when I opened it early this morning:*

"Possible to get those little shampoo bottle samples they have in hotels?"

"French Toast like mam-mam used to make in the commissary?"

"Would it be a possibility we could be allowed to roll around in the fresh prison laundry while still warm?"

"Cafeteria suggestion: prison sushi Saturday?"

"Can we learn a new trade? Instead of auto mechanics, could we learn something more useful for the world, like how to avoid paying taxes and shit?"

Of course, all of these suggestions had been made up by me! But I do want to hear <u>your</u> suggestions for this column! Or for prison! Let me *know! And I'll include them in the next column! Once again, this is Skippy writing from the Jungle House and I hope you enjoyed what I had to say!*

The column was a *huge* hit!

"Prison sushi this Saturday?" I would hear while out on the yard, the person laughing hysterically.

"Ready to roll in the fresh prison laundry?" I'd hear from a guard in the common area.

"Mam-man's French toast for Sunday brunch?" would be another quip someone would yell over to me outside in the yard.

Prisoners are surprisingly shy when it comes to giving another prisoner a compliment but not in my case.

All day, every day I kept hearing how funny my column was. And the looks in these prisoners' eyes and the smiles on their faces only added to my appreciation of *their* appreciation.

Things were going really well.

And things then got even *better*: I finally heard back from the warden about my improv class idea.

Or I should say my *father's lawyer* heard back, as he had been the one who had brought suit against the warden as well as the entire Maryland prison system.

Does that sound aggressive? That I sued the very warden of the prison where I was staying? Hear me out:

How much time did I have to waste? Not much. Granted, it was the ACLU that got me here to begin with, so why not have them get me *out* of the prison?

Meanwhile there was still no word from any one of the conservative groups I had reached out to with questions and requests.

Thanks again, assholes!

How quickly and easily one is forgotten when they're laboring behind prison walls making two cents an hour producing widgets of some sort. (Not me … but the other poor shmucks who were unable to pay their way out.)

My father visited me a few times, which I appreciated, even if he did look uncomfortable and out of sorts in his Brooks brothers suit and Prada necktie.

My mother would write often but didn't have the "heart" to see her youngest in jail. *Thanks, mom*. I would write back and our relationship remained civil enough. As I mentioned earlier, she never really did share my sense of humor, finding it too harsh or edgy or whatever. Her favorite humor was *Lake Woebegon*. Barf. I've heard similar things about a lot of parents of brilliant comedic minds. Their parents just don't *get* it. Which I guess makes sense. Did Einstein's mother ever understand his calculations?

No word from my older brother or his bitch of a wife.

Flammer would sometimes write. Or, more accurately, he would send dirty postcards of nude women with just a few words on the back: *Miss Pussy A lot?*

Shit, at least the guy was writing to me!

I heard from an old high school pal.

Once.

Whatever. I would have probably done the same thing. There was a life to live out there. And they were living it.

It's like writing your best friend from summer camp.

You do it once. And then never again.

That's just what happens.

So I was fine with that.

But I kept thinking ... who had come to my aid in prison?

Was it the Koch brothers and the Americans for Prosperity?

Was it the Heritage Foundation?

Was it the NRA, even after I made so many members laugh by pretending to having just been shot but blaming gas pains?

Nope.

Nada.

Zilcho.

No, it was the dreaded ACLU and the liberals who had come through for me.

Who would have predicted that?!

Not me, I'd be the first to admit.

I could feel my allegiances switching and I felt a little dizzy.

The ground was moving beneath me.

Could this *really* be happening? I mean, I had a good thing going on the outside. Why fuck that up because the ACLU was a little nice to me and the conservative organizations were not?

I was going to think about this more, but meanwhile ... I had a new prison comedy improv program to run!

You remember my Neo-Nazi cellie?

He was still *super* into the idea of doing improv. Maybe a little *too* into the idea, in retrospect. But with him on board, and the good doctor acting as my teaching assistant, I was off and running.

How to advertise?

I figured I'd let the underground internet of gang gossip lead the way. So I let it be known that a very special event would be happening this upcoming Friday afternoon at 2:00 P.M., in the Devotional Space, and that if any prisoner ever had a dream of performing comedy or improv comedy or just wanted to make some new friends, this would be THE place to be.

Before I knew it, prisoners were approaching with questions. It's amazing how quickly the jailhouse internet can spread information, both for good and bad.

The good would be an improv class to be taught to all prisoners for free.

The bad would be hearing that the head of the Mexican gang wanted to behead you.

Luckily for me, I was paying off *el jefe* with six cartons of cigarettes a day.

Guy sure could *smoke*!

This was all very exciting. I had four days to prepare, and I did so from lights on to lights off.

I came up with some prompts that we could use. And I came up with some suggestions for the improvisers that would help them not only with comedy but with life on the outside.

I fashioned an "improv stick" out of two long cardboard tubes used to hold Pringles. Whoever was the one holding the stick had the stage. There would be no interrupting, unless the stick was handed over to *another* improviser. I wanted there to be as little cross-talk as possible so that all voices, regardless of color or religion or race or what have you, could be heard.

I felt that this was only fair.

Comedy is like music.

If you're a musician and you're talented, it doesn't matter to the rest of the musicians whether you're black, white, red or yellow.

Same thing holds true for comedy. It's a family, regardless of your background. I wanted this to be the Switzerland of the prison. A place that was safe and where people could explore their deepest needs, desires and regrets, where *everyone* mattered *equally*.

Read that again please:

Where. *Everyone*. Mattered. *Equally*.

A *true* safe space.

Not some bullshit "safe space" at a college with stuffed bunnies and a cozy blanket for adult children.

And I meant it. I was changing. Why couldn't the rest of the prison? Maybe it was the ACLU helping but I could feel my mind clear a little, and all hostilities that I had held before were now kind of wiped away.

Being nice to *everyone* started to make more sense.

A few days before the first improv class, one of the leaders of the Black Guerilla Nation, a black prison gang, beckoned for me to follow him into the laundry room.

Typically not a smart thing to do: follow a leader of the Black Guerilla Nation into a laundry room.

I did anyway.

I was already paying him off daily with dozens of Cremora non-dairy creamers and plastic squeeze ReaLemons.

"Holmes, what's this shit all about?"

"The class?" I asked.

He nodded.

I explained to him my intentions.

He smiled and walked away.

Interesting, I thought. A man of few words. And if he *does* decide to show up, how effective would he be at improv?

Who knows! He could be a latent genius!

There are *plenty* of actors who, in their youth, spent time in prison. And they're fucking good!

I received a lot of questions about this upcoming improv class.

I always tried to stop whatever I was doing to answer them. This was going to be a good thing, I kept telling myself. And selfishly, it could also make for a terrific story later on, after I got out of this shit hole.

The afternoon arrived. I showed up early to the Dev Room (basically a room that served as a non-denominational devotion room) and I set about arranging the chairs and the "stage", which was really just a raised platform two feet off the ground that was big enough to hold a small group of improvisers.

The first student walked in, someone I knew to be high up in the ranks of *La eMe*, the Mexican Mafia gang.

He didn't strike me as anyone with a particularly strong or nuanced sense of humor.

Or for that matter, someone who wanted to learn more about themselves, let alone the craft of improv … but who was I to judge? I nodded and thanked him for coming. He took a seat without a word. I thought: *Yet another guy who might (or might not) be any good at this very strange and mysterious art form.*

Well, we'd see soon enough, wouldn't we …

The room was packed when the class was due to start, with maybe twenty prisoners and three or so bulls leaning against the back wall, amused and waiting anxiously to see what these killers and rapists and muggers and bank robbers would do when it came time to make people laugh.

Maybe these guards didn't have confidence in the prisoners' ability. Maybe it was racism. Who knows what it was. They were snickering. Some were giggling.

But fuck them.

I was here to prove them all wrong.

I could see in the audience the leaders of the six prison gangs, which I took to be a good sign.

Comedy is an emollient, a word I learned from one of my prison books. Emollient means "something that brings everything together."

I learned this word in a biography of Richard Nixon, and the emollient was G. Gordon Liddy.

Just you watch, I wanted to tell the bulls leaning against the walls, smirking. *Just you fucking watch! Comedy is magic! And you know nothing about it!*

I'm basing what happened next on surveillance video footage (and audio) that was recorded, as well as court testimony during the trial that would take place December 2014 through August 2015.

I started off by telling the crowd: "It's *so* great to see you all here this afternoon. You can put your trust in me. And I hope that I can repay that trust by offering you a guide into a world you might never have known you could enter. But you *can*! I mean, why *not*? Let me tell you a story: one of the greatest minds in comedy grew up in a whorehouse in Arkansas. By a show of hands, how many people here grew up in a whorehouse? Nobody? I'm surprised. What I'm saying is that if this great comedian, Richard Pryor, could do it, then so can you, right? Because you have something that professional comedians and actors do *not* have. And that's real world experience. Do you know how valuable that is to have? No, your lives might not have been easy. Yes, you're now in prison. But you won't be here forever. And when you do get out, you'll have stories under your belt that no one else will have. And who knows? Maybe one day you can actually *make a living* at comedy. How *cool* would that be?!"

I paused to gauge their reaction. I had 'em right where I wanted 'em.

I continued:

"Anyone can do this. If I can do this, then you can do this. It just takes concentration. And focus. Okay, let's get started. I'm going to ask *you*, and *you*, and *you* to come up on stage."

Three men came up on stage, a bit *too* eagerly I thought, although I didn't pay it much mind. I just took it to be a sign that they were anxious to get started. Not one was a gang leader but one was Hispanic, one was black, and the third was a Nazi dude (not my roommate or Steele).

Unity in comedy! I *liked* where this was headed!

"Okay, fellas," I continued, my long, cardboard improv stick at the ready, all dolled up with fun and glittery items glued to it. I had taped messages on the stick, like:

GO 4 IT

U CAN DO IT

YASSS!!!

It was fun and I thought the prisoners would enjoy the encouragement.

"I'm going to give you what I call a 'prompt,'" I announced, "which is basically just a suggestion on where to take a particular scene. By 'take a scene,' I refer to what to do when you improvise up on stage."

I felt, if anything, that I had to *over* explain what I was teaching. These weren't exactly *experts* at the craft.

Up on stage, they nodded. The audience, too, remained quiet. The bulls against the wall were smiling as if to say, *Let's see what you got. And good luck, asshole!*

"Let's start with *this* prompt," I said. "I'll throw one out ... your parents bring you to an orthodontist to see if you need braces ... but the orthodontist is a barber from the 15th century."

No one on the stage made a move. I was puzzled.

What was happening—

Oh. They were waiting for the improv stick. I handed it over to the Hispanic.

He took it. But still no one made a move to launch into improv.

Strange.

Okay then, let's try something else ...

"You need to return an expensive shirt for a refund at, say, a Nordstrom's but you forgot the receipt and the sales person is deaf."

No one made a move. *Fuck is happening?!,* I thought.

I became a little more aggressive. I grabbed the stick back.

"This thing that I'm up here holding is an improv stick, okay? So whoever I pass it on to, I just want you to start improvising. Let's start simple, all right? You're selling your house to a young couple—"

"But you ain't the motherfucking owner!" the Nazi on stage screamed at the Hispanic.

Jesus. *Finally*. Someone *willing* to play. I handed him the improv baton.

"Good," I said. "Now go with *that*."

Hey, this was working!

"Um ... fuck are you doing here, assholes?" the Nazi improvised. "I invite you? I didn't. Get the *fuck* off my lawn."

The black prisoner on stage stepped toward the Nazi. "Why you saying all that shit? I saw it being sold on the internet. Why you lying?"

Now the Hispanic joined in with the improvisation.

"Why you call me asshole, asshole? You listed the house. Now I'm here. What you going to do about it?"

Good, I thought. *Let's see where this leads ...*

"I ain't listed shit," said the Nazi. "I was invited here. Now I living here. Deal with it."

"Then why you put that sign on the grass outside?" said the Hispanic.

"Sign don't say shit," said the Nazi.

"Sign says you *selling*," said the black. "Saw it myself."

"Asshole must have put it there. Have no idea," said the Nazi.

"Anyway, get out. My house now."

Someone called out from the crowd. I looked over. It was my neo-Nazi cellie! Nice! He was getting involved!

"Neighbor listening to all this shit and all upset. He *know* the house gonna be sold."

I motioned him to get on stage. He jumped up on to it.

"Saw that sign," he said, now next to the other improvisers. "Said as clear as fucking day: NOT SELLING."

"Must be blind," said the Hispanic. "I'm telling you it says you SELLING."

Someone stepped forth from the audience. It was the leader of the Black Guerilla Nation who had asked me into the laundromat!

I loved it!

"And then a police arrives," he said, loudly.

Wow! He was certainly coming to this craft quickly and *confidently*!

"I'm the police," he continued. "What's happening?"

"Bitch says I'm selling. I'm *not*," said the Nazi.

Now a new improviser jumped up onto the stage. It was the leader of *La eMe*, the Mexican Mafia gang.

"Saw that you are. So you *will*," he announced.

"Yeah," said the other Hispanic. "You will."

"I ain't doing shit," said the Nazi. "This is *my* place now."

"And then he calls his homies in," said another black in the crowd.

I motioned for him, too, to get up on stage, now growing a bit, how should one say?, crowded.

"He told me it's selling," he said, once up there. "And I *believe* him. He's my *holmie*."

"Don't believe shit," said the Nazi.

"Better believe *this* shit," said one of the Hispanics.

This is when time seemed to *slow*.

The Hispanic pulled out his own improv stick—or what I *thought* was an improv stick.

It wasn't.

It was a very long, metallic shank.

"Hey, guys," I said. "Um, let's maybe start with a different prompt—"

"Fuck your bitch, cunt!" screamed a Nazi.

"Suck my cunt ball!" screamed another Nazi.

Thankfully, they weren't yelling at me … but at a black prisoner.

I looked over to the bulls against the wall.

They were smirking.

As if to say, *We told you so!*

That's all well and good, I thought. *But could you get off the fucking wall and help drain some of this here performance intensity?*

They didn't move. Not an inch. And I'll tell you why:

Because they were looking at me as being a "hug-a-thug."

Someone who only wanted to help others. In effect, they were thinking like *I* had thought before I had entered prison.

I pitied them.

The metallic shank went whooshing through the air and caught the Nazi in his neck. Blood spurted up to the dropped ceiling.

Uh oh. This really isn't good.

"Guys, *guys*! This is supposed to be *fun*," I started, but I perhaps already knew that it was maybe too late. It was just a sense.

All six leaders of the prison gangs were now hopping on to the stage. They began swinging.

Meanwhile, the Nazi was crouching on all fours, blood gurgling through his neck wound, which was in the shape of a huge smile. The rest of the audience rushed the stage. The noise was tremendous. I thought I even heard applause.

What happened next has been discussed many times.

It has been informally called the "Great Comedy Improv Prison Riot."

More officially: "The Hagerstown Facility Disaster."

And I suppose for good reason.

The fight began on stage but soon spread through the rest of the prison, and within an hour, the entire prison complex was nearly up in flames, with everyone shanking, cutting, hacking each other to bits.

By everyone, I mean everyone but the guards and the warden who had hightailed it the fuck out of there to safety.

Smart move.

Before the national guard arrived to calm down the masses, there were twenty-five dead, sixty-three wounded, and one unlucky guy beheaded (a Nazi by the name of Peckerwood. Someone, I can't remember, joked that at least he didn't lose the *first part* of his name.)

As for myself, I successfully hid in the library, beneath one of the reading tables. I paid a murderer named Roundabout to protect me for $5,000.

Not a good day.

I will say this: the fellas did what I had asked of them … but *maybe* took it a *little* too far? There was some good material in the beginning which would have worked anywhere else.

Have to know your audience, I guess.

And I'll also say this: if I may pat myself on the back, I did get a huge laugh years later when I told other comedy writers and comedians that I had called *"And … scene!"* moments before one of the improvisers was shot to death by another prisoner with a homemade gun.

The joke was sort of missed at the time I said it, but I *still* think it's a good one.

Evidence later came out that all this had been planned from the get go, the opportunity to get up close and real personal (and violent) with fellow prisoners one might not have otherwise had another opportunity to ever get close to.

Was I so naïve to have missed this?

Not sure, in retrospect. One could say it was the warden's fault for allowing any of this to happen.

Sure, one could also say that the warden was *forced* by court order to hold this improv class. But he really was the one who signed off on the class and he certainly knew the prison better than I did.

I look at it this way: *it was fun while it lasted.*

It could have ended so differently.

Friends for life, bonding over a deep love for comedy that would ultimately change their lives for the better.

But no, that didn't happen.

What I *will* say is that after the troops arrived, after the television crews left, after the shock of that afternoon wore off, a week or so later, something good *did* happen to me: I received a visit from a guard I knew named Rico.

Now Rico was a huge fan of Moon Lodge Stuffed Jalapenos, which I always helpfully supplied him with.

The guy liked me.

He really liked me.

In fact, I had once performed a comedy act in order to divert his attention from another prisoner receiving a blow job in the visiting room.

This was how *that* routine went:

"'Sup, Rico? How are you doing? I'm fine. Did you see Warden ____ today? He was being fucked behind the laundry cart. But he kept saying that the situation was 'normal, everyone back to their cells.' [HUGE LAUGH] The rumor is that it's Dead Man's Inc. But the guy needed very specific instructions from a capo. So they think it's an Aryan. [HUGE LAUGH] You know, *not the brightest.* [LAUGH] I'm just kidding, Rico. He's fine. What are you up to today? Anything *new* happening? Anyone visiting Steele today? Or was that *last* year? [HUGE LAUGH] Nah, I love Steele. Like a brother. A brother who'd slit my throat and fuck me in the ass. [HUGE LAUGH] You're a fantastic audience, Rico. A great sense of humor, so rare in here! Hey! Did you have the corned hash meal last night? Looked like someone had it before us, and we got it on the way *out.* [HUGE LAUGH] Won't be the last piece of shit to escape this place. [HUGE LAUGH]."

Rico was now standing before my cell, grinning.

"Hey, Mister Comedy, looks like you're sprung. You're *out.* Pack your shit and head to R&R."

My father's lawyer had worked *more* of his magic and had gotten a judge to release me early.

In the end, I did six months, three days, and four hours. Not that I was counting.

I said goodbye to all my friends.

Steele, in particular, was upset I was leaving but he understood.

Huff N' Puff was upset I was leaving but he didn't seem to understand why—he *still* wanted his snacks.

But guess what?!

That was no longer my concern!

I was headed back out into the real world.

And I couldn't wait.

You're on your own now, fellas! Best of luck to all of youse!

I hugged the good doctor goodbye, promised I'd keep in touch (boy, did we ever, maybe *too* much), and left without saying a word to anyone I had been paying off.

Let them rely on some new asshole to buy their tuna and non-dairy milk creamers!

When I emerged back into the real world, outside the prison, holding a plastic bag, wearing the clothes that I had arrived with months before, now blinking against the sunshine, I was a new man.

Waiting for my father to pick me up in his BMW 760, I thought back on *all* I had been through.

It was a lot for any man to have experienced.

Strangely, I felt lighter. Almost re-born.

And I knew, even then, that my comedy had to *change* to suit my new personality.

Instead of politics, I'd now have to concentrate on something that would appeal to *everyone*. Maybe a fresh form of comedy that wasn't as angry. That could bring people *together* instead of to *divide*.

Like all the greats, I now had to re-invent myself. Carlin did it. So did Pryor. So did Lenny Bruce. So did Gallagher. So did Jeff Dunham and Achmed the Dead Terrorist.

One word kept repeating itself in my head.

Beyond, of course, *freedom*.

And as I climbed into my father's car and fist-bumped him, the word resounded:

Goodness.

It was time to put politics behind me and to concentrate on being a *good* person.

In both my life and in comedy.

I never wanted to head back into that goddamn prison.

Ever!

This was my future.

No longer prisoner 64684-947.

Back to being just plain ol' Skippy Battison, comedy persona extraordinaire.

Funny to think about all of this now but I *still* have over $23,000 in that prison commissary, which is just fine.

It's non-taxable.

Safe as a trust in a crust.

But what was about to arrive for me was a future I never could have predicted.

Events that would change the course of my life forever.

And not necessarily for the better ....

★ **Chapter Nineteen** ★

WHAT'S MINE IS YOURS AND WHAT'S YOURS IS DEFINITELY MINE

There are a ton of well-known facts about me that have circulated for years in show business.

You've read a few already.

That I'm a "smart" comedy writer. That I'm a "joke machine." That I always show up for a gig and always give it *everything* I have.

But here's one fact you might not have heard:

That I happen to have a propensity for coming up with a million ideas for television shows and movies that others have later stolen.

It's the truth.

I'll give you a few examples.

Ever see *Ted Lasso?*

Crazy Rich Asians?

Breaking Bad?

How about the 2008 Clint Eastwood movie *Gran Torino?*

Netflix's award-winning show *Orange is the New Black?*

All mine.

Each and every one.

Of course, the "creators" of these shows deny it. Too much money is at stake. Too much Hollywood "rep." Too much pussy.

But I'm declaring, right here and now, in black and white print (or in my luxurious voice if you're listening to the audiobook version), that I created *all* of those shows.

And *more*.
How about any of these tasty little yummies?
Succession?
Big Mouth?
Bo-Jack Horseman?
Glow?
All mine.
Each and every one.
Avatar?
Pixar's *Inside Out?*
Pixar's *Toy Story 4?*
All mine.
This isn't bragging. This is the truth: I'm an idea machine.
Every day, every minute, every hour of every single day of every single month of every single year, ideas simply *pour* out of me.
Some of these ideas I'll work into scripts, such as the original versions of *Crazy Rich Asians* or *Toy Story 4*. Some I'll just tell friends about. Some I'll pitch in emails to producers. Some I'll just think about when buying a donut.
But it's pretty clear to me—and to many others that I've told this to, including prosecution lawyers and such—that most, if not all, of the ideas were either stolen outright, or "plucked from the ether," as one friend put it to me, just floating out there in the zeitgeist.
Whether this is my own damn fault or not is up for debate.
I'm a generous person and sometimes I don't know my own damn vulnerabilities.
I tend to be *too* generous.
Let's start with *Crazy Rich Asians*.
If you're not reading this book on fucking Pluto, you'll know that *Crazy Rich Asians* was a hit movie from 2018 about a young couple who travel to an Asian country and the woman learns that her boyfriend's parents are rich as shit. I haven't seen the movie but I've heard a lot about it, believe me.
In my particular idea, a young white woman hooks up with a lifeguard who basically lives in a shack by the beach. She likes him but doesn't yet love him. He invites her home for Thanksgiving and she's picturing a real shit house in the suburbs. What she finds instead is a mansion. The dude is rich as shit and he's just taking a year off before working at his dad's successful business. It's sort of based on some people I knew growing up.
You would think they were poor but they were just temporarily slumming it.
The script was called *Rich as Fawks*.

The Fawks was the last name of the lifeguard's family.

That was another thing that had been stolen!

About fourteen years before even finishing *this* script, I came up with the idea for a family to be named the Fawks.

Lo and behold I find a movie coming out called *Meet the Fockers*.

Totally stolen.

Fact.

The producer of *that* movie, someone whose name I won't mention as we're still in litigation, is a friend of a friend. I foolishly told this dipshit my idea and he told his friend and so on.

Before I knew it, I'm fucked out of the millions, if not billions, that I deserve.

Ain't that nice?

So, actually, I was screwed over *twice* for the same idea.

Now obviously the family in my script wasn't Asian. They were just normal white folks from Virginia Beach. But beyond that, it was all pretty much the same.

When I brought litigation against the producers, they claimed that the story was based on a 2013 novel called *Crazy Rich Asians*—five years before the movie came out.

But here's the problem: I came up with the idea back in 2004 when on vacation in Myrtle Beach, *way* earlier.

In retrospect, I should have gone with the minority angle.

But that's really easy to say now, right?

I went with what was in my heart, which is always a bad choice in a world driven by marketing.

More examples:

Naked and Afraid was an idea I had come up with *years* earlier called *Being Chased on a Deserted Island Totally Buck-Ass Nude*.

Dog Whisperer with Cesar Millan was an idea I had that was called *Control Your Pets the Third-World Way*.

Big Mouth was originally *Batty's Pube Years*.

Toy Story 4 was *Sex Toys Come to Life*.

Of course, there were some *slight* differences in my original ideas and what later appeared on television and on movie screens, but, let's face it, they were *exactly* the same.

But "in essence" doesn't count.

What matters is, basically, who you know.

This would also hold true for individual jokes that I've submitted to late-night shows over the years when I'd inevitably recognize the *very same damn joke* I had sent via fax or email a few days before.

I'll give you an example.

On a *Jimmy Kimmel* show in June 2016, there was this joke that he told to much applause:

"How great is it that Caitlyn Jenner is doing what she's doing? Honestly, I think it's great. I expect our golf excursion to be a whole lot chattier now but I'm all for it."

And here is the joke I had faxed the day before:

"Caitlyn Jenner is no longer a resident of Sacramento, as she no longer has a sack."

Notice any difference?
I don't.
Not much anyway.
And that's it.
They had stolen my joke.
Here's another example:
On a *Real Time with Bill Maher* show from August 2011, there was this joke:
I'm all for gay marriage. It's the gay destination weddings I'm not looking forward to.
And *here* is the joke I had emailed the show a few days before:
If gays want to get married, that's on them. I just don't want to pay to travel down to the Bahamas for the wedding.
Pretty damn similar, if not outright stolen. Clearly.
Hundreds, if not thousands, of jokes were stolen from me over the years from any of the countless late-night shows. I could go on and on and the list would run pages.
But I'm over that now. I'm no longer angry.
If I were to ever write a book about how to make it in Hollywood, it'd consist of one page and that page would read: "Know people."
Even better: "Have successful friends."
My problem is that I've always known people, a ton of people — but not necessarily the ass-kissers who *can get shit made*.
The problem with me, and with all of my best buddies in the business, is that we don't give a shit.
We don't attend the "necessary" parties, the ones with the Hollywood Fluffernutters who have zero talent for comedy, but *mucho* talent for kissing the right asses.
I never did have *that* talent.

In high school, I could have *easily* been the most popular student. But I decided to hang with my wackadoodle nutjobber group of friends who made me laugh and who I made laugh.

If someone didn't laugh at me, no matter how cool they were, I didn't want to have anything to do with them.

Life is too short to spend with others who don't find you funny all the time.

And yes, I know that friends can have different senses of humor but guess what? I don't want them to be my friends.

What can I say? That's just how this testicle rolls.

Which brings me to Marc Maron.

Marc and I have a long history, dating back to me asking for advice to get on *SNL*. I also remember seeing him perform on stage and I was drinking at the bar. After his set, I complimented him on his material but told him his delivery needed some work. He laughed, thinking I was telling a joke. But I wasn't. We didn't talk again for months. But when we did see each other again, when we were both out in L.A., I told him again what I felt needed to be accomplished on his part to *really* push himself and his material to the next level.

I think there was a hesitancy at first but he eventually came around.

We got to talking. And we found that we had more in common than might have first been apparent:

Always the funniest in our schools.

Always driven to want to create and to achieve something that we didn't yet have a name for.

Both frustrated with the indignities of Hollywood.

Both wanting our own sitcoms.

We talked for about five minutes and then we went our separate ways. Truthfully, I did most of the talking but we equally went our separate ways.

And lo and behold, we ran into each other yet again, now at a deli in Pasedena! This was around February 2008.

This time he *did* recognize me and pretended at first not to notice me, which I took to mean that he didn't want to bother me, as I was with a very beautiful actress who, ironically, ended up later that night headed home with Marc!

Life is funnier than anything you could sometimes "make up."

I bought Marc a corned beef sandwich and invited him to sit at the table with my date. He asked what I was up to and I told him that I was thinking of starting a radio show where I would talk with fellow comedy writers and comedians about comedy and about the business.

"Would never work," he said.

"And why not?"

"Too inside baseball. Would be better talking about politics."

Marc, at this time, was an on-air host of a political show on *Air America*, a liberal syndicated radio network.

"Disagree," I said. "Trust me. I'm from D.C. I grew up with that shit. It's exhausting already. Audiences want you to interview celebrities and people in the comedy world. It's a can't miss."

Marc shook his head as if he'd heard it all before.

"Sticking with politics," I could have sworn he said and would now swear on the holy Bible (or the Cliffs notes version) if we ever did end up in court, which we won't because I really admire the guy.

"Then how about instead, just record in your bedroom or something and then post it online?" I then think I asked between bites of my omelet.

"Like pirate radio but for the Web?" I think he asked.

"Exactly," I'm pretty sure I replied. "Like CB radio but for the modern age."

He looked at me, I'm almost 100% sure, as if I was crazy.

And that was that. Marc finished his sandwich, motioned to my date, and they both left. Whatever. She didn't have much of a personality anyway. (She ended up becoming one of the actresses on *black-ish*, a show I never really understood. And, actually, that was *another* idea that was stolen from me, except my show was called *white-like me*. And I had come up with that idea back in 2002. Notice all of the lowercasing. Look familiar? Yup.)

Marc and I didn't talk again until years later.

But when we did ... *whoo boy*.

Explosion.

I'll get to that later.

So after I got out of prison, I doubled down and worked as hard as I ever had in order to get a ton of projects I had percolating in me ol' brain off the sandy ground.

That most of these ideas would later be stolen was something I didn't know at the time. To be honest, I might *not* have worked so hard if I *had* known that they'd all be taken by *other* people.

But in another sense, it did me a lot of good to keep working.

It took my mind off my prison time and all the torturous things I had seen and experienced.

And it got me back into the working weave. Of getting up every morning at 11:30 or so and working until 3:00 and then taking a long walk on my parents' property until dinner.

I was back in the real world. I now had to act like it.

One of the ideas I had when I first got out of the clink was about a little girl who becomes a backgammon prodigy. It was sort of based on this chick I had known back in Maryland who was real quiet, not too attractive, and she had only a grandmother to take care of her. I never talked to her at school, never felt the need, as I just assumed her sense of humor was very poor. Her name was Mary Beckons.

One night at a house party in Bethesda, when everyone else was swimming in a giant backyard pool, I went into the pool house to change.

I found Mary sitting all alone, playing backgammon. She had been invited to the party because the host's mother felt sorry for her and knew Mary's grandmother from church. Mary hadn't even changed into a bathing suit but was just sitting there with a cheap terrycloth onesie. She barely looked up when I entered.

I'm a nice guy, so I approached and introduced myself. I asked her what she was up to. She said she was practicing for a backgammon tournament to be held in a few weeks. Seems that there was good money to be made on the circuit and Mary needed it for "clothes" and "food" for herself and her grandmother.

I smelled bullshit but I stayed to chat anyway. I asked her to teach me how to play. Over the next two or so hours, I sat there transfixed as Mary beat me over and over again. I was worried that the others at the party would think Mary and I were hooking up. But what Mary was doing with the backgammon board was incredible. She was an artist. It's hard to explain what I saw, but it's like she almost *knew* what I was going to do *before* I ever did it.

It was spooky.

She beat me four or five times, or maybe even more.

I thought about coming on to her but, again, I'm a nice guy. I thanked her and returned to the party just as the sun was setting and the burgers were being served. She stayed behind, practicing.

It's something I never forgot.

The reason why I'm telling you this story is that years later, searching for a "family" movie idea, I hit upon writing a script with a lead character like Mary. The script was titled: "The Lover's Leap," which is a rollout move in backgammon that one can make at the beginning of a game to improve one's chances.

The movie was about a young woman without parents who teaches herself backgammon and soon becomes a prodigy, supporting herself as she travels across the world, winning tournaments. She's also smoking hot, which definitely helps. Along the way, she meets other backgammon players, some young, some old, some gorgeous, some not, and keeps going until the world championship. I won't give away the ending but it's half sad and half funny and it would have hit really well with audiences of all ages.

I sent it out to a million agents and producers, and never heard back.

Years later, I was looking for something on cable when I came across *The Queen's Gambit*. I started to watch and soon became very upset.

This was *my* idea!

Not just my general idea but *everything*: characters, dialogue, specific details. I am talking *everything*.

I was so upset I was shaking.

Literally *shaking*.

The chick I was dating at the time thought I was having a reaction to her meat lasagna. Granted, it fucking sucked but it had nothing to do with what I was eating.

I watched through the credits and paused to take down all of the names. This was *too* close for comfort.

Someone *had* to have stolen this idea.

I then compared all of the names on the credits with the list of people I had sent out the script to years before and there it was:

"Adam Rickperoff, key grip"

It took me awhile to connect all the dots but after I did, it became *very* easy to see exactly what had happened.

Adam was a guy I knew from around town (the town being, of course, "Hollywood") who would sell pills and pot, and when he wasn't dealing drugs, he'd work as a key grip on various television and movie productions, whatever the fuck that meant. Typically it meant holding a boom mic or something.

I had bought some pills from him years ago before I was sober and would hang out with some mutual friends at a bar in Pasadena. One of our mutual friends, a guy named Danny, was a wannabe screenwriter. At the time—and this was before my confidence as a writer grew—I was looking to find a writing partner for scripts. To pass ideas back and forth, create dialogue through conversation, etc. I told Danny about my backgammon idea and he didn't seem overly interested.

Fine.

Not everyone has to "get it."

I didn't think about it again. Until I saw Adam Rickerpoff's name in the end credits.

This fucker had been told about the idea by Danny and years later, he used it to his advantage in order to tell a writer friend about it so that *he* could secure a job as a key grip on a major television production.

It was all so *clear*.

Hollywood is a sniper's nest where people are capable of *anything* in order to advance their careers.

I'll give you another example:

Do you like the McLovin' joke in *Superbad*?

Of course you do.

Well, can you guess who came up with that joke first?

Right. You're looking at him right now. That would be me.

In 1999, as a gag, I went to one of those shitty T-shirt shops in Venice Beach and I had a fake license/ID made for myself just to make women laugh in bars. Instead of creating a fake ID that would make me *older* than I was (something I had done back in high school) or instead of creating a fake license to pretend I lived on a certain street in order to avoid rush-hour traffic, I created this fake persona to be much younger than I really was.

So young, in fact, that I was too young to drink.

The joke, and it's a great one, is that I was making a fake ID for no real purpose *but* to get a laugh from a made-up name.

And, quite frankly, if I happened to hook up with someone a hell of a lot younger, all the better.

The photo was of me when I was young, and the name on the ID read:

Beefy McBeefy

When I'd meet a girl at a bar, and she'd ask me for my contact info, or even *before* she asked me for my contact info, I'd hand over the card and wait for the laugh.

It always arrived.

Always.

One night, I was at a bar in Inglewood and I was talking to a hot woman. Before she even said a word, I handed over my ID.

She laughed very, very hard.

When she stopped laughing, who comes walking over but a big lump of a dude, asking what I thought I was doing. I explained that it was all just a joke and that everything was cool and could I buy the guy a drink?

Guess who this guy turned out to be?

Seth Rogen.

At least, looking back, I *think* it was Seth Rogen.

Shit, it *had* to be Seth Rogen.

If you're an academic and you never leave the university and teach your screenwriting courses to people who will never make a living at what you're teaching, well, you might believe things like this don't happen.

But in the real world, I am here to tell you that they do ... and I'd love for you to prove me wrong.

Batty's Pube Years was an animated pitch I made to many executives between 2004 and 2007, and it would have been about my years in junior high school when I first started to sprout pubes. The hormones would have been voiced by myself and one who would have looked like the mascot to the Philadelphia Phillies.

That was stolen.

Watch *Big Mouth* and tell me differently.

Grand Torino was a 2006 action adventure script I had written called *Hatred for Others*. Fuck, I even suggested in the goddamn screenplay itself that Clint Eastwood play the lead character, Kurt!

In his version, his character's name was Walt.

Yeah.

I traced that particular hoist to a guy I knew who worked as Clint's son's daughter's math tutor, a guy I used to drink with at a bar in Redondo Beach.

He *had* to have told Clint's son, who then *had* to have told Clint.

Sigh.

Ain't that nice?

I'm not complaining, as no one forced me to get into making others laugh for a living. I *own* that decision.

But ... I don't know. Things could have certainly been *easier* for me.

Again, not that I'm complaining.

But did you love the *Dave Chapelle Show* like the rest of the world?

That was *my* idea.

Not the one starring Dave but a similar show starring me.

Laugh if you want, but it *was*.

"I'm Rick James, bitch"?

Remember that?

My version was "I'm Huey Lewis, cunt!"

What I am saying is that many of the shows and movies that you've been watching and enjoying over the years were based on my ideas.

Which brings me back to Marc Maron and "his" podcast, *WTF with Marc Maron*.

In 2011, two years after he "created" his podcast, I got in touch with Marc and I asked if we could meet for a late-night snack at a diner we both frequented in Hollywood.

He claimed at first that he was too busy but after some cajoling on my part, he finally agreed.

After we sat down and ordered coffee, the conversation went like this:

Me: "Thanks for coming."

Marc: "What's going on?"

Me: "Straight to the chase."

Marc: "Always. What's up?"

Me: "I want to talk to you about your podcast."

Marc: "Okay."

Me: "Remember when we spoke last?"

Marc: "I don't."

Me: "I think you do."

Marc: "I don't."

Me: "I told you that you should interview people in comedy. Comedians and writers and stuff. You said you'd rather stick to politics."

Marc: "I don't remember saying that."

Me: "I can assure you that you did."

Marc: "All right. So what?"

Me: "Okay. Do you remember me telling you about a CB radio for the Web?"

Marc: "No. What are you trying to say? That you … you invented podcasting?"

Me: "Yes."

Marc: "And that you came up with my podcasting idea first?"

Me: "Yes."

What happened next was reported, at the time, on various websites, but thankfully without the video. This was before people could film very easily.

As I told you at the beginning of this book, I'm an honest guy.

And I'm not going to sugarcoat what came next.

Marc and I stepped outside and proceeded to beat the shit out of each other. Him beating me more than I beat him.

When you see me in photos these days, you might notice that while my face looks perfectly great, my nose is a tad off center.

Marc broke it that day.

I've told this story a ton on my own podcast and satellite radio show. But here's something that I have never before told:

As I was lying on the ground, clutching my nose, blood spurting onto the sidewalk, passersby watching intently, including a tiny dog and its ugly middle-aged owner, Marc leaned down to me and whispered, I'm pretty sure:

"Maybe you did invent the podcast. Maybe you did come up with the idea for interviewing comedy writers and comedians first. But so what?"

Ain't that nice?!

Marc will swear up and down that he *never* said any such thing and that the fight didn't even happen and that I only made up the entire experience later to create a "fake" rivalry to boost my own ratings.

That's all a lie.

Marc knows how it all happened.

I *know* how it went down.

Do I mind that this story is not better known?

Not really. I still actually like the guy a lot. I think he's funny and he was great as an actor on *Glow*, another show whose idea I came up with first (in my version, it was a group of female mud wrestlers taking on a college wrestling team ... and *winning*).

But the fact of the matter is that I *did* invent podcasting and I *did* invent the comedy interview podcasting idea before anyone else.

And let's face it: if I hadn't gotten smacked around by Marc that night, I wouldn't have started lifting weights and becoming a "master" at the self-defense and fighting system known as krav maga (or krav MAGA, as I like to refer to it).

So I have Marc to thank for me looking hot as hell and being in shape and, I guess, having a slightly off-center nose.

No hard feelings.

And, Marc, if you're reading or listening to this book, my invitation for you to come on my show and apologize still stands. I have more listeners than you now anyways.

Yeah, everything turned out just fine.

But when I walked out of the Maryland Correctional Institution in Hagerstown on November 3, 2005, things were about to get *weird*.

In ways I never could have forecast.

But in ways that I would have to deal with regardless.

Whether I wanted to or not.

I didn't.

But I had very little choice.

As you shall soon see ....

★ Chapter Twenty ★
REDEMPTION THONG

Ever hear that song by Bob Marley (although I think it was written by Eric Clapton) called "Redemption Song"?

I never understood the lyrics but I always loved the title: "Redemption Song."

Real simple, real meaningful.

It's just a song about redemption, as simple as that, no matter what the hell the lyrics are talking about.

I think of that song whenever I look back at emerging into the real world after my hard stint in prison.

I wanted to redeem myself.

How best to go about that?

I had much to think about. So I hit my parents' pool and had Miss Benda cook me up some lick-smacking BBQ ribs (her specialty) and a few drinks that really sang, and I floated the afternoon away.

By the time the sun went down, and the meaty ribs had turned into a carcass that sat by the side of the pool waiting to be picked up, I had come up with a plan.

If I may say so, it was a *damn* good plan.

I'd hire a batch of hispanic and black actors and I'd tour schools, libraries, maybe even institutions that held young "troubled" teens, and give a fun, enlightening production about the realities of prison.

A lot of ex cons did this.

They just didn't do it *well*.

Or funny.

I remember seeing a few of these types of productions back in high school, mostly concerning not doing drugs or not raping a classmate. I remembered them as being dry and performed by people who didn't have the greatest comedic chops.

I also remember thinking that I'd have learned so much *more* if the performers had made me laugh rather than just preaching to me.

Why couldn't I now do otherwise? Put on a kick-ass, funny show about not necessarily the "crime" I was accused of committing, but an authentic look at what you'd find if you ever were unlucky enough to enter prison?

I got to work immediately and published an ad online that I sent to all of the local acting websites I could find in the D.C. area:

Looking for Black and Hispanic Looking Criminals Types
to Entertain Kids and Teach Them
How to Survive Prison

Within a few hours, I had a stack of actor's headshots and a few regular photos.

Here's the funny thing about Washington: there's really not too many opportunities for actors. So when there *is* an opportunity, they go haywire.

Especially at a *great* opportunity.

I didn't want to let it be known who I was just yet.

I figured that once I told them, they'd be pretty happy that a successful working comedy writer and comedian had shown an interest in them. But for those who weren't picked, I wasn't looking forward to a million emails begging to get on the project.

Let them, for now, just think I was a rando moron looking for talent.

After whittling down the stack, I chose two blacks and two hispanics, which pretty well represented the average ratio in prison.

All four were local actors, looking for a big break.

I won't use any of their real names, as I'm still in litigation with three of them, but to make it easy, I'll just use the following: Leroy (black), Lamonte (black), Javier (hispanic), Josefe (hispanic).

I got to work immediately on writing a fresh and exciting act that would appeal to high school kids and that could be performed in a tidy 10 to 15 minutes. I wanted to keep it short. I remembered how limited my attention span had been as a kid.

We could perform the bit and the rest of the actors would leave the stage. I'd then be alone to accept the applause and to answer any questions from the kids in the audience.

I wrote the script which I called "Prison Reality" and my group, which I named *The Battisons,* began to practice.

And practice.

And *practice.*

There were some complaints from the actors that I was driving them too hard but I wanted this *perfect.*

There was also a few complaints about "payment."

When are you going to pay us?

How is there any money in this?

I can't eat without you paying us!

My daughter needs to go to the doctor, could you please pay me?

You get the idea.

I suppose I can't blame them, in retrospect. All were working odd jobs to support their acting dreams. I've talked to a few people about this and they all say I should have kicked some money their way.

I guess I should have but I wasn't exactly rolling in the green myself.

So should I have thrown them some bones?

Sure.

But my intention was to redeem myself.

And is there any specific monetary amount you can attach to *that* goal?

No really.

After I was completely happy with how the group was clicking, we were ready to hit the road and enlighten today's youth.

First stop: a high school close to where I grew up. It was called Winston Churchill High School.

Maybe it still is.

I know that there's now a certain element of our good population who want to change the name as they find that the *real* Winston Churchill isn't quite up to their moral standards. Seems that ol' Winston isn't a guy they'd want to hang out with or trust with their children.

It wasn't as if saving the *entire world* during World War II should have any bearing on that choice.

Nah, *anyone* could have saved the world!

Regardless, I'll save all this for my next book, which will be an "alternative history" in which Hitler and Churchill team up to deliver a six-pack of Coors across state lines in 1977.

Back to the performance ...

I can't now say, in all honesty (and I did promise to be *fully honest* at the beginning of this book), that our first performance went over great.

In fact, there *were* a few glitches.

The first glitch was that the school had not given us permission to perform.

The second was that we arrived at the school and set up shop on the front grassy quad area just as the kids were coming out for lunch.

I guess the third glitch was that even before the show started, Josefe was seen making out with one of the juniors behind a school dumpster.

So Josefe was out. And the show never took place, as we were hastily escorted off the property.

And Julio (not his real name but also a hispanic) was hired at the last minute to replace Josefe for our *next* show, which took place at *another* high school not too far away. I won't name the school, as there's *still* litigation, but it begins with a "W."

All public high schools in Maryland seem to begin with a W.

We dusted ourselves off, asked permission this time, and performed for the kids inside their gym.

WJLA-TV in Washington later reported on our production.

It seems that one of the station's reporters had a daughter who was a senior at the school.

Let me correct some errors in that particular report which later became so popular on the internet that viewership reached more than two million on Youtube.

I wasn't nude.

I wasn't cursing.

We didn't use ethnic slurs.

We didn't re-enact a prison rape.

We didn't do *any* of that.

Here is what we *did* teach:

That if you ever get in trouble, hire a *really good* lawyer.

We taught the kids the *reality* of prison. And that if you had to pay your way out of being raped, well, that's just what you had to do.

Prison wine was another subject we hit on. If you're going to head off to prison, the chances are pretty damn good that you're either going to do drugs or drink.

Should I have recommended that they take up a drug habit? Or drink hooch cooked in their own toilet?

It's a close call but I chose the hooch.

At least they would know *where the wine was coming from!*

With your typical "Scared Straight" approach, we might have lied and said that prison was the worst thing that could ever happen to you. But we never did.

What I was trying to point out was this:

That there are *far* worse things that can happen to you. Like, say, working as a temp for $12 an hour at an office park off I-270.

That's *forever*.

Prison isn't forever. Or *typically* isn't forever.

Again, hire a *really* good lawyer!

I taught them, through sketches, what snacks are the best to purchase at the commissary.

I taught them the best ways to disinfect a prison pay phone before using it (bleach and *lots* of it).

I taught them how to properly pay off guards.

I taught them to be nice to the judge and to not bend over backwards to make him laugh. (And definitely don't bend over backwards in prison!)

I taught them to not bring much money into the prison when you check in, as you might not see that money when you check *out*.

I taught them that if you're white, the neo-Nazi gang would probably be your best bet. If you were black, the black gangs were probably your best bet.

But, again, I was realistic about it all.

Let's face it: 95% of the kids in that audience would never go to prison.

Probably 100% *thought* they would never go to prison.

If I had been sitting in that audience, or *had* been sitting in that audience, I would have thought the same.

But guess what?

I fucking *went* to prison.

So even if they didn't *think* they'd be going to prison, some *would*. About 5%, right?

As for this 5%, they'd be thanking me later.

I thought our first full performance went really well.

We presented our bit which lasted about 20 minutes and then we took some questions.

The first question, of course, was why was I sent to prison.

I told them I had been falsely accused and then charged with a crime I'd rather not talk about.

The next question, of course, was "Why not?"

I had prepared for this.

I began to speak but before I could get a word out, Julio ran up to me in character and pretended that he was going to hit me. He said, real loud, "A snitch who tells on another snitch is just a snitch. Even if it's on your *own* damn self!"

"And that's *another* lesson," I said, as if none of this had been planned before the show. "*Never* talk about your crimes in prison, yo. You feel me? But *especially* after you leave prison."

That worked. The crowd quieted down and they asked some more questions. After a few, we left the gym to a huge round of applause. I made my way with the group to the principal's office to ask for our money.

He expressed surprise. "I thought this would be for *free*," he said.

"Ain't nothing for free," said Julio.

Wow, that's pretty intense, I thought at the time. This guy can *really* act scary.

I said, "No, this takes time and effort and we traveled a long way for it."

Not true but that was okay. I wanted at least *something* for our efforts.

"Well, I'm sorry," said the principal. "You said nothing about money. I only allowed you to perform because I know Ed at the Montgomery school department who knows your father who vouched for you."

"We want our money," said Julio.

Jesus, I thought. This fucker is taking this role *real* seriously!

"Okay, okay," said the principal. "Would $20 be enough? For each of you?"

Julio looked at him and shook his head. "Make it $200. For each of us."

"I'll see what I can do," said the principal.

"Need it *now*," said Julio.

"I don't have that type of money on me," said the principal.

Quite frankly, I thought $20 a person was more than fair. But Julio seemed … quite intent on getting that money.

"Then *find* it," said Julio.

"Let me talk with Alice," said the principal.

"Who's Alice?" asked Julio.

"Special ed teacher. Hang on. I just saw her walk past."

The principal scooted out of the office, leaving us standing there. He never returned. A security guard came over and escorted us off the property but not before Julio went charging back into the school to find the principal.

As I was leaving, Julio was *still* in the building. The principal later suffered a broken wrist and a compound fracture in both femurs.

That was the last time we ever performed. Julio was arrested and the group disbanded, leaving me alone once again to make my own damn way in the world.

Turns out Julio wasn't just an actor playing a criminal.

Julio *was* an actual criminal.

Just my luck! Geez!

I guess I hadn't done *too* thorough a job vetting the kid's criminal history, as he did turn out to be the famous "Duct Tape and Kite String Murderer of 2003 - 2007."

This was all very frustrating.

My father suggested I leave town for a bit, as I was still under probation.

At first I fought it.

But when the TV report aired on WJLA—and I started seeing reporters show up at my parents' house—I *really* knew it was time to bid D.C. farewell.

Sayonara, assholes. Best of luck in your swamp!

There was really only one other place to head:

And that was back to L.A. (It didn't help my cause that some rich dickhead high schooler had an early version of the digital camera and had videotaped the *entire* proceedings, including Julio chasing after the principal. I told them at the beginning of the performance to put down any cameras or phones they might have on them. Well, one didn't listen and it cost me.)

After the second, third and fourth report aired, I was thankful that I was already three thousand miles away. My father had purchased for me a first-class plane ticket back to La La land.

I could never see myself living in New York City. Too dirty. Too dangerous. Too many goddamn surprises. Every day was a surprise.

So Los Angeles it was!

I bought back my Malibu house from the couple I had sold it to (for a bit more than they had bought it for) so it was an easy decision for all of us.

When I arrived in Los Angeles in March of 2006, I hit the ground running.

Or, I should say, *walking*.

I took a ton of walks on Malibu's beach trying to think of what my next step would be. Obviously, redemption wasn't as easy as I thought when I left that prison!

So in what direction should I *now* head?

I was being given yet another chance.

I wasn't going to fuck *this* one up!

There were a ton of comedy websites I could have written for around this time.

But that was too low-hanging fruit for me.

Twitter, however, *did* look interesting. If I could back up here for a second …

Beep, beep, beep …

I'd like to talk a little about Twitter and just exactly how I became a *forerunner* in many ways when it comes to social platforms and the problems that surround them. (There's a lot of specifics I'm not allowed to talk about but I'll try my best …)

Twitter began in 2006.

Around 2007 or so, Twitter became kind of the hip place for comedy people to post jokes.

I had heard of TV comedy writers already getting gigs based on what they had posted on Twitter, and I thought I'd give it a try.

I signed up and used the name @theprimreaper, The Prim Reaper. Not sure why I came up with that particular name but I stuck to it.

Within the year I had more than 25,000 followers.

By the end of the following year, 250,000 followers.

Right before I was shut down by Twitter, 500,000 followers.

The closest thing I can compare it to is a plant that buds and then grows completely out of control, soon taking over the entire town.

A lot of my followers I did actually pay for, to be honest.

But not all.

What was meant to be fun at first, to get the word out about my comedic talents, soon became a pain in the ass. Half my days were spent answering assholes who challenged my jokes or who took offense at *everything* that I'd say.

Things started out innocent, with Tweets like this one:

I love marinated flank steak stuffed with blue cheese.

That wasn't even a joke. I just really liked that particular meal!

Or this one:

What exactly is the Edge of U2 hiding under that knitted cap of his?

Or this one:

I hate Seinfeld. He's a pompous fucking asshole.

But then it occurred to me that I was wasting my possibly very powerful vehicle of expression on statements that really didn't matter.

I decided to always either make a societal point or to make a really funny joke.

Here was one that had a point:

Just read Christopher Hitchens' Women Aren't Funny piece. Have to say that I agree with some of it. There are some funny (1/2) women but I'd rather like a woman than laugh at her. Most guys would. (2/2)

Or this one, which was just purely a joke:

Anyone know how to get mac and cheese off a jock strap? Seriously. Long story!

Or this:

I think if I ever found my "spirit animal," it would be a lazy cat lying on a comfy couch, next to the A.C., licking itself

Or this one:

Out of all military occupations, fighter pilots have the best nicknames. The worst: Soldiers who have retired from the bomb squad with one missing limb

These were all really great, solid jokes and observations. The problems started to arise soon enough when younger women began to join the platform and became offended at literally everything they would read. Here's one of mine that offended a lot of these do-gooders:

For all those ladies into dinosaur sex, do the short little arms really not bother you?

It's a fucking solid-ass joke. But of course there were the typical female complaints:

What kind of women are actually into dinosaur sex?

What does the length of a limb have to do with the happiness in a relationship?

And then I'd write back something like:

A lot of women would love to fuck a dino. There are books all about it. As far as arm length, no, you're (1/2)

right. Midgets are good at fucking also (2/2)

And then all hell would break loose.

I'd then write something else and they'd jump on me even harder.

When I look back at all this now, this really was the beginning of me turning against the liberalism I had adopted in prison.

I mean, I was on *their* side!

And *this* is how they treated me?

There would be times when I answered a question that a woman had Tweeted and I'd be blamed for "mansplaning."

How about just "explaining"?

If I was a woman doing the explaining, would it *still* have been offensive?

Someone once wrote:

Women can have as many orgasms as they are entitled to.

I wrote back:

Even after the guy falls asleep?

Then I received this:
Who the fuck are you to tell us (me) how many orgasms we can have?!
Whose to say a woman has to sleep with a man?!
Is it so wrong for a woman to cum before a man?!
And then there was this Tweet that a woman wrote:
On the rag today, feel like shit.
And I wrote back:
Heard taking a bath helps, if that helps!
I wasn't even joking! I sincerely heard that taking a bath helped with menstrual cramps.
Jesus!
I can't win here!
And then all hell would break loose again.
Fuck! I was just explaining what I knew about menstruation. I didn't call myself a fucking expert!
Soon, every damn thing I said was a cause for blow-up from at least one person on Twitter.
I'd post certain recurring gags that became the forerunner for bits that I'd later use on my satellite radio show and podcast.
These were early versions of radio bits that you no doubt know:
Things like "Fugliest Bride," in which I'd Tweet a daily newspaper photo of the ugliest bride I could find in newspaper wedding announcements.
Or "The Problem With Da Women" bit, in which I'd Tweet the news to highlight why a lot of societal problems are directly connected to women (whether they want to admit as much or not).
And there was that famous Twitter fight I got into with Chelsea Clinton. I forget what that one was about.
There was the fight I got into with the English musician Billy Bragg, who I called Billy Fagg.
There was the fight I got into with the head of marketing for a vegan hot dog company.
There was the Twitter fight I got into with the head of marketing for a woman's-centric sex toy company.
There was the fight I got into with a female music journalist over Lou Reed using the lyrics "colored girls" in "Walk on the Wild Side."
God, so many Twitter fights!
Everything I wrote, gag or not, became a fight!
But to me it was all in the name of fun.
Isn't this what the internet was invented for?!
By the time I started my new writing gig at the TV sitcom *Samantha Who?* in September 2007, my Twitter account had reached cruising altitude and new subscribers were coming in every day.

I'd love to tell you a long, boring story of how I got the gig writing for *Samantha Who?*, but unlike Bill Cosby, I hate putting people to sleep.

Here's the quick version: I would loan money to a guy and never really ask for any of it back.

This was a plan of mine that I had in case this dipshit ever made it in the industry and I could then come back and he would then be *forced* to do me a favor.

In this case, it worked.

I won't mention his name because we're still in litigation but he was an executive producer of a few shows in the 2000s, or the aughts as assholes call them, and somehow he had worked his way up to running his own show.

And that show was *Gossip Girl*, a hit sitcom that would run from 2007 until 2012.

He didn't get me a gig on *that* show.

No, he got me a gig on a show called *Samantha Who?* that ran on ABC for a little less than two seasons.

Did I want to write for television?

Not really.

But I kind of felt as if I was stuck in what I now refer to as "the La La Brea Tar Pits of my career."

I'd just sit at home, Tweeting. And getting into Twitter fights. Maybe take a walk or two. Or pitch a joke or movie or television idea.

But I needed to keep *busy*.

My brain just works too quickly. It's like a high-end Tandy computer from Radio Shack.

I suppose you could say that this is when I officially "sold out." If that's what you want to say, that's okay.

Because I *did* sell out, and *gladly*.

I think *everyone* should sell out to Hollywood at some point in their careers, if only to later appreciate the freedom you'll feel when you choose your *own* creative path.

You need to go through hell to reach paradise.

You need to work "for the man" to eventually "work for yourself."

With that said, I knew I was in trouble the first day I showed up to work at *Samantha Who?* Only to find the writers' room filled with eight women and two men, one of who was I.

Great, I remember thinking sarcastically. *This should be most interesting indeed!*

The first thing I was forced to do after arriving at the Burbank office was to sit down in a room with the rest of the writers and watch a VHS video about proper work etiquette and how *not* to commit any sexually offensive acts against colleagues. Seems that on a previous

ABC sitcom a writer had been fired for offensive remarks and some "inappropriate behavior" aimed at female colleagues. I won't give you his name but I will say that he later went on to win an Emmy for an NBC sitcom. His career was hardly ruined.

And yet I, and the rest of the male writers in television, would have to pay the price for this dickhead's behavior.

This is never mentioned but ten years before that fat fuck Harvey Winestein was MeToo'ed out of Hollywood, there was *already* a movement afoot to make life difficult for the male, white comedy writer.

No one talks about this but I can assure you that I experienced the hate *long* before most younger writers now working. I dealt with this garbage from the beginning and I am here to tell you that it wasn't fun.

If you've listened to my podcast and satellite radio show, you'll have heard the many parodies I've performed based on these horrible workplace anti-harassment videos.

I can promise you that the parody isn't far off from the truth.

In one that I was shown on that first day at *Samantha Who?*, the dialogue went something like this:

Man: "I like your dress."

Woman: "Thank you."

Man: "Maybe I can see you one day without it."

Woman: "That's hurtful. I don't feel comfortable with you saying that!"

Man: "Gosh! I'm so sorry! I meant nothing by it!"

Another video went like this:

Man: "I hear you'd like a promotion."

Woman: "I've been working hard and think I deserve one."

Man: "Maybe you should stop by my apartment later and prove to me that you deserve it."

Woman: "I won't do anything of the sort. That's an outrageous request to ask of an underling!"

Man: *"Wow, I apologize! I had no idea!"*

These are *real* samples of the dialogue I heard on these videos.
Who the fuck talks like this? No one in the real world!
And besides … so what if they *do* talk like that? What guy who talks like this would ever get laid in the real world? It's survival of the fittest out there! If you talk like this, you won't get laid.
And then guess what?
You'll eventually *stop* talking like that!
It's *very* effective. Consider it the Darwinism of Office Mating Rituals.
Why inflict our own rules? Let nature takes its own damn course!
My point is that we don't need to hear what's "appropriate" or "inappropriate."
We *know* already. That's why we're *writers*.
Do you understand the irony?
We're writers hired to create funny and great dialogue … and we're forced to listen to crap dialogue written by hack writers in order to "learn a lesson."
It'd be like a master chef arriving on his first day at a fancy restaurant and being forced to eat a fast food lunch.
It was absurd!
But it had to be done.
You know why?
Well, I'll now tell you why:
Because it makes the 15% happy.
If you are an avid listener to my shows, you'll *already* know what the 15% means but I'll do my best to explain it here:
75% of the world goes about their everyday business not bothering anyone, heading to work, having a family, saving some money, maybe going out to eat once in a while.
The other 15% are the "pain in the asses."
The ones who are *never* happy.
The ones who are *always* complaining.
The ones who are *always* suing over sexual harassment.
You'll never please *this* 15%.
Ever.
So why even fucking try? (Wait. Make it 85% and not 75% who go about their every day business. I'm terrible at math.)
You're not *ever* going to win them over. In the meantime, the rest of us assholes have to sit through this shit, pretending we're interested, doling out our best fakes smiles to show that we're learning something.
Sure we are.

On that first day on the new job, I took a look around at the other writers in the room.

Was anyone else hating this also? There had to be at least a few, right?

I tried to make eye contact with them.

Jesus.

No. They seemed *fascinated* by it all.

Knew right then and there I was in trouble.

And that was just the *first* day.

I knew pretty quickly I was in trouble.

Samantha Who? was about a woman (played by Christina Applegate) who gets hit by a car, experiences amnesia, and then slowly comes to learn that she was hated *before* the accident, that her *new* persona is so much nicer than the one that previously existed.

A clever enough idea, I guess.

When I first heard the idea, I thought it'd be fun to *really* play with that: to show what a better person she was after the accident ... but then to pull a U-turn and show that, actually, when she was "mean" and "aggressive" and "selfish" before the accident, she was actually much *more* interesting.

Wouldn't that have been cool? And just what the audience *wouldn't* have expected?

And so much more *true to life*?

And yet you would have thought I had recommended putting her in a *Playboy* bunny suit and parading her before a group of male ABC executives.

Things only got worse from there.

(I should point out that I never had any problems with Christina Applegate or any of the other actors. They were wonderful. It was the comedy writers I had a problem with. I've pointed this out so many times but reporters never mention this. So ... now *you* know.)

I was tasked with working on the third episode. The first two episodes, including the pilot, had already been written. After batting around some ideas, we all thought the concept of Samantha attending a wedding as a bride's maid would be a funny concept.

We banged out a story frame for me to work with and I went off to my house to begin writing it. I took a long walk on the Malibu beach that day, I had much to think about.

When I returned to the house a few hours later, I had the entire episode mapped out in my head:

Samantha sees an email that asks her to be a bridesmaid. She shows up at the wedding and learns that everyone who knew her from before the accident thought she was an asshole. She sets out to prove how much nicer she is *now*. But she ends up fucking the groom (this happens during the commercial break, obviously). The bride confronts Samantha in front of the entire wedding party.

They get to yelling.

Then comes the twist: the bride is an even *bigger* bitch.

In the final act, the groom asks Samantha if *she'll* marry him. It seems that he doesn't like the bride-to-be. He prefers Samantha.

But being the nice person Samantha is (and actually always was) she tells him no, that he *must* marry the bitch because that's what he had promised. And he can't go back on his word.

Samantha is taking one for the team, falling on that grenade, even though she knows she'd be very happy with the groom. It's an act of selflessness that everyone (except for the selfish bitch of a bride) looks at with great wonder. But before the marriage, Samantha sleeps with the groom, just for the hell of it.

Why not? She's not so innocent after all.

It was an amazing script, and I was very happy with it. Beyond the plot, of course, I had sprinkled in a ton of really incredible jokes that truly reinforced the character of Samantha. Here's one:

Samantha
I hate chocolate.

Dana (Samantha's best friend)
No you don't.

Samantha
I don't?

Dana
You absolutely love chocolate.

Samantha
What else do I love?

Dana
Gerald, for one.

Samantha
Do I?

Dana
You don't remember?

Samantha
About what?

Dana
You don't remember washing his underwear after your trip to Mexico?

Samantha
(slowly)
Oh yes. That I <u>do</u> remember!!

I adored that last joke. I actually laughed out loud when I wrote it. If it had been accepted, I can guarantee you that the laugh would have been long and (ahem) *explosive*. I turned in the script and then anxiously attended the first read-through the next morning to go over what worked and what didn't work and how certain jokes could be improved and how certain jokes should be removed entirely and replaced with new ones.

The rest of the writers shuffled into the room. I looked over at them for a wink or a thumb's up but none came. I sensed this was not going to go as well as I had thought.

The complaints did not come at first. Things started slow, with some hesitancy but then quickly built up steam once the first complaint was launched.

A bunch of clucking hens. Fast and furious and high-pitched and grating:

"This deviates from our sensibility and tone."

"I mean, there were parts I liked. But, like, why overcomplicate it? She was a jerk and now she's not? But she is again? Or she wasn't but now she is? I'm confused!"

"When we originally plotted this episode out we had nothing about Samantha having slept with the groom, right?"

"A lot of these jokes are offensive. The network would never accept anything like this, I wouldn't think, right? A *gynecological* joke?!"

"Needs a total rewrite. Gut it and start over."

I held my tongue and merely nodded. Inside, though, I was thinking: *Why the fuck did they hire me? And if they wanted something "edgy" and they got it, why were they now complaining?*

After the meeting, the show runner took me into her office and closed the door.

"Rough start," she said.

"Yeah," I replied, faking my laugh.

"May take a while to get the hang of it."

"Excuse me?"

"The hang of it."

"Why would it take a while?"

"This isn't easy."

"You talk like I haven't done this before. I have."

"I'm sorry. But different shows have different sensibilities. You'll catch on, I'm confident of it."

"Gee, thanks."

"Don't worry, it'll work out," she said. "And don't forget the party at Erica's tonight. It'll be a good way to bond."

I silently nodded and went back to my own office, leaving more than a little bothered. It was up to me to catch on? Catch on to what exactly? More comedic network pap that would amuse no one, least of all anybody with a well-developed sense of humor?

The party that night was in the Hollywood hills, thrown by one of the female writers at her and her husband's house overlooking Hollywood Boulevard. If one were to produce a lame rom-com (and what rom-com *isn't* lame?) this would be *the* house they'd choose.

It was gorgeous, mostly glass, with a kick-ass deck and a backyard pool that, although small, was lit up beautifully.

I arrived stag and within the hour I was already hammered.

Let me re-emphasize: this was *way* before I gave up drinking and became addicted to vaping bubble-gum flavored THC.

Let's just say it didn't take long for me to get whoofered. Especially when I was digging into the hard liquor, like rum and whisky.

I've always been a lightweight and yet I've always been a "fun drunk," meaning I've always had more fun when tipsy, rather than becoming belligerent or emotional like some guys and most women. I've never cried when drunk (I *have* cried when I've woken up the next morning after a bender, but never cried *while* surfing that buzz).

To my surprise, I found that all of the writers were being pretty nice to me. I have to be honest here: they were welcoming even *after* the disastrous script reading earlier in the day. Maybe they wanted to overcompensate for their rudeness. Whatever the case, we were soon all standing around the lit pool, drinking, have a great time. While there really wasn't much we had in common, beyond comedy, the conversation did flow freely and there were a lot of laughs, mostly from things I was saying.

The conversation eventually turned to current events, which in California, of course, had to do with the wildfires then happening.

All the women were clicking and clacking about what a shame it all was and how global warming *definitely* had something to do with it and the loss of property and the loss of life and all that shit.

"Who told 'em to move here?" I asked, quite reasonably.

"What?" asked one of the woman writing assistants, I'm forgetting her name.

"They have the entire fucking state — no, *country* — to move and they chose the driest, most dangerous area for fires?" I asked. "Who forced them to move there?"

"No one, I guess," said another woman writer, "but don't you think it's sad that they have to go through all this?"

"I think it's sad when people move too close to the ocean and then complain when there's a hurricane and their house falls into the ocean. Or they move too close to a super dry area that always catches on fire and then it catches on fire and then they complain. Shit, I live in Malibu. My house could fall into the fucking ocean. That's the chance I took."

"Big chance," said someone.

"Yeah, it is," I corrected him. "But you ain't gonna find me bitching if anything happens to the house. Besides that, I wouldn't want to put firefighters in harm's way. And I sure as shit wouldn't want other taxpayers to pay for *my* fuck up."

"Are you serious?" some other asshole asked.

"As a shit attack," I said, grinning. "You guys ever read Ayn Rand?"

"Oh god," someone said.

"What?" I asked. "Have you or not?"

"Are you one of *those*?" a guy asked.

"Those what?" I asked.

"People," he said. "One of those types."

"Actually, if anything, I'm a libertarian," I replied.

"But you like Ayn Rand."

"I do, yes. Have read everything she's written. Have you?"

"I always avoided it."

"Why?"

"Don't think I'd like what she had to say."

"Give it a shot," I said. "Maybe you will."

"Doubt it," he said.

"Do you not respect people who like Ayn Rand?" I asked.

"Probably not," he said. "Just being honest."

"How about those who would rather not have the government in our lives?" I asked.

"Conservatives? To be honest, no. I don't agree with a lot of conservative viewpoints. I didn't agree with the war in Iraq. I don't agree with lack of abortion rights for women. No, I don't agree with any of it."

It's *impossible* in Hollywood to have any opinion beyond the far-left liberal one.

Look at what happens to just about any conservative actor or top-shelf talent working in Hollywood, whether they're Scott Baio or Rob Schneider or James Woods or Kirstie Alley.

They're dead in the water.

Dead!

I've talked about this on my shows with Kirstie and Rob and James and Scott.

And we all agree.

You are literally unable to express *any* political opinion ... *unless it's liberal.*

That's it.

End of story.

I was truly taken aback by the reaction of the people at this party. Here I was, thinking I was a goddamn reasonable person, too! They had no idea about my past nor would they for years to come. But a little respect would have been nice: not only for my experience in the comedy world but also for my political opinions.

I think *all* political opinions should be respected.

Especially if they're mine.

It was a real eye opener.

Keep in mind this was *years* before Trump became President.

The nation was most definitely divided ... but not like it is now.

I guess I stupidly assumed that we were a team or something.

Or a platoon of soldiers, all in this *together*.

In actuality, I *was* on the front lines in a war: but it was a cultural war.

I'm not familiar with anyone else at the time who suffered like I did for my political views in Hollywood. There were a few actors, as I mentioned, but their careers had already seemed to flame out anyway.

(Sorry, guys. Just being honest.)

Mine was on the rise.

A *steep* fucking rise.

The conversation at the party then took a turn into showbiz and comedy, which it inevitably does at these parties, but I knew my hide was already roasted.

I knew I was a goner.

There's been so much written about what happened next that I hesitate to even write about it myself, but it's unavoidable I suppose. How many podcast episodes are devoted to what happened next?

Jesus, it sometimes feels as if it's been analyzed more closely than the fucking *Zapruder Film*.

I've spoken about it many times but I've never put pen down to paper and explained it in detail.

So here we go.

After the conversation about politics, I wandered over to another area of the pool and began talking with a young woman (I'll call her Jan) who worked as a production assistant but wanted nothing more than to one day write comedy. Turns out we shared a lot of the same likes and dislikes. We sat on some pool furniture and began to discuss comedy in detail. She had had a few opinions and I *definitely* had more than a few. She announced suddenly that she had to go to the bathroom.

I asked if I could go first, would that be possible? I told her that the conversation was so fascinating that I'd been putting off using the toilet for what seemed like hours.

She said sure.

I used the bathroom, returned and then she took off for the bathroom.

When she returned, we launched right back into the conversation we were having before the bathroom breaks.

But we were soon interrupted when a writer whose name I won't mention came out of the house carrying a cell phone.

"Who's is *this*?" she asked.

We all looked at her and then around the pool. No one seemed to be claiming it.

"No one left a cell phone in the bathroom?" she asked.

"Oh, that could be mine," I replied, feeling my pockets. "I used the bathroom earlier."

"Any reason it was facing the toilet and videotaping?"

"Huh?" I asked, genuinely confused.

"Is there any reason this phone was videotaping facing the toilet?"

Jesus, what a night, I remember thinking. *Can I catch a break here or what?*

"I must have placed it down while I was washing my hands," I said.

"*Beneath* the sink?" she asked.

"Shit, I don't know. Where was I supposed to place it? On *top* of the toilet?"

"So why was it recording?"

"It wasn't when I left. There's no way. I barely know how to operate this thing. I just got it!"

"What even is it?" someone asked. A crowd had begun to form.

"It's called an Iphone," I said. "It just came out from Apple."

"And it has a video recorder?" someone asked.

"I guess so," I said, shrugging.

"Let's just see," said the jerk holding the phone. "Let's just see what's recorded on here."

She pressed a few buttons. Amazingly, for someone who had never so much as seen an iPhone, she did remarkably well for herself.

"Is that me?" asked Jan, the woman I had just been talking to.

"Yes," said the woman holding the phone. "And you're urinating."

"What the fuck?!" I exclaimed. "Bullshit! Get that off my phone *immediately!*"

I went to grab for the phone but the woman who was running the party reached for it and stated all importantly, "Keeping for evidence."

I reached for the phone and grabbed it ... but in doing so I mistakenly pushed this party host into the pool. Another woman touched my shoulder. Before I knew it, I had turned and reflexively pushed *her* into the pool. Someone else, another woman, went to grab me by my elbow, and by turning in such a way, I accidentally broke her hand. She went to fall into the pool. But when I tried to catch her, I ended up breaking her *other* hand.

I then carelessly dropped the $599 iPhone into the water, which is a shame.

A first generation iPhone is now worth a *fortune*.

Everything on the phone was ruined.

And there was no way to prove that I had videotaped a woman using the bathroom. Of course, there was also no way to prove that I *hadn't*.

But I'm here to tell you that I didn't!

So many fake videotapes have been connected with me over the years. You'll see them on porn sites. Some horrible voyeur video of a woman taking a leak and then it'll have something like "This video shot by Skippy Battison."

Ha ha. Real funny.

Not one is mine, I can *assure* you.

Anthony and Opie even posted a few, claiming that I had taken them.

Not mine, fellas.

Joe Rogan posted a few. For all I know, he took them of himself. Not mine, pal.

I can honestly say that I was the first person with an iPhone to be mistakenly charged with taking a video of a woman urinating without her permission. What I think *actually* happened, in retrospect, is that the iPhone was all so new and so exciting and just different, that people sort of lost their minds when they saw it on the bathroom floor.

When Jan asked, "Is that me pissing?", she was not much different from the first movie audiences in 1911 who were afraid the train on the movie screen was going to burst out and come directly at them.

Think about it. She had never seen an iPhone video before. How would she have known that it was her being videotaped?
I hold no ill way towards Jill!
And I still don't believe anything was captured on that video and even if it was, I had nothing to do with it.
How did it get below the sink, aimed at the toilet?
I was drunk. How the fuck do I know? I probably dropped it and it landed in the right position. Drunk people have a knack for doing stupid things in the correct way.
The party ended and I was ready to forget all about the incident—but ABC was not.
On Monday morning, the head of ABC's human resource department called me into her office on the Burbank lot. I'm forgetting her name.
"Can you tell me what happened?"
"Yeah. I was drunk and left my cell phone in the bathroom. I was accused of videotaping someone using the toilet. That's ridiculous!"
"And did you?"
"No, definitely not."
"I've been told differently."
"You were told wrong."
"I'm afraid that I will have to discuss this with the higher ups."
"You're going to investigate?"
"Yes."
"In the meantime, can I have my phone back?"
"We're seeing if anything can be saved."
"First of all, you can't do that. It's my phone. Second, I want it back. It's *my* property."
"Do you have anything else you'd like to tell me?"
"I think I'm being framed."
"And why would that be?"
"Because ..."
She was waiting.
"Because I'm a conservative."
"A conservative? What does that have to do with what you're being accused of doing?"
"No one else on staff is a conservative. I'm being railroaded. They don't like me."
I was speaking the truth.
Why had I ever really considered myself a liberal?
Or even a libertarian, for that matter?
A conservative is what I *was*!
Why didn't I just admit to this earlier?!!!!!!!

Yes, I had to do what I had to do in jail to get through—and maybe that was to pretend I was a liberal—but this here was the *real* world ...

And in the real world I was a conservative.

End of story.

"I hardly think that's the case," this idiot woman stated.

"Oh, I think it's very much the case," I replied. "Am I allowed back to the writers' room?"

"Not until we figure this out," she said.

"Figure *what* out?"

"Figure out what exactly occurred."

"I can tell you *exactly* what happened. I got drunk, the phone *fell*. The video recording came on and it must have recorded someone on the toilet. I never even saw it. Shit, if I had recorded it, don't you think I would have taken the phone with me?"

"Not if you wanted to record someone else. Or others."

"Jesus. What do you take me for?"

"I suppose this is partly our fault. We didn't background check you."

"And what is that supposed to mean?"

"You didn't inform us that you had a prison record."

"I didn't know I *had* to."

"And we've read over your Twitter profile. There's a lot to be offended by on there."

"I'm a comedy writer. Not a goddamn accountant."

And that was that.

I left her office and drove back to my house.

I knew it wasn't even worth heading back to the office to clear out my desk.

I was as good as gone.

I was no idiot.

Gone from the show.

Great.

And here I was actually beginning to even like my co-writers!

I had a thought.

No, it couldn't possibly work.

Or could it?

I called the ACLU and I told them the situation.

It was a last-ditch effort, a Hail Mary, but in the end, I still wanted this shit job.

The show sucked.

The people sucked.

The network sucked.

But the money ... *oh, that money* ...

I got in touch with a nice young ACLU lawyer, I'm forgetting her name:

Would it be legal to fire someone based only on their political affiliations?

Absolutely not.

Would you be interested in taking on this case?

Well, we're backed up and it could take a while.

What would you need?

Not sure, I'd have to look at this particular case.

I'm conservative now. And no one else seems to be in Hollywood, or not many. I feel very alone.

There are plenty of people in Hollywood who are conservative. But have they been fired for their beliefs? Or just not hired?

Good point.

I mean (laughing) would it help if I was a racist? I'm not but I'm just asking.

That's a terrible question. But I'm not sure. We've never represented a racist comedy writer who was being held back because of their beliefs.

So racism helps?

I wouldn't say it helps ... but we believe all people of all different beliefs are allowed their voice and shouldn't be prejudiced.

I thanked her and hung up. What a strange world she inhabited! They didn't believe in racism but they *defended* those who did.

I mean, you had to hand it to them, I suppose.

I then took a long walk on the Malibu beach. I had much to think about. By the time I arrived home, I had my answer.

I kept in touch with a ton of people I had known from prison, other outliers in this ridiculous game called life.

One was Steele, the Neo-Nazi without most of a tongue who communicated with only finger and hand gestures unrelated to official sign language.

Steele was now out on parole and working as a motorcycle mechanic in Idaho.

I'm always asked about my relationship with Steele, who's a frequent and hard-to-understand caller to my show.

Why do you have Neo-Nazi friends and so few gay friends?

How could you befriend someone with such beliefs?

Do you believe what he believes? You couldn't possibly, right?

The answers to these questions are ...

I have a lot of gay friends!

I'm friends with Steele because he's a good friend and loyal!

And no, I don't believe in neo-Nazi beliefs, just like I don't believe in the pro-African beliefs my friend Richard believes in or the pro-Chinese socialist beliefs my friend Kim believes in.

Friends are allowed to have *different* opinions about things.

But they're *still* friends.

And Steele is one of the most loyal friends I've ever met.

After I got out of jail, I continued to feed Steele's prison commissary fund. And when he left jail, I continued to send him some much-needed cash.

That's what friends do for each other.

Some might claim I did this out of fear for my life and safety.

I'd counter that this is what one does for people who are *good* to you.

And who don't murder you when they had the chance.

And fuck it.

He's my *friend*.

I help him.

He helps *me*.

I gave Steele a call and left a message with one of his co-workers at the garage.

A few days later, Steele got back to me.

The first thing he asked, after I got through all of the small-talk and the catching up and all the bullshit and trying really hard to decipher what the fuck he was saying, was: "How can I help you?"

I thought that was pretty cool.

Like I said, the dude is *loyal*.

I told him what I needed, he said fine, we said goodbye and I immediately called back the ACLU. I was put through to a different lawyer, this one sounding even younger.

I laid out my situation: I had been fired for my conservative views. ABC owed me not only for back pay but also for my brand-new iPhone which they had ruined at a work-related party.

She expressed some interest but said she'd have to get back to me. I told her to hang on a sec, that she hadn't heard it *all*.

Here's another thing, I said:

Did you know that my agent is a Neo-Nazi? Without the majority of his tongue? I wonder if that might have anything to do with my firing?

"A Neo-Nazi?" she asked. "As your Hollywood agent?"

"Yeah," I said, nonchalantly. "Those are his beliefs. I don't necessarily agree with them but he's a great agent."

"A Neo-Nazi?" she asked again.

"Yup," I replied, as if no big deal. As if this happened all the time in Hollywood.

"And the network knows this?" she asked.

"I guess so," I said, not quite truthfully.

"And do you think that's preventing you from keeping your job?" she asked.

"Yes," I said. "Definitely."

"I'll be in touch," she replied.

And that was how Steele, a devoted and convicted Neo-Nazi, became my Hollywood agent.

I'd like to stop here for a moment in order to reiterate the following: I have not, and have never been, a racist, an anti-Semitic, a hater of foreigners, gays, Asians or anyone else who is different from me.

Not at all.

I have a ton of friends who are gay, Asian, Jew, black and everything in between, including a few you would never have ever dreamed existed or even *wanted* to exist.

I love *everyone* equally.

I also hate everyone equally.

I'm an equal opportunity hater.

The hiring of Steele at first was, I'll be the first to admit, a bit of a stunt.

I wanted to truly entice the ACLU to defend my god-given rights as a conservative American white male.

Because I wanted to win!

Hell, I could *now* admit it: I was a conservative!

I was who I was. And probably *always* had been. Maybe even *born* that way. I couldn't *help* who I was!

I gave the other side a chance but I was now back where I belonged.

There was never any other choice for me.

I won't lie to you:

I was super pissed about the situation at *Samantha Who?*

If I didn't think I had been screwed when the party incident first occurred, and if I didn't necessarily feel that my firing had mostly to do with my conservative views, I certainly came around to eventually believing that I had been prejudiced against.

The ACLU got back to me within a few days. They were interested in my case.

Of course they were. How would this *not* have interested them? This story was practically *made* for a front headline.

Actually, it *was* later used as a headline on Gawker:

Nazi-Repped Conservative Comedy Writer Given the Heave Heil!

My ACLU lawyer, whose name I'm forgetting, went about trying to get me back on the show as a writer.

She also attempted to have my iPhone returned to me, even though I knew it wouldn't work.

I wanted it anyway.

I planned to take it straight to Apple to complain that it had broken for no reason.

(Try pulling *that* off today. There's no way it would work! But back then, when the iPhone was brand new, Apple didn't know what the hell caused malfunctions. As it turned out, this *did* work for me. After a few months, the network returned my cell phone, I immediately took it to an Apple store claiming ignorance, and they gave me a brand new one, although it was second generation and probably not as historically valuable as the first generation that it was replacing. Regardless, ABC couldn't find anything incriminating on the phone, as I knew they wouldn't, so that was good news.)

Was Steele really my agent? Not really. He was still back in Idaho working at the motorcycle repair shop and receiving calls and messages on the shop's pay phone. He wasn't making a living as my agent, that's for sure, but he always did have time to talk to an ACLU lawyer, or a reporter, or a lawyer for ABC or anyone else for that matter, barely understood by all.

Instead of hiring me back on the show, ABC paid me a very nice settlement, and I of course forwarded Steele his 15%, which he loved.

I think, in the end, ABC just didn't want the aggravation of having to explain why they had hired a writer who had been to prison and who was been repped by a Neo-Nazi.

And that's fine with me. The cash settlement came out to even *more* than I would have made if I had stayed on that show producing lines like, "I had no idea that everyone hated my previous self this much!"

Jesus. Kill me.

The civil trial involving the woman who accused me of videotaping her taking a leak was settled out of court with a little help from an old friend.

You're asking: wait, who is this old friend?

Steele?

No.

Think back to the beginning of this book when I was still an innocent high school student.

Remember when I befriended an older lawyer at a pool party in high school and he asked what I wanted to do and I told him comedy and I told him a few jokes and he laughed and was very supportive?

And I said to him, "I'll tell you what. One day when you're one of the top judges at the Supreme Court, I'll write you jokes that you can read from the bench"?

And then we both laughed and shook on it?

Well, that person was not yet a Supreme Court justice, he was still only a judge on the (and I'm quoting from Wikipedia here) "United States Court of Appeals for the District of Columbia Circuit."

So a big-wig.

Incredibly, when I reached out to him, he not only got back to me right away but he *remembered* me!

It had been practically decades!

"Where are my jokes?" he asked when I called and got put through.

"You *remember*!" I said. "I *can't* believe it!"

"I never forget a good joke teller," he said. "There's plenty of other things I don't remember but not that!"

We both laughed very hard, maybe him more than me. I was astonished that his memory was so sharp. This was no dummy, we were talking about. This was someone who came from little ol' Bethesda, Maryland, from the same private high school as me (granted, years before) to then attend Yale as an undergrad and then Yale law for a higher degree.

Like I said, no dummy.

He asked what I needed.

Loyal dude.

I told him about the pickle I was in and he sighed.

"Boy, I hate when things like this happen," he said. "So what *did* happen?"

I told him everything and he again sighed. "Frustrating. Very, very frustrating."

"So what should I do?" I asked.

I won't say what happened next.

I just can't.

But I *can* say this:

The case disappeared.

Poof!

Gone.

Sayonara!

See ya!

It's sort of like taking a crap.

You do your business and then you flush.

Where it goes next you have no idea and you don't *want* to know.

You just want it gone.

Well, same as with this stinky situation.

To this day, I don't know what happened and I still don't *want* to know.

I just never want to smell that stink again.

This is not to say that I wasn't shy about telling the world my side of the story and to brag (if that's even the right word) when things went my way.

I had, at this point, over 200,000 followers on Twitter, not all of who were my friends or on my side.

I got the feeling, even back then, that half the people who followed me were doing so because they hated me. Now this is common. But back then, I might have been the *first* on Twitter to have "hate followers."

But I knew even then that this could be a *good* thing.

I received a ton of criticism on Twitter about "attacking" ABC and the specific woman who had done me wrong. I even heard from this idiot woman's lawyers to stop what I was doing.

No way.

Who did they think they were dealing with here?

If anything, I *ramped* it up on Twitter.

Some Tweets meant more than others. I'll give you an example:

On February 2, 2008, I wrote out this Tweet:

Hounds been called off my trail. Thank you to a certain judge who will go unnamed. Can now get back to writing jokes!!

And here are some of the responses:

Fuck you asshole. Get back to sucking my dick.

You know you did it fucker. Where do you get off? Besides bathrooms with video running?

Guilty as shit of taking that piss video. Just admit it. Asshole!

Fine, whatever. Doesn't mean a thing.

Who gives a shit?

But when I wrote this Tweet:

Applying to write on more shows. Hope I get a spot!

Someone wrote back:

Best of luck to you and your neo-Nazi fuck agent in pulling THAT off!

But it wasn't just any "someone."

No.

It was a producer for a new CBS sitcom called *Worst Week*, based on a British sitcom called *The Worst Week of My Life*.

Off to the ACLU I went, where I lodged a formal complaint. I then called my judge friend in D.C. Three weeks later, I was hired for the writing staff of *Worst Week*.

It really was that simple.

That particular show didn't make it past the pilot, which was just fine with me.

The writing staff sucked. They were, in ways, and if you can believe it, even *more* difficult to work with than the staff for *Samantha Who?*

But it paid well and I had a new show to put on my CV.

In November 2008, I cast out another Tweet and waited for the little fishies to bite:

Looking for a new show after Worst Week wasn't picked up!

And then I thankfully received this response:

Your a hack and always will be a hack and youre a creep to boot!

That lovely response came from a writer for a new show called *Blue Mountain State* on the Spike channel about football players at a small mountain college somewhere in the Appalachian area.

I worked one episode, got a few jokes in and then was let go for reasons having zero to do with my writing ability. But that's fine. I was locked into a yearly rate and left pretty well insulated with cash.

Steele got his 15% and was very happy, which was always important.

On and on this went for the next two years. Some sitcoms made it beyond the pilot, some did not:

The Bill Engvall Show on TBS

Eastwick on ABC

Sons of Tuscon on Fox

Blonde Charity Mafia on CW

the forgotten on ABC (an aptly titled show if there ever was one)

Refuse to Lose on CBS

Matty's Choice on TNT

Renay Rocks on Fox

Ruby & the Rockits (ABC Family)

Happy Wife, Happy Wife (NBC)

Defying Reality (ABC Family)

$ecurity on Fox

And that doesn't even count the shows that Steele and I pitched on our own that never made it to air:

Girls Gone Gyno

The Juice Is In the Squeeze

Hunting Human Beings Through a Forest

REAL Sex in Prison

For any of the shows that actually *did* make it to air, you might find one or two jokes that I wrote. The rest were cut or later deleted after I'd be fired.

It was a good system and it put me on solid financial footing, and later allowed me to go after all of my dreams and to eventually achieve them, which is why you're now holding this book (or listening to it).

Because it definitely ain't cause I wrote a joke or two for *The Bill Engvall Show*, I can assure you!

In August of 2010, I did some Tweet fishing and grabbed a great gig, which was a spot on the writing staff of CBS's *$h*! My Dad Says*.

The Tweet that got me the gig was this one:

Fired from yet another gig. Are they lying or me? Well, it aint me!

To which a show runner at *$h*! My Dad Says* wrote back:

You're vile! And a liar. I believe the women! Also, fuck you and your shit politics! And say hi to your Nazi agent!

This fishy was *real* easy to catch and hook!

So it's October 2010.

And I'm a staff writer on *$h*! My Dad Says*.

To rehash what I wrote in the beginning of this book (and I'm *not* going to rewrite what I wrote back then as it was just perfectly fine the first time):

Inside the writing room at *$h*! My Dad Says*, where I'm perched on an uncomfortable chair bought in bulk at Office Depot, in front of a huge, leaning tower of styrofoam boxes (this back when we were still allowed to store hot food in a container that actually kept the food, you know, *hot*), things are only getting hotter.

It's already 2:00 P.M., five hours into the day, and we've been arguing since ten about the same joke in an episode we're writing.

You may even remember the episode. The middle-aged character of Ed, played by the great (*ahem*) William Shatner, is mistakenly invited to an orgy and is asked by a young female attendee to get the party started. But there's a problem. He can't. He left his reading glasses back at home and is now unable to decipher the directions on the three-speed vibrator that he's clutching.

Do you have a magnifying glass? asks Ed.

Looking down at Ed's crotch, the woman replies, *That bad, eh?*

It's a great joke and it would have killed, but there's a reason you don't remember it.

It was cut.

No shit.

Hollywood *never* could handle my brand of humor.

This was my first day on the job.

I wouldn't last but two more weeks.

In January 2011, I decided to officially call it quits writing for TV.

I no longer found it fulfilling, for one.

I just found it exhausting, dealing with all the madness.

I didn't get into comedy writing because I liked going to court or fighting on Twitter.

I got into comedy to be creative and to make people laugh. And to get some of that wild, sluicy pink.

Television was just a grind.

Granted, it was a well-paid grind, but *still* a grind.

My jokes never seemed to make the cut. And there was always, of course, the *likability factor* for characters and situations which I never could fully understand.

More than that was the bullshit I had to deal with, the creeping rot of "wokeness" which was just beginning to rear its ugly, pernicious head. It was becoming clear that Skippy Battison and an office environment were not a good mix. When I wasn't watching my inclusive language and avoiding biases, slang, or expressions that might discriminate against groups of people based on race, gender, or socioeconomic status, I barely had time to breathe.

And from what I've heard, it's only gotten so much *fucking worse*.

If you're a white man and above the age of twenty-two and want to write for a sitcom, good fucking luck to ya!

Seriously. Hit the goddamn road and go drive a truck or something. You'll be better off.

As Joe Biden might say, "No. I *mean* that. I'm not *kidding*!"

Because I *mean* it. And I'm *not* kidding. You are fucked.

More than that, if you can get hired *at all*, a near miracle, good luck actually being *funny*!

I never for one moment—not once, not *ever*—regretted pulling the rip-cord from television writing. There's a great piece of serious dialogue in my favorite all-time movie *Heavyweights* that goes: "I was just saying we need a little rest." And the other character responds: "Good idea. Let's take an hour meditation break."

In January 2011, I took a break, a little rest, a little meditation break.

And it's lasted up to today, as I dictate this book into a digital recorder and have some poor slob over in India transcribe it into cohesive form.

If I hadn't taken a break, I'd still be popping out lame lines and you never would have heard about me. You certainly wouldn't be reading a book I'd written, right?

Truthfully, there were *other* factors that led me out of television comedy writing, one of which was that I was deep in litigation on a number of cases, some of which are still ongoing.

And on January 25, 2011, Steele was accused of attempted kidnapping of a judge and his assistants and threatening them with being buried alive. Great. *There goes my agent!*

Actually, forget "threatening." You might have read about the murders as they made the international news and a few A&E movies.

Also, around now Twitter finally decided to kick me off for good.

Again, way ahead of my time.

To beat Trump by a full ten or so years?

(Regardless, I now have more than a million followers on Parler, even more than Trump himself, including some very famous, wonderful people. So, for that, I'm *super* proud.)

As for the Twitter debacle, and why I was kicked off, you've no doubt heard what happened as the entire comedy community talked about it. I mean, Twitter hadn't been happy with me for a long time, but what no one mentions is that it all came down to one somewhat simple misunderstanding.

That's right.

A simple misunderstanding.

Let me explain, as no one else seems to have ever gotten this right: My Twitter account really was the forerunner for my future satellite radio show and podcast. It was sort of the 1.0 version of what would later reach practically into infinity. Some bits worked. Others didn't.

One that definitely *did* work was a bit that I had I come up with called:

A Zagat's Guide to People I Fucked

Everything about it was funny. (Remember, please, that this was back when *Zagat's* was huge. Would the bit work today? No. Which is why I've since changed it to *Yelp Reviews of People I've Fucked.*)

Reading over the entries now still make me laugh.

My mistake, in retrospect, was to use *real names* of real women I had fucked.

Another mistake was to link to *real* Twitter accounts.

And to use photos I probably shouldn't have had of people I took without first "asking permission," photos I'd find online or in newspapers or yearbooks or on company's websites or what have you.

Granted, everything I Tweeted was true and, if anything, I'd use a rating that was *more positive* than it had any right to be!

Ain't that nice?

Like I said earlier: I'm a nice guy.

I am!

I never understood being a jerk to women.

If you want to get laid, shouldn't you be *nice*?

And *funny*?

Maybe that's where the confusion lies. Too many men try just too hard to be funny and thereby ruin their chances in the process.

This Twitter bit (*Zagat's for Sex*) was always done in good fun and innocence.

I was *never* complaining about the experiences.

I was forever *accentuating* what I *liked* most and what I remembered most *fondly* about all of these women!

And I guess yet *another* mistake I made was to rate a woman I fucked who had a father who was the mayor of a town in Maryland.

Whoopsy!

That was dumb.

Real dumb.

But I still laugh when I see the rating I gave her:

Sex **29**

Décor of Apartment **19**

Quality of Service **28**

Cost **$17 for beer and Bugles**

Like I said, that's a really good ranking! And the reason I gave her apartment décor such a negative review had to do with all of the stupid baby pictures of *herself* that she had sprinkled throughout.

Who the fuck does that?

Were you *that* gorgeous as a baby that you need to constantly see *yourself* at four years old? How egotistical is *that*?

And I'm not talking about a family photo or a photo of you with your dead grandmother.

I'm talking about *just* a photo of you and *only* you.

That bothered me. Hence the low score.

But she was good in the feathers, had a nice sexual style, and the entire evening came in at under four hours.

A win/win.

I mean, I gave her a fucking *29* for the sex!

Only *one point* prevented her from achieving that perfect and rare *30*!

(There *were* a few women who achieved a perfect 30. One was a whore, a professional fucker. It was almost unfair. She was a fuck ringer.)

But, again, it was a mistake on my part to link this mayor's daughter to her real account and to include a photo of her from the evening of our date that she claimed she didn't give me permission to take.

So here I was:

A thirty-three-year-old man without a job, without a future, and without a social media presence.

Alone against the world.

No job.

No Twitter feed.

No agent.

Shit out of luck.

And then I received news that my father had just suffered a stroke. He was in a coma.

Could I perhaps come home?

Christ, what the fuck now?!

Did I need this?! Of all fucking times!!
I knew instantly that things were about to take a serious change.
And not necessarily for the better.
And I would just be along for the crazy-ass ride ... here we go now....

★ Chapter Twenty-One ★
A DEATH AND A REBIRTH

There we all stood around my father's bed, in Suburban Hospital, down in Maryland, me on one side, my brother Doc Tim on the other, with his lousy wife next to him, all staring at a man we hardly recognized.

What does one say to a dying man?

Well, you did the best you could, maybe we'll see you down the road?

My father was a good man. I loved him very much. It was the rest of the family that I could have done without.

My brother and I hadn't spoken in years, since the Thanksgiving dustup at the Bethesda house over a fight we had both long forgotten the reason for, if we had ever known to begin with.

My brother and I just didn't get along. Never had.

I always joked that my tombstone would one day read:

He Just Liked to Have Fun

While *his* would read:

He Just Liked to Prevent Others From Having Fun

Never into pranks, never into jokes, never into cutting up, never into Judd Apatow movies, my brother was straight edge with solid A's but with nary a story to tell about his childhood after he matured (if you can even say that he *did*) into an adult.

He was an ophthalmologist surgeon specializing in issues pertaining to the retina and he taught at the University of Maryland medical school, whatever the fuck that means.

He had a huge office on Old Georgetown Road in Bethesda, a house in Chevy Chase, a membership to the Chevy Chase Country Club, oh, my brother had signed up for *everything* my parents had ever wanted for him!

Two week vacations at Bethany Beach, a time-share down in St. Barts, no surprises, no laughs, no spark, no edge, Brooks Brothers socks with Gucci loafers, a facial tan that ended at his forehead as he always wore a hat, Halloween decorations every October bought from Nordstrom's.

You know the type. *Every* family has one.

I don't remember if I wrote this earlier in the book but I'm too lazy to go back to the beginning and check if I *did* write this.

But here's a story:

I'm eleven, he's nine. We're down by the creek off Tuckerman Road, searching for "pirate's gold." A crowd of kids form around us. They want to see what we can find. I tell my brother to keep digging, I'll be right back. I run to my parent's house, grab a gold bracelet my mother owns and race back. I dig a small hole not far from where everyone else watches my brother dig with his tiny little shovel.

I throw the bracelet into the hole and scream, *"I found gold! I found gold!"*

All the kids run my way. "Gold!" they scream. "He found gold!"

"We want to find gold!" they scream. "We want to find gold!"

"I can tell you where," I said. "If you *really* want to find gold."

"Where? *Where?!*"

"First you have to give me silver. From your house. And then I'll tell you where you can find gold!"

The kids start to run off to find silver bracelets, watches, cups, whatever the hell their parents own and would never have noticed was missing.

What would I have done with the silver objects if they *had* given them to me?

I have no idea. But it would have been fun to figure out. And a nice story to tell people at school.

But my brother steps forth: "He's joking. He put that gold in the hole from our house. He doesn't know where to *really* find gold!"

I shot him a look.

Are you serious?!

They're just about to run off and hand over their silver to me and you have to go and tell them that I'm just making up the pirate gold story?

Cut to years later:

As my brother and I stood across from each other in a hospital room, I thought back on that incident. *Boy, nothing's really changed. Still the same asshole he ever was!*

"So we need to discuss best options for dad," he said, popping me out of my revelry.

"No shit," I said.

"Boys," said my mother. "*Please.*"

"Can I finish my story?" I asked. "I was telling dad some jokes. About our past. And about the pirate gold story."

"He's not listening," said my brother.

"They say that they actually can hear *everything*," I said. "I saw it in a magazine."

"Ooooh, a *magazine*," said my sister in law.

"*Maxim*?" asked my brother.

"Actually, *Gear*," I said.

"Uh huh," said my brother.

"Another jerkoff rag for people in the military," said my sister in law.

"You let her talk to me like that?" I asked my brother.

"Why not?" my brother said.

Now I was *steaming*.

"Boys, *boys*," said my mother, exasperated.

"I'm going to have to ask you all to leave," I declared.

"Are you fucking serious?" asked my brother. "Dad's about to die."

"Serious as a stroke," I said, pointing to dad.

"Hilarious," said my sister in law.

"Wasn't trying to be funny. But I need to be alone now."

"Are you—" my brother started.

"Out!" I declared. "Or I'll sue all your asses ... and you also, mom!"

They *knew* I meant it. They all left. My brother grumbling all the way.

I wasn't to be triffled with.

Now it was just me and my father.

What happened next was spooky, almost as if I was but a vessel and the god of comedy was communicating *through* me.

Over the next ten minutes, I performed the best comedy set I've *ever* performed, and perhaps *anybody* has ever performed. My only regret is that I didn't tape it. I think about this all the fucking time. I touched on practically everything that my father and I had experienced as father and son, from the time I was only a little baby, up until that very moment. It was if I had entered straight into a fever dream, our entire relationship as depicted through jokes. I stopped at *nothing*. Maybe it took a bravery to do this. I don't know.

There is no doubt that my father heard every word, every joke.

And I just know that inwardly my pops was laughing hysterically. He had to be. He always loved my sense of humor, always loved me.

In a way, this was my gift to him.

He had his problems, as all fathers do.

He was a workaholic.

We didn't always see eye to eye when it came to a lot of things, including humor.

But there are *always* differences between parents and children.

And we were no exception.

He never understood my career path but he also *never* tried to discourage it. My mother did, god bless her soul as she now plays golf as I'm typing this, but my father *never* tried to discourage me.

He was my old man and we had our differences.

I would never forgive him for just giving me six months to achieve success when I first started out.

Who can achieve success in only six months?! Especially in this crazy business?!

But I forgave him. He just didn't know from this world.

As I stood over him, I finished my routine, throwing everything I had into the performance, everything I had learned over the past ten years, every nuance and every facet of the complicated skillset I had learned since I began my crazy journey just after high school graduation.

Ten minutes turned into thirty, which turned into forty.

Which turned into an hour.

I couldn't stop. I'd motion to the nurses and concerned doctors to leave. I'd motion to my brother who kept inching his way back into the room to *get the fuck out and now!*

I needed more time. *I needed to get this out of my system!*

The improvised routine was coming to an end after 90 or so minutes.

And it was going to end as it only could have: it was going to end with a big laugh!

Yes!

But also a promise.

A promise from one son to his father that I would *never* give up on my quest to become a success, to make the world (or most of it) laugh and be entertained. To have enough money to live comfortably and maybe give a little to conservative charity. To hold my head high when I walked down the street, knowing that I had devoted my life to a worthy cause.

My father died before I could finish.

Shit. Just minutes from my final lines, too.

Damnit!

So close!

I motioned for the nurses and doctors to now come in. My family followed. And yet they had nothing more to say. *Choke!*

I walked out of the hospital room and then out of the hospital itself. I got into my car and drove away.

I never did end up talking to any of my family again, except for my mother.

My brother and his stupid wife were "furious" with me.

Was it that I kicked them out as my father lay dying? Was it because they were drinking coffee in a hospital hallway as he passed away forever, and they never had a chance to say goodbye?

Maybe.

But I think more than anything, it was jealousy.

My father never *once* laughed at anything my brother said—at least something that my brother *meant* to be funny.

Our politics, our philosophy, the way we looked at the world never really connected.

After our father's death, things only grew worse between us.

I know that he's been interviewed for local (as well as national) publications about his relationship with me. And I know that he's expressed his "disappointment" with how my politics and philosophy "turned out."

I can only express disappointment right back at him.

But with that said ... I also hope to one day bridge our differences and come together again. If only for a dinner or a barbecue. Or just a hug.

I've said some pretty fierce things about him on my podcast and satellite radio show. If I had to do it over, I probably wouldn't have.

A brother doesn't talk bad about another brother, at last in front of millions.

For the first time, and maybe not for the last, I'm going to say:

Brother, I apologize.

I look back with some events with regret, like kicking you and your wife out of the hospital room as dad lay dying.

And yet, and yet ...

For those 90 minutes, with me telling stories and jokes and even using props like a throw up pan and a rectal thermometer, this was my joyful tribute to the only father I ever knew, in the only *way* that I knew.

It was a singer singing an aria. A painter creating his final panoramic vista. A musician playing a rousing, heavenly melody on his violin or guitar or skin flute.

I was a porn star waving his dig ol' bick around and around and around like a goddamn lasso.

That was my gift to my father, and if my brother was a "friendly fire casualty," then so be it.

I mourned for a few days, and then got right back to work on my career.

In truth, I didn't even need to try that hard.

My father had willed me a nice chunk of change and I could have coasted for a while after working so hard for so many years.

But for me, it was about *so* much more than money!

It was a matter of principle. I was going to *fucking make it.*

It was just a matter of how.

And by what means.

And in what medium.

I didn't exactly have a love affair with television.

Movies were a big pain in the ass.

I've always hated to read, so books and magazines weren't exactly at the top of my list.

In the past, there had been Twitter.

But I was no longer on Twitter.

As for the rest of the internet … it paid shit.

What else *was* there?

Stand-up again?

Ugh, maybe. But did I really want to jump through all those stupid hoops?

I thought back to my childhood.

What was I good at?

From the get go?

Well, for one, I could always make friends laugh like crazy.

And I could always pull off very clever pranks that would make not only people laugh but maybe also *learn* a little bit about themselves.

I could always talk and converse and shoot the shit: about life, comedy, politics. Sitting inside the cafeteria at school, or later at a bar, and just talking about all things American. All things history. How societies evolved. How civilizations formed. And ultimately ended. And having a *good time* doing it.

An idea started to form in my mind, growing, hardening, solidifying.

As Spring 2013 turned into Summer 2014, I had my answer.

I had a vision for the next and final stage of my career. Things were about to ramp up big time.

And things were about to grow *real* interesting.

In ways that I *never* could have predicted.

But in ways that I'd come to appreciate regardless.

The shackles were off, motherfuckers!

And *anything* could happen.

And pretty much everything did ....

★ Chapter Twenty-Two ★

OPERATION MAYHEM

One of my favorite non-comedies is *Fight Club,* which I think is a *perfect* movie. I was around twenty-one when I first saw it, so maybe I was the precise demographic they were aiming for. Regardless, it made a *huge* fucking impression on me at the time and no doubt later influenced my decision to become an expert at krav maga (or krav MAGA, as I like to refer to it), the Hebrew-invented self-defense fighting system that I've since mastered.

Surround. And pound!

If I may blow my own cock (and sadly I can't do this in real life, only on the page), I took to the system more quickly than most. I had tried other martial arts in the past, but I hated them. Judo was boring and I had to memorize *way* too many Japanese phrases and numbers. Karate also bored the shit out of me: the studio always smelled like smelly feet and ass.

But the Krav always impressed me because you could basically learn all you needed to know in two minutes. It's real fucking simple. Just do whatever the fuck it takes to bring down your opponent. If that means kicking them in the balls, do it. If that means jabbing them in the adam's apple, do it. Hit their knees, their neck, nose, their tits, their face, it doesn't matter. Throw dirt in their eyes. Grab a rock and bash it over their head. It's all perfectly legal ... and *encouraged*!

How cool is that?!

I mean, honestly. No memorized moves. No reading. No fucking ancient bullshit.

Just make it happen.

Which is how I've always managed my career.

Do anything that needs to be done.

Just.

Make.

It.

Fucking.

Happen!

I *love* that.
And you do, too!
How do I know?
Because you're reading this book!
And you've no doubt purchased at least one piece of my *Passing on the Right* T-shirt gear.
On the front:

Pass on the Right!

And on the back:

Just Make It Fucking Happen!

$29.95 and 10% off if you use this code:

MakeItFuckingHappen69

Anyway, I could very well still be back in Bethesda or Ocean City, picking my fine butt, watching television.
Instead, I grabbed life by the horns and steered it in the direction I wanted to head.
Am I proud of everything I've done?
Yeah, why not?
Gives a flying shit?
As with most things, sometimes things had to get a little ... messy.
To get back to *Fight Club* ... there's a character named Tyler (played by the great Brad Pitt) who is a fucking bad ass. He does a lot of cool things. And he kicks off an anti-capitalist campaign called

"Project Mayhem." I never liked the anti-capitalist aspect of it. I always thought it should be anti-*socialist* or anti-*communist* instead.

What I loved was the *attitude* surrounding it.

Bring down *everything*.

And start fresh.

Which is what I had to do with my career.

Fuck Hollywood. It was time to begin something new. And the only way to do that was to ruin everyone and everything that tried to bring me down.

Not literally.

But have some fun with them.

To my *benefit*.

I decided to create my own Youtube prank show that would get back at everyone who never hired me, anyone who ever rewrote something I'd written, anyone who ever fired me, who treated me with the lack of respect that I found (and still find) incomprehensible.

Hey, if I could no longer do it online, why not do it in real life? Time for a little quiz:

Have you ever seen or enjoyed *any* of the following shows?

MTV's Tom Greene Show

Tim and Eric

Borat

Crank Yankers

Punk'd

Jerky Boys

Anything by *Spike Jonze*

Yes?

Well, I invented them.

I invented *all* of their characters and concepts.

Think back to the beginning of this book when I told you about my high school adventures with the fun-time pranks, whether it was filling a teacher's backyard hot tub with Surge soda or renting a horse under a fake name and leaving it in the shopping mall's one handicapped spot, or toilet-papering the house of a foreign exchange student.

I was doing this shit before anyone.

That's just a fact.

What I sadly hadn't done was capture it on film or video, not that this was such an easy thing to do back in the '90s.

But come 2014, it suddenly became a *whole* lot easier.

When it comes to the pranks you're about to read, the victims *still* don't know that they were the victims.

This will be the *first time* they'll learn that Skippy Batty Battison was behind the event that they just could never quite figure out. I'm imagining many won't be happy and might even sue. I don't really care. The footage has all been erased, thrown out.

True, more than a million people have seen these videos on Youtube.

They were really the first videos to ever go "viral," but there's nothing out there now to prove that it was me who did any of it.

Maybe I'm lying when I said I did them, who knows, right?

Some of the videos I posted were only up there for an hour! Some were up for a day or more. None was up there longer than, at most, two days. The purpose wasn't to embarrass anyone. The purpose was payback. And to get my name out there as someone capable of entertaining a new generation in a fresh and original way.

The first video went up August 3, 2014.

It depicts Billy Crystal eating at the Crossroads restaurant in West Hollywood. He's just ordered when a phone call comes in for him at the front desk. He leaves the table (never was sure who he was sitting with, maybe his agent) and takes the call and he screams. He races out of the restaurant. He's just learned that his grandson has suffered a seizure. The agent is left wondering where Billy went, with a very puzzled look on his face.

The second video went up on September 10, 2014. It shows the executive producer of the *Wayans Bros* show coming out of a movie theater where he just watched *The Wolf of Wall Street*. He discovers that his Lexus RX 350 has been shot at with a .22 rifle with a note on his windshield that says "Karma." The bullet holes are only stickers, much to his ultimate and great relief.

The third video takes place in the D.C. area and was posted on October 1, 2014. A middle-aged man comes out of his house in the morning to see his entire yard has been "toilet papered" and that his car has been covered in shaving cream. His mentally challenged daughter comes out to see what's happening. She's no longer 15 but she's now 18. She no longer works as a bagger at the Giant Grocery. You can see a slight smile play on her face.

Maybe she knows who did this and why?

The fourth also takes place down in Maryland. A certain judge emerges from his chambers in a Montgomery county courthouse to use the bathroom. When he walks in, he discovers a "dead person" on the floor, covered in "blood." He runs out screaming, yelling for security. When he returns with the security guards, there is no more dead man. Just an empty bathroom. Is he going mad?

This judge looks familiar. Maybe he once took it upon himself to send an innocent young man to prison for something that was hardly a crime?

More pranks:

A certain manager of a certain comedy club in Ocean City, Maryland is anonymously accused of rape. A local TV news crew shows up to interview him about the very specific allegations.

He's confused. *What is happening?! Does he deserve this?! Who would do this to him?! Is his business and life ruined? Will his wife ever believe him?*

The head writer of *The Simpsons* is inside a Los Angeles grocery store, strolling down an aisle. He exits the aisle, only to have a grocery cart slam into him at high speed. He's out for a full ten minutes.

Again, don't bother to look up these prank videos, as they were all taken off the Web by yours truly.

I only wanted to give the nation a taste of what a certain someone was capable of pulling off.

None had to do with politics. All were just done in the name of entertainment.

And yes, I suppose, a little payback for the way I was treated.

It was all in good fun. Really it was.

More videos followed, so many videos, and I soon began to build up a loyal following. Later, some of my fans would become famously associated with certain political groups or historical events, including a certain event down in Charlottesville, Virginia.

But I found this ironic, as again, my video pranks had *nothing* to do with politics!

Maybe it was merely the *spirit* of the videos that appealed to a lot of these young men.

I don't know.

What I do know is that while I never put my real name on the videos (I only went by the moniker DaShitRipper), I sort of became an "in" thing in Hollywood.

Which I soon managed to leverage to my advantage.

Sure, not *everyone* was happy with these videos but, as with most things in my life, I tell it like it is. If you can't handle my comedic power, get out of the way.

I'll be passing you ... on the right!

That's not to say there weren't a few wrinkles along the way.

The specific incident that nearly brought everything crashing to the ground was the infamous "magazine prank with Janeane Garofalo" in November 2014.

Let me explain.

Whoo boy.

Where do I start with this gem?

Let me start by saying that I've never liked Janeane Garofalo. Never felt she was funny. Never thought she was a good actor. Never thought she was overly smart, certainly when it came to politics.

For a few years she yapped away on a horrible liberal radio network called Air America. The same network Marc Maron had been on.

It was insufferable. She never shut up. She sounded like a fucking clucking hen, like a stuttering mental patient: "*Yippity yap, yappity yip!*"

Ugh. *She drove me fucking crazy!*

Beyond that, I once wrote a comedy movie script for her when she was at the height of her fame. I figured that even though I didn't like her, I could use her fame for myself. When she never got back to me about the script, which I mailed to her certified, *which was definitely not cheap,* I can assure you, I blew my damn lid. I went kamikaze, yo.

The script was about an ugly-ish woman who grows up with a friend who's the most beautiful woman in their hometown. This beautiful woman gets in a car accident and becomes scarred and hideous. Her ugly best friend drops her because she's now uglier than *she* is. When she's called out on this by her mother, she goes for a long walk, she has much to think about. A very handsome man then moves into town but he *also* gets into a car accident right in front of the ugly woman going for a walk. She saves his life. He's now scarred and he, too, is also ugly.

The movie then becomes a love triangle between all three.

It's a rom com with a very modern flavor. Who will hook up with who, especially now that they're *all* ugly?

I had reached out to Janeane a few additional times (maybe eight total?) but, again, never heard back.

By late 2014, I had finally had it.

I devised my most complicated prank to date. In order to do this, I paid the Flammer to fly from Maryland to Los Angeles.

The Flammer was *still* working as a fucking house painter in Ocean City and *still* living in my apartment. The guy owed me. Beyond that, we worked well together and I think he missed being creative, to have those comedic juices flowing through his vains.

He performed a little stand-up here and there, but nothing that took up too much of his time. He was my age and was already having a career crisis. Did he really want to get up on a ladder in the middle of winter and paint the trim beneath second floor windows for the rest of his life? Beyond that, we had kept in touch and he had followed my career closely, with some admitted jealousy. That I could have escaped Ocean City to emerge as a successful comedy writer and personality was no minor feet.

The comedy gang back in Ocean City would often talk about me as if I was some sort of mythical creature who wandered away from home and became giant-sized. Like the monster in that Israeli script I wrote. I always loved to hear stories of people back home telling stories about my success. If they had any idea that I'd grow *even larger* in stature as the years progressed, I think their heads would have exploded. But they were way proud of a local boy made good and I was thrilled that I could make their lives that much more interesting.

Flammer flew out to meet me in L.A. and when he arrived, we took a long walk, we had much to talk about. By the time we returned to my house, the idea for the prank had been created ... and it was a *doozy*.

And by no means easy to pull off.

But we felt that it was doable ... if we had the right amount of good people to help. I called Kevin Reynolds, who you might know as The Rim Rambler or Da Executioner from my satellite radio show, a proud member of my Passing Posse for years now. I had first met Kevin, if you'll remember, while auditioning for *Last Comic Standing*, and we had hit it off and he became a member of the Comin' At Ya Harders.

Kevin would later say that my call to him was the best thing that ever happened in his life, and I believe it. The guy was a disaster, living out of a car in a parking lot at Venice Beach. It don't get much lower than that. He had fallen out of comedy and taken to assorted odd jobs and low-level drug dealing. He later told me that after I called, he broke down and cried.

Again, I *believe* it.

I also hired some guy I met through a temp agency. I hired him for the day. I'm forgetting his name.

Having three accomplices would free me up so that I could actually operate the hidden video camera that I had in my carry on.

The edited version of the prank would run for more than twenty minutes on Youtube and was about as complicated as landing in enemy territory to engage in war.

The video begins with Janeane sitting in a waiting area at Hollywood Burbank Airport looking at her phone.

Someone sits across from her, holding a magazine.

Janeane looks up, glances back at the phone and then looks up again.

She reads the magazine cover and puts a hand over her mouth. She says to the person across from her (the Flammer), "Where did you *get* that?" He shrugs and points: "The magazine stand."

She walks over and sees nothing. She returns to the waiting area and takes the same seat. A different man (Kevin) is now sitting in front of her reading *another* magazine.

Her mouth drops. "Where did you get *that*?" she exclaims.

He points and mumbles, "Magazine stand."

Janeane marches over to the magazine stand and talks loudly with the woman working there. "Have you seen any magazines with me on the cover?" she asks.

The woman shakes her head. *What the fuck is this crazy woman going on about?*

Janeane marches *back* to the waiting area. A third man (the temp I hired) is sitting and he too is reading yet another magazine. She walks right up to the man and takes a look at the cover.

"Okay," she says, fed up. "What's going on here?"

"What do you mean?" asks the man.

"Let me see that magazine," she says.

"No," the man says. "Who the fuck are you?"

"Janeane Garofalo," she says. "I'm on the cover. I'm on *all* the covers—the other people were reading—they, I was on all the covers."

The man shrugs, stands and walks towards the men's room.

You can see Garofalo stewing in her chair. Eventually she boards the plane, still shaking her head.

Cut-to a close-up of three different magazine covers. The first is *People* magazine with a picture of Janeane and a fake headline that reads:

Comedic Star Janeane Garofalo Breaks Silence About Death of Career

The second close-up is of an issue of *US* magazine with a photo of Jeaneane and this fake headline:

Failing Comedy Star Regrets Liberal Claptrap

The third close-up is of an issue of the *National Enquirer* with Jeaneane as the cover star and a fake headline that reads:

Jeaneane On Her New Conservative Future with Newt Gingrich

"It's the best sex I ever had!!!"

The final scene of the prank, really my favorite part, would take place at a vegan restaurant on Santa Monica Boulevard. It's a week later. Janeane is back from wherever she traveled. She's eating outside alone. Her phone rings. She looks at the number that pops up and lets it go straight to voicemail.

The phone rings again. She again lets it go to voicemail.

Her phone rings for a third time. Now she answers, a bit angrily.

"Hello."

"Hi. Is this Janeane*?"*

(irritated) "Yes."

"This is Newt. Wondering when we're getting together again to fuck."

"Who is this?!"

"Newt. Newt Gingrich. We've had the best sex you've ever had—"

"Goddamnit," Janeane screams, and then uses a phrase that would soon become a meme and then a short animated online video and then lyrics to a song by an alternative group called Lawrence Arabia and then a throw away joke (that was bleeped) on *SNL*, and then a line used in just about every stand-up's set for the next five years.

The line went like this:

"Goddamnit to my fucking butter licking shit fuck hell Jesus!"

This could have been my most popular prank, at least amongst a certain subset of comedy fans.

This entire prank was later stolen by a German advertising firm (of all places) hawking deodorant, although their commercial was far more complicated than mine, with fake news on the airport *televisions* broadcasting above the waiting passengers.

You've heard about what happened next after the Garafalo prank, no doubt. There was the TMZ story. There was Garofalo on talk shows and all that shit.

Those were fine but what was *amazing*—truly life changing—is what happened after all of *that* died down.

Cut to April of 2015. I'm in my house, cooking up some fresh pranks in my head. I'm considering going after Bratt Pitt for never returning my scripts that I had sent him back in 2008. My cell rings.

"Skippy Battison?"

"Yes?"

"I'm glad I have the right number."

"Well, it's the right number. Who is this?"

"I'm glad of that."

"How can I help you?"

"My name isn't important but I'd like to extend an offer on behalf of an organization that I'll call The Foundation."

"The *Foundation*?"

"Yes."

"What is it?"

"A syndicate of sorts. We'd love to talk with you."

"About what?"

"About your future."

"Your number is listed as Private."

"That's right."

"Is this a prank?"

(laughing incredibly hard) "No. No prank."

"Then what do you want?"

"We'd like to work with you."

"Work with me how?"

"We're admirers of your talent, your ability to prank. And we think we can work well together. Would you be free to fly out to Washington D.C. in two weeks?"

"I guess so. I have family there. I could visit friends. This is truly for real? How do I know?"

"You're from D.C., is that right?"

"Yes."

"Then you've heard of The Foundation. You just don't yet know it."

He was right. I *had* heard of The Foundation. I had met members. I had seen their handiwork. I just didn't yet *know* it.

Just like *you* don't yet know it. But you will, dear reader or listener.

Two weeks later, on a warm spring afternoon, I was in Washington D.C., pulling a rental car up to a large (and I'm telling you, a *very* large) house in the Dupont Circle area of the city, driving through security gates that had been opened as if by magic, and parking in front of one of the largest front doors I've ever seen. It was Disney castle big.

The gates at the bottom of the winding driveway shut behind me with a loud clank.

What happened next would forever change my life.

In more ways than I could ever imagine.

Not only changing my life, but obviously *yours* as well.

In ways we *both* could never have predicted.

Ready?
Let's go all in … hang on tight ….

★ Chapter Twenty-Three ★
GOING ALL IN

If you've gotten this far in the book, and I know you have because you're reading or listening to this sentence, you can rest assured that it's now my chance to talk about my hit satellite radio show and my smash weekly podcast.

Why did it take so long for me to get to all this? Clearly, I had a ton of things that I had to first get off my chest.

Also, and in all honesty, I'm constantly being asked the same questions about my past, questions I've grown tired of answering or ignoring.

The book that you hold in your hands (or are now listening to) is *the* definitive version of my life.

Nothing will ever be written again, especially if it's unauthorized, that will come *close* to explaining how I became the man and beloved celebrity I am today.

Everything you've just read has been 100% true and accurate.

I told you from the beginning of this book that I'd never lie to you and I've kept my promise.

I intend to *keep* to that very promise as I finish off my story.

A lot has been written about my origins in satellite radio and podcasting, most of it completely wrong. I have to wonder where people come up with some of these stories they invent!

Here are a few:

Mohammed bin Salman, the head of Saudi Arabia, encouraged me. *False.*

The once-head of the Republican National Committee, Reince Priebus, encouraged me.

False. Reince and I are very good friends but definitely not true!

Liz Cheney persuaded me so that I could bring in an entire *new* generation of young people into the conservative fold.

Again, *false*. Liz and I are on friendly terms, although hardly the best of pals. But again, not true.

And here's a real doozy:

I am a product of "the deep state," chosen by a secret cabal of unnamed conservatives to help spread misinformation and half-truths to millions through an appealing combination of comedy and laughter.

Definitely not true!

The real truth is a whole lot more mundane, even if the *New Republic* attempted to decipher the origins a few times, as did that joker at the *New Yorker,* Frank Sinatra's son, Ronan.

Here's the *real* story:

Like most cities—but maybe *more* so—D.C. is operated *behind* the scenes, in board rooms, offices, secret meting places, town homes that you'd pass every day and never think twice about.

It's a ghost city with phantoms running the show.

As I walked through those giants doors and into that mansion in the Dupont Circle area of the city, I knew I had entered a realm that few would ever see with their own eyes.

If you've seen the Kubrick movie *Eyes Wide Shut*, you'll know what this place looked like, although there were no naked women with their crotches blurred out. Just six men in very expensive suits, ties, and leather wingtip footwear all sitting on two couches.

They rose when I entered. They didn't bother to shake my hand.

I was led into a grand hall and then into a connected room, smaller, almost like a library. Actually, it *was* a library but I couldn't make out the books. No Stephen King paperbacks here, though.

"Have a seat," said one.

I did so. The chair was incredibly plush and I sank right into it.

"Good trip over?" asked another.

"Very good," I said. "Thank you for the tickets."

"We tried getting you first class, but they were already sold out."

"That's okay," I said, meaning it. "It was nice."

I was served an alcoholic drink. And over the next few hours I learned all about this mysterious group.

They were called The Foundation. They had been working behind the scenes in Washington for nearly seventeen years, but really came on strong after Obama had been voted into office in 2008.

The group consisted of exactly one representative from each of the six largest conservative think tanks in the country, forming a sort of "Seal Team Six" of conservative policy advisors.

They told me their names but I won't mention them. If I did, I'd be ruined. Possibly even dead. And I'm not joking. Not even close.

Suffice it to say, I recognized a few of these middle-aged men from when I performed my act at political events a few years back. They had been super impressed with my comedy then and had been following my career closely since, apparently.

"We want you to become the spearhead of a new movement," said one.

"Meaning?"

"We want you to shine a much-needed light on ignorance through transgressive comedy."

Although this sounded interesting, I wasn't *truly* comprehending what they were telling me.

I asked them to translate.

By the time they finished, I knew my life had taken a fresh and swift curve directly into virgin territory.

I'm often asked by reporters if I'm paid by The Foundation.

Can't answer that.

But I can tell you that The Foundation launched my career as a broadcaster on satellite radio and in podcasting. Without them, I'd probably still be pulling Youtube pranks.

The Foundation knows *everyone*. I'm not exaggerating.

I mean *any one* of any importance, whether conservative or liberal. Or *whatever*.

Everyone!

I can't tell you much more than that but I *can* say that the Foundation introduced me to the then head of the satellite radio company where I now work and persuaded him to give me a shot.

And this guy wasn't necessarily conservative. Just a dude who liked to do well for his shareholders. And moneyed friends.

I can also say that the Foundation introduced me to the head of iHeartRadio and persuaded *him* to give me a shot for having my own podcast. The Foundation *always* has had my back.

Let me also dispel this myth:

That I'm merely a talking head and have *no say* in what the radio show or podcast talks about. That it's the Foundation really in charge. WRONG!

The Foundation and I *do* trade ideas, concepts, political opinions back and forth but I've never—*ever, ever, ever!*—been told what I *had* to say or *couldn't* say.

The name of my show, *Passing on the Right*, was their idea, and I loved it immediately.

They encouraged me to think of my show as a conservative Morning Zoo.

I loved that idea, also.

The concept for the show, they said, was two-fold:

Make young conservatives laugh.

And root out dark money and deep-state actions through bits and sketches with me playing various characters on air.

I loved those ideas, too!

We were *clearly* on the same page on so many issues!

I *did* have a few suggestions, one being that I'd be able to hire two of my old pals, The Flammer and Da Executioner.

The first radio producer they gave me was a guy named Rex Simard, long since fired. He was a good guy who had previously worked for Glenn Beck at BlazeTV.

Again, nice guy. Just not a solid fit.

You now know my producer to be Teddy Frantz. As in Teddy Frantz, Just Give Him a Chance!

I really liked Rex but our comedy didn't always mesh and I managed to convince the Foundation to hire Teddy after I saw some jokes he put up on Twitter just after the Unite the Right Rally (it was a photo of a protestor being thrown into the air by a car and the tagline: "Too micro-aggressive for you?").

From the get go, I did insist on hiring the good doctor (remember him from prison?) as an "intern," which only meant that he had no experience in showbiz and would be working for cheap. (Not to say that I don't "accidentally" slide some extra dough his way now and again. Don't tell the IRS!)

Everything came together so quickly that I really didn't have time to grow nervous. I barely had time to move back into my childhood house and reunite with old friends and Miss Benda. All of my time, or most of it, was taken up planning for those first shows.

My first radio show aired on March 2, 2015. And from the very start, I felt as if I was *born* to play this role.

I'm not saying there weren't *some* speed bumps along the way…

There was maybe too much reliance on phone pranks, such as the one we pulled on Steven Spielberg in which I pretended I was the president of the Nobel Prize commission, awarding him an honorary medal for all his peaceful work bringing space aliens and human beings together in harmony.

He accepted very humbly. But, my god, was he pissed when he found out it was just a gag!

Fuck it, right?

His movies *suck*!

Many of the bits that you'd recognize today came from the early days. Some haven't changed at all and some a lot.

From the beginning, I was super lucky to have a ton of great writers working on material for the show. Quite a few came from various think tanks around the D.C. area, employees who were wonks who always harbored a secret desire to write comedy.

This was a great outlet for them. And I was so happy to provide it.

One writer, Marc Richards, known to our listeners as Marky Marc with a C, became one of my most consistent contributors, coming up with a few classic and recurring bits, such as "Liberal Jeopardy," "Liberal Ancient History," "If Left was Right," "If a Lib Landed on the Moon," and many other classic bits, including my perennial favorite "I'm Dreaming of a Lefty Christmas."

Another of the show's writers from very early on later went on to write comedy for the hilarious *Gutfeld!* on Fox and is now working with James Woods on a comedic full-length movie about the liberal system that tried (and failed) to prevent the great Lee Atwater from succeeding, and the travails that poor Lee had to go through in order to ultimately *triumph*. He's also the "comedic advisor" to the great Jesse Watters on Fox. *Not bad!*

Today, my radio show has ten writers. For the podcast, I have another four writers. I have one of the *best* writing teams in comedy. I like to refer to them by their group moniker, Unite the Laugh.

I've gotten some shit online about having no women writers and that all of my writers just happen to be white men, but what can I tell you? I've looked far and wide for women comedy writers who could write in my style ... and I've yet to find one.

Shit, I can pretend that I found one, but that's not good enough for my audience or for me. There's another host of a satellite radio program, I won't use his name, who once told me that he did end up hiring a minority woman as a writer.

Guess what? There was trouble from the beginning.

Claims of racism and misogyny flew right from the start. Nothing was ever good enough for this woman. Beyond that, her jokes were lame, all having to do with being a liberal twenty-something Indian-American lesbian. After a few weeks, she left the show and then sued for $5 million for various reasons, one having to do with a sexual harassment claim that another writer pinched her ass and said, "I love me some unleavened pumpernickel bread."

$5 million for that?!

In the end, after the trial was settled out of court, she ended up getting about $100,000 which was probably $100,000 more than she was worth.

I've heard she later went on to write for a show I've never seen but looks terrible: it's about two teenagers on Hulu called *Pen15*. And that, amazingly, she won an Emmy.

Best of luck to her.

No, my writing team is just as I want them. In my mind the team has a really nice and diverse mixture of people from different backgrounds: three of the guys are from down south, which I love, two are from out west, six are from the northeast, two are from Texas and one is even from Britain.

That's pretty goddamn *diverse*.

And none are from the *Harvard Lampoon*!

To stay on this topic a little longer ... if you're out there and you're young and you're a female and you're ethnic and you're a fan of my shows, I'd *love* for you to contribute!

Honestly, I would *love* that!

But you have to *listen* to the show before you submit!

I can't tell you how many submission packets I've received that would be better suited for Samantha Bee or Stephen Colbert or Jimmy Kimmel or Jimmy Fallon.

I'm not saying they're bad. I'm just saying that the style isn't for me. And I'm saying they're not right for me or my show or my sensibility or my sense of humor.

They're not. End of story.

No one admits this but it's often not worth hiring a minority or a woman.

Why would anyone want to open themselves up for litigation by hiring a minority writer who's not up to par?

No. Fucking. Thank. You.

Beyond that, I have another friend who's a well-known radio personality. Against his best wishes, he went and hired a woman writer. Two weeks later, she announces she's pregnant.

Good luck firing her *then*, my friend!

I mean, honestly: *good fucking luck!*

You're stuck and out of goddamn luck. The entire show can be gummed up for years because of this one woman's decision. Who needs it?

My main focus is to put together an amazing satellite radio show four days a week and a podcast on the remaining day. It's all pretty simple.

In theory, at least.

You try putting together two-and-a-half hours of comedic bits and characters and interviews with top political wonks every day and then keep that up for forty weeks a year!

Seriously, *try* it.

It ain't easy.

I can't tell you how many people I'll see out and about in Vegas or wherever I'm traveling who tell me (really, *beg* me to believe them) that they could *easily* do what I do.

You can't.

Everything you hear on my show has been written and analyzed to death.

Beyond that, there are a million tiny decisions that I make on the fly that you know *nothing* about: jokes that might not work, questions I could have asked but now feel would take away from the flow, decisions about when to break for a commercial, when to cut away from an interview subject who's droning on and on about nothing.

Should we use a bit today or hold it for tomorrow when it might not be as relevant?

A million tiny decisions!

It's the game inside the game. And it has to run like clockwork every day, for forty weeks a year, without fail.

You try that.

Beyond the material for the show itself, there's everything *else* we're in charge of coming up with, such as the T-shirt slogans, bumper sticker jokes, the things written across coffee mugs, *everything*.

Do you have a *Passing on the Right* beer koozie? Does it say something funny? Well, guess who took the time to write that funny beer koozie slogan?

Us!

Who the fuck else?

Did you buy and enjoy the "LIB NOT ON BOARD!" car sign?

Or the bumper sticker of Calvin pissing on Obama's profile?

Or the T-shirts that read: "If It Was a *Real* Insurrection, We'd Have Won" and on the back "We Just Passed You On the ... *Right*"?

Or have you worn any of the millions of pieces of Batty Swag that we sell online and at live events?

If yes, those didn't grow on fucking trees, people!

All this swag is *surprisingly* difficult to write but we absolutely *love* to make that extra effort for our fans.

All proceeds, by the way, go straight into the charitable endowment that I set up, *The Passing on the Right Fund,* which collects money to be dispersed to PR firms in order to assist those conservatives who are victims of liberal whitewashing.

Steve Bannon, Roger Stone, Michael Flynn, and Lil Wayne are just some of the more noteworthy recipients.

So it's a *tremendous* amount of work.

Over the years, we've had amazing successes. And also some … um, perhaps less than amazing successes. Maybe even downright disasters. But to achieve greatness you have to fly *close* to the sun.

To start, here are a few of the better known successes, with some *bonus* information thrown in that you've never read or heard about!

Again, *this* alone would be worth the price of this book!

You're not finding this info *anywhere* else, folks!

"The Malia Obama Prom Night Prank"

This one got a ton of attention and for good reason: we pulled it off spectacularly. You know the gist already: I managed to find (with a little help from The Foundation) the cell number for Malia Obama. I called her on the day of her prom, acting as the owner of the limo company that was supposed to later pick her and her date up. I told her that the limo was cancelled. When she asked why, I said one of the engine parts was made in China and it broke. We captured audio of her crying and asking a ton of questions and then calling for her mother, who, sadly, never got on the phone. Neither did her father, which also was disappointing. So that was the gag. But here's what we never played for legal reasons but will include as an outtake on our upcoming "Just the *Right* Bitties" CD on our Patreon page. What you didn't hear was a secret service agent getting on the line, where we managed to keep him for over an hour as we "fixed" the problem and made our way (not really) over to the Obama house, asking directions the entire time. Like, *a ton of directions*. To the point where the agent was nearly crying. By the end, it simply becomes fucking hilarious. The poor asshole stammers and nearly screams "left", "right", "no, *straight!!!*" before we tell him that his African-born boss sucks and that it's all been just a gag. We did later receive a visit from the secret service. But what are they gonna do? We didn't say we were gonna kill anyone! Just harmless fun!

[A word about our Patreon page: There have been a lot of complaints we've been hearing about this page, that even when members do go to cancel their membership, they're not allowed to do so and, in fact, will then be automatically signed up for a monthly charge from now until eternity. We're not sure what's happening but we think it's the same thing that happened to our "DONATE TO" page in 2020 on our website. It's weird. We'll look into it!]

"Cock Tales"

As you know, this is an ongoing bit that our "Marky Marc with a C" came up with and it's proven to be one of our most popular. The premise is this: we invent three fake rumors about liberal actors' cocks as told by former lovers. But only *one* of the former lovers is actually a *true* former lover with all the goods on the down-under info. There was one specific instance of this game that was particularly amazing. Here was the "Cock Lineup" that we had that day: Richard Dreyfus, George Clooney, Jake Gyllenhaal, and Leonard Di Caprio. The rumors were the following: "spotted," "bent," "a very thin mushroom," and "so large that it has its own gravitational force." I won't tell you who the real one was here. Just go back and listen, it's incredible. But I *will* say that once she was off the air, the woman told us that she had slept with *another* particular, very well-known liberal actor not mentioned on the show (but I mean, you'd *know* him, without a doubt) who had a "micro penis" two inches long. Here's a hint: Cheers. Bartender. Bye.

"Inclusion Teacher"

Here's another ongoing bit, one that I'm proud to say I came up with. The premise is really quite simple: I play the role of a diversity equity and inclusion teacher named Mr. Playwell and I call the workplaces *least* receptive to such an asshole, such as a boxing ring, an inner-city Detroit hospital emergency room on Halloween eve, and a Hell's Angels clubhouse in Omaha, Nebraska. The results have been pretty *astonishing*, if I may say so myself. It's fun to hear a Hell's Angel, cranked out of his fucking skull on speed, respond to the recommendation that when kicking the shit out of a new member in a hazing situation, he should always be mindful of not cursing or shouting out implicit biases that could emotionally hurt the young man being initiated. It's super fun to hear the chaos of a Detroit hospital room as you insist that the doctor on call use an appropriate workplace conversational style for the incoming gun-victims that is devoid of "exclusive" language. And talking to brain dead boxers about *anything* is fucking hilarious. But here's something that's never been revealed: in 2019, we were sued (unsuccessfully) by a meat packing plant in Nebraska after we insisted that the slaughterhouse workers not refer to any of the animals in any way that would imply a certain age, gender, educational background, or social class. The reason we were sued is because the foreman actually *did* insist on this for a week, which so tied up the slaughtering of so many of the animals that the company's stock fell 35% in one week. Sorry!

"Retard At a Stockholders Meeting"

The Foundation and I despise companies that pretend to be "woke" just to earn themselves more money and to appease their liberal shareholders. In fact, this perhaps bothers me more than *anything* else. How to get back at these bullshit companies? Well, one way is to send a retarded guy named Bunx (actually one of our writers who's not retarded) into these shareholder meetings to ask inane questions until he's dragged away by security. Here are a few gems that you might not have heard for legal reasons: "Has Ronald McDonald ever killed anyone? (McDonald's shareholder meeting, 2018); "Does Bill Gates have *one* black friend?" (Microsoft, 2019); "How tall do you have to be to ride Selena Gomez?" (Disney, 2020).

"Abe Wellingham, Movie PC Critic"

Abe Wellington was a character that Da Executioner came up with in 2019 and it's one of my very favorites. I play this character as a cross between Roger Ebert and that smug asshole on *ABC's Good Morning America*, I'm forgetting his name but he's a jackass. My character is overly confident about his own ability to suss out inappropriate jokes or characters or plots from classic movies. To give you but one example, Abe has rewatched *Casablanca* recently and he feels that there's way too much drinking and smoking and meanness between racial and demographic groups. He proposes that they film a remake, shot in the present day, in which a disparate group comes together to beat the bad guys through initiative, smarts and cunning. No drinking, no smoking, no negativity.

The joke is that the script would last less than fifteen minutes. Abe has also loudly complained about *Blazing Saddles, Foul Play* (the dwarf and albino characters, in particular), *9 to 5* (the dope smoking scene), the original *Bad News Bears* (for the use of the dreaded word whose name I'm not allowed to write, let alone even *think*), and many others. Here's the irony: one of Abe's ideas for a movie was later stolen and actually became a *real* television show, the new *Fantasy Island*!

It's true! Mr. Rourke turned into *Miss* Roarke and the ethnic midget sidekick turned into an ethnic sidekick of *normal* height. It *bombed*.

"Realistic Trigger Warnings"

This one was created by me one day while watching college porn on PornHub. *Whoops! Can I mention that?! That I have sexual cravings for young, healthy women?!* So these would be realistic warnings about life for college students, such as: "You have to work hard" and "No one will put up with your childish bullshit out in the real world." This one worked out well, with a few students actually crying when we called them at random in their dorms and spoke to them in a realistic, real-world manner. *Deal with it, kids. Life ain't easy!* (Here's a fun fact: one of the college students later became an intern for us. You might remember him as the guy we sent to throw cartons of Ben & Jerry's Ice Cream at the socialist Bernie Sanders. That never ran for legal reasons because Bernie did end up injured, which we regret. The name of our fake ice cream was "Taste the Bern.")

"Jerry Mandering"

A character named "Jerry Mandering" says funny shit that makes Democrats look like idiots. I play Jerry. That's it.

"How Much Realistically?"

Pretty simple in concept but amazingly fun to play. How much realistically would it take for you to fuck Nancy Pelosi? How much realistically would it take for you to drive across country with Chuck Schumer? How much realistically would it take to wear a bullshit "Covid" mask for one month straight? How much to go down on Rachel Maddow? We once came up with an entire bit devoted only to Alec Baldwin: "How much would it realistically take to be stuck in an elevator for one evening with Alec Baldwin?" We never ran this one because Alec is a maniac who will sue *anyone* at the drop of a hat. But who cares. I now get to talk about him here in my memoir. So suck on *that*, Alec. Maybe I should leave you an obnoxious message on your cell like you did with your *own* daughter?

Not every bit we've performed on *Passing on the Right* has been a grand-slam success. There *have* been a few clunkers over the years and I take full responsibility for them, as opposed to most liberals who never seem to take responsibility for *anything*.

Here are a few, all of which have been wiped off our archives:

"Is Jim Gaffigan a Fag?"

He's not and it wouldn't matter if he is, I guess. But we might have gone too far with this one when we cold-called his grandmother with dementia.

"Ted Danson, 'I'm Your *Biggest* Fan!'"

This was a one-off, an attempt to convince lib Ted that we were his *biggest* fans by calling him on his cell endlessly and questioning his views on everything from "global warming" to "gun rights." He was surprisingly chatty and agreeable. But after the sixth or so call, we discovered that it was a different Ted Danson, an accountant in Gary, Indiana with, let's just say, a few *extreme* views on Jews and homosexuals. Anyway, we made a new friend and listener but we never called him back for that seventh conversation …

"Win A Weekend on Jeffrey Epstein's Island"

This sounded like a good idea at the time but unfortunately it later came out that Jeffrey enjoyed the young women a little *too* much. Sad because he really was a funny and great guy, as well as a very generous contributor to *Passing on the Right*. RIP.

"Black *Schindler's List*"

I love the idea for this one (replacing all the Jewish character in *Schindler's List* with black characters) but it just ended up falling a bit flat, probably because we had so little time to work on it before rushing it out to coincide with the Oscars in 2018. The little girl in the red coat becomes a hip-hop dancer. With that said, we very well might take another crack at it. There's a lot of milk left in this particular coconut!

It's not all about fun and games, however. Over the years, I've conducted *hundreds* of interviews with the most elite conservative minds this country has to offer, whether from Nations in Action

Globally, Judicial Crisis Network, Turning Point Action, Heritage Action, Advancing American Democracy, the Right Stuff, Americans United in Life, Center for Medical Progress, Election Transparency Initiative, Center for Bio-Ethical Reform, The Susan B. Anthony List, or the American Principles Project, all of who are generous donors of both time and money to my satellite radio show and podcast.

Things were cruising along really nicely those first few years! I had a ton of listeners and fans and accolades and really terrific notices and all the rest of it.

I even had an idea for a *Passing on the Right* college tour that finally came together in 2018, which I was really happy with. The conceit was this:

I was going to announce a list of colleges that I hoped to speak at. Word would get out that I was coming and the inevitable protests would start. I'd then leak further word about my appearance: it was going to be incredibly offensive to just about any college group that one could possibly imagine existing on campus. Near riots would take place, the shows would attract international attention. The tour would become an absolute sensation, one *everyone* would be talking about.

But here was the twist: when it came time for me to *actually* give a lecture, it would be the most milquetoast performance imaginable. I'd offend *no one*.

How delicious would that have been?

Ultimately, I was too lazy to travel but this would have killed.

Instead I did what the rest of the country tended to do after the Covid "pandemic" hit. I never left my studio and would just communicate via Zoom and FaceTime to Republican female college students around the country for a very high fee.

It was fun, kept me youthful and, truthfully, introduced me to a few yummy little lovelies I ended up convincing to come to the suburbs of Washington to visit me in my tiny 14,000-square-foot humble abode overlooking the Potomac River.

Suck on that, naysayers!

To teach a younger generation about conservative values and comedy is just a great honor and I'm internally grateful ...

Most of the controversy in the last few years has not been connected to my radio show. Most of the dissension has to do with my *podcast*.

I look at my podcast, *Podding on the Right*, as being a more free-form version of my satellite radio show, where I can let it *all* hang out, test new material, take more chances, practice bits that I might still have some lingering doubts about, just have fun with.

It's the difference between a rock band in the studio and a band in a garage just fucking around.

As popular as the satellite radio show has become, the podcast has become even *more* popular, which is hard to believe. While stats for the radio show are hard to come by, I do know that downloads for *Podding on the Right* quickly reached more than 500,000 a month, which is good by *any* standard.

So much has been said about my podcast! And typically from people who've never even heard it!

If you've heard the podcast mentioned or talked about on the smarmy *Daily Show* or the insufferable *Tonight Show* or the supposedly factual *CNN News*, I *can* tell you that what you've heard about me is most likely *incorrect*.

Here's a snippet of advice for you: *don't believe a thing you see or hear on mainstream television*.

Honestly. None of it is true.

And if it was, would you want to believe it anyway?

In the end, I'm just really nothing more than a very talented guy going about his life and work not trying to bother *anyone*. I'm no more than a version of someone on the left trying to entertain young listeners through his humor, and if they happen to learn something from my political sensibility, all the better for it.

I just happen to be on the right ... and *in* the right.

I'm not asking for the world here, people.

If you don't like my politics or my humor, there's *plenty* of other shit out there for you to quasi-enjoy. Believe me. *Plenty* of choices.

Over the past few years, I've been called "the giggling devil," "a horror show," "the worst the right has to offer," "Trump's flying monkey," "jester of dissemination," "Bill O'Smiley," and many other names I've since forgotten and never gave a shit about to begin with.

Advertisers have pulled out of my podcast to the point where I'm left with just one, but it's a good one and I'm not complaining at all. I'm fortunate to have this sponsor and I can tell you that their product *definitely* works:

Stiff Nights Herbal Supplements

Seriously. If you're a dude, *try* 'em. Worse comes to worse, you have a boner for a few hours. Could come in handy. Like *literally*.

My show and podcasts are *huge* hits. And yet I *keep* getting knocked down. Or at least people are *trying* to knock me down.

Here's but one example:

On September 5, 2018, I was seen in *The Washington Compost*, front cover of the fucking *Style* section, a photo of me lunching with a good pal.

Was this *really* news worthy?

I can tell you exactly where I was and what I was saying when the photo was shot.

It was taken a few days before a certain Senate Judiciary Committee hearing.

This friend was ... Brett Kavanaugh and he was *this* close to becoming a fucking Supreme Court Justice.

Not bad for a kid from the streets of Bethesda!

Brett is an amazing guy and an loyal friend. When he was at his lowest I took him out to eat at one of our favorite restaurants in the Woodley Park area of D.C.

And I was giving him some advice. Really, it was the *least* I could do for all the help he'd given me over the years.

I will not tell you exactly what we were talking about.

It's none of your fucking business.

But I can tell you, in general terms, what I was saying.

The poor guy needed some assistance, especially coming from a trusted friend who was a professional entertainer and a performer.

Be amusing, I told him.

No one wants to see a dour guy groveling for a vote!

Get your ass off the floor, pick yourself up like a man, and then make the entire world smile!

I've been there, bro. But look at where I am today, okay?

Stop feeling sorry for yourself over one bullshit accusation. Remember what it was like to grow up in Bethesda, not knowing anyone.

This is your life, bro. No one else's.

Making it fucking happen.

I told him that instead of crying before the television cameras (which I feared he would do, as I knew the guy to be an easy weeper), just try telling some jokes!

Everyone loves jokes!

Seriously. It doesn't matter what fucking political party you're from, humans just love to laugh!

I recommended a bunch of jokes and "off the cuff" remarks that would have brought the temperature down in that room and across the nation.

For whatever reason, my pal chose not to go that route, which doesn't mean I don't love him any less.

I hate to say it, but the jokes would have made him ... *more likable*.

It's true.

But I hate to say it.

I *still* hate that term.

There have been a ton of people in the conservative world who have reached out to me for help when they needed it, and I've always done my best to come through for them.

Lindsey Graham is one. I won't tell you why. But I did get him out of a potentially very rough pickle by suggesting a certain joke having to do with a ladybug.

I've helped a lot of people.

The Koch brothers would often ask that I punch up their speeches with funnier material and I would. One brother had a better sense of humor than the other, but I'm not saying which.

Rudy Giuliani has a *terrific* sense of humor but if you hear him say something funny–anything *exceedingly* funny–it was probably written by me. (And no, I did not write his speech when his hair dye leaked or neither did I have anything to do with the speech he gave outside a Philadelphia sex shop. I wrote speeches that made fun of those speeches, but I had nothing to do with that one in particular, thank goodness. Credit where credit is due, right?)

Roger Stone is a stone-cold lunatic and has just an *insane* sense of humor. He doesn't need my help with comedy (only with money donations, I guess). But I have written a few gags he's told over the years, including the famous joke he told on *Newsmax* about the rabbi and the capital gains tax.

Ginni Thomas is funny as hell and has often asked for zingers on her Twitter feed. She also called me before she let loose on Anita Hill's voicemail. What you've heard on those voicemails is probably mine.

The NRA sought me out for the fifth anniversary of Sandy Hook in 2017. That wasn't my easiest gig but it ended up going just fine.

More recently, Governor DeSantis and a group of anti-vaxxers in Florida hired me to spice up some slogans that they yelled at masked teachers entering public schools.

This isn't even for extra money on my part, just something I do to help some friends and at the request of some friends who help me.

A few of these aren't even politicians.

One friend has been Edgar Welch, otherwise known as the "Pizzagate shooter," although he never shot at anything and is as harmless as a church mouse.

I've kept in touch with Eddie since he was arrested and have been sending him care packages and books that I think he might find amusing. I might even send him this book. He's a good guy who might have taken a wrong turn in life but through no fault of his own.

Do I believe in the Pizzagate conspiracies?

Let's just say that there are too many coincidences to overlook a connection between that specific pizza restaurant and all of the thousands of links to pedophilia in the D.C. community.

I'll leave it at that.

I'm also proud to declare that *my* show broke a lot of news stories over the years *before* anyone else.

And this would be *way* before the mainstream media, or even other conservative outlets, came to learn about them.

We sniffed out the Hunter Biden situation years before anyone else. One of our listeners knew Biden from the Delaware party scene and found his cell number. Pretending that we were a crack-smoking Delaware young skank, we left all sorts of messages, some of which were returned by a very high Hunter. That eventually became our ongoing "Hunting Hunter" series, which became really popular around 2018 when we broke it wide.

Now that I think about it, a *tremendous* amount of breaking stories has come from our show!

We broke the story in October 2017 that "economic inequality" is basically a load of mainstream media invented bullshit.

What else?

The announcement that Bill Barr would take over Jeff Session's role as U.S. Attorney General was announced on our radio show *live* when we interviewed Bill in his car on the way to the White House to meet with Trump.

Similarly, the announcement that Bill Barr would be stepping *down* as the U.S. Attorney General was later announced as Bill *left* the White House after talking with Trump.

Score two for us!

Another huge exclusive came when Mitchell McKenney, the head lobbyist for Perdue Pharma, called our show to announce that the company was tired of fighting the ridiculous allegations concerning OxyContin and would just be paying a settlement to not have to deal with any of the madness anymore.

Another major score!

There was also an exclusive interview with Timothy Oliphert, the college student who threw a tomato at "doctor" Anthony Fauci.

What else did we break over the years?

Milo Yiannopoulos called us on our podcast to announce that his ghostwritten biography *Dangerous* was being killed by Simon & Schuster for no reason at all.

Rand(y) Paul called us live on the air to give us an exclusive about the efficacy of hydroxychloroquine and also to tell us about the effectiveness of *generic* deworming medication, which is cheaper than "over-the-counter" deworming meds from the veterinarian.

Uh oh! We just pinched out a truth bomb!

Jim Jordan is a longtime friend of the show and we were the *first* outlet he called in order to deny allegations of college-age wrestling sexual allegations that he continues to deny to this day on our show.

Joe Manchin calls every time a report is released about the silliness of solar power, which, to be honest, can get a little tiring. I love the guy but ...

Who else?

Ron Johnson will call whenever there's a huge snow in Wisconsin to gently remind us that global warming is a crock of shit.

Tons of people!

We have a lot of fun. And we also manage to *inform*. *That's* not an easy formula.

But we do manage to do it. Day after day, year after year, forty weeks a year.

Beyond all that, as if that's not enough, the *Passing on the Right* crew has even got into the *digital game*.

In 2019, we created our own iPhone app called "Rad Dads."

Don't for one second think we love Apple.

We don't.

But money's money and Apple's Apple.

What can ya do?

You've no doubt read about this app. Hell, maybe you even *own* it!

It wasn't my idea (it was one of our listeners') but we put our name on it and it became a huge smash.

The idea was that there's absolutely no reason why conservative dads can't be as funny as liberal dads, which was a complaint I've heard for years and years.

"Conservatives aren't funny!"

"It's impossible to be a hilarious conservative!"

"There's no such thing as a right-wing funny person!"

Bullshit! Our show proves them 100% wrong *every goddamn day*!

I dare you to compare our joke-to-laugh ratio to *any* liberal late-night "comedy" show.

We'd destroy them *all*.

But it did occur to me that the regular, conservative Average Joe could perhaps become a *little* funnier with our help, which is why we created the app.

For $4.99 a month we provide responses and quips and even small talk that will amuse the fuck out of your co-workers and friends, while also remaining true to your conservative values.

Here are a few examples:

Them: "God, I *hate* conservatives."
Response: "Your breath stinks."

Them: "I don't understand why people *wouldn't* want more illegal aliens coming into this country!"
Response: "And I don't understand why you're so fucking ugly."

Them: "I don't believe in prayer in school."
Response: "Suck my shlong."

The point is to have fun with their ignorance while also making your own point known.

So far it's proven to be a huge success, even talked about on *The View* and other lib shows.

Things were chugging along swimmingly. With the illness that Rush Limbaugh sadly experienced (always a supporter of our show, always a mensch), we were lucky enough to inherit a lot of his lovely fans on those sad days when Rush was too ill to perform.

By October 2019, we were at the top of the conservative podcasting charts, and blowing it out of the ratings waters with our satellite radio show.

I couldn't have been happier.

Okay, great, you're saying.

Wonderful, just wonderful. But we *know* this already!

You're thinking:

Are you (or are you not) going to get to it already?!

The thing that everyone is talking about?

You know, *that* thing?

The reason why we bought this damn book?

Are you ever going to discuss *that*?

Or are you going to save that for *another* book?

You know what we're talking about! We're talking about that certain "ex" President!

Please!!!! you're screaming.

Just get to it!

Okay, okay, I *got* it!

I'll *get* to it! *Just fucking stop screaming please!*

Right off the bat, I want to say a few things, none of which I've told anyone publicly as I've been warned not to by my lawyers.

But fuck it, Viking and Random House ain't publishing this book no more and I'm free to say whatever the hell I want.

There's *so much* I can write about the events of January 6th but I'll just limit it all to my specific role. Beyond that, I'm now being sued by Trump and his lawyers. Yes. It's true.

Trump and his team are claiming they don't know me, never met me, that I never helped write jokes for him, that I never made Trump laugh at any dinner party I attended at Mar-A-Lago, never went baby giraffe hunting with his kids, never helped him with Twitter responses, never did *this*, never did *that* and all the rest of the bullshit.

I really don't care if they *do* continue to sue me. I'm just stating a fact: I knew Trump, he knew me, I helped him, he thanked me in various ways.

That's it. Nothing more, nothing less.

Do I think he won the 2020 election?

I do.

And even if I didn't, who cares? That's my position and I'm sticking by it.

Sometimes the teams you root for just aren't the nicest.

That's life.

I hope that we again become friends–I truly and deeply do–and that we can find a way to somehow bridge our differences, which I would love to do before he wins in 2024 (for the *third* time).

There were so many tragedies on January 6th, so so many.

One of the worst tragedies might have been the assassination of Ashli Babbitt and the rest of the American patriots who were murdered by armed thugs paid for by the government to protect nothing but their own thug reputations.

Ashli was a longtime listener to *Passing on the Right,* both the satellite radio show and my podcast, and a lovely person. She was a true Bang Banger, one of my Fanatic Fans that I loved speaking with her about politics, philosophy and war.

I honor her beautiful spirit.

But I think the *biggest* tragedy about that day was the way I was treated. You wouldn't find war criminals treated worse than I was (and still am).

I've been accused of more shit than Jesus Christ, Himself.

I've been accused of harboring the January 6th "attackers" at my Great Falls mansion.

I've been accused of feeding and sheltering hundreds for a week leading up to the January 6th event.

I've been accused of feeding the "insurrectionists" with fancy food and expensive booze and all the rest of it.

But nothing comes close to what I want to talk about now. Again, you'll be the first in the world to read about what *exactly* happened and not what *supposedly* happened.

So here goes. All in:

One could argue from now until eternity as to whether Trump encouraged his followers (many of who were my fans and listeners) to attack the Capitol. I'd rather not get lost in the weeds of all that shit.

One could argue from now until eternity whether I had been given a tour of the Capitol the day before by Jim Jordan.

Would rather not get into that, also.

One could also argue from now until forever whether I did or did not call Trump and Matt as the situation unfolded with updates.

Likewise, I would rather not get into that.

No, I'll stick with my own individual narrative, which began very early on the morning of January 6th, maybe as early as 5:00 A.M.

After waking, I went downstairs to check on my hundred or so guests. Most were already up, anxious and eager for the day to begin. They ate breakfast (just eggs and bagels and a few pounds of lox and Russian caviar that I provided, and Brut champagne and freshly-squeezed sumo citrus oranges from Sicily) and then we got to work on the signs we were going to carry at this huge event.

A lot of my guests needed help "punching up" their signs, making them shorter, simpler and, most of all, *funny*.

For instance, a lot of signs just read "STOP THE STEAL."

That was fine but a worldwide audience was going to see these signs. And you want to waste your signage on *that*?

We could do better.

A whole lot better.

How about something that just immediately *grabs you*? Something like:

> *I'd Rather Be a Conservative Nut Job …*
> *Than a Liberal With No Job or Nuts!*

Or:

> *Conservative Because Not Everybody Can Be a Freeloader!*

I mean, there's no reason *not* to make the world laugh while teaching them a lesson, right? I do it every day on my show.

From there, we all boarded the first-class jitneys I had rented to take us from Great Falls to the Capitol area where the speeches were being held. There was no grand plan to "attack." There was no grand plan for *anything* except to listen quietly to speeches and to silently protest our disgust with the way the election was stolen.

It was still early, maybe 8:00 A.M, when we arrived. The skies were cloudy and a wind was kicking up as we made our way to where the other gentle patriots were gathering.

To help keep everyone warm, I passed around bulletproof vests and helmets, and also gas masks in case the celebratory fireworks became too much to bear.

Everyone seemed bored and the speeches weren't set to start for another hour. To keep everyone entertained, I hauled out the wood guillotines and the fake gallows I had had delivered the day before, and everyone seemed to enjoy all of those very much, posing in front of them for photos and just for laughs.

Can only Democrats have a sense of humor?

I mean, think about what's seen at a liberal protest: the signs, the statements, the dirty photos, and all the rest of it. In comparison, a conservative protest is *mild*.

Especially this one. Seriously. Check out the nudity in the signs carried at Democrat rallies. The majority are rated R or X.

We had *none* of that.

It soon became clear that the only danger to us would be the *counter protestors* who were starting to arrive.

To protect ourselves, I handed out canisters of mace and pepper spray.

There was no yelling, no screaming, no pushing, no shoving.

Everyone was on their *very best* behavior and I defy any reporter to tell me otherwise.

Were *you* there? Probably not.

I was.

Have you ever been to Disney World? Or to one of the national parks? Or to New Orleans during Mardi Gras?

Have you seen the way *those* tourists act?

Animals.

We were as gentle as kittens.

The morning just grew colder. The wind whipped even harder and I began to shiver. To warm myself, I began to walk around and interview some in the crowd.

I would be going live for my podcast at precisely 12:00 P.M. (two and a half hours earlier than normal) but I figured I'd delve into one of my characters, "Dr. Slauci," to get on tape.

"Dr. Slauci" is a very funny character I created who is supposedly Dr. Fauci's former assistant and really dumb. The premise was that I was a fucking idiot who learned everything from my former boss.

I figured that the character was an easy one to play.

I'd use these excerpts for a comedic bit for a show down the road.

Many in the crowd recognized me and I had no problem getting enough material. I received a thousand hugs.

Is *that* ever reported?

I called my studio to give Da Executioner and the Flammer the latest, and I then set off towards the front of the action, to be close to the stage, where Rudy was already speaking.

I told you earlier that I've written jokes for Rudy and I have.

We're friends. I've been to his house, he to mine. He's a great guy, an American hero.

With that said, I won't say whether or not I wrote any of the jokes in this January 6th speech.

But I *will* say that it wasn't the best speech he's ever given. Maybe it was the cold outside. Perhaps he was hungry. Maybe he was even a bit tipsy (the guy does like to drink and that's no condemnation on my part! God knows I *used* to love to have a few refreshments!)

I don't know if he was buzzed and I never asked. But I'd give his speech a B.

Maybe a B plus.

I recognized a fan and a frequent caller, "Charlie the Cuck," who's always good for a laugh or two. He was standing next to me. His shtick is that *everything* offends him, but he's too much of a pussy to do anything about it. We exchanged pleasantries, I asked him a few questions, and then he went back to waving his gigantic Trump flag. Standing behind me was another guy with a gigantic flag with *Passing on the Right* on it.

When he recognized me he started screaming in excitement.

I screamed back.

It was cute.

But God it was cold!

So fucking *cold* and *windy*! Maybe that had something to do with it all.

I saw another fan of my show, "Early Voting Earl," who does a great imitation of a Democrat showing up two weeks early to vote. The call usually ends with him being at the wrong location. We spoke for about thirty minutes and I then turned my attention to the stage.

It looked like Trump was just about to come out.

And this is when I went live.

Trump emerged onto the stage, looking confident, looking strong. The crowd (and it had to be over a million, maybe even two million, at a minimum) cheered wildly. The cheers and applause reminded me of my stand-up days. Trump scanned the crowd, finally landing on my thumb's up. He smiled. I won't say whether I helped him with this particular speech, or the jokes in it.

But I will say that it was one of the *best* speeches I've ever seen the man give. The crowd was euphoric.

I'd rate it an A, maybe at worst an A minus.

It had everything. Highs, lows, anger, nurturing, jokes, sadness. I could see a look in his eyes I've never seen. Nothing was going to stop him from delivering this speech the way *he* wanted it delivered.

That is to say with energy, with conviction, persuasiveness.

He used the words "sword," "fire" and "blood."

He spoke about "enemies."

He spoke about "socialists," "liberals" and other assholes.

I stood there spellbound.

And then came his famous *improvised* last lines: "So we're going to walk down Pennsylvania Avenue. We're going to try and give our Republicans the kind of pride and boldness that they need to take back our country. So let's walk down Pennsylvania Avenue."

I did not write that, contrary to many reports.

It was all improvised by Trump.

I *assure* you.

If I had written it, I would have ended the speech with a joke. And a *good* one, at that.

What happened next was *also* improvised.

By me.

And I blame my days back when I was deeply immersed in the comedy improv world. When I would "read" the crowd and then do what was necessary to get them on to my side. The only difference now was that the crowd was in the millions and not eleven or so.

Small difference, right?

Now, I have to be honest, some of what happened next *did* have to do with me wanting to get the fuck out of that cold and wind.

I hate cold weather. I like dat nasty hot and sticky swamp!

So without even thinking, I looked up at Trump and he looked down at me. I could have sworn he winked. This was my cue, unspoken but no less implied.

I took off, still live on the air, weaving my way through the crowd, making my way east and towards the Capitol. I seemed to have been the first, or one of the first, to leave the speech.

I began to run.

I looked to the guy next to me. He wordlessly handed over his *Passing on the Right* flag on a giant stick. A passing-of-the-baton of sorts.

A true hero.

I held it high above, proudly. I get chills just writing this. Where else was I supposed to head? Back home?

Now let me pause here and tell you what I told investigators and everyone else who's asked:

This was a joke.

It was a gag.

It was shtick, a *routine*.

Live, performed during my podcast.

I was "leading the comedic charge."

The people following me as I made my way across the Mall were fucking *laughing*.

Can I even begin to express how many thumb's ups and smiles I received along the way?

Laughing.

Giggling.

Grinning like mad!

Having a wonderful time!

All my fans, not bothering anyone, *millions*! It was heaven!

I assure you that there wasn't *one* angry person in that crowd, and if there was, I didn't see or hear them.

And that is the truth.

It all started as a lark. That's what I do! I provide comedy!

And yet ... I *can* admit that when we finally did reach the Capitol, things took a turn ... for the different.

It wasn't a bad situation. Just a *different* situation.

I was one of the first to arrive at the Capitol steps, if not the very first.

When I turned around, smiling, ready to interview the first person behind me, I was overtaken by an energy that I hadn't expected.

Again, it wasn't angry. Just ... *different*.

It's hard to explain. I guess it's like being in the winning crowd at a World Series game, ready to overtake the ball field.

Eager. Ready. Excited. Confident.

Confident that you are in the right. That your actions need no excusing.

Now here's the tricky part which I was told *not* to talk about by my lawyers but I will anyway because even though the case has yet to go to court, I'm *that* confident that I'll prove that I was *not* in the wrong.

The crowd behind me literally *pushed* me *into* the Capitol.

I had *zero* choice. None. It'd be like trying to hold back a beach wave.

I was through a broken window and into the Capitol and there was nothing I could do about it. It was pre-ordained. (This was the last I ever saw of Ashli Babbitt. She was right behind me, smiling so innocently. I miss her ...)

Once in, I was taken aback by how calm everything suddenly became!

People were taking pictures, giving each other the high five, smiling, laughing. I interviewed a few who were just so happy and excited to see me and who said hi and then they went about their business. Keep in mind, I was *still* recording and it was still *live*!

Nothing was untoward. *Nothing!*

Even if I had *wanted* to exit, I wouldn't have been able to. All of the exits were now blocked by armed guards. That's one thing never reported. We were *locked* in! It was, in essence, a prison!

From there, things grow a little hazy.

I suppose the fact that I was still podcasting live didn't help my cause, in retrospect.

But listening to the show again recently, I can only ask: Was I there to *attack*? Is that what attackers do? Crack jokes and make sarcastic quips?

Is this what the Huns did when attacking Europe in the 5th century? Crack a ton of jokes, making others smile?

Or *entertain*?

I'm guessing no. But that's what *I* was doing.

Maybe I just have a "weird" sense of humor. Which leads me to my next point:

I've *always* found it funny (when at a woman's house) to sort of just stroll out of her bedroom (when she's in the kitchen, typically) and then wait until she sees me, and I'd be totally nude, save for wearing *her* bra and panties, pretending to play with my penis.

I'm not sure why. We all have our "comedic Achilles heel." A friend of mine is unable to stop laughing whenever he sees an old person stumble.

That's *his* thing.

Another friend finds it hilarious to see videos of men getting hit in the nuts with a baseball bat. He will literally fall to the floor crying, much like a guy who's just been hit in the nuts with a baseball bat.

Again, no criticism on my part!

That's just what they find funny.

Humor is such a strange thing, isn't it? So subjective and dependent on someone's mood.

And I guess so is sexuality.

Let's just get this out of the way now.

After January 6th, a ton of women came out of the woodwork and claimed that I had tried various things with them over the years.

All nonsense!

I've *never* had a fetish for amputees or women who pretended to be amputees!

Not true!

I never got "off" by sucking someone's nose!

Seriously?!

I've never asked anyone to stutter dirty to me!

I hate when people stutter, let alone find it sexy!

I've never achieved sexual climax by insisting someone tickle my nipples with their feet! *I mean, really …*

And I've never found it kinky to watch someone else who's watching birthing documentaries!

If anything, I find that gross!

My sex life is private and I intend to keep it that way.

So many accusations over the years, and I will continue to deny them all, unless you have specific evidence that can prove otherwise.

The allegations have only grown worse and more frequent the more famous I've become.

There was that woman who accused me of pulling up next to her car, in *my* car, and jacking off with Ace of Base blasting.

There was that pair of teenage twins who accused me of flashing them inside a Forever 21 store.

There was that 80-something woman down in Florida who accused me of saying that I wanted to fuck her folds.

There was a 17-year-old in Jacksonville, Florida who claimed that I had sent her a selfie of my asshole via some app.

There was an entire cheerleading team at a high school in the midwest who claimed that I sent them a cock shot with my pubic hair shaved into a Shazam lightning bolt.

I defy *anyone* to prove that any of these things were sent by me on my cell phone and not someone else impersonating me and somehow using my number as the callback digits.

I'd defy *anyone* so goddamn hard that I'd immediately fucking take them to court if anyone ever said as much—and I have, numerous times.

What I'm saying is that when you become famous, there's a bull's-eye on your back.

And the bull's-eye only grows *bigger* if you are a *conservative* celebrity. What I mean is this: The accusations have only grown stranger over the years, perhaps culminating with a charge in 2018 that I hid in a dressing room at a JC Penny's in Baltimore and watched a pre-teen change into a swimsuit.

That charge was thrown out of court. It was never proved that I was in JC Penny's, although I *will* admit that I *was* in the mall shopping for a new diving watch and hunting knife.

Sure, there are a few things that turn my on sexually, and I've already discussed one: shrimping a woman's *faux*-gina, just basically her forearm.

Harmless. And I invented it myself.

So there's that special X factor to it. Or triple-X factor.

I *love* women!

What can I say?!

At least I ain't a "cuck," am-I-right?

I've shrimped a lot of women in my day.

And I've fucked a lot of women, too.

I adore them. I never married because I never wanted to. My goal in life is to make people laugh. Anything else, to me, just seems besides the point. My bride is your smile.

Do I have to apologize?

Does Justice Kavanaugh?

If so, *why*?

When he was in high school, Brett liked women. So what? He *still* likes women. Half of his staff, supposedly—if not *more*—are women!

He coaches girl's basketball for his daughters!

Anyway, I don't blame Trump for anything that happened to me on January 6th. If anything, I consider it an "optics issue."

Maybe the photos taken of me by security were too much for people to handle without a long, detailed explanation.

I also don't blame Trump for what happened to *anyone* at the Capitol or to those who died that day.

Nor do I blame myself.

Yes, it was me in Nancy Pelosi's office, allegedly masturbating with women's undergarments over my face, or maybe even two, which might have been Nancy's or it might have been someone else's.

And yes, I was nude, save for one of my fun T-shirts, that read:

Age Has Its Advantages!
Too Bad I Can't Remember What They Are!

The T-shirt was super clever and a bit self-deprecating and people *loved* it.

Or they would have loved it if I hadn't been wearing a coat and bullet-proof vest earlier.

As for what I was allegedly *doing* …

So what?

I had to do *something* interesting for my fans who were listening live!

Have *you* ever had to fill hours worth of live air time?

I've never thought about myself as someone who is a *victim*.

I'm an *entertainer*. And I was doing what *entertainers* do.

Would I do it again?

That is *allegedly* masturbating with undergarments over my face in Nancy Pelosi's office, which might have been Nancy's undergarments or it might have been someone else's?

Probably not. But who knows?

What's ironic is that when the news came out about all this (thanks Anderson Cooper—er, I mean *Snooper*), I began receiving criticism from *both* fucking sides:

The libs thought it was disgusting that I would ever do such a thing inside the Capitol of the United States with undergarments that were, allegedly, not mine.

Meanwhile, the conservatives (my goddamn *supposed* friends!) were giving me a ton of grief for covering my face, as if I was afraid of Covid, as if I was using these undergarments as a Covid mask!

I mean, I couldn't *win*!

I found that very funny.

Other things I don't find so funny.

Like the upcoming trial. And the possibility that I might again have to do hard time. Christ. That's all I need.

The future remains uncertain but I stand proud.

I'm a man and I stand proud.

As you've read, I always have.

And I always will.

I want to end with a story:

There's a working class guy. Say his name is "Joe."

Let's call him "Joe the working class guy." He works a shit job, laying brick at construction sites, maybe. He's exhausted. He gets up every morning at, say, five. (Can you *imagine* doing that? I get up at 10:00 A.M. and I'm *still* fucking fried.) But let's just say he gets up at 5:00 A.M. It's cold out, he's miserable, he says goodbye to his horrible wife and snot-nosed children. He gets into his car and he drives to his shit job, where he proceeds to work his ass off all day, out in the raw, nasty elements.

By 3:30 or 4:00 in the afternoon he's finally done. He's exhausted. His hands have calluses. His bones ache. He doesn't want to head back home. He doesn't want to yet drive over to his favorite bar. He just wants to sit in his truck and relax a little.

He wants to laugh, he wants to learn.

He doesn't want to pay taxes on all the money that his children will one day inherit. And he doesn't want his children to have to pay taxes on the $1 million cabin in Lake Tahoe that he purchased for $5,000 and fixed up himself and plans to one day leave to his children and to *their* children. In fact, this man doesn't want to pay taxes on *anything*! And why *should* he?

He doesn't want to have to buy a new "environmentally safe" car that has zero room to store his tools. What a joke!

This imaginary Joe doesn't need to wait in line at a socialist's health office in case he ever, god forbid, breaks an arm while laying bricks.

He doesn't want to then be *literally* forced to take a vaccine for a disease that might or might not even exist, a vaccine that very well could be *harmful*, a vaccine that just might make him even *sicker* than the mysterious "disease" ever could to begin with, again, if it ever even existed.

This Average Joe doesn't want to be told to do *anything* by the government. He can *barely* abide his own wife telling him what to do!

Can't he just be given a goddamn break here?

He turns the radio up even louder. On it is a very funny man speaking.

Joe smiles widely.

This man on the radio is doing a bit called "How Much Realistically?"

This man is a talented entertainer, going out of his way each and every weekday to make this Average Joe's life just a *little* better.

Average Joe *lives* for this guy and the comedy he creates.

Today, Joe seems to need it just that *much* more.

For his part, the entertainer has braved huge crowds and the frigid cold to bring some levity into Average Joe's life.

But what's this entertainer now saying?

Joe turns up the radio even louder and listens.

The entertainer is claiming that he's in the office of the dreaded Nancy Pelosi. And now he's asking his listeners, "How much realistically to jerk off in Nancy Pelosi's office? Would you do it for $10,000? $5,000? How about for *free*?"

Is this man really doing this?! He *couldn't* be, right?!

The man on the radio is saying, "How about for free? And how about I pull these little ol' panties and bras from out of this here drawer and put them over my face and take off my own damn pants?"

Joe the working class guy is exhausted, plum worn out from a very difficult day of blue-collar labor. But he can't help but laugh. How could he *resist*?

Maybe the world isn't so bad after all!

And for the next ten minutes, as this entertainer makes life worth living again, this Average Joe shall sit in his truck and laugh until he cries and he'll turn up the heat and just thank the Lord above that there are actually real people out there who devote their lives to make *his* life a whole lot better.

It's a selfless act.

Joe the working class guy smiles. His life hasn't worked out, that much is true. But another's *has*. And he's so so *so* grateful for that. So, so, *so* grateful.

But the entertainer on the radio isn't yet finished. In fact, he's just getting warmed up. He launches into jokes about women talking way too much and men not being able to follow what the fuck they're saying, jokes about how expensive bras are to buy as gifts, how pricey tampons are to purchase for wives and girlfriends but you have to buy them anyway ... all while jerking off *live* on the air, wearing what could be Nancy Pelosi's underwear and bra over his face!

Average Joe has simple needs. He wants his children to be safe and not attacked by, say, armed Muslims coming into this country from other countries. And he definitely doesn't want his children to have to be taught silly race theories, and if they are, can he not be critical about it? He just wants his wonderful American kids to receive a great, *real* education and not to have to work a job like *he's* working.

Joe the working class guy is sitting in that car, and he's rubbing his hands to produce warmth, and he allows himself to laugh for the first time today. And he's listening and he's laughing and he's learning and time no longer has any meaning. It's just Joe and the entertainer talking over the airwaves and that's it.

Is this heaven? Maybe. It *has* to be, right? If this isn't, what the hell *is*?

And as I recuperate from Covid in Sibley Hospital in suburban Maryland, I only wish all of you, my listeners and fans, the very best.

Will I be convicted for the January 6th charges I'm unfairly saddled with? I doubt it. The judge taking the case is someone I fondly recall as have guffawed when I wrote him some jokes at a Federalist Society Grand Ball event, back in 2017.

(And remember, I always have that one other very special judge friend in my back pocket, if need be. *Semper Fi*.)

What you can't knock down, only pops back up, as stubborn as a goddamn weed!

My name is Skippy "Batty" Battison and this has been my story ...

A man who came from nothing to reach the very top of his profession.

And man who, for one terrible night, slept in his car in his parent's driveway because they didn't *understand* him.

A man who's met every comedian on the planet, presidents of countries, representatives from North Korea to Switzerland, someone who's spoken on the phone with Steven Spielberg, spelunked into a

West Virginia mine with Joe Manchin, shook hands with Rush
Limbaugh on his death bed, went yachting with Ron Johnson,
interviewed representatives from the Taliban about their favorite jokes,
had a falling out with Judd Apatow (but hopes to soon bridge it!), and
all the rest of it.

A guy who's never perfect but *always* tries his best.

A common man.

An average Joe himself.

There's *so* much more to come.

And I hope you will join me for *every step* of the journey.

Here. Grab my hand. And help me hoist this giant *Passing on the
Right* flag on the top of the Capitol, *our* Capitol.

Ain't that nice?!

And let's head together into the future.

Come with me.

My name is Skippy "Batty" Battison.

And this has been my story.

If you don't want to join me, then just get the fuck out of the way.

Cause I'll just be passin' you on the goddamn right ....

Skippy's Comedy Advice

When performing improv, if you don't like where the other performer is headed, just nod your head no. And then go wherever the hell you wanted to from the beginning.

It's so much more important to be funny than it is to be nice. No one remembers *nice*.

Never work at the top of your intelligence. It can only lead to zero laughs.

There's nothing wrong with getting into comedy to make a ton of money. It's no worse than anyone going into medicine to become really fucking rich. And bang nurses. In our case, waitresses.

Look at comedy as a competition, no different from baseball or basketball or boxing. There is no team. Do not feel bad if you have to fuck over people to get *where* you want and to get *what* you want.

Sometimes you just have to wait for the muse to arrive. If this takes a week or a month or even a year, so be it. Ask your parents for money, if need be.

Either you're good at comedy or you're not. No need to be an asshole and practice it. This ain't classical piano!

Reading is for suckers. If you can get away with listening to an audiobook, that's better. You should always multi-task.

I see nothing wrong with "punching down." If someone's an idiot, they're an idiot. What's this have to do with you?

If you achieve success, don't think, *Why me?* Why the fuck *not* you?!

Only treat people who can actually *help* you in your career with respect. Otherwise, it's too exhausting and a bit of a waste of time.

When you try to acquire an agent, always try to be as funny as possible to impress him, even if this requires a very long cover letter or a cold-call on his cell phone late at night or on a religious holiday.

If you're trying to get a book published, send a gift along with the book pitch. If it's a woman agent, send flowers.

Fancy or funny fonts are *always* a good idea in pitch letters.

No one gives a shit about basic rules of grammar or spelling. People just want to read whatever you wrote that's *funny*.

Include as much of your work as possible when seeking out a literary agent, even if this includes a few unpublished book manuscripts.

If you're able to afford the flights, always show up in person if you're looking for a literary agent.

Always be super, *super* confident, even if you're being incredibly obnoxious. Be persistent to the point of being overbearing. It's truly the best way to get ahead, especially when dealing with television producers.

Never write a children's book, unless you want to be looked at as being an asshole.

Life is a short race. If things aren't going well, you might as well just quit. You probably don't have that special "it" factor.

More specifically, if you sense that the rest of the writing room for a television show is made up of idiots who don't understand good comedy, just quit. Why waste your time and effort?

Just do whatever the fuck you want and never let anyone stop you.

Have fun!

Acknowledgments

I really only want to thank a few people:

My father, the Flammer, Brett K, Rudy G, Donald, Donald Jr, Eric, Roger, Bill B, Da Executioner, all of our listeners and Patreon members, Bill B, Mike P, Mick M, Stevie B, Sean S, Reince P, Stevie, Mitchy, Goetzy, Peter N., Joshy Hawley, Kevy McCarthy, my Fanatic Fans, Miss Benda, the Peanutters Gallery, my entire POTR crew, Steele (RIP), Tuck Tuck to the Maxy Max, the Right-of-Wayers, and, yes, even my "Staller Callers."

But I was told by some friends that I had to thank more women. So here are some random generated names I found online:

Deborah Aguilar, Krista Page, my mother, Debra Cooper, Sue Barnett, Donna Peters, Kelvin Mendez, Jeannie Flowers, Candice Schwartz, Flora Graham, Kristen Ramsey, Melody Terry, Georgia Robertson, Rita Potter, Rosie Ford, Carmen Holmes, Mercedes Powell, Violet Tate, Kara Sutton, Jane Reyes, Kristin Banks, Jana Miles, Carrie Jensen, Bessie Herrera, Robyn Snyder, Tonya Scott, Lela Morales, Irene Murphy, Lorena Gutierrez, Catherine Walters, Belinda Taylor, Velma Underwood, Loretta Greer, Sara Hawkins, Joy Reynolds, Stacy Hubbard, Marianne Maxwell, Jacqueline Ellis, Jody Pena, Meghan French, Bridget Reid, Meredith Chambers, Jenna Dennis, Naomi Mason, Tricia Fitzgerald, Blanche Thomas, Katie Sharp, Elsie Wood, Dana Jackson, Shannon McDonald, Heather Logan, Cindy Myers, Kelley Holland, Jennifer Simmons, Margaret Perry, Elizabeth Walker, Judy Adams, Sandra Morgan, Helen Butler, Donna Wright, Lori Rogers, Andrea Davis, Sharon Sanchez, Cynthia Cox, Julie Smith, Norma Lopez, Denise Young, Nicole Taylor, Anne Nelson, Tammy Bailey, Carol Bryant, Shirley Collins, Marilyn, Anna Mitchell, Sarah Rodriguez, Michelle Gray, Amy Watson, Janice King, Diana Scott, Karen Miller, Ann Diaz and Betty Ramirez.

battybattison@gmail.com

CPSIA information can be obtained
at www.ICGtesting.com
Printed in the USA
BVHW080727090222
628414BV00002B/2